PLANNING DECISIONS

2, MITRE COURT BUILDINGS,
TEMPLE, LONDON, EC4Y 7BY
TEL: 01-583 1355

AUSTRALIA AND NEW ZEALAND
The Law Book Company Ltd.
Sydney: Melbourne: Perth

CANADA AND U.S.A.
The Carswell Company Ltd.
Agincourt, Ontario

INDIA
N.M. Tripathi Private Ltd.
Bombay
and
Eastern Law House Private Ltd.
Calcutta and Delhi
M.P.P. House
Bangalore

ISRAEL
Steimatzky's Agency Ltd.
Jerusalem : Tel-Aviv : Haifa

MALAYSIA : SINGAPORE : BRUNEI
Malayan Law Journal (Pte.) Ltd.
Singapore and Kuala Lumpur

PAKISTAN
Pakistan Law House
Karachi

PLANNING DECISIONS DIGEST

by

MICHAEL PURDUE, LL.M.
Solicitor, Lecturer in Law, University of East Anglia

VINCENT FRASER, M.A.
Barrister

LONDON
SWEET & MAXWELL
1987

Published in 1987 by
Sweet & Maxwell Limited
of 11 New Fetter Lane, London.
Computerset by Promenade Graphics Ltd., Cheltenham.
Printed in Great Britain by
Page Bros. (Norwich) Limited.

British Library Cataloguing in Publication Data

Purdue, Michael
   Planning decisions digest.
   1. City planning and redevelopment law—
   England—Cases   2. Regional planning—
   Law and legislation—England—Cases
   3. Zoning law—England—Cases
   I. Title   II. Fraser, Vincent
   344.2064′5′0264   KD1125.A7

ISBN 0-421 32570-4

All rights reserved.
No part of this publication may be
reproduced or transmitted, in any form
or by any means, electronic, mechanical, photocopying,
recording or otherwise, or stored in any retrieval
system of any nature, without the written permission
of the copyright holder and the publisher, application
for which shall be made to the publisher.

©
Sweet & Maxwell
1987

PREFACE

Every year there are thousands of disputes over both the application and the meaning of the Town and Country Planning Act 1971. The appellate structure provided by the Act means that the Secretary of State and his inspectors carry out a quasi-judicial function in determining these disputes. These decisions may in turn be challenged on a point of law in the High Court. However, the courts have made clear that while ministerial decisions cannot be treated as binding precedents their content is important for various reasons. First, although the courts have the last say on the meaning of the legislation and on other matters of law, they have tended to confirm principles and concepts built up by ministerial decisions. Such decisions are therefore an important indication of what the law is likely to be held to be. Secondly, it has now been established that while the meaning of the legislation is a matter of law, the actual decision as to whether the factual circumstances comes within that meaning will usually be a question of fact and degree for the minister or his inspector. This means that ministerial decisions as to whether an action is or is not within the definition of development or whatever are very likely to be followed in the future. Thirdly, this last consequence has been underpinned by the fact that it has been held by the courts that a previous ministerial decision is a relevant consideration in a planning appeal and it may be that an inspector should give reasons if he disagreed with a previous decision; see Forbes J. in *Rockhold Ltd. v. Secretary of State for the Environment and South Oxfordshire District Council* [1986] J.P.L. 130. In particular where a policy line is laid down by the minister, this should be followed by inspectors until it is changed or repudiated.

So while judicial decisions expand on and explain the basic structure provided by the 1971 Act, ministerial decisions provide the key to how the system is operated in practice. The aim of this book is therefore to provide practitioners and others with a means of quickly finding out the judicial pronouncements on a particular provision along with a selection of the more important ministerial decisions. We have tried to include all the reported decisions of the English High Court on the main Act since the passing of the 1947 Act: although, no doubt, a few have escaped our notice. This inevitably means that some of the cases digested are obsolete or have been overturned but we thought it important to try to be comprehensive and where possible we have indicated the changes. As to ministerial decisions their vast number made selection mandatory and we have tended to restrict our selection to decisions that turn on the interpretation or application of the Act rather than on a question of policy. By their nature, ministerial decisions must be treated cautiously and not be vested with the inevitability of the laws of the Medes and the Persians. As the decisions on Class VI of the classes of permitted development reveal, ministerial views on the meaning of provisions can change and rechange. In our selection, we have not attempted to make editorial judgements as to which are the "correct" decisions and which are "incorrect." This is not the purpose of this book, which is to provide access to the raw material on the meaning and application of any particular provision. Our only incursion into the raw material is that, where there are a vast number of decisions on a particular provision, we have attempted to group them under what we hope are sensible and useful headings.

The layout of the book follows the structure of the 1971 Act and under each section and subsection are digested the relevant judicial and ministerial decisions. Judicial decisions are drawn from all the standard law reports and detailed citations are given in the table in the front of the book. Ministerial decisions are taken from the Journal of Planning and Environment Law and so this is the standard reference except when the decision was reported in the Planning and Compensation Law Reports. Both judicial and ministerial decisions are listed under the relevant heading in the chronological order in which they were reported; but judicial decisions are grouped first and then are followed by ministerial decisions.

PREFACE

A detailed contents page is provided so that readers can identify the particular point in which they are interested. Where relevant, the contents page breaks down the different sub-divisions that have been made in the material.

The work of compiling this book has been divided between us. The researching and digesting of the decisions was mainly carried out by Vincent Fraser. The organisation and selection was carried out by Michael Purdue.

The work was completed in June 1986 and is intended to represent the cases that were available at that date.

MICHAEL PURDUE
VINCENT FRASER

June 1986

CONTENTS

Preface v
Table of Cases xvii
Table of Statutes xlviii

Town and Country Planning Act 1971

PART II. DEVELOPMENT PLANS

Section 9. Approval or Rejection of Structure Plan by Secretary of State	9–01
Section 11. Preparation of Local Plans	11–01
Section 13. Inquiries with Respect to Local Plans	13–01
Section 14. Adoption and Approval of Local Plans	14–01
Decisions on Old-style Development Plans	14–02

PART III. GENERAL PLANNING CONTROL

Section 22. Meaning of Development	22–01
A. The General Concept of Development	22–01
B. Operational Development	22–02
Meaning of operational development; acts of demolition; examples of building, engineering and mining operations; other operations	
C. Material Change of Use	22–90
1. What amounts to a material change of use	22–90
General principles; concurrent and composite uses; incidental or ancillary uses; Planning Unit and subdivision thereof; cessation of use—intensification	
Categories of ministerial decisions as to what amounts to a material change of use	22–129
(a) Changes relating to residential type uses	22–129
(b) Changes relating to shop/restaurant type uses	22–160
(c) Changes relating to agricultural type uses	22–180
(d) Changes relating to haulage uses	22–188
(e) Changes relating to office type uses	22–194
(f) Changes relating to industrial type uses	22–200
(g) Changes relating to social/recreational type uses	22–205
(h) Changes relating to storage/parking type uses	22–215
(i) Changes relating to uses concerned with motor vehicles	22–235
(j) Changes relating to tipping/dumping uses	22–244
(k) Changes relating to the mooring and other use of boats	22–246
(l) Changes relating to general commercial uses	22–253
2. The distinction between primary and ancillary or incidental uses	22–263

3. Intensification as material change of use	22–310
Judicial decisions on intensification	22–310
Ministerial decisions on intensification	22–328a
(a) Intensification resulting in a material change of use	22–328a
(b) Intensification not involving a material change of use	22–347
4. The identification of the correct planning unit	22–371
5. Material change of use due to loss of established use	22–417
(a) Loss of existing use rights by change to another use	22–417
(b) Loss by abandonment	22–424
(As to the abandonment of planning permission, see judicial decisions on section 45)	
(c) Loss by radical change in planning history	22–464
(For judicial decisions on conditions restricting existing user rights, see planning conditions)	
D. Operations and Uses not Involving Development: section 22(2)	22–474
1. Maintenance, improvement or other alteration of a building: section 22(2)(a)	22–474
2. Uses incidental to a dwelling-house within its curtilage: section 22(2)(d)	22–492
3. Use of land for agricultural and forestry purposes: section 22(2)(e)	22–556
4. Use classes—section 22(2)(f)	22–581
(a) General approach to use classes	22–581
(b) Uses which are sui generis	22–593
(c) The specific classes	22–604
Class I: Shops	22–604
Class II: Offices	22–614
Classes III and IV: Light and general industrial buildings	22–620
Class V: Special industrial buildings	22–643
Class X: Wholesale warehouses and repositories	22–644
Class XI: Boarding and guest houses and hotels	22–655
Class XIV: Use as home or institution	22–665
E. Changes of Use which are Development: section 22(3)	22–668
1. Use as two or more separate dwelling-houses: section 22(3)(a)	22–668
2. Extension of refuse tips	22–670
Section 23. Development Requiring Planning Permission	23–01
A. Planning Permission is Required for the Carrying Out of Development: section 23(1)	23–01
B. Rights to Revert to Former Uses of Land: section 23(3)–(10)	23–03
Section 24. Development Orders	
A. General Approach to Development Orders	24–01
B. Particular Categories of Permitted Development under the General Development Order	24–07

1. Class 1: Development within the curtilage of a dwelling-house	24–07
2. Class II: Sundry minor operations	24–73
3. Class III	24–85
4. Class V: Temporary buildings and uses	24–88
5. Class VI: Agricultural buildings, works and uses	24–95
6. Class VII	24–135
7. Class VIII: Development for industrial purposes	24–137
8. Class IX: Repairs to unadopted streets and private ways	24–143
9. Class X	24–144
10. Class XII: Development under local private acts	24–145
11. Class XV	24–147
12. Class XVII	24–148
13. Class XVIII: Development by statutory undertakers	24–149
14. Class XIX: Development by mineral undertakers	24–153
15. Class XXII: Use as a caravan site	24–155

Section 25. Form and Content of Applications   25–01

A. General   25–01
B. Outline Applications
   Ambit of; applications for approval of reserved matters; interpretation of outline permissions   25–07
C. Informal Applications and Estoppel   25–36

Section 26. Publication of Notices of Application   26–01

Section 27. Notification of Applications to Owners and Agricultural Tenants   27–01

Section 29. Determination of Applications   29–01

A. The Procedures for Determining a Planning Application   29–01
   Time limits; validity; legal effect of; notification of decision; fairness in decision-taking process
B. The Factors to be Considered in Determining the Planning Application: section 29(1)   29–17
  1. The development plan   29–17
  2. Development plans in preparation and non-statutory plans   29–35
  3. The policy of a presumption in favour of granting permission   29–59
  4. Government policies   29–65
  5. Other Material considerations   29–86
    (a) The general approach to what are planning considerations   29–86
    (b) Matters regulated by other statutes   29–89
    (c) Protection of private interests   29–102
    (d) Desirability of retaining existing use or promoting different use   29–109
    (e) Section 52 agreements   29–117
    (f) The need for "planning gain"   29–119
    (g) Water and sewerage problems   29–127
    (h) Housing standards   29–140
    (i) Economic considerations   29–148

CONTENTS

(j) Planning rights and general planning background	29–165
(k) Hardship and other exceptional circumstances	29–203
(l) Alternative sites for the proposed development	29–218
(m) Fear of precedent	29–226
(n) Moral considerations	29–233
(o) Educational considerations	29–237
(p) Shopping policies	29–239
(q) Public development needs	29–250
(r) Noise and pollution	29–254
(s) Car parking needs	29–262
(t) Traffic and safety problems	29–268
(u) Miscellaneous	29–280
C. Conditional Planning Permission	29–297
1. General approach	29–297
2. Conditions must be imposed for a planning purpose	29–301
3. Conditions must fairly and reasonably relate to the proposed development	29–316
4. Conditions must not be totally unreasonable	29–344
5. Conditions must not be hopelessly uncertain	29–396
6. Severance of invalid conditions	29–415
7. Examples of ministerial policies towards conditions	29–421
(a) General	29–421
(b) Conditions relating to section 52 agreements	29–427
(c) Personal conditions	29–432
(d) Occupancy conditions	29–441
D. The Interpretation of Planning Permissions	29–471
E. Judicial Review of the Determination of Planning Applications	29–540
F. Liability Tort Arising from the Determination of a Planning Application	29–553
Section 30. Conditional Grant of Planning Permission Special Cases	30–01
A. Conditions Relating to Land under the Control of the Applicant: section 30(1)(a)	30–01
B. Limited Period Conditions: section 30(1)(b)	30–09
Section 31. Direction as to Method of Dealing with Applications	30–01
Section 33. Provisions as to Effect of Planning Permission	33–01
A. Permissions Enure for the Benefit of the Land: section 33(1)	33–01
B. The Purposes for which Buildings may be Used: section 33(2)	33–02
Section 34. Register of Applications and Decisions	34–01
Section 35. Reference of Applications to Secretary of State	35–01
Section 36. Appeals Against Planning Decisions	36–01
A. The Powers and Duties of Secretary of State on Appeal	36–01
B. Appeals Decided by Written Representations	36–28
C. Appeals Decided Following Public Local Inquiry	36–32
1. Rules governing pre-inquiry procedure	36–32

2. Rules governing the conduct of the inquiry	36–34
3. Rules governing post-inquiry procedures	36–55
(a) Inspector's report or decision letter	36–55
(b) Disagreements between the inspector and Secretary of State on findings of fact, the taking into account of new evidence or issues of fact, and the rules of natural justice generally	36–70
(c) Duty to give reasons	36–103
Section 41. Time Limits on the Life of Full Planning Permission	41–01
Section 42. Time Limits on Outline Planning Permission	42–01
Section 43. Provisions Supplement to Sections 41 and 42	43–01
Section 44. Completion Notices	44–01
Section 45. Power to Revoke or Modify Planning Permission	45–01
Section 51. Discontinuance Orders	51–01
Section 52. Agreements Regulating Development or Use of Land	52–01
Section 53. Applications to Determine Whether Planning Permission Required	53–01

PART IV. ADDITIONAL CONTROL IN SPECIAL CASES

Section 54. List of Buildings of Special Architectural or Historic Interest	54–01
Section 55. Control of Works For Demolition, Alteration or Extension of Listed Building	
A. The Extent of Control	55–01
B. Applications for Listed Building Consent	55–08
Section 56. Provisions Supplemental to Section 55	56–01
Section 60. Tree Preservation Orders	60–01
Section 63. Control of Advertisements	63–01
Section 65. Proper Maintenance of Waste Land	65–01

PART V. ENFORCEMENT OF CONTROL UNDER PARTS III AND IV

Section 87. Power to Serve Enforcement Notice	87–01
A. The Discretionary Power to Issue a Notice: section 87(1).	87–01
B. What Amounts to a Breach of Planning Control: section 87(3)	87–11
C. The Operation of the Four Year Rule: section 87(4)	87–27

CONTENTS

D. The Requirements for Service of a Notice: section 87(5)	87–47
E. The Contents of the Notice	87–66
1. Matters alleged to constitute breach of planning control: section 87(6)	87–66
2. Specifying the steps required to be taken: section 87(7) and (10)	87–120
(a) The notice must only require those steps necessary to remedy the breach of planning control and should safeguard existing user rights	87–120
(b) Question of "under-enforcement"	87–141
3. The date notice is to take effect and the period for compliance: section 87(8) and (13)	87–158
F. Enforcement of Planning Control by Injunction	87–166
Section 88. Appeals Against Enforcement Notices	88–01
A. The Grounds of Appeal: section 88(2)	88–01
B. The Procedures for Making an Appeal	88–18
C. Inquiries and the Decision-Making Procedure	88–37
Section 88A. Appeals Against Enforcement Notices—The Powers of the Secretary of State with Regard to the Enforcement Notice	88A–01
A. The Powers of Correction and Variation: section 88A(1) and (2)	88A–01
B. Power to Disregard Failure to Service Notice on Required Persons: section 88A(3)	88A–47
Section 88B. Other Powers of the Secretary of State on Appeal	88B–01
Section 89. Penalties for Non-Compliance with Enforcement Notice	89–01
A. General Approach to section 89	89–01
B. Failure by the Owner to Carry out Steps Required by the Notice: section 89(1) to (4)	89–02
C. The Use or Permitting of Uses Contrary to the Notice: section 89(5)	89–07
Section 90. Stop Notices	90–01
Section 91. Execution and Costs of Works Required by Enforcement Notice	91–01
Section 92. Effect of Grant of Planning Permission on Enforcement Notice	92–01
Section 93. Enforcement Notice to Have Effect Against Subsequent Development	93–01
Section 94. Certification of Established Use	94–01
Section 95. Grant of Certificate of Established Use by Secretary of State	95–01
Sections 96, 97, and 97A. Power to Issue Listed Building Enforcement Notices and Appeals	96/97/97A–01

Section 101. Urgent Works for Preservation of Unoccupied Buildings	101–01
Section 102. Penalties for Non-Compliance with Tree Preservation Order	102–01
Section 105. Penalties for Non-Compliance with Notice as to Waste Land	105–01
Section 109. Enforcement of Control of Advertisements	109–01

PART IV. ACQUISITION AND APPROPRIATION OF LAND AND RELATED PROVISIONS

Section 112. Compulsory Acquisition of Land in Connection with Development and for Other Planning Purposes	112–01
Section 121. Appropriation of Land Forming Part of a Common	121–01
Section 123. Disposal of Land Held for Planning Purposes	123–01
Section 127. Powers to Override Easements and Other Rights	127–01

PART VII. COMPENSATION FOR PLANNING DECISIONS RESTRICTING NEW DEVELOPMENT

Section 136. Original Unexpended Balance of Established Development Value	136–01
Section 137. Claim Holdings, their Areas and Values	137–01
Section 146. General Provisions as to Right to Compensation	146–01
Section 147. Planning Decisions not Ranking for Compensation	147–01
Section 148. No Compensation if Certain Other Development Permitted	148–01
Section 152. General Provisions as to Amount of Compensation	152–01
Section 158. Apportionment and Registration of Compensation	158–01

PART VIII. COMPENSATION FOR OTHER PLANNING RESTRICTIONS

Section 164. Compensation where Planning Permission Revoked or Modified	164–01
Section 165. Application of Section 164 to Special Cases	165–01
Section 169. Compensation for Planning Decisions Restricting Development other than New Development	169–01
Section 170. Compensation in Respect of Discontinuance Orders	170–01

CONTENTS

Section 174. Compensation in Respect of Tree Preservation Order	174–01
Section 177. Compensation for Loss due to Stop Notice	177–01
Section 178. General Provisions as to Compensation for Depreciation Under Part VIII	178–01

PART IX. PROVISIONS ENABLING OWNER TO REQUIRE PURCHASE OF HIS INTEREST

Section 180. Purchase Notice on Refusal or Conditional Grant of Planning Permission	180–01
Section 181. Action by Council on Whom Purchase Notice is Served	181–01
The Consequences of Confirmation of Purchase Notice	181–01
Section 182. Procedure on Reference of Purchase Notice to Secretary of State	182–01
Section 184. Power to Refuse to Confirm Purchase Notice where Land has Restricted Use by Virtue of Previous Planning Permission	184–01
Section 186. Effect of Secretary of State's Action in Relation to Purchase Notice	186–01
Section 190. Purchase Notice on Refusal or Conditional Grant of Listed Building Consent	190–01
Section 192. Blight Notices: The Qualifying Land and Interests	192–01
Section 193. Power to Serve Blight Notice	193–01
Section 194. Objection to Blight Notice	194–01
Section 195. Reference of Objection to Lands Tribunal	195–01
Section 203. Meaning of "Owner Occupier" and "Resident Occupier"	203–01

PART X. HIGHWAYS

Section 209. Highways Affected by Development: Orders by Secretary of State	209–01
Section 210. Footpaths and Bridleway Affected by Development Order by Local Planning Authorities	210–01
Section 212. Order Extinguishing Right to Use Vehicles on Highway	212–01

PART XI. STATUTORY UNDERTAKERS

Section 222. Meaning of "Operational Land"	222–01
Section 238. Measure of Compensation to Statutory Undertakers	238–01

PART XII. VALIDITY OF PLANNING INSTRUMENTS AND DECISIONS AND PROCEEDINGS RELATING THERETO

Section 242. Validity of Development Plant and Certain Orders, Decisions and Directions	242–01
Section 243. Validity of Enforcement Notices and Similar Notices	243–01
Section 244. Proceedings for Questioning Validity of Development Plans	244–01
Section 245. Proceedings for Questioning Validity of Other Orders, Decisions and Directions	245–01
A. Who can Bring Proceedings under section 245 and the Period for Challenge	245–01
B. Grounds of Challenge and the Procedures and Powers of the Court.	245–07
Section 246. Appeals to High Court Relating to Enforcement Notices	246–01

PART XIV. APPLICATION OF ACT TO SPECIAL CASES

Section 266. Exercise of Powers in Relation to Crown Land	266–01
Section 270. Application to Local Planning Authorities of Planning Control and Enforcement	270–01

PART XV. MISCELLANEOUS AND SUPPLEMENTARY PROVISIONS

Section 276. Default Orders	276–01
Section 277. Control of Demolition in Conservation Areas	277–01
Sections 280 and 281. Rights of Entry	280/81–01
Section 282. Local Inquiries	282–01
A. Award of Costs under section 250(5) of the Local Government Act 1972	282–01
Section 283. Service of Notices	283–01
Section 287. Regulations and Orders	281–01
Section 290. Interpretation	290–01
Section 292. Transitional Provisions	292–01

TABLE OF CASES

A.B. Motor Co. of Hull v. Minister of Housing and Local Government (1969) 211 E.G. 281 36–56
A.I. & P. (Stratford) v. London Borough of Tower Hamlets [1976] J.P.L. 234; (1975) 237 E.G. 416 29–319
Abbey Homesteads (Developments) Ltd. v. Northamptonshire County Council (1986) 130 S.J. 482; (1986) 278 E.G. 1249; (1986) 83 L.S.Gaz. 1902 52–15
Accountancy Tuition Centre, The v. Secretary of State for the Environment and London Borough of Hackney [1977] J.P.L. 792 .... 36–40, 36–107
Adams & Wade Ltd. v. Minister of Housing and Local Government (1965) 18 P. & C.R. 60 180–04
Alderson v. Secretary of State for the Environment (1984) 49 P. & C.R. 307; (1984) 270 E.G. 225; [1984] J.P.L. 429; (1984) 81 L.S.Gaz. 975, C.A.; reversing *The Times*, October 10, 1983 29–402
Alexandra Transport v. Secretary of State for Scotland (1973) 27 P. & C.R. 352; 1974 S.L.T. 81 22–672
Allen v. Corporation of the City of London [1981] J.P.L. 685; (1981) 79 L.G.R. 273 29–42
Allen & Allen v. Marple Urban District Council (1972) 23 P. & C.R. 368 192–13
Allnat London Properties v. Middlesex County Council (1964) 15 P. & C.R. 288; [1964] R.V.R. 357; (1964) 62 L.G.R. 304; 189 E.G. 791 .... 29–347, 29–418
Amalgamated Investment & Property Co. Ltd. v. Walker (John) & Sons Ltd. [1977] 1 W.L.R. 164; (1976) 32 P. & C.R. 278 54–05
Ames (L.A.H.) Ltd. v. North Bedfordshire Borough Council [1980] J.P.L. 183; (1979) 253 E.G. 55 .... 29–498, 41–01
Anglia Building Society v. Secretary of State for the Environment and Medina Borough Council [1984] J.P.L. 175 .... 29–228, 29–285
Anns v. Merton London Borough Council [1978] A.C. 228; [1977] 2 W.L.R. 1024; (1977) 121 S.J. 377; (1977) 75 L.G.R. 555; [1977] J.P.L. 514; (1977) 243 E.G. 523; *sub nom.* Anns v. London Borough of Merton [1977] 2 All E.R. 492 ... 29–555
Arcam Demolition and Construction Co. Ltd. v. Worcestershire County Council [1964] 1 W.L.R. 661; 128 J.P. 344; 108 S.J. 424; [1964] 2 All E.R. 286; 62 L.G.R. 363; 16 P. & C.R. 39 91–02
Argyll and Bute District Council v. Secretary of State for Scotland, 1977 S.L.T. 33 23–02
Arlington Securities Ltd. v. Secretary of State for the Environment and Bromley London Borough Council [1985] J.P.L. 550 29–63
Ashbridge Investments Ltd. v. Minister of Housing and Local Government [1965] 1 W.L.R. 1320; 129 J.P. 580; 109 S.J. 595; [1965] 3 All E.R. 371; 63 L.G.R. 400, C.A.; reversing (1965) 109 S.J. 474 245–08
Ashby v. Secretary of State for the Environment [1980] 1 W.L.R. 673; 124 S.J. 185; [1980] 1 All E.R. 508; (1979) 78 L.G.R. 226; [1980] J.P.L. 178; (1979) 40 P. & C.R. 262, C.A.; affirming (1978) 37 P. & C.R. 197 209–01
Associated Provincial Picture Houses v. Wednesbury Corporation [1948] 1 K.B. 223; [1948] L.J.R. 190; 177 L.T. 641; 63 T.L.R. 623; 112 J.P. 55; 92 S.J. 26; [1947] 2 All E.R. 680; 45 L.G.R. 635, C.A.; affirming [1947] L.J.R. 678 35–03
Aston v. Secretary of State for the Environment (1982) 43 P. & C.R. 331 . 22–465, 23–391
Atkinson v. Secretary of State for the Environment and Leeds City Council [1983] J.P.L. 599 .... 29–365, 30–04
Att.-Gen. v. Bastow [1957] 1 Q.B. 514; [1957] 2 W.L.R. 340; 121 J.P. 171; 101 S.J. 192; [1957] 1 All E.R. 497; 8 P. & C.R. 168; 55 L.G.R. 122 87–116
Att.-Gen. *ex rel.* Bedfordshire County Council v. Howard United Reformed Church Trustees, Bedford [1976] A.C. 363; [1975] 2 W.L.R. 961; 119 S.J. 376; [1975] 2 All E.R. 337; 73 L.G.R. 364; 30 P. & C.R. 47, H.L.; reversing [1975] Q.B. 41 56–02
Att.-Gen. v. Melville Construction Co. Ltd., 112 S.J. 725; (1968) 20 P. & C.R. 131; 67 L.G.R. 309 60–01
—— v. Morris [1973] J.P.L. 429; (1973) 227 E.G. 991 87–168
—— v. Smith [1958] 2 Q.B. 173; [1958] 3 W.L.R. 81; 122 J.P. 367; 102 S.J. 490; [1958] 2 All E.R. 557; 56 L.G.R. 295; 9 P. & C.R. 439 87–167
Att.-Gen. *ex rel.*; Sutcliffe, Rouse and Hughes v. Calderdale Borough Council (1983) 46 P. & C.R. 399; [1983] J.P.L. 310 54–05

TABLE OF CASES

Att.-Gen. *ex rel.* Turley v. Greater London Council (1976) 239 E.G. 893 270–01
Augier v. Secretary of State for the Environment (1978) 38 P. & C.R. 219; *sub nom.*
    Hildenborough Village Preservation Association v. Secretary of State for the
    Environment and Hall Aggregates (South East) [1978] J.P.L. 708 ...... 29–357, 52–10
Avon County Council v. Millard (1985) 50 P. & C.R. 275; (1985) 129 S.J 269; (1985) 83
    L.G.R. 597; (1985) 274 E.G. 1025; (1985) 82 L.S.Gaz. 1173 87–176
Ayles v. Romsey and Stockbridge Rural District Council (1944) 108 J.P. 175 27–01

Backer v. Secretary of State for the Environment (1984) 47 P. & C.R. 149; [1983] J.P.L.
    167; (1982) 264 E.G. 535 22–121
—— v. —— [1983] 1 W.L.R. 1485; 127 S.J. 748; [1983] 2 All E.R. 1021; (1963) 46 P. &
    C.R. 357; [1983] J.P.L. 602 87–87
—— v. Uckfield Rural District Council (1970) 114 S.J. 666; 21 P. & C.R. 526; (1970) 68
    L.G.R. 596 89–12
Balco Transport Services Ltd. v. Secretary of State for the Environment (1983) 45 P. &
    C.R. 216; [1982] J.P.L. 177 .... 22–431, 23–09
Balco Transport Services v. Secretary of State for the Environment and Maidstone
    Borough Council [1986] 1 W.L.R. 88; [1985] 3 All E.R. 689; (1985) 50 P. & C.R.
    423; [1986] J.P.L. 123 .... 180–13, 180–14
Bambury v. Hounslow London Borough Council [1966] 2 Q.B. 204; [1966] 2 W.L.R.
    1294; 130 J.P. 314; 110 S.J. 370; [1966] 2 All E.R. 532; 18 P. & C.R. 365; 64
    L.G.R. 314 87–160
Banks Horticultural Products Ltd. v. Secretary of State for the Environment [1980]
    J.P.L. 33; (1979) 252 E.G. 811 36–64
Barling (David W.) v. Secretary of State for the Environment and Swale District Council
    [1980] J.P.L. 594 22–272
Barnet London Borough Council v. Eastern Electricity Board [1973] 1 W.L.R. 430; 117
    S.J. 245; [1973] 2 All E.R. 319; 71 L.G.R. 254; 25 P. & C.R. 261; [1973]
    Crim.L.R. 255 102–02
Barnham v. Secretary of State for the Environment and Hertfordshire County Council;
    Pye v. Same [1985] J.P.L. 861 9–02
Barratt Developments (Eastern) Ltd. v. Secretary of State for the Environment and
    Oadby and Wigston Borough Council [1982] J.P.L. 648 29–105
Barrs v. Bethell [1982] Ch. 294; [1981] 3 W.L.R. 874; (1981) 125 S.J. 808; [1982] 1 All
    E.R. 106; (1982) 80 L.G.R. 269 29–547
Barvis Ltd. v. Secretary of State for the Environment (1971) 22 P. & C.R. 710 22–08
Bates v. Secretary of State for the Environment [1975] J.P.L. 156; (1974) 233 E.G. 157 .. 60–03
Bath City Council v. Secretary of State for the Environment and Grosvenor Hotel
    (Bath) (1984) 47 P. & C.R. 663; [1983] F.S.R. 737; [1983] J.P.L. 737 87–139,
    96/97/97A–02
Beaconsfield District Council v. Gams (1974) 234 E.G. 749 87–169
Bedfordia Plant Ltd. v. Secretary of State for the Environment and North Bedfordshire
    District Council [1981] J.P.L. 122 .... 25–41, 94–04
Bedfordshire County Council v. Central Electricity Generating Board, South of
    Scotland Electricity Board, United Kingdom Atomic Energy Authority; British
    Nuclear Fuels; Same v. Natural Environment Research Council [1985] J.P.L. 48,
    C.A.; affirming [1985] J.P.L. 43 .... 22–19, 87–175
—— v. Secretary of State for the Environment (1972) 71 L.G.R. 420 292–06
Beecham Group Ltd.'s Application, *Re* (1980) 41 P. & C.R. 369; [1981] J.P.L. 55;
    (1980) 256 E.G. 829 52–13
Behrman v. Secretary of State for the Environment and East Devon District Council
    [1979] J.P.L. 677 .... 36–46, 245–24
Bell & Colvill v. Secretary of State for the Environment and Guildford Borough Council
    [1980] J.P.L. 823 36–119
Bellway v. Strathclyde Regional Council [1980] J.P.L 683 29–544
Belmont Farm Ltd. v. Minister of Housing & Local Government (1962) 106 S.J. 469;
    (1962) 13 P. & C.R. 417; 60 L.G.R. 319; [1963] J.P.L. 256 .... 22–556, 24–95,
    24–99, 290–03
Ben Jay Auto Sales v. Minister of Housing & Local Government, 108 S.J. 381; (1964) 16
    P. & C.R. 50; (1964) 62 L.G.R. 360 22–97
Bendles Motors Ltd. v. Bristol Corporation [1963] 1 W.L.R. 247; 127 J.P. 203; 107 S.J.
    77; [1963] 1 All E.R. 578; 14 P. & C.R. 128; 61 L.G.R. 205 22–372

Bevan v. Secretary of State for Wales (1969) 211 E.G. 1245 .... 88A–04
Biggs v. Buckinghamshire County Council (1953) 8 P. & C.R. 404 164–05
Bilboe (J.F.) v. Secretary of State for the Environment and West Lancashire District
 Council; Bilboe (J.F.) and Bilboe (J.F.) (Junior) v. Secretary of State for the
 Environment and West Lancashire District Council (1980) 39 P. & C.R. 495;
 [1980] J.P.L. 330; (1980) 78 L.G.R. 357; (1980) 254 E.G. 607, C.A.; reversing
 [1979] J.P.L. 100 .... 22–675, 87–28
Birmingham Corporation v. Minister of Housing and Local Government and Habib
 Ullah; Same v. Same and Khan [1964] 1 Q.B. 178; [1963] 3 W.L.R. 937; 128 J.P.
 33; 107 S.J. 812; [1963] 3 All E.R. 668; 15 P. & C.R. 404; 61 L.G.R. 623; [1963]
 R.V.R. 712 .... 22–669, 28–98
Birnie v. Banff County Council, 1954 S.L.T. 90; 70 Sh.Ct.Rep. 246 29–344
Bizony v. Secretary of State for the Environment [1976] J.P.L. 306; (1975) 239 E.G.
 281 .... 29–397, 245–04
Blackpool Borough Council v. Secretary of State for the Environment and Keenan
 (1980) 40 P. & C.R. 104; [1980] J.P.L. 527 22–116
Blakemore v. Heron Service Stations. See Heron Service Stations v. Coupe.
Blankey v. Minister of Housing and Local Goverrnment (1967) 205 E.G. 109 36–70
Blow v. Norfolk County Council [1967] 1 W.L.R. 1280; 131 J.P. 6; 111 S.J. 811; [1966] 3
 All E.R. 579; 66 L.G.R. 1; [1966] R.V.R. 557, C.A.; reversing (1965) 16 P. &
 C.R. 342 170–02
Bolivian and General Tin Trust Ltd. v. Secretary of State for the Environment [1972] 1
 W.L.R. 1481; 116 S.J. 862; [1972] 3 All E.R. 918; 24 P. & C.R. 323; 71 L.G.R.
 39 94–01
Bollans v. Surrey County Council (1968) 20 P. & C.R. 745; [1969] J.P.L. 285 174–01
Bolton Corporation v. Owen [1962] 1 Q.B. 470; [1962] 2 W.L.R. 307; 126 J.P. 68; 105
 S.J. 1105; [1962] 1 All E.R. 101; (1961) 13 P. & C.R. 231; 61 L.G.R. 7; [1962]
 R.V.R. 25 192–02
Bone v. Staines Urban District Council (1964) 15 P. & C.R. 450 192–04
Borg v. Khan (1965) 109 S.J. 435; (1965) 63 L.G.R. 309; 17 P. & C.R. 144 87–70
Borthwick-Norton v. Collier [1950] 2 K.B. 594; 66 T.L.R. (Pt. 2) 131; 94 S.J. 404; [1950]
 2 All E.R. 204; 1 P. & C.R. 147; 48 L.G.R. 429 290–01
Bosies v. Secretary of State for the Environment, The Times, May 10, 1983 36–125
Bovis Homes (Scotland) Ltd. v. Inverclyde District Council [1983] J.P.L. 171 29–12
Bowers Farm Products v. Essex County Council [1985] J.P.L. 857 24–102
Bowling v. Leeds County Borough Council; Kitchen (E. & H.) v. Leeds County
 Borough Council; Hicks v. Leeds County Borough Council (1974) 27 P. & C.R.
 531 192–17
Boyer (William) & Sons v. Minister of Housing and Local Government. See William
 Boyer & Sons v. Minister of Housing and Local Government.
Braddon (Edward) v. Secretary of State for the Environment and Dacorum District
 Council [1976] J.P.L. 508 22–113
Bradford City Metropolitan Council v. Secretary of State for the Environment [1980]
 J.P.L. 752 29–71
Bradford Metropolitan Council v. Secretary of State for the Environment. See City of
 Bradford Metropolitan Council v. Secretary of State for the Environment.
Bradford Metropolitan District Council v. Secretary of State for the Environment
 (1977) 76 L.G.R. 454; (1977) 35 P. & C.R. 387; [1978] J.P.L. 177; (1977) 245
 E.G. 573 .... 22–477, 24–09
Bradley (Edwin H.) & Sons v. Secretary of State for the Environment (1984) 47 P. &
 C.R. 374 9–01
Bradwell Instrustrial Aggregates v. Secretary of State for the Environment [1981] J.P.L.
 276 29–88
Brayhead (Ascot) Ltd. v. Berkshire County Council [1964] 2 Q.B. 303; [1964] 2 W.L.R.
 507; 128 J.P. 167; 108 S.J. 178; [1964] 1 All E.R. 149; 15 P. & C.R. 423; 62 L.G.R.
 162 29–01
Brazil (Concrete) v. Amersham Rural District Council (1967) 111 S.J. 497; (1967) 65
 L.G.R. 365; 18 P. & C.R. 396; 202 E.G. 413 .... 22–374, 22–623
Breachberry v. Secretary of State for the Environment and Shepway District Council
 [1985] J.P.L. 180 22–660
Bridger v. Minister of Housing and Local Government (1960) 11 P. & C.R. 335 146–02
—— v. Shoreham-by-the-Sea Urban District Council (1956) 6 P. & C.R. 291 52–05

TABLE OF CASES

Briggs v. Central Land Board (1956) 6 P. & C.R. 451 152–01
Brighton Borough Council v. Secretary of State for the Environment (1978) 39 P. &
    C.R. 46; [1979] J.P.L. 173; (1978) 249 E.G. 747 29–152
Bristol Stadium Ltd. v. Brown [1980] J.P.L. 107; (1979) 252 E.G. 803 .... 87–81, 90–02
Britannia (Cheltenham) v. Secretary of State. *See* Hitchins (Robert) Builders v.
    Secretary of State for the Environment.
British Airports Authority v. Secretary of State for Scotland, 1979 S.L.T. 197 290–04,
    29–358
British Paper and Board Industry Research Association v. Croydon Borough Council.
    See 88, Winifred, Welcomes Road, Kenley, Surrey.
Britt v. Buckinghamshire County Council [1964] 1 Q.B. 77; [1963] 2 W.L.R. 722; 127
    J.P. 389; 107 S.J. 153; [1963] 2 All E.R. 175; 14 P. & C.R. 318; 61 L.G.R. 223;
    [1963] R.V.R. 215 65–03
Bromley London Borough v. Hoeltschi (George) & Son and the Secretary of State for
    the Environment [1978] J.P.L. 45; (1977) 244 E.G. 49 22–269
Bromsgrove District Council v. Carthy (1975) 30 P. & C.R. 34 89–14
—— v. Secretary of State for the Environment [1977] J.P.L. 797 22–384
Brookdene Investments Ltd. v. Minister of Housing and Local Government (1969) 21 P.
    & C.R. 545 180–07
Brooks v. Gloucestershire County Council (1967) 19 P. & C.R. 90; 66 L.G.R. 386;
    sub nom. Brooks v. Ministry of Housing and Local Government (1967) 205
    E.G. 16 .... 22–100, 22–316, 22–376
Brooks & Burton v. Secretary of State for the Environment [1977] 1 W.L.R. 1294;
    (1977) 35 P. & C.R. 27; [1977] J.P.L. 720; 244 E.G. 715, C.A.; reversing (1976)
    75 L.G.R. 285 .... 22–323, 22–584, 24–37, 25–39, 88A–12
Brown v. Hayes & Harlington Urban District Council (1963) 107 S.J. 931; 15 P. & C.R.
    284; (1963) 62 L.G.R. 66; 188 E.G. 785 24–88
—— v. Secretary of State for the Environment (1978) 40 P. & C.R. 285; *sub nom.*
    Brown and Gilston Estates v. Secretary of State for the Environment [1979]
    J.P.L. 454 36–89
Broxbourne Borough Council v. Secretary of State for the Environment [1980] Q.B. 1;
    [1979] 2 W.L.R. 846; (1978) 123 S.J. 34; [1979] 2 All E.R. 13; (1978) 249 E.G.
    959; [1979] J.P.L. 308; (1978) 77 L.G.R. 381; (1978) 38 P. & C.R. 381 93–01,
    94–02, 246–09
Bryant & Bryant v. City of Bristol (1969) 20 P. & C.R. 742 192–08
Buckinghamshire County Council v. Callingham [1952] 2 Q.B. 515; 116 J.P. 303; 96 S.J.
    296; [1952] 1 All E.R. 1166; 2 P. & C.R. 400; 50 L.G.R. 329, C.A.; affirming
    [1951] W.N. 522 22–02
—— v. Hall Aggregates (Thames Valley) Ltd. and Sand and Gravel Association [1985]
    J.P.L. 634 .... 11–02, 13–02
Bullock v. Secretary of State for the Environment (1980) 40 P. & C.R. 246; (1980) 254
    E.G. 1097; [1980] J.P.L. 461 60–06
Bunce (R.P.) & Bunce (E.W.) v. Minister of Housing and Local Government (1957) 9
    P. & C.R. 105 136–02
Burdle v. Secretary of State for the Environment [1972] 1 W.L.R. 1207; 116 S.J. 507;
    [1972] 3 All E.R. 240; (1972) 24 P. & C.R. 174; 70 L.G.R. 511 .... 22–377, 88A–06
Burgess v. Jarvis and Sevenoaks Rural District Council [1952] Q.B. 41; [1952] 1 T.L.R.
    580; 116 J.P. 161; 96 S.J. 194; [1952] 1 All E.R. 592; 50 L.G.R. 213; 2 P. & C.R.
    377 87–158
Burkmar v. Secretary of State for the Environment (1984) 271 E.G. 377 21–126
Burlin v. Manchester City Council (1976) 32 P. & C.R. 115; (1976) 283 E.G. 891 .. 178–02
Burnam v. 58, Albans Corporation (1961) 12 P. & C.R. 360 169–05
Burner, Burner and Burner v. Secretary of State for the Environment and the South
    Hams District Council [1983] J.P.L. 459 .... 88A–21
Burns v. Secretary of State for the Environment (1971) 219 E.G. 586 .... 87–74, 87–124
Burwood (Caterers) Ltd. v. Secretary of State for the Environment (1972) 224 E.G.
    2021 36–58
Bushell v. Secretary of State for the Environment [1981] A.C. 75; [1980] 3 W.L.R. 22;
    (1980) 125 S.J. 168; [1980] 2 All E.R. 608; (1980) 40 P. & C.R. 51; (1980) 78
    L.G.R. 269; [1980] J.P.L. 458, H.L. 36–48
Button v. Jenkins (1975) 119 S.J. 697; [1975] 3 All E.R. 585; (1975) 74 L.G.R. 48 88–21,
    246–04

Buxton v. Minister of Housing and Local Government [1961] 1 Q.B. 278; [1960] 3 W.L.R. 866; 124 J.P. 489; 104 S.J. 935; [1960] 3 All E.R. 408; 12 P. & C.R. 77; 59 L.G.R. 45 .... 245–02, 245–04

Calcaria Construction Co. (York) Ltd. v. Secretary of State for the Environment (1974) 118 S.J. 421; (1974) 27 P. & C.R. 435; 72 L.G.R. 398 25–11
Caledonian Terminal Investments Ltd. v. Edinburgh Corporation [1970] S.C. 271 45–02
Calflane Ltd. v. Secretary of State for the Environment and Westminster City Council [1981] J.P.L 879; (1981) 260 E.G. 1191 29–155
Camden London Borough v. Backer & Aird [1982] J.P.L. 516 87–30
—— v. Secretary of State for the Environment and EMI and EMI Cinema Properties [1975] J.P.L. 662 36–76
—— v. Secretary of State for the Environment and Allen Marsdon [1979] J.P.L. 311; (1978) 252 E.G. 275 22–386
—— v. Secretary of State for the Environment and Herwald [1980] J.P.L. 31 36–117
Campbell (A.G.) (Arcam) v. Worcestershire County Council (1963) 61 L.G.R. 321; 16 P. & C.R. 1 292–03
Caravans & Automobiles v. Southall Borough Council [1963] 1 W.L.R. 690; 127 J.P. 415; 107 S.J. 375; [1963] 2 All E.R. 533; 15 P. & C.R. 5; 61 L.G.R. 365; [1963] R.V.R. 408; [1963] R.A. 164 87–47
Cardiff Corporation v. Secretary of State for Wales (1971) 115 S.J. 187; (1971) 22 P. & C.R. 718 25–09
Cardiff Rating Authority v. Guest Keen Baldwin's Iron and Steel Co. [1949] 1 K.B. 385; [1949] L.J.R. 713; 65 T.L.R. 159; 113 J.P. 78; 93 S.J. 117; [1949] 1 All E.R. 27; 47 L.G.R. 159; 42 R. & I.T. 2 22–08
Carnall v. Jones (1966) 65 L.G.R. 217 29–399
Carpet Decor (Guildford) Ltd. v. Secretary of State for the Environment and Guildford Borough Council (1982) 261 E.G. 56; [1981] J.P.L. 806 .... 22–587, 29–360, 29–501
Cartwright v. Dudley County Borough Council [1968] R.V.R. 396; sub nom. Cartwright v. County Borough of Dudley (1968) 206 E.G. 1303 170–03
—— v. Minister of Housing and Local Government (1967) 111 S.J. 605; 18 P. & C.R. 499; (1967) 65 L.G.R. 384 242–02
Casburn and Casburn v. Secretary of State for the Environment and South Buckinghamshire District Council [1984] J.P.L. 501 245–34
Cass v. Platford; Cass v. Charles Griffiths (1968) 20 P. & C.R. 58; 67 L.G.R. 283; [1969] J.P.L. 274 54–01
Cater v. Essex County Council [1960] 1 Q.B. 424; [1959] 2 W.L.R. 739; 123 J.P. 301; 103 S.J. 414; [1959] 2 All E.R. 213; 57 L.G.R. 188; 10 P. & C.R. 269 .... 24–90, 87–17
Catton (Arnold) v. Secretary of State for the Environment and Ellesmere Port Borough Council [1976] J.P.L. 633 245–12
Cawoods Aggregates (South Eastern) v. Southwark London Borough (1982) 264 E.G. 1087; (1983) 23 R.V.R. 79 164–14
Cedar Holdings v. Walsall Metropolitan Borough Council (1979) 38 P. & C.R. 715 195–06
Central Land Board v. Saxone Shoe Co. [1956] 1 Q.B. 288; [1955] 3 W.L.R. 614; 120 J.P. 30; 99 S.J. 793; [1955] 3 All E.R. 415; 5 P. & C.R. 320; 54 L.G.R. 41, C.A.; affirming (1954) 5 P. & C.R. 39 22–604
Centre Hotels (Cransdon) Ltd. v. Secretary of State for the Environment and the London Borough of Hammersmith and Fulham Council [1982] J.P.L. 108 .... 25–17, 29–503
Chadburn (Walter) & Son v. Leeds Corporation (1969) 113 S.J. 72; (1969) 20 P. & C.R. 241 22–624
Chalgray Ltd. v. Secretary of State for the Environment (1976) 33 P. & C.R. 10; [1977] J.P.L. 176 .... 25–13, 29–493, 36–13, 242–06
Chelmsford Borough Council v. Secretary of State for the Environment and Alexander (E.R.) [1985] J.P.L. 316 29–76
—— v. Secretary of State for the Environment and the Halifax Building Society [1985] J.P.L. 555 29–45
—— v. Secretary of State for the Environment and E.R. Alexander Ltd. [1986] J.P.L. 112 29–27
Chelmsford Corporation v. Secretary of State for the Environment (1971) 22 P. & C.R. 880; 70 L.G.R. 89 25–10

xxi

Chelmsford Rural District Council v. Powell [1963] 1 W.L.R. 123; 127 J.P. 157; 107 S.J. 56; [1963] 1 All E.R. 150; 14 P. & C.R. 102; 61 L.G.R. 96; [1963] R.V.R. 71 88–02

Cheshire County Council v. Secretary of State for the Environment (1971) 222 E.G. 35 .... 22–106, 22–319

—— v. Woodward [1962] 2 Q.B. 126; [1962] 2 W.L.R. 636; 126 J.P. 186; 106 S.J. 222; [1962] 1 All E.R. 517; 13 P. & C.R. 157; 60 L.G.R. 180; [1962] R.V.R. 148 22–04

Chichester District Council v. Secretary of State for the Environment and Hall Aggregates (South Coast) [1981] J.P.L. 591 .... 36–122, 245–28

Chiltern District Council v. Hodgetts. See Hodgetts v. Chiltern District Council.

Choudhury v. Secretary of State for the Environment [1983] J.P.L. 231; (1983) 265 E.G. 345 87–137

Chris Fashionware (West End) v. Secretary of State for the Environment and Tower Hamlets London Borough [1980] J.P.L. 678; (1980) 256 E.G. 1009 29–173

Chrysanthou v. Secretary of State for the Environment and London Borough of Haringey [1976] J.P.L. 371 22–112

Church (Charles) v. Secretary of State for the Environment (1979) 251 E.G. 674; [1979] J.P.L. 769 29–39

City of Bradford Metropolitan Council v. Secretary of State for the Environment and McLean Homes Northern [1986] J.P.L. 292; (1986) 278 E.G. 1473 .... 29–367, 52–14

City of Glasgow District Council v. Secretary of State for Scotland [1982] J.P.L. 374, H.L. 22–15

City of London Corporation v. Secretary of State for the Environment (1971) 23 P. & C.R. 169; (1971) 71 L.G.R. 28 .... 22–582, 29–351

City of Westminster v. British Waterways Board. See Westminster City Council v. British Waterways Board.

Clare & Ridgway Ltd. v. Minister of Health and Local Government (1970) 217 E.G. 873 87–123

Clarke v. Caterham & Warlingham Urban District Council. See Clarke v. Minister of Housing and Local Government.

—— v. Minister of Housing and Local Government (1966) 18 P. & C.R. 82; 64 L.G.R. 346; *sub nom.* Clarke v. Caterham & Warlingham Urban District Council, 198 E.G. 583 .... 22–102, 22–129, 22–669

Cleaver v. Secretary of State for the Environment and Warwick District Council [1981] J.P.L. 38 87–131

Clwyd County Council v. Secretary of State for Wales and Welsh Aggregates; R. v. Secretary of State for Wales, *ex p.* Welsh Aggregates; Welsh Aggregates v. Clwyd County Council [1962] J.P.L. 696 .... 23–10, 29–326, 29–506, 43–05, 90–03, 177–01

Clyde & Co. v. Secretary of State for the Environment [1977] 1 W.L.R. 926; (1977) 121 S.J. 512; [1977] 3 All E.R. 1123; (1977) 35 P. & C.R. 410; (1977) 75 L.G.R. 660; [1977] J.P.L. 521; (1977) 244 E.G. 1024, H.L.; reversing [1972] 1 All E.R. 333 .... 29–109, 29–110

Cohen (George) 600 Group v. Minister of Housing and Local Government [1961] 1 W.L.R. 944; 125 J.P. 474; 105 S.J. 611; [1961] 2 All E.R. 682; 12 P. & C.R. 341; 59 L.G.R. 406 22–643

Cole v. Somerset County Council [1957] 1 Q.B. 23; [1956] 3 W.L.R. 814; 120 J.P. 582; [1956] 3 All E.R. 531; 54 L.G.R. 616; 8 P. & C.R. 161 24–02

Coleshill and District Investment Co. Ltd. v. Minister of Housing and Local Government [1969] 1 W.L.R. 746; 133 J.P. 385; 113 S.J. 469; [1969] 2 All E.R. 525; 20 P. & C.R. 679; 68 L.G.R. 334, H.L.; affirming [1968] 1 W.L.R. 600 22–07

Collis Radio Ltd. v. Secretary of State for the Environment (1975) 119 S.J. 302; (1975) 73 L.G.R. 211; (1975) 29 P. & C.R. 390 .... 29–226, 29–228

Comben Homes (Midlands) Ltd. v. Secretary of State for the Environment and Blaby District Council [1985] J.P.L. 321 29–75

Comley and Comley v. Kent County Council (1977) 34 P. & C.R. 218 192–16

Commercial and Residential Property Development Co. Ltd. v. Secretary of State for the Environment and Kensington and Chelsea Royal Borough [1982] J.P.L. 513; (1982) 80 L.G.R. 443 .... 22–659, 29–363

Company Developments (Property) Ltd. v. Secretary of State for the Environment and Salisbury District Council [1978] J.P.L. 107 112–01

Continental Sprays v. Minister of Housing and Local Government (1968) 112 S.J. 640; (1968) 19 P. & C.R. 774; 67 L.G.R. 147 245–10
Cook v. Secretary of State for the Environment and Penrith District Council [1982] J.P.L. 644 22–119
—— v. Secretary of State for Wales (1970) 220 E.G. 1433 22–104
Cookham Rural District Council v. Bull (1972) 222 E.G. 2104 88–19
Cooper v. Bailey (1956) 6 P. & C.R. 261 63–05
Co-operative Retail Services v. Taff-Ely Borough Council (1981) 42 P. & C.R. 1, H.L.; affirming (1979) 39 P. & C.R. 223; *sub nom.* Att.-Gen., *ex rel.* Co-operative Retail Services (1979) 250 E.G. 757; [1979] J.P.L. 466, C.A.; reversing (1978) 38 P. & C.R. 156 .... 29–09, 29–10, 31–01
Co-operative Services v. Secretary of State for the Environment and City of Wakefield Metropolitan District Council and William Morrison Supermarkets [1980] 1 W.L.R. 271; (1979) 124 S.J. 81; [1980] 1 All E.R. 449; (1979) 39 P. & C.R. 428; (1979) 78 L.G.R. 158; (1979) 254 E.G. 401; [1980] J.P.L. 111 . 36–14, 36–45, 242–06
Copeland Borough Council v. Secretary of State for the Environment (1976) 31 P. & C.R. 403; [1976] J.P.L. 304; (1976) 239 E.G. 503 .... 87–18, 87–142
Cord v. Secretary of State for the Environment and Torbay Borough Council [1981] J.P.L. 40 87–132
Corthorn Land and Timber Co. v. Minister of Housing and Local Government (1965) 63 L.G.R. 490; (1966) 17 P. & C.R. 210; [1965] C.L.Y. 3778 54–03
Cotswold District Council v. Secretary of State for the Environment [1985] J.P.L. 407 54–06
Cottrell v. Secretary of State for the Environment and Tonbridge and Malling District Council [1982] J.P.L. 443 95–01
Country Dwellings v. Ministry of Housing and Local Government [1959] C.L.Y. 3251 147–03
Courtney-Southan v. Crawley Urban District Council [1967] 2 Q.B. 930; [1967] 3 W.L.R. 57; 131 J.P. 330; [1967] 2 All E.R. 246; 65 L.G.R. 270; 18 P. & C.R. 477 87–48
Covent Garden Community Association Ltd. v. Greater London Council [1981] J.P.L. 183 29–549
Crabtree (A.) & Co. Ltd. v. Minister of Housing and Local Government (1965) 109 S.J. 921; (1965) 17 P. & C.R. 232; 64 L.G.R. 104; [1965] C.L.Y. 532 123–01
Creighton Estates v. London County Council [1958] C.L.Y. 3319 29–472
Crisp from the Fens Ltd. v. Rutland County Council [1950] W.N. 72; 114 J.P. 105; 94 S.J. 177; (1950) 1 P. & C.R. 48; 48 L.G.R. 210, C.A.; affirming (1949) 113 J.P. 426 29–471
Crittenden (Warren Park) v. Surrey County Council [1966] 1 W.L.R. 25; 130 J.P. 81; 109 S.J. 852; [1965] 3 All E.R. 917; 64 L.G.R. 326; [1965] C.L.Y. 3787 52–07
Crowborough Parish Council v. Secretary of State for the Environment and Wealdon District Council (1982) 43 P. & C.R. 229; [1981] J.P.L. 281 .... 22–562, 290–05
Curtis v. O'Morgan (Ted) and Test Valley Borough Council [1982] J.P.L. 581 29–505
Cynon Valley Borough Council v. Secretary of State for Wales [1986] J.P.L. 283 .... 23–13, 24–85, 29–514

D.F.P. (Midlands) Ltd. v. Secretary of State [1978] J.P.L. 319 36–110
D'Alessio v. Enfield Urban District Council [1951] W.N. 503; [1951] 2 T.L.R. 859; 115 J.P. 573; 95 S.J. 670; [1951] 2 All E.R. 754; (1951) 2 P. & C.R. 166; 49 L.G.R. 821 292–02
David (Thomas) (Porthcawl) Ltd. v. Penybont Rural District Council [1972] 1 W.L.R. 1526; 116 S.J. 785; [1972] 3 All E.R. 1092; 24 P. & C.R. 309; 71 L.G.R. 89, C.A.; affirming [1972] 1 W.L.R. 354 .... 22–09, 87–27
Davies v. Hammersmith & Fulham London Borough [1981] J.L.P. 682 29–43
—— v. Secretary of State for Wales (1976) 33 P. & C.R. 330; [1977] J.P.L. 102 ... 35–01, 36–32, 242–05
Davis v. Miller [1956] 1 W.L.R. 1013; 120 J.P. 503; 100 S.J. 588; [1956] 3 All E.R. 109; 54 L.G.R. 537; 6 P. & C.R. 410 87–02
Davy v. Spelthorne Borough Council [1984] A.C. 262; [1983] 3 W.L.R. 742; (1983) 127 S.J. 733; [1983] 3 All E.R. 278; [1984] J.P.L. 269; (1983) 133 New L.J. 1015, H.L.; affirming (1983) 127 S.J. 156 243–05
Dawson v. Secretary of State for the Environment and London Borough of Barnet [1983] J.P.L. 544 24–10

Day v. Secretary of State for the Environment (1979) 251 E.G. 163; *sub nom.* Day and Mid-Warwickshire Motors v. Secretary of State for the Environment and Solihull Metropolitan District Council (1979) 78 L.G.R. 27; [1979] J.P.L. 538 .... 23–08, 25–588, 87–128
Day and Mid-Warwickshire Motors v. Secretary of State for the Environment and Solihull Metropolitan District Council. *See* Day v. Secretary of State for the Environment.
Deasy v. Minister of Housing and Local Government (1970) 214 E.G. 415 36–57
Debenhams plc v. Westminster City Council (1986) 130 S.J. 483; (1986) 278 E.G. 974; (1986) 83 L.S.Gaz. 1479 54–06
Decorative & Caravan Paints Ltd. v. Minister of Housing and Local Government (1970) 214 E.G. 1355 .... 22–645, 87–122
De Mulder v. Secretary of State for the Environment [1974] Q.B. 792; [1974] 2 W.L.R. 533; (1973) 118 S.J. 185; [1974] 1 All E.R. 776; (1973) 27 P. & C.R. 369; (1973) 72 L.G.R. 371 .... 22–321, 22–379, 23–392, 87–05
Denham Developments v. Secretary of State for the Environment and Brentwood District Council (1984) 47 P. & C.R. 598; [1984] J.P.L. 347 87–138
Devonshire County Council v. Horton (1962) 14 P. & C.R. 444; (1962) 61 L.G.R. 60; [1963] J.P.L. 258 22–95
Devotwill Investments v. Margate Corporation. *See* Margate Corporation v. Devotwill Investments.
Dimsdale Developments (South East) Ltd. v. Secretary of State for the Environment and Hounslow London Borough Council [1986] J.P.L. 276; (1985) 275 E.G. 58 .... 29–78, 36–133
Dominant Sites Ltd. v. Hendon Borough Council [1952] W.N. 516; [1952] 2 T.L.R. 914; 117 J.P. 29; 96 S.J. 784; [1952] 2 All E.R. 899; (1952) 3 P. & C.R. 245; 51 L.G.R. 56 63–02
Dorking & Horley Rural District Council v. Fry (1960) 11 P. & C.R. 289; 59 L.G.R. 132 29–476
Dover District Council v. McKeen (1985) 50 P. & C.R. 250; (1985) 149 J.P. 486; [1985] J.P.L. 627; (1985) 276 E.G. 493 .... 88–18, 88–28, 88–30
Dowty Boulton Paul v. Wolverhampton Corporation (No. 2); Same v. Same [1976] Ch. 13; [1973] 2 W.L.R. 618; 117 S.J. 304; 71 L.G.R. 323; 25 P. & C.R. 282; *sub nom.* Dowty Boulton Paul v. Wolverhampton Corporation (No. 2) [1973] 2 All E.R. 491, C.A.; affirming [1973] Ch. 94 127–01
Draco v. Oxfordshire County Council (1972) 224 E.G. 1037 22–427
Duckworth v. Haslingdon Urban District Council [1973] J.P.L. 196 22–673
Dudley Borough Council v. Secretary of State for the Environment and Electronic and Mechanical Engineering Co. [1980] J.P.L. 181 92–01
Dudley Bowers Amusements Enterprises v. Secretary of State for the Environment (1986) 278 E.G. 313 .... 87–154, 246–18
Duffy v. Pilling 120 S.J. 504; (1976) 33 P. & C.R. 85; [1976] J.P.L. 575 .... 22–98, 87–80
—— v. Secretary of State for the Environment (1981) 259 E.G. 1081; *sub nom.* Duffy, Zetterlund, Forsyth-Saunders v. Secretary of State for the Environment and Westminster London Borough Council [1981] J.P.L. 811 23–370
Duke of Wellington Social Club and Institute Ltd. v. Blyth Borough Council (1964) 15 P. & C.R. 212 195–02
Dunton Park Caravan Site Ltd. v. Secretary of State for the Environment and Basildon District Council [1981] J.P.L. 511 .... 88A–16
Dyble v. Minister of Health and Local Government (1966) 197 E.G. 457 22–312

Eales-Johnson v. Minister of Housing and Local Government and Kilton (1958) 9 P. & C.R. 350 158–02
Ealing Borough Council v. Minister of Housing and Local Government [1952] Ch. 856; [1952] 2 T.L.R. 490; 116 J.P. 525; [1952] 2 All E.R. 639; 3 P. & C.R. 173; 50 L.G.R. 699 182–01
Ealing Corporation v. Jones [1959] 1 Q.B. 384; [1959] 2 W.L.R. 194; [1959] 1 All E.R. 286; 57 L.G.R. 86; 10 P. & C.R. 100; *sub nom.* Jones v. Ealing Borough Council, 123 J.P. 148 245–01
—— v. Ryan [1965] 2 Q.B. 486; [1965] 2 W.L.R. 223; 129 J.P. 164; 109 S.J. 74; [1965] 1 All E.R. 137; 63 L.G.R. 148; 17 P. & C.R. 15 22–669

East Barnet Urban District Council v. British Transport Commission [1962] Q.B. 484; [1962] 2 W.L.R. 134; 126 J.P. 1; 106 S.J. 76; [1961] 3 All E.R. 878; 13 P. & C.R. 127; 60 L.G.R. 41 .... 22–92, 222–02, 24–149
East Hampshire District Council v. Secretary of State for the Environment and Josephi (C.H.) [1979] J.P.L. 533; (1979) 257 E.G. 763, C.A.; affirming [1978] J.P.L. 182; (1978) 248 E.G. 43 .... 36–63, 245–18
East Riding County Council v. Park Estate (Bridlington) Ltd. [1957] A.C. 223; [1956] 3 W.L.R. 812; 120 J.P. 380; 100 S.J. 489; [1956] 2 All E.R. 669; 54 L.G.R. 363; 6 P. & C.R. 231, H.L. 87–66
East Suffolk County Council v. Secretary of State for the Environment (1972) 70 L.G.R. 595 .... 29–302, 53–02, 87–16
Easter Ross Land Use Committee v. Secretary of State for Scotland and the County Council of Ross and Cromarty, [1970] S.L.T. 317 14–02
Eckersley v. Secretary of State for the Environment and Southwark London Borough (1977) 121 S.J. 593; (1977) 34 P. & C.R. 124; 76 L.G.R. 245; [1977] J.P.L. 580; 244 E.G. 299 245–14
Edgwarebury Park Investment Ltd. v. Minister of Housing and Local Government [1963] 2 Q.B. 408; [1963] 2 W.L.R. 257; 127 J.P. 165; [1963] 1 All E.R. 124; 14 P. & C.R. 114; 61 L.G.R. 184 53–01
Edmunds v. Cardiganshire County Council (1969) 113 S.J. 406; 67 L.G.R. 528, C.A.; reversing (1968) 67 L.G.R. 158 29–486
—— v. Secretary of State for Wales and Powys County Council [1981] J.P.L. 52 .... 25–04, 29–499
Edwick v. Sunbury-on-Thames Urban District Council (No. 2) [1962] 1 Q.B. 229; [1961] 3 W.L.R. 553; 125 J.P. 551; 105 S.J. 724; [1961] 3 All E.R. 10; 12 P. & C.R. 355; 59 L.G.R. 428 29–03
—— v. —— (1965) 109 S.J. 214; 64 L.G.R. 204; 17 P. & C.R. 1; 193 E.G. 933, C.A.; affirming (1964) 16 P. & C.R. 128 87–03
Eldon Garages Ltd. v. Kingston-upon-Hull County Borough Council [1974] 1 W.L.R. 276; (1973) 117 S.J. 853; [1974] 1 All E.R. 358; (1973) 27 P. & C.R. 48; (1973) 72 L.G.R. 456 87–76
Ellinas v. Department of the Environment and Torbay Borough Council [1977] J.P.L. 249 36–83
Ellis v. Secretary of State for the Environment (1974) 31 P. & C.R. 130 36–105
—— v. Worcestershire County Council (1961) 12 P. & C.R. 178 .... 29–477, 164–07
Elmbridge Borough Council v. Secretary of State for the Environment (1980) 124 S.J. 273; (1980) 39 P. & C.R. 543; (1980) 78 L.G.R. 637; [1980] J.P.L. 463 . 245–25
Emma Hotels v. Secretary of State for the Environment (1980) 41 P. & C.R. 255; (1980) 258 E.G. 64; [1981] J.P.L. 283; [1979] J.P.L. 390; (1979) 250 E.G. 157 .... 22–585, 22–658, 22–271
Enfield London Borough Council v. Secretary of State for the Environment [1975] J.P.L. 155; (1974) 233 E.G. 53 29–18
English v. Dedham Vale Properties [1978] 1 W.L.R. 93; (1977) 121 S.J. 320; [1978] 1 All E.R. 382; (1977) 35 P. & C.R. 148; 245 E.G. 747, 839; sub nom. English v. Denham Vale Properties [1978] J.P.L. 315 27–05
—— v. Denham Vale Properties. See English v. Dedham Vale Properties.
English Clays Lovering Pochin & Co. v. Plymouth Corporation [1974] 1 W.L.R. 742; 118 S.J. 388; [1974] 2 All E.R. 239; 27 P. & C.R. 447; 72 L.G.R. 413, C.A.; affirming [1973] 1 W.L.R. 1346 24–153
English-Speaking Union of the Commonwealth v. Westminster London Borough Council (1973) 26 P. & C.R. 575; (1973) 72 L.G.R. 132 .... 22–657, 53–04
Enticott & Fullite v. Secretary of State for the Environment [1981] J.P.L. 759 29–175
Epping Forest District Council v. Scott [1986] J.P.L. 603 243–09
Erroll v. Essex County Council (1962) 14 P. & C.R. 95; (1962) 185 E.G. 15 22–417
Esdell Caravan Parks Ltd. v. Hemel Hempstead Rural District Council [1966] 1 Q.B. 895; [1965] 3 W.L.R. 1238; 130 J.P. 66; 109 S.J. 901; [1965] 3 All E.R. 737; 18 P. & C.R. 200; 64 L.G.R. 1, C.A.; reversing [1966] 1 Q.B. 895 .... 22–314, 29–86
Essex Construction Co. v. East Ham Borough Council (1963) 61 L.G.R. 452; 16 P. & C.R. 220 292–04
Essex County Council v. Essex Incorporated Congregational Church Union [1963] A.C. 808; [1963] 2 W.L.R. 802; 127 J.P. 182; 107 S.J. 112; [1963] 1 All E.R. 326; 14 P. & C.R. 237; [1963] R.V.R. 151, H.L. 195–01

TABLE OF CASES

Essex County Council v. Minister of Housing and Local Government (1967) 111 S.J. 635; sub nom. Essex County Council v. Minstry of Housing and Local Government (1967) 18 P. & C.R. 531 24–01
—— v. Secretary of State for the Environment [1974] J.P.L. 286; (1973) 229 E.G. 1733 22–625
Etheridge v. Secretary of State for the Environment (1984) 48 P. & C.R. 35; [1984] J.P.L. 340 25–19
Evans v. Cheshire County Council (1952) 3 P. & C.R. 50 164–03
—— v. London County Council (1960) 12 P. & C.R. 172 29–553
Ewen Developments Ltd. v. Secretary of State for the Environment and North Norfolk District Council [1980] J.P.L. 404 .... 22–13, 22–74, 87–29

Fairmount Investments v. Secretary of State for the Environment (1976) 120 S.J. 801; [1976] 2 All E.R. 865; sub nom. Fairmount Investments and Southwark London Borough Council v. Secretary of State for the Environment [1976] 1 W.L.R. 1255, H.L. 36–81
Farm Facilities and Prunadand Investments v. Secretary of State for the Environment and South Oxfordshire District Council [1981] J.P.L. 42 22–595
Farrington (Phillip) Properties v. Secretary of State for the Environment and Lewes District Council [1982] J.P.L. 638; (1983) 265 E.G. 47 22–118
Fawcett Properties v. Buckingham County Council [1961] A.C. 636; [1960] 3 W.L.R. 831; 125 J.P. 8; 104 S.J. 912; [1960] 3 All E.R. 503; 12 P. & C.R. 1; 59 L.G.R. 69, H.L.; affirming [1959] Ch. 543, C.A.; reversing [1958] 1 W.L.R. 1161 .... 29–298, 29–301
Fayrewood Fish Farms v. Secretary of State for the Environment [1981] J.P.L. 135 22–57
—— v. —— [1984] J.P.L. 267 .... 22–18, 24–97
Federated Estates Ltd. v. Secretary of State for the Environment and Gillingham Borough Council [1983] J.P.L. 812 .... 29-62, 36–50
Felton & Sons (Motors) v. Secretary of State for the Environment (1973) 227 E.G. 1475, D.C. 88A–08
Findlow v. Lewis [1963] 1 Q.B. 151; [1962] 3 W.L.R. 429; 126 J.P. 398; 106 S.J. 572; [1962] 3 All E.R. 7; 13 P. & C.R. 302; 60 L.G.R. 313 87–68
Finlay (M.) v. Secretary of State for the Environment and London Borough of Islington [1983] J.P.L. 802 .... 29–233, 36–94
Finn (L.O.) & Co. v. Secretary of State for the Environment and Barnet London Borough [1984] J.P.L. 734 29–157
Flashman v. Camden London Borough (1979) 130 New L.J. 885 243–04
Fogg v. Birkenhead County Borough Council (1970) 22 P. & C.R. 208 192–12
Fordham v. Elstree Rural District Council (1968) 207 E.G. 893 87–121
Forkhurst v. Secretary of State for the Environment and Brentwood District Council (1982) 46 P. & C.R. 89; [1982] J.P.L. 448 .... 22–583, 22–591, 246–11
Fourth Investments v. Bury Metropolitan Borough Council and Secretary of State for the Environment [1985] J.P.L. 185 13–01
Francis v. Minister of Housing and Local Government (1959) 10 P. & C.R. 151 148–02
—— v. Yiewsley and West Drayton Urban District Council [1958] 1 Q.B. 478; [1957] 3 W.L.R. 919; 122 J.P. 31; 101 S.J. 920; [1957] 3 All E.R. 529; 56 L.G.R. 1; 9 P. & C.R. 38, C.A.; affirming [1957] 2 Q.B. 136 .... 24–90, 87–14
French Kier Developments Ltd. v. Secretary of State for the Environment [1977] J.P.L. 30 .... 29–68, 36–106
Frescat v. Walker [1975] I.R. 177 27–03
Frith v. Minister of Housing and Local Government (1969) 210 E.G. 213 22–103
Fry v. Essex County Council (1959) 11 P. & C.R. 21 169–03
Fullman v. Minister of Housing and Local Government (1958) 9 P. & C.R. 358 158–02
Furmston v. Secretary of State for the Environment and Kent County Council [1982] J.P.L. 49 36–96
Fyson v. Buckinghamshire County Council; Metal Recovery and Storage Co. v. Same [1958] 1 W.L.R. 634; 122 J.P. 333; 102 S.J. 420; [1958] 2 All E.R. 286n.; 56 L.G.R. 310; 9 P. & C.R. 301 .... 22, 424

Gabbitas v. Secretary of State for the Environment and Newham Borough Council [1985] J.P.L. 630 36–69

Gardiner v. Central Land Board (1957) 8 P. & C.R. 215 137–01
Garland v. Minister of Housing & Local Government (1968) 112 S.J. 841; (1968) 20 P. &
 C.R. 93; 67 L.G.R. 77, C.A. 24–04, 87–73
—— v. Westminster City London Borough Council (1970) 68 L.G.R. 587; 114 S.J.
 434; *sub nom.* Garland v. Westminster City Council, 21 P. & C.R. 555 88–18
Gee v. National Trust for Places of Historic Interest or Natural Beauty, The [1966] 1
 W.L.R. 170; 109 S.J. 935; (1965) 17 P. & C.R. 6, C.A.; reversing *sub nom.* Gee
 (Gordon)'s Application, *Re*, 17 P. & C.R. 90 52–06
General Accident Fire and Life Assurance Corporation v. Secretary of State for the
 Environment [1977] J.P.L. 588; (1977) 241 E.G. 842 36–85
General Estates Co. Ltd. v. Minister of Housing and Local Government (1967) 194
 E.G. 201 180–05
General Poster and Publicity Co. v. Secretary of State for Scotland, 1961 S.L.T. 62, 1960
 S.C. 266 36–34
George v. Secretary of State for the Environment (1979) 77 L.G.R. 689; (1979) 38 P. &
 C.R. 609; (1979) 250 E.G. 339; [1979] J.P.L. 382, C.A.; reversing (1979) 37 P. &
 C.R. 188 245–23
Ghafoor (Abdul) v. Secretary of State for Wales [1976] J.P.L. 95 36–36
Gill v. Secretary of State for the Environment [1978] J.P.L. 373 36–42
—— v. Secretary of State for the Environment and North Warwickshire District
 Council [1985] J.P.L. 710 .... 22–565, 29–329, 245–35, 246–09, 290–06
Givaudan & Co. v. Minister of Housing and Local Government [1967] 1 W.L.R. 250;
 131
 J.P. 79; 110 S.J. 371; [1966] 3 All E.R. 696; 18 P. & C.R. 88; 64 L.G.R. 352; 198
 E.G. 585 36–104
Glacier Metal Co. Ltd. v. Hillingdon London Borough [1976] J.P.L. 165; (1975) 239
 E.G. 573 36–05
Glamorgan County Council v. Carter [1963] 1 W.L.R. 1; 127 J.P. 28; 106 S.J. 1069;
 [1962] 3 All E.R. 866; (1963) 14 P. & C.R. 88; 61 L.G.R. 50, D.C. .. 22–313, 23–03
Glodwick Mutual Institute and Social Club v. Oldham Metropolitan Borough
 Council [1979] R.V.R. 197 193–04
Glover v. Secretary of State for the Environment [1981] J.P.L. 110 245–25
Goodbarne v. Buck [1940] 1 K.B. 771; [1940] 1 All E.R. 613; 109 L.J.K.B. 837; 162 L.T.
 259; 56 T.L.R. 433; 84 S.J. 380; 31 Cox.C.C. 380; 66 Ll.L.Rep. 129 89–07
Gorston v. Sevenoaks Urban District Council (1962) 13 P. & C.R. 449 23–14
Grainger v. Secretary of State for the Environment [1978] J.P.L. 631 36–113
Grampian Regional Council v. City of Aberdeen District Council, (1984) 47 P. & C.R.
 633; [1984] F.S.R. 590; 1984 S.L.T. 197 29–366
Granada Theatres v. Secretary of State for the Environment [1976] J.P.L. 96 29–109,
 36–79
—— v. —— (1982) 43 P. & C.R. 258; (1980) 257 E.G. 1154; [1981] J.P.L. 278 29–111
Gransden (E. C.) v. Secretary of State for the Environment [1986] J.P.L. 519 .... 29–79a
Gravesham Borough Council v. Secretary of State for the Environment and Michael W.
 O'Brien (1984) 47 P. & C.R. 142; [1983] J.P.L. 307 24–13
Gray v. Minister of Housing and Local Government (1970) 68 L.G.R. 15 22–464
—— v. Oxfordshire County Council (1963) 15 P. & C.R. 1, D.C. 22–96
Graysmark (George Thomas) v. Secretary of State for the Environment [1984] J.P.L.
 115 245–31
Great Portland Estates v. Westminster City Council. *See* Westminster City Council v.
 Great Portland Estates.
Greater London Council v. Secretary of State for the Environment [1983] J.L.P. 793 36–33
—— v. —— [1984] J.P.L. 424 287–01
—— v. Secretary of State for the Environment and Harrow London Borough Council
 [1985] J.P.L. 868 246–15
—— v. Secretary of State for the Environment and London Docklands Development
 Corporation and Cablecross Projects; Tower Hamlets London Borough Council
 v. Same [1986] J.P.L. 193 29–223
Greater London Council, London Borough of Lambeth, London Borough of
 Southwark, *ex p.* Bernadette Spain v. Secretary of State for the Environment and
 Greycoat Commercial Estates. *See* Southwark; London Borough of v. Secre-
 tary of State for the Environment.
Green v. Birmingham Corporation (1951) 2 P. & C.R. 220 169–01

xxvii

Green v. Minister of Housing and Local Government [1967] 2 Q.B. 606; [1967] 2
W.L.R. 192; 131 J.P. 95; 111 S.J. 75; [1966] 3 All E.R. 942; 18 P. & C.R. 270; 65
L.G.R. 35 246–02
Green (Peter Hembrow) v. Secretary of State for the Environment and the Calerdale
Borough Council [1985] J.P.L. 323 .... 24–100, 87–140
Greenwich London Borough v. Secretary of State for the Environment and Spar
Environments [1981] J.P.L. 809 36–120
Gregory v. Camden London Borough Council [1966] 1 W.L.R. 899; 110 S.J. 213; 18 P.
& C.R. 69; 64 L.G.R. 215; 197 E.G. 19; sub nom. Gregory v. London Borough of
Camden, 130 J.P. 244 29–541
Grenfell-Baines (Sir George) v. Secretary of State for the Environment and Sheffield
City Council [1985] J.P.L. 256 36–30
Greycoat Commercial Estates v. Radmore, The Times, July 14, 1981, C.A.; affirming
The Times, June 12, 1981 36–47
Griffiths v. Secretary of State for the Environment [1983] 2 A.C. 51; [1983] 2 W.L.R.
172; 127 S.J. 87; [1983] 1 All E.R. 439; (1983) 45 P. & C.R. 299; [1983] J.P.L.
237; (1983) 81 L.G.R. 369; (1983) 266 E.G. 623; (1983) 133 New L.J. 105,
H.L. 245–05, 246–08
Grillo v. Minister of Housing and Local Government (1968) 208 E.G. 1201 22–421
Grinham v. Minister of Housing and Local Government (1958) 9 P. & C.R. 359 147–04
Guildford Rural District Council v. Fortescue. Same v. Penny [1959] 2 Q.B. 112; [1959]
2 W.L.R. 643; 123 J.P. 286; 103 S.J. 350; [1959] 2 All E.R. 111; 57 L.G.R. 169; 10
P. & C.R. 232 22–310

Haigh v. Secretary of State for the Environment and Kirlees Borough Council [1983]
J.P.L. 40 87–136
Halford v. Oxfordshire County Council (1952) 2 P. & C.R. 358 164–02
Hale v. Lichfield District Council [1979] J.P.L. 425 22–429
Halifax Building Society v. Secretary of State for the Environment [1983] J.P.L. 816;
(1983) 267 E.G. 679 .... 36–51, 36–67
Hall & Co. Ltd. v. Shoreham-by-Sea Urban District Council [1964] 1 W.L.R. 240; 128
J.P. 120; 107 S.J. 1001; [1964] 1 All E.R. 1; 15 P. & C.R. 119; 62 L.G.R.
206 .... 29–346, 29–356, 29–398, 29–482
Hambledon & Chidding Parish Council v. Secretary of State for the Environment [1976]
J.P.L. 502 .... 29–149, 36–77
Hamblett v. Flintshire County Council (1960) 11 P. & C.R. 284; 59 L.G.R.
128 22–425
Hamilton v. West Sussex County Council [1958] 2 Q.B. 286; [1958] 2 W.L.R. 873; 122
J.P. 294; 102 S.J. 364; [1958] 2 All E.R. 174; 56 L.G.R. 275; 9 P. & C.R.
279 .... 25–07, 25–08
Hammersmith & Fulham London Borough Council v. Secretary of State for the
Environment [1980] J.P.L. 750 25–16
Hammersmith London Borough Council v. Magnum Automated Forecourts [1978] 1
W.L.R. 50; 121 S.J. 529; [1977] 1 All E.R. 401; (1977) 76 L.G.R. 159; [1978]
J.P.L. 106 87–170
—— v. Secretary of State for the Environment (1975) 119 S.J. 591; 73 L.G.R. 288;
(1975) 30 P. & C.R. 19 .... 22–111, 88A–10
—— v. Winner Investments Ltd. (1968) 20 P. & C.R. 971 283–04
Hammond v. Minister of Housing and Local Government (1957) 8 P. & C.R.
398 148–01
Hanily v. Minister of Local Government and Planning [1951] 2 K.B. 917; 115 J.P. 547; 95
S.J. 577; [1951] 2 All E.R. 749; 2 P. & C.R. 161; 49 L.G.R. 769 245–07
—— v. —— [1952] 2 Q.B. 444 [1952] 1 T.L.R. 1304; 116 J.P. 321; 96 S.J. 328; [1952] 1
All E.R. 1293; 3 P. & C.R. 6; 50 L.G.R. 437 27–02
Hansford v. Minister of Housing and Local Government (1969) 114 S.J. 33; (1969) 214
E.G. 33 .... 88B–01
Harding v. Secretary of State for the Environment and Bridgnorth District Council
[1984] J.P.L. 503 24–99
Harlow v. Minister of Transport [1951] 2 K.B. 98; 66 T.L.R. (Pt. 2) 1037; 114 J.P. 603;
94 S.J. 821; [1950] 2 All E.R. 1005; (1950) 1 P. & C.R. 271; 49 L.G.R. 59, C.A.;
reversing [1950] 2 K.B. 175 209–02
Harrison v. Gloucester County Council (1953) 4 P. & C.R. 99 170–01

Hartley v. Minister of Housing and Local Government [1970] 1 Q.B. 413; [1970] 2 W.L.R. 1; 113 S.J. 900; [1969] 3 All E.R. 1958; 21 P. & C.R. 1, C.A.; affirming [1969] 2 Q.B. 46 22–426
Harwich Harbour Conservancy Board v. Secretary of State for the Environment (1974) 118 S.J. 755; [1974] J.P.L. 724; 233 E.G. 263; [1975] 1 Lloyd's Rep. 334, C.A.; affirming (1973) 118 S.J. 184; *sub nom.* Harwich Harbour Conservancy Board v. Secretary of State for the Environment, East Suffolk County Council and Stour River Estate [1974] 1 Lloyd's Rep. 140 29–281
Hasluck (decd.), *Re*; Sully v. Duffin [1957] 1 W.L.R. 1135; 101 S.J. 868; [1957] 3 All E.R. 371; (1957) 9 P. & C.R. 70 136–01
Hatfield Construction v. Secretary of State for the Environment [1983] J.P.L. 605 .... 29–283, 36–12
Hartnell v. Minister of Housing and Local Govenment [1965] A.C. 1134; [1965] 2 W.L.R. 474; 109 S.J. 156; *sub nom.* Minister of Housing and Local Government v. Hartnell, 129 J.P. 234, H.L.; affirming [1964] 2 Q.B. 510, C.A.; affirming [1963] 1 W.L.R. 1141 29–349
Havering London Borough v. Secretary of State for the Environment [1983] J.L.P. 665 24–11
—— v. Secretary of State for the Environment and Smith MacDonald & Co. and MacDonald Evans & MacDonald (1983) 45 P. & C.R. 258; [1983] J.P.L. 240 92–02
Hawes v. Thornton Cleveleys Urban District Council (1965) 109 S.J. 197; 63 L.G.R. 213; (1965) 17 P. & C.R. 22; 193 E.G. 837 22–149
Hawkey v. Secretary of State for the Environment (1971) 22 P. & C.R. 610 .... 23–392, 87–75, 88A–05
Hawking v. Minister of Housing and Local Government (1962) 14 P. & C.R. 44 148–03
Hayns v. Secretary of State for the Environment (1977) 36 P. & C.R. 317; [1977] J.P.L.663; (1978) 245 E.G. 53 30–01
Hermans (Walter) & Sons v. Secretary of State for the Environment [1975] J.L.P. 351; (1974) 234 E.G. 47 29–166
Heron Corporation v. Manchester City Corporation [1978] 1 W.L.R. 937; (1978) 122 S.J. 316; [1978] 3 All E.R. 1240; (1978) 37 P. & C.R. 44; (1978) 76 L.G.R. 665; [1978] J.P.L. 471; 247 E.G. 379, C.A.; affirming (1976) 33 P. & C.R. 268 .... 25–15, 25–21a
Heron Service Stations v. Coupe [1973] 1 W.L.R. 502; 117 S.J. 305; [1973] 2 All E.R. 110; 25 P. & C.R. 349; 71 L.G.R. 313, H.L.; affirming *sub nom.* Blakemore v. Heron Service Stations (1971) 22 P. & C.R. 601 .... 63–07, 63–08
Hewitt v. Leicester Corporation [1969] 1 W.L.R. 855; 113 S.J. 346; 62 L.G.R. 436; (1969) 20 P. & C.R. 629; 210 E.G. 459; *sub nom.* Hewitt v. Leicester City Council, 133 J.P. 452; affirming 19 P. & C.R. 809 283–05
Hewlett v. Secretary of State for the Environment [1985] J.P.L. 404; (1985) 273 E.G. 401 .... 22–480, 36–128
—— v. Secretary of State for the Environment and Brentwood County Council [1983] J.P.L. 105 245–29
—— v. Secretary of State for the Environment and Brentwood District Council [1981] J.P.L. 187 88–25
Hibernian Property Co. Ltd. v. Secretary of State for the Environment (1973) 72 L.G.R. 350; (1972) 27 P. & C.R. 197 36–75
Hidderley v. Warwickshire County Council (1963) 107 S.J. 156; 14 P. & C.R. 134; (1963) 61 L.G.R. 266; 185 E.G. 759 .... 22–94, 22–559
High Peak Borough Council v. Secretary of State for the Environment and Courtdale Developments [1981] J.P.L. 366 43–02
Hilliard v. Secretary of State for the Environment (1979) 37 P. & C.R. 129; (1978) 248 E.G. 225 .... 22–114, 22–325
Hipsey v. Secretary of State for the Environment and Thurrock Borough Council [1984] J.P.L. 806 .... 22–327, 94–05
Hitchins (Robert) Builders v. Secretary of State for the Environment (1983) 265 E.G. 696 36–95
Hitchins (Robert) Builders Ltd. v. Secretary of State for the Environment; Britannia (Cheltenham) v. Same [1979] J.P.L. 534; (1979) 251 E.G. 467, C.A.; affirming (1978) 247 E.G. 301; *sub nom.* Britannia (Cheltenham) v. Secretary of State for the Environment [1978] J.P.L. 554 .... 25–03, 29–321, 29–356, 29–400, 36–07
Hobbs (Quarries) Ltd. v. Somerset County Council (1975) 30 P. & C.R. 286 .... 164–11, 178–01, 178–02

TABLE OF CASES

Hoddesdon Urban District Council *v.* Secretary of State for the Environment (1971) 115 S.J. 187 180–09
Hodgetts *v.* Chiltern District Council [1983] A.C. 120; [1983] 2 W.L.R. 577; 147 J.P. 372; [1983] 1 All E.R. 1057; (1983) 45 P. & C.R. 402; [1983] J.P.L. 377, H.L. 89–01, 89–04, 89–09, 89–15
Hodgkinson (Ringway) Ltd. *v.* Bucklow Rural District Council (1972) 225 E.G. 2105 .... 29–65, 36–74
Hollis *v.* Secretary of State for the Environment [1983] J.P.L. 164; (1983) 265 E.G. 476 .... 245–05, 2435–30
Holmes *v.* Bradfield Rural District Council [1949] 2 K.B. 1; [1949] L.J.R. 978; 65 T.L.R. 195; 113 J.P. 140; 93 S.J. 183; [1949] 1 All E.R. 381; 47 L.G.R. 278 164–01
—— *v.* Knowsley Borough Council (1977) 35 P. & C.R. 119 203–05
Holmes and Trustees of the Kingston Meeting Rooms Trust *v.* Secretary of State for the Environment and the London Borough of Hounslow [1983] J.P.L. 476 29–21
Holtby *v.* Stretford Borough Council (1964) 108 S.J. 158; 189 E.G. 517 87–71
Hooper *v.* Slater [1978] J.P.L. 252; (1977) 245 E.G. 573 .... 22–648, 29–495
Hope *v.* Secretary of State for the Environment (1975) 31 P. & C.R. 120 ...... 36–59, 52–09
—— *v.* —— [1979] J.P.L. 104 29–69
Horsham District Council *v.* Fisher [1977] J.P.L. 178 246–06
Horwitz *v.* Rowson [1960] 1 W.L.R. 803; 124 J.P. 424; 104 S.J. 606; [1960] 2 All E.R. 881; 11 P. & C.R. 411; 58 L.G.R. 252 .... 22–607, 22–621
Hoser *v.* Minister of Housing and Local Government [1963] Ch. 428; [1962] 3 W.L.R. 1337; 127 J.P. 24; 106 S.J. 1010; [1962] 3 All E.R. 945; 14 P. & C.R. 36; 60 L.G.R. 542 246–01
Hounslow London Borough Council *v.* Secretary of State for the Environment and Indian Gymkhana Club [1981] J.P.L. 510 87–150
Hoveringham Gravels *v.* Secretary of State for the Environment [1975] Q.B. 754; [1975] 2 W.L.R. 897; 119 S.J. 355; [1975] 2 All E.R. 931; 73 L.G.R. 238; 30 P. & C.R. 151, C.A.; reversing (1974) 27 P. & C.R. 549 29–90
Howard *v.* Secretary of State for the Environment [1975] Q.B. 235; [1974] 2 W.L.R. 459; (1973) 117 S.J. 853; [1974] 1 All E.R. 644; (1973) 27 P. & C.R. 131; (1973) 72 L.G.R. 325, C.A.; reversing [1973] Q.B. 481 88–20
Howell *v.* Sunbury-on-Thames Urban District Council (1963) 107 S.J. 909; 62 L.G.R. 119; 114 L.J. 121; 188 E.G. 689, C.A.; affirming (1963) 15 P. & C.R. 26; 61 L.G.R. 477; 187 E.G. 393 .... 22–06, 22–605
Howes *v.* Secretary of State for the Environment [1984] J.P.L. 439 87–32
Hudson (D.E.) *v.* Secretary of State for the Environment and Leeds City Council [1984] J.P.L. 258 36–98
Hughes (H.T.) & Sons Ltd. *v.* Secretary of State for the Environment and Fareham Borough Council (1985) 51 P. & C.R. 134; [1985] J.P.L. 486 .... 88A–23
Hussain *v.* Secretary of State for the Environment (1971) 23 P. & C.R. 330; *sub nom.* Hussain *v.* City of Birmingham (1971) 221 E.G. 627 .... 22–606, 22–267
Hutchinson *v.* Firetto [1973] J.P.L. 314 243–09
Hyndburn Borough Council *v.* Secretary of State for the Environment [1979] J.P.L. 536; (1979) 251 E.G. 473 .... 36–92, 88–40

Iddenden *v.* Secretary of State for the Environment [1972] 1 W.L.R. 1433; 116 S.J. 665; [1972] 3 All E.R. 883; 71 L.G.R. 20; 26 P. & C.R. 553, C.A.; affirming [1972] 3 All E.R. 722 .... 22–10, 87–141
Impey *v.* Secretary of State for the Environment; Lake District Special Planning Board *v.* Secretary of State for the Environment (1984) 47 P. & C.R. 157 22–15
Ipswich County Borough Council *v.* Secretary of State for the Environment (1972) 225 E.G. 797 .... 87–125, 88A–07
Inland Revenue Commissioners *v.* Metrolands (Property Finance) [1982] 1 W.L.R. 341; 126 S.J. 188; [1982] 2 All E.R. 557; [1982] J.P.L. 570; (1982) 80 L.G.R. 553; [1984] T.C. 679, H.L.; reversing [1981] 1 W.L.R. 637 181–06
—— *v.* National Federation of Self-Employed and Small Businesses Ltd. [1982] A.C. 617; [1981] 2 W.L.R. 722; 125 S.J. 325; [1981] 2 All E.R. 93; [1984] T.C. 133; [1981] S.T.C. 260, H.L.; reversing *sub nom.* R. *v.* I.R.C., *ex p.* National Federation of Self-Employed and Small Businesses [1980] Q.B. 407 29–546
Irlam Brick Co. *v.* Warrington Borough Council (1982) 126 S.J. 244; [1982] J.P.L. 709 .... 29–361, 29–507

Inverclyde District Council *v.* Inverkip Building Co. [1983] J.P.L. 118; [1983] F.S.R. 118 29–327
—— *v.* Lord Advocate (1982) 43 P. & C.R. 375; [1982] J.P.L. 313, H.L. 25–18
Iveagh *v.* Minister of Housing and Local Government [1964] 1 Q.B. 395; [1963] 3 W.L.R. 974; 128 J.P. 70; 107 S.J. 790; 851; [1963] 3 All E.R. 817; 15 P. & C.R. 233; 62 L.G.R. 32; [1963] R.V.R. 791, C.A.; affirming [1962] 2 Q.B. 147 54–02
Ivens & Sons (Timber Merchants) Ltd. *v.* Daventry District Council (1976) 31 P. & C.R. 480 169–08
Ivory *v.* Secretary of State for the Environment and North Hertfordshire District Council [1985] J.P.L. 796 87–153

J.R.M.C. Management Services Ltd. *v.* Secretary of State for the Environment (1972) 222 E.G. 1593 29–104
James *v.* Brecon County Council (1963) 15 P. & C.R. 20 22–05
—— *v.* Minister of Housing and Local Government. *See* James *v.* Secretary of State for Wales.
—— *v.* Secretary of State for Wales (formerly the Minister of Housing and Local Government) [1968] A.C. 409; [1967] 1 W.L.R. 171; 131 J.P. 122; 111 S.J. 55; [1966] 3 All E.R. 964; 18 P. & C.R. 165; 65 L.G.R. 171, H.L. 22–315, 29–03
Jeary *v.* Chailey Rural District Council (1973) 26 P. & C.R. 280 .... 87–04, 243–02
Jelson *v.* Minister of Housing and Local Government; George Wimpey & Co. *v.* Minister of Housing and Local Government [1970] 1 Q.B. 243; [1969] 3 W.L.R. 282; 133 J.P. 564; 113 S.J. 427; [1969] 3 All E.R. 147; 20 P. & C.R. 663; 67 L.G.R. 543 181–02
Jennings Motors Ltd. *v.* Secretary of State for the Environment and New Forest District Council [1982] Q.B. 541; [1982] 2 W.L.R. 131; [1982] 1 All E.R. 471; (1982) 43 P. & C.R. 316; [1982] J.P.L. 181; (1982) 80 L.G.R. 226; (1982) 261 E.G. 994 .... 22–464, 22–465, 22–466, 22–467, 23–391, 23–392
Jillings *v.* Secretary of State for the Environment and the Broads Authority [1984] J.P.L. 32 .... 22–274, 36–97
John *v.* Reveille Newspapers (1955) 5 P. & C.R. 95 63–03
Johnston *v.* Secretary of State for the Environment (1974) 118 S.J. 717; (1974) 28 P. & C.R. 424; 73 L.G.R. 22 .... 22–322, 22–380, 89–13
Joiner *v.* Guildford Corporation (1954) 5 P. & C.R. 50 91–01
Jones *v.* Merioneth County Council (1968) 112 S.J. 881; (1969) 20 P. & C.R. 106; 67 L.G.R. 203 63–06
—— *v.* Secretary of State for the Environment (1974) 28 P. & C.R. 362, D.C. 22–108
—— *v.* Secretary of State for Wales (1974) 28 P. & C.R. 280; 72 L.G.R. 583, C.A. 52–08
—— *v.* Stockport Metropolitan Borough Council (1983) 50 P. & C.R. 229; [1984] J.P.L. 274; (1984) 269 E.G. 408; (1984) 24 R.V.R. 35 .... 24–98, 165–01
Joyce *v.* West Sussex County Council (1965) 17 P. & C.R. 34 164–10
Joyce Shopfitters *v.* Secretary of State for the Environment [1976] J.P.L. 236; (1975) 237 E.G. 576 22–382

K. & B. Metals Ltd. *v.* Birmingham City Council (1976) 33 P. & C.R. 135; (1976) 240 E.G. 876 170–04
Kember (Robert Frederick) *v.* Secretary of State for the Environment and the Tunbridge Wells Borough Council [1982] J.P.L. 383 .... 29–325, 30–03
Kensington and Chelsea (Royal) London Borough *v.* Secretary of State for the Environment and Mua Carla [1981] J.P.L. 50 .... 22–326, 88A–15
Kensington and Chelsea Royal London Borough Council *v.* C.G. Hotels (1980) 41 P. & C.R. 40; [1981] J.P.L. 190 .... 22–14, 22–479
Kent *v.* Guildford Rural District Council (1959) 11 P. & C.R. 255 29–474
Kent County Council *v.* Batchelor (1976) 33 P. & C.R. 185; [1976] J.P.L. 754 60–05
—— *v.* —— (No. 2) [1979] 1 W.L.R. 213; (1977) 122 S.J. 47; [1978] 3 All E.R. 980; (1978) 38 P. & C.R. 185; (1977) 76 L.G.R. 714; [1978] J.P.L. 179 60–04
—— *v.* Kingsway Investments (Kent); Same *v.* Kenworthy [1971] A.C. 72; [1970] 2 W.L.R. 397; 114 S.J. 73; [1970] 1 All E.R. 70; 68 L.G.R. 301; 21 P. & C.R. 58, H.L.; reversing *sub nom.* Kingsway Investments (Kent) *v.* Kent C.C.; Kenworthy *v.* Kent C.C. [1969] 2 Q.B. 332 .... 29–350, 29–416, 29–417

xxxi

TABLE OF CASES

Kent County Council v. Secretary of State for the Environment and Burmah-Total Refineries Trust (1976) 33 P. & C.R. 70; [1976] J.P.L. 755; (1976) 241 E.G. 83; (1976) 75 L.G.R. 452 .... 25–02, 29–66, 29–318, 36–78, 245–13

Kent Messenger Ltd. v. Secretary of State for the Environment [1976] J.P.L. 372; (1976) 241 E.G. 25 55–09

Kentucky Fried Chicken (G.B.) v. Secretary of State for the Environment and Borough of Lambeth [1977] J.P.L. 727; (1977) 245 E.G. 839 36–62

Kenwood (Travel, Employment and Estates) and Z.I. Gourgey v. Secretary of State for the Environment, Westminster City Council [1984] J.P.L. 36 .... 14–01, 29–25

Kerrier District Council v. Secretary of State for the Environment and Brewer (1980) 41 P. & C.R. 284; [1981] J.P.L. 193 .... 87–12, 87–20, 87–82

King & King v. Secretary of State for the Environment and the Nuneaton Borough Council [1981] J.P.L. 813 87–162

Kingdon v. Minister of Housing and Local Government [1968] 1 Q.B. 257; [1967] 3 W.L.R. 990; 132 J.P. 1; 111 S.J. 543; [1967] 3 All E.R. 614; 65 L.G.R. 457; 18 P. & C.R. 507 23–05

Kingston-upon-Thames Royal London Borough Council v. Secretary of State for the Environment [1973] 1 W.L.R. 1549; 117 S.J. 794; [1974] 1 All E.R. 193; (1973) 26 P. & C.R. 480; (1973) 72 L.G.R. 206 .... 29–317, 29–352

Kingsway Investments (Kent) v. Kent County Council; Kenworthy v. Kent County Council. See Kent County Council v. Kingsway Investments (Kent).

Klein v. Whistable Urban District Council (1958) 10 P. & C.R. 6 89–08

Knight v. Secretary of State for the Environment (1971) 219 E.G. 586 88–38

Knights Motors v. Secretary of State for the Environment and Leicester City Council [1984] J.P.L. 584 .... 36–52, 36–152

Krueger v. Secretary of State for the Environment and Congleton Borough Council [1983] J.P.L. 233 87–85

Kwik Save Discount Group v. Secretary of State for Wales, Kwik Save Discount Group v. Secretary of State for the Environment (1981) 42 P. & C.R. 166; (1980) 79 L.G.R. 310; (1980) 257 E.G. 169; [1981] J.P.L. 198 .... 22–385, 22–589, 29–500

LG Buildings Materials v. Secretary of State for the Environment (1980) 41 P. & C.R. 243 23–392

LTSS Print and Supply Services Ltd. v. Hackney London Borough Council [1976] Q.B. 663; [1976] 2 W.L.R. 253; (1975) 119 S.J. 866; [1976] 1 All E.R. 311; (1975) 31 P. & C.R. 133; 74 L.G.R. 210, C.A.; reversing [1975] 1 W.L.R. 138 .... 22–646, 23–06, 23–07, 23–12, 246–05

LWT Contractors v. Secretary of State for the Environment and Broxborne Borough Council [1981] J.P.L. 815 88–07

Ladbroke (Rentals) Ltd. v. Secretary of State for the Environment [1981] J.P.L. 427; (1981) 258 E.G. 973 29–92

Lade & Lade v. Brighton Corporation (1970) 22 P. & C.R. 737 193–02

Laing (John) & Son Ltd. v. Buckinghamshire County Council (1960) 11 P. & C.R. 114 164–06

Lake v. Cheshire County Council (1976) 32 P. & C.R. 143 192–14

Lake District Special Planning Board v. Secretary of State for the Environment, 119 S.J. 187; [1975] J.L.P. 220; 236 E.G. 417 36–80

Lamb (W.T.) & Sons v. Secretary of State for the Environment [1975] 2 All E.R. 1117; (1975) 30 P. & C.R. 371 23–06

Lamb (W.T.) Properties v. Secretary of State for the Environment and Crawley Borough Council [1983] J.P.L. 303 22–626

Lamplugh, Re (1967) 19 P. & C.R. 125; sub nom. Watch House, Boswinger, Re (1967) 66 I.G.R. 6 51–01

Langley (Thomas) Group v. Warwick District Council (formerly Leamington Spa Borough Council) (1974) L.G.R. 171; (1974) 29 P. & C.R. 358, C.A.; affirming (1973) 26 P. & C.R. 416 45–04

Larkin (C.W.) v. Basildon District Council and Secretary of State for the Environment [1980] J.P.L. 407; (1980) 256 E.G. 381 22–478

Lavender (H.) & Sons Ltd. v. Minister of Housing and Local Government [1970] 1 W.L.R. 1231; 114 S.J. 636; (1969) 68 L.G.R. 408; [1970] 3 All E.R. 871 36–02

Lee v. Bromley London Borough Council (1983) 45 P. & C.R. 342; [1983] J.P.L. 778 87–151

xxxii

Leighton & Newman Car Sales Ltd. *v.* Secretary of State for the Environment (1976) 32 P. & C.R. 1; [1976] J.P.L. 369; (1976) 240 E.G. 931, C.A.; affirming (1975) 30 P. & C.R. 23 29–353
Lenlyn *v.* Secretary of State for the Environment [1973] J.P.L. 666 88–34
—— *v.* —— (1984) 40 P. & C.R. 129; [1985] J.P.L. 482; (1985) 82 L.S.Gaz. 358 .... 88–27, 246–14
Leominster Borough Council *v.* Minister of Housing and Local Government (1971) 218 E.G. 1419 .... 180–08, 190–01
Lever Finances Ltd. *v.* Westminster (City) London Borough Council [1971] 1 Q.B. 222; [1971] 1 W.L.R. 732; 68 L.G.R. 757; *sub nom.* Lever Finance *v.* Westminster Corporation, 21 P. & C.R. 778, C.A. 25–38
Lewis *v.* Secretary of State for the Environment (1971) 23 P. & C.R. 125; 70 L.G.R. 291 .... 22–105, 22–317
Lewstar *v.* Secretary of State for the Environment (1985) 273 E.G. 303, C.A.; affirming [1984] J.P.L. 116 29–179
Link *v.* Worcestershire County Council (1965) 16 P. & C.R. 255 192–05
Link Homes *v.* Basildon District Council and the Secretary of State for the Environment [1977] J.P.L. 310; (1977) 242 E.G. 545 29–67
—— *v.* Secretary of State for the Environment [1976] J.P.L. 430 29–38
Lipson *v.* Secretary of State for the Environment (1976) 75 L.G.R. 361; (1976) 33 P. & C.R. 95; (1976) 242 E.G. 1049 .... 22–98, 87–79, 87–80, 87–127, 87–147
Lloyd-Jones *v.* Minister of Housing and Local Government (1967) 204 E.G. 1200 .... 88A–03
Lloyd Jones *v.* Minister of Health and Local Govenment (1967) 204 E.G. 49 22–264
Lobb *v.* Secretary of State for the Environment and South Wight Borough Council [1984] J.P.L. 336 .... 25–20, 29–511
Lockers Estates (Holdings) Ltd. *v.* Cadby Urban District Council; Fine Fare *v.* Oadby Urban District Council (1970) 21 P. & C.R. 836 .... 194–02, 195–03
Logue *v.* London County Council (1964) 192 E.G. 281 22–263
London Ballast Co. Ltd. *v.* Buckinghamshire County Council (1966) 111 S.J. 36; 65 L.G.R. 227; (1966) 18 P. & C.R. 446; [1966] C.L.Y. 11905 29–02
London Borough of Richmond-upon-Thames *v.* Secretary of State for the Environment. *See* Richmond, London Borough of *v.* Secretary of State for the Environment and Hutchinson & Locke & Monk.
London Corporation *v.* Cusack-Smith [1955] A.C. 337; [1955] 2 W.L.R. 363; 119 J.P. 172; 99 S.J. 108; [1955] 1 All E.R. 302; 5 P. & C.R. 65; 53 L.G.R. 209, H.L.; reversing *sub nom.* R. *v.* Minister of Housing and Local Government, *ex p.* London Corporation [1954] 2 W.L.R. 103 .... 180–01, 290–02
London C.C. *v.* Marks & Spencer [1953] A.C. 535; [1953] 2 W.L.R. 932; 117 J.P. 261; 97 S.J. 315; [1953] 1 All E.R. 1095; 3 P. & C.R. 409; 51 L.G.R. 329 22–03
London Parachuting Ltd. *v.* Rectory Farm (Pampisford) Ltd. *v.* Secretary of State for the Environment and South Cambridgeshire District Council [1986] J.P.L. 279 88–30
—— *v.* —— [1986] J.P.L. 428 246–17
Lord Mayor and Citizens of the City of Westminster *v.* Secretary of State for the Environment [1983] J.P.L. 602 .... 87–86, 88A–22
Loromah Estates Ltd. *v.* London Borough of Haringey (1978) 38 P. & C.R. 234; [1979] J.P.L. 107; (1978) 248 E.G. 877 .... 164–12, 178–03
Louisiville Investments Ltd. *v.* Basingstoke District Council; Planned Properties *v.* Basingstoke District Council (1976) 32 P. & C.R. 419; (1976) 240 E.G. 637 195–04
Lovelock *v.* Secretary of State for Transport (1979) 123 S.J. 80; (1979) 39 P. & C.R. 468; [1979] R.T.R. 250; [1979] J.P.L. 456 36–44
Lucas (F.) & Sons *v.* Dorking & Horley Rural District Council (1964) 62 L.G.R. 491; 17 P. & C.R. 111 29–481
Luke (Lord) of Pavenham *v.* Minister of Housing and Local Government [1968] 1 Q.B. 172; [1967] 3 W.L.R. 801; 131 J.P. 425; 111 S.J. 398; [1967] 2 All E.R. 1066; 18 P. & C.R. 333; 65 L.G.R. 393 36–71
Lydcare *v.* Secretary of State for the Environment [1985] L.G.R. 33; (1985) 49 P. & C.R. 186; (1984) 272 E.G. 175, C.A.; affirming [1984] J.P.L. 39 ...... 22–275, 22–607
Lyons *v.* Booth (F.W.) (Contractors) and Maidstone Borough Council (1982) 262 E.G. 981 29–555

TABLE OF CASES

Margate Corporation v. Devotwill Investments [1970] 3 All E.R. 864; 22 P. & C.R. 328; 69 L.G.R. 271, H.L.; reversing sub nom. Devotwill Investments v. Margate Corporation [1969] 2 All E.R. 97, C.A.; affirming 19 P. & C.R. 458 181–01
McDaid v. Clydebank District Council [1984] J.P.L. 579 .... 243–06, 243–08a
McDermott v. Department of Transport (1984) 48 P. & C.R. 351; (1984) 25 R.V.R. 116; [1984] J.P.L. 596 194–05
Macdonald v. Glasgow Corporation (1960) 11 P. & C.R. 318; [1960] J.P.L. 492; 1960 S.L.T. (Sh.Ct.) 21; 76 Sh.Ct.Rep. 115 22–670
McDonald v. Howard Cook Advertising [1972] 1 W.L.R. 90; 115 S.J. 950; 22 P. & C.R. 1078; 70 L.G.R. 186 63–09
McKellan v. Minister of Housing and Local Government (1966) 198 E.G. 683 ...... 22–418, 22–557
McKinnon Campbell v. Greater Manchester Council (1976) 33 P. & C.R. 110 192–15
McLaren v. Secretary of State for the Environment [1981] J.P.L. 423 .... 29–118, 36–09
Macpherson v. Secretary of State for Scotland [1985] J.P.L. 788 24–101
Maddern v. Secretary of State for the Environment and Thurrock Borough Council [1980] J.P.L. 676 22–115
Magoa Services v. Secretary of State for the Environment and Bromley London Borough [1978] J.P.L. 383 29–170
Maidstone Borough Council v. Mortimer [1980] 3 All E.R. 552; (1982) 43 P. & C.R. 67; [1981] J.P.L. 112; (1980) 256 E.G. 1013 102–01
Main v. Swansea City Council (1985) 49 P. & C.R. 26; [1985] J.P.L. 558 .... 27–04, 27–06
Maltglade Ltd. v. St. Albans Rural District Council [1972] 1 W.L.R. 1230; 116 S.J. 468; [1972] 3 All E.R. 129; 24 P. & C.R. 32; 70 L.G.R. 490 283–06
Malvern Hills District Council v. Secretary of State for the Environment (1983) 81 L.G.R. 13; (1983) 46 P. & C.R. 58; [1982] J.P.L. 439; (1983) 263 E.G. 1190 43–04
Mancini v. Coventry City Council (1983) 49 P. & C.R. 127; (1985) 25 R.V.R. 132, C.A.; affirming (1982) 44 P. & C.R. 114 .... 36–130/131, 195–02
Mansi v. Elstree Rural District Council (1964) 16 P. & C.R. 154 .... 22–321, 87–120
Markovits (Alan) v. Hove Borough Council (1958) 9 P. & C.R. 292 .... 29–345, 87–11, 87–67
Marning (Christine) v. Secretary of State for the Environment [1976] J.P.L. 634, C.A. 29–492
Marrable Estates v. Secretary of State for the Environment (1973) 229 E.G. 967 29–36
Marshall v. Nottingham Corporation [1960] 1 W.L.R. 707; 124 J.P. 222; 104 S.J. 546; [1960] 1 All E.R. 659; 11 P. & C.R. 270; 58 L.G.R. 226 22–93
Marshallsay v. Minister of Housing and Local Government (1967) 204 E.G. 695 22–101
Mason v. Secretary of State for the Environment and Bromsgrove District Council [1984] J.P.L. 332 .... 36–68, 245–32
Mayflower Cambridge Ltd. v. Secretary of State for the Environment (1975) 119 S.J. 590; (1975) 30 P. & C.R. 28; 73 L.G.R. 517 .... 22–110, 22–656
Mead v. Chelmsford Rural District Council [1953] 1 Q.B. 32; 3 P. & C.R. 239; sub nom. Mead v. Plumtree [1952] 2 T.L.R. 700; 116 J.P. 589; 96 S.J. 696; [1952] 2 All E.R. 723; 50 L.G.R. 690 87–158
Meadows v. Secretary of State for the Environment and Gloucester City Council [1983] J.P.L. 538 .... 22–650, 29–509
Mercer v. Manchester Corporation (1964) 15 P. & C.R. 321 192–03
—— v. Uckfield District Council (1962) 106 S.J. 311; 14 P. & C.R. 32; 60 L.G.R. 226; [1962] R.V.R. 326; sub nom. Mercer v. Minister of Housing and Local Government, 182 E.G. 941 88–01
Meravale Builders Ltd. v. Secretary of State for the Environment (1978) 36 P. & C.R. 87; (1978) 77 L.G.R. 365; [1978] J.P.L. 699 .... 36–87, 36–108
Metallic Protectives Ltd. v. Secretary of State for the Environment [1976] J.P.L. 166 87–148
Michell v. Minister of Housing and Local Government (1957) 8 P. & C.R. 248 147–01
Millard v. Secretary of State for the Environment (1979) 254 E.G. 733 ...... 29–171, 36–115
Miller v. Weymouth and Melcombe Regis Corporation (1974) 118 S.J. 421; (1974) 27 P. & C.R. 468 .... 36–04, 51–02, 245–11
Miller (T.A.) v. Minister of Housing and Local Government [1968] 1 W.L.R. 992; 112 S.J. 522; [1968] 2 All E.R. 633; (1968) 19 P. & C.R. 263; 66 L.G.R. 39 .... 36–35, 246–03

Miller Mead v. Minister of Housing and Local Government [1963] 2 Q.B. 196; [1963] 2 W.L.R. 225; 127 J.P. 122; 106 S.J. 1052; [1963] 1 All E.R. 459; 14 P. & C.R. 266; 61 L.G.R. 152 .... 24–90, 29–485, 87–69, 88A–01

Mills & Allen Ltd. v. City of Glasgow District Council [1980] J.P.L. 409 63–10

Minister of Agriculture, Fisheries and Food v. Appleton [1970] 1 Q.B. 221; [1969] 3 W.L.R. 755; 113 S.J. 738; [1969] 3 All E.R. 105; 7 K.I.R. 232; [1969] 1 T.R. 341 22–558

—— v. Jenkins [1963] 2 Q.B. 317; [1963] 2 W.L.R. 906; 107 S.J. 234; [1963] 2 All E.R. 147 .... 23–01, 266–01

Minister of Housing and Local Government v. Sharp [1970] Q.B. 223; [1970] 2 W.L.R. 802; 114 S.J. 109; [1970] 1 All E.R. 1009; 68 L.G.R. 187; 21 P. & C.R. 166, C.A.; reversing [1969] 3 W.L.R. 1020 158–04

Ministry of Transport v. Holland (1962) 14 P. & C.R. 259; 9 R.R.C. 228; [1962] R.A. 396; 183 E.G. 541; (1962) 61 L.G.R. 134; sub nom. Holland v. Minister of Transport [1962] R.V.R. 552, C.A.; reversing (1961) 13 P. & C.R. 42 203–01

Mixman's Properties v. Chertsey Urban District Council [1965] A.C. 735; [1964] 2 W.L.R. 1210; [1964] R.V.R. 632; sub nom. Chertsey Urban District Council v. Mixman's Properties, 15 P. & C.R. 331 .... 29–396, 29–348

Moldene v. Secretary of State for the Environment [1979] J.P.L. 177; (1978) 248 E.G. 43 .... 88B–03

Molton Builders Ltd. v. Westminster London Borough Council (1975) 119 S.J. 627; (1975) 30 P. & C.R. 182, C.A.; affirming [1974] J.P.L. 600 266–02

Monomart (Warehouses) v. Secretary of State for the Environment (1977) 34 P. & C.R. 305; [1977] J.P.L. 524; (1977) 242 E.G. 881 22–647

Moody v. Godstone Rural District Council [1966] 1 W.L.R. 1085; 130 J.P. 332; 110 S.J. 687; [1966] 2 All E.R. 696; 18 P. & C.R. 249 283–03

More O'Ferrall v. Harrow Urban District Council [1947] K.B. 66; [1947] L.J.R. 520; 175 L.T. 277; 62 T.L.R. 604; 110 J.P. 357; 90 S.J. 490; [1946] 2 All E.R. 489 63–01

Morecambe and Heysham Corporation v. Warwick (1958) 56 L.G.R. 283; 9 P. & C.R. 307 283–02

Mornford Investments Ltd. v. Minister of Housing and Local Government [1970] 2 All E.R. 253; 21 P. & C.R. 609 22–653

Morris v. Secretary of State for the Environment (1975) 31 P. & C.R. 216 . 23–392, 87–78, 88A–09

—— v. Secretary of State for the Environment [1986] J.P.L. 62 22–415

Mounsdon v. Weymouth and Melcombe Rehs Corporation [1960] 1 Q.B. 645; [1960] 2 W.L.R. 484; 124 J.P. 231; 104 S.J. 232; [1960] 1 All E.R. 538; 58 L.G.R. 144; 11 P. & C.R. 103 87–12

Moxey v. Hertford Rural District Council (1973) 27 P. & C.R. 274 169–07

Murfitt v. Secretary of State for the Environment and East Cambridgeshire District Council (1980) 40 P. & C.R. 254; [1980] J.P.L. 598 .... 87–129, 87–134, 88A–14

Murphy (J) & Sons v. Secretary of State for the Environment; Same v. Same [1973] 1 W.L.R. 560; [1973] 2 All E.R. 26; sub nom. Murphy v. Secretary of State for the Environment, 117 S.J. 304; sub nom. Murphy (J.) & Sons v. Secretary of State for the Environment (1973) 71 L.G.R. 273 .... 29–148, 29–149

Myton v. Minister of Housing and Local Government (1963) 61 L.G.R. 556; 16 P. & C.R. 240; [1963] R.V.R. 775 29–35

Nash v. Secretary of State for the Environment and Epping District Council [1986] J.P.L. 128 29–181

National Carriers Ltd. v. Secretary of State for Transport (1978) 35 P. & C.R. 245 238–01

National Provincial Bank v. Portsmouth Corporation (1959) 58 L.G.R. 115; (1959) 11 P. & C.R. 6, C.A.; affirming (1958) 10 P. & C.R. 60 .... 22–474, 169–02

National Trust v. Midlands Electricity Board [1952] Ch. 380; [1952] 1 T.L.R. 74; 116 J.P. 65; 96 S.J. 29; [1952] 1 All E.R. 298 52–03

Nelsolvil Ltd. v. Minister of Housing and Local Government [1962] 1 W.L.R. 404; 126 J.P. 108; 106 S.J. 310; [1962] 1 All E.R. 423; 13 P. & C.R. 151; 60 L.G.R. 83; [1962] R.V.R. 344 88–37

New Forest District Council v. Secretary of State for the Environment and Clarke (J.F.H.) [1984] J.P.L. 178 .... 29–204, 36–11

Newbury District Council v. Secretary of State for the Environment; Same v.
  International Synthetic Rubber Co. [1981] A.C. 578; [1980] 2 W.L.R. 379; (1980)
  124 S.J. 186; [1980] 1 All E.R. 731; (1980) 78 L.G.R. 306; (1980) 40 P. & C.R.
  148; [1980] J.P.L. 325, H.L.; reversing [1978] 1 W.L.R. 1241 .... 22–464, 22–468,
  22–649, 23–389, 29–297, 29–323, 30–08, 266–03
—— v. Secretary of State for the Environment [1983] J.P.L. 281 29–177
Newham London Borough v. Secretary of State for the Environment and East London
  Housing Association [1986] J.P.L. 607 .... 29–93, 29–254
Newport v. Secretary of State for the Environment and Bromley London Borough
  (1980) 40 P. & C.R. 261; [1980] J.P.L. 596 87–130
Niarchos (London) Ltd. v. Secretary of State for the Environment and Westminster
  City Council (1977) 76 L.G.R. 480; (1977) 35 P. & C.R. 259; (1977) 245
  E.G. 847; [1977] J.P.L. 247 .... 29–19, 29–151, 36–08
Nicholls and Nicholls v. Secretary of State for the Environment and Bristol City Council
  [1981] J.P.L. 890 22–430
Nicholls (A.H.) & Sons v. Hertford Rural District Council (1964) 15 P. & C.R.
  330 .... 88A–02
Nicholson v. Secretary of State for Energy (1977) 76 L.G.R. 693; [1978] J.P.L. 39;
  (1977) 245 E.G. 139 36–39
Norfolk County Council v. Secretary of State for the Environment [1973] 1 W.l.R. 1400;
  117 S.J. 650; [1973] 3 All E.R. 673; 23 P. & C.R. 23; 72 L.G.R. 44 28–07
North Norfolk District Council v. Long [1984] J.P.L. 45; (1983) 267 E.G. 251 29–508
North Sea Land Equipment v. Secretary of State for the Environment and Thurrock
  Borough Council [1982] J.P.L. 384; (1982) 263 E.G. 668 87–135
North Surrey Water Co.. v. Secretary of State for the Environment (1967) 45 P. & C.R.
  140; [1977] J.P.L. 100 .... 29–167, 36–61
North Warwickshire Borough Council v. Secretary of State for the Environment and
  Amrik Singh Gill (1983) 50 P. & C.R. 47; [1984] J.P.L. 435 22–564
North West Leicestershire District Council v. Secretary of State for the Environment
  and Lees (Barry J. and Margaret) (1983) 46 P. & C.R. 154; [1982] J.P.L. 777 24–12
Northavon District Council v. Secretary of State for the Environment (1980) 40 P. &
  C.R. 332; [1981] J.P.L. 114 .... 22–12, 24–96
Nowell (Executor) v. Kirkburton Urban District Council (1970) 21 P. & C.R.
  832 192–10

O'Reilly v. Mackman; Millbanks v. Secretary of State for the Home Department [1983]
  2 A.C. 237; [1983] 3 W.L.R. 1096; (1982) 126 S.J. 820; [1982] 3 All E.R. 1124,
  H.L.; affirming O'Reilly v. Mackman; Derbyshire v. Same; Dougan v. Same;
  Millbanks v. Home Office [1982] 3 W.L.R. 604 29–550
Ormston v. Horsham Rural District Council (1965) 109 S.J. 701; (1965) 63 L.G.R. 452;
  17 P. & C.R. 105; [1965] C.L.Y. 3809, C.A. 87–72, 87–145
Ostreicher v. Secretary of State for the Environment [1978] 1 W.L.R. 810; (1978) 122
  S.J. 194; [1978] 3 All E.R. 82; 76 L.G.R. 445; (1978) 37 P. & C.R. 9; [1978] J.P.L.
  539 36–41
Overland v. Minister of Housing and Local Government (1957) 8 P. & C.R. 389 ... 147–02
Oxley v. Keighley Corporation (1960) 11 P. & C.R. 465 192–01

P.A.D. Entertainments v. Secretary of State for the Environment [1982] J.P.L. 706;
  (1982) 264 E.G. 1005 88–26
Page v. Mayor, Aldermen and Burgesses of the Borough of Gillingham (1970) 21 P.
  & C.R. 973 192–11
Panayi v. Secretary of State for the Environment and Hackney London Borough
  Council (1985) 49 P. & C.R. 109; [1985] J.P.L. 783 22–128
Pardes House School Trustees v. Hendon Borough Council (1964) 15 P. & C.R.
  326 29–480
Parker & Parker v. West Midlands County Council (1978) 38 P. & C.R. 720; [1979]
  J.P.L. 178 .... 194–04, 195–05
Parker Bros. (Farms) v. Minister of Housing and Local Government (1969) 210 E.G.
  825 88–03
Parkes v. Secretary of State for the Environment [1978] 1 W.L.R. 1308; (1978) 122 S.J.
  349; [1979] 1 All E.R. 211; (1978) 36 P. & C.R. 387; (1978) 77 L.G.R. 39;
  (1978) 248 E.G. 595; [1979] J.P.L. 33 .... 22–01, 51–03

Parry (decd.) v. Forest of Dean District Council (1976) 34 P. & C.R. 209; [1977] J.P.L. 728; (1978) 241 E.G. 387 89–15
Patel v. Betts [1978] J.P.L. 109; (1977) 243 E.G. 1003 .... 88A–13
Paultons Square Properties v. London County Council (1965) 63 L.G.R. 158 . 96/97/9A–01
Peacock Homes v. Secretary of State for the Environment (1984) 48 P. & C.R. 20; [1984] F.S.R. 729; (1984) 83 L.G.R. 686 87–33
Peak Park Joint Planning Board v. Secretary of State for the Environment and Cyril Kay [1979] J.P.L. 618 .... 29–70, 29–172, 235–22
—— v. Secretary of State for the Environment and Imperial Chemical Industries (1979) 39 P. & C.R. 361; [1980] J.P.L. 114 .... 29–322, 29–359
Peake v. Secretary of State for Wales (1971) 115 S.J. 507; (1971) 22 P. & C.R. 889; (1971) 70 L.G.R. 98 .... 22–266, 22–320
Peaktop Properties (Hampstead) v. Camden London Borough Council (1983) 46 P. & C.R. 177, C.A.; reversing (1982) 44 P. & C.R. 233 169–09
Pennine Raceway v. Kirklees Metropolitan Council [1983] Q.B. 382; [1982] 3 W.L.R. 987; (1982) 126 S.J. 449; [1982] 3 All E.R. 628; (1983) 45 P. & C.R. 313; (1983) 81 L.G.R. 89; (1984) 24 R.V.R. 85; [1982] J.P.L. 780; (1982) 263 E.G. 712; (1984) 134 New L.J. 969; (1982) 79 L.S.Gaz. 921 .... 52–11, 164–13
Penwith District Council v. Secretary of State for the Environment (1977) 34 P. & C.R. 269; [1977] J.P.L. 371 29–320
—— v. Secretary of State for the Environment and Mainstreet Marketing Ltd. [1986] J.P.L. 432; (1985) 277 E.G. 194 .... 29–79, 29–403
Performance Cars Ltd. v. Secretary of State for the Environment (1977) 34 P. & C.R. 92; (1977) 246 E.G. 563; [1977] J.P.L. 585, C.A.; reversing (1976) 240 E.G. 51 .... 36–38, 245–15
Perkins v. Secretary of State for the Environment and the Rother District Council [1981] J.P.L. 755 87–134
—— v. West Wiltshire District Council (1975) 31 P. & C.R. 427 193–03
Perris v. Minister of Housing and Local Government (1959) 11 P. & C.R. 112 146–01
—— v. Stanborough (Developments) Ltd. [1978] J.P.L. 36; (1977) 244 E.G. 551 87–07
Petticoat Lane Rentals Ltd. v. Secretary of State for the Environment [1971] 1 W.L.R. 1112; [1971] 2 All E.R. 793; 69 L.G.R. 504; 22 P. & C.R. 703; sub nom. Petticoat Lane Rentals v. Minister of Housing and Local Government, 115 S.J. 487 22–466
Philglow v. Secretary of State for the Environment and London Borough of Hillingdon [1985] J.P.L. 318; (1984) 270 E.G. 1192, C.A.; reversing [1984] J.P.L. 111 .... 22–127, 22–328
Phillips v. Minister of Housing and Local Government [1965] 1 Q.B. 156; [1964] 3 W.L.R. 378; 128 J.P. 507; 108 S.J. 423; [1964] 2 All E.R. 824; 15 P. & C.R. 376; 62 L.G.R. 616; [1964] R.V.R. 470, C.A.; reversing [1964] 2 W.L.R. 1 56–01
Pilkington v. Secretary of State for the Environment [1973] 1 W.L.R. 1527; 117 S.J. 894; [1974] 1 All E.R. 283; (1973) 26 P. & C.R. 508; (1973) 72 L.G.R. 303 .... 25–01, 29–512, 87–77
Pioneer Aggregates (U.K.) Ltd. v. Secretary of State for the Environment [1985] A.C. 132; [1984] 3 W.L.R. 32; (1984) 128 S.J. 416; [1984] 2 All E.R. 358; (1984) 48 P. & C.R. 95; [1984] J.P.L. 651; (1984) 82 L.G.R. 488; (1984) 272 E.G. 425; (1984) 81 L.S.Gaz. 2148, H.L. 29–512, 33–01, 45–01, 45–05
Plymouth Corporation v. Secretary of State for the Environment [1972] 1 W.L.R. 1347; 116 S.J. 565; [1972] 3 All E.R. 225; 24 P. & C.R. 88; sub nom. Plymouth City Corporation v. Secretary of State for the Environment (1972) 70 L.G.R. 567 184–01
Pollock v. Secretary of State for the Environment and Greenwich London Borough (1979) 40 P. & C.R. 94; [1979] J.P.L. 680; (1979) 252 E.G. 914 22–270
—— v. Secretary of State for the Environment [1981] J.P.L. 420 .... 36–93, 88–43, 88–44
Postill v. East Riding County Council [1956] 2 Q.B. 386; [1956] 3 W.L.R. 334; 120 J.P. 376; 100 S.J. 490; [1956] 2 All E.R. 685; 54 L.G.R. 415; 6 P. & C.R. 400 .... 24–90, 87–13
Poyser and Mills' Arbitration, Re [1964] 2 Q.B. 467; [1963] 2 W.L.R. 1309; [1963] 1 All E.R. 612; sub nom. Poyser v. Mills, 107 S.J. 115 36–103
Preece & Preece v. Worcester Corporation (1966) 18 P. & C.R. 103; [1967] J.P.L. 162 192–07

TABLE OF CASES

Prengate Properties v. Secretary of State for the Environment (1973) 25 P. & C.R. 311;
  71 L.G.R. 373 24–73
Preston District Council v. Secretary of State for the Environment and E.L.S.
  Wholesale (Wolverhampton) [1978] J.P.L. 548 .... 36–112, 245–19
Price Bros. (Rode Heath) v. Secretary of State for the Environment (1979) 38 P. & C.R.
  579; [1979] J.P.L. 387; 252 E.G. 595 .... 36–06, 36–111, 245–21
Property Investment Holdings v. Secretary of State for the Environment and Reigate
  and Banstead Borough Council [1984] J.P.L. 587 .... 29–364, 53–06
Prosser v. Sharp [1985] J.P.L. 717; (1985) 274 E.G. 1249 .... 89–06, 243–08
Provincial Properties (London) v. Caterham and Warlingham Urban District Council
  [1972] 1 Q.B. 453; [1972] 2 W.L.R. 44; 115 S.J. 832; [1972] 1 All E.R. 60; 23 P. &
  C.R. 8; 70 L.G.R. 151 181–03
Purbeck District Council v. Secretary of State for the Environment (1983) 46 P. & C.R.
  1; (1982) 263 E.G. 261; [1982] J.P.L. 640; (1982) 80 L.G.R. 545 ...... 180–13, 180–14
Pye (J.A.) (Oxford) Estates Ltd. v. Secretary of State for the Environment and
  Cherwell District Council [1982] J.P.L. 180 36–123
—— v. West Oxfordshire District Council and Secretary of State for the Environment
  [1982] J.P.L. 577; (1982) 264 E.G. 533 .... 29–61, 29–73
—— v. Wychavon District Council and Secretary of State for the Environment [1982]
  J.P.L. 575 28–64
Pyrford Properties Ltd. v. Secretary of State for the Environment (1977) 36 P. & C.R.
  28; [1977] J.P.L. 724; (1977) 244 E.G. 383 36–84
Pyx Granite Co. v. Minister of Housing and Local Government [1960] A.C. 260; [1959] 3
  W.L.R. 346; 123 J.P. 429; 103 S.J. 633; [1959] 3 All E.R. 1; 10 P. & C.R. 319; 58
  L.G.R. 1, H.L.; reversing [1958] 1 Q.B. 554 .... 24–145, 29–316, 29–415

R. v. Amber Valley District Council, ex p. Jackson [1985] 1 W.L.R. 298; (1983) 49
  P. & C.R. 136; [1984] 3 All E.R. 501; (1984) 128 S.J. 853 29–14
—— v. Berkshire County Council, ex p. Mangall. See R. v. Royal County of Berkshire,
  ex p. Mangall.
—— v. Beverley Borough Council, ex p. Wilson [1983] C.L.Y. 3721 29–158
—— v. Bolton Metropolitan Borough Council, ex p. Whitecroft [1984] J.P.L. 875 36–99
—— v. Bournemouth Justices, ex p. Bournemouth Corporation (1970) 114 S.J. 150; 68
  L.G.R. 261; (1970) 21 P. & C.R. 163 60–02
—— v. Bradford-on-Avon U.D.C., ex p. Boulton [1964] 1 W.L.R. 1136; 128 J.P. 339;
  108 S.J. 710; [1964] 2 All E.R. 492; 15 P. & C.R. 304; 62 L.G.R. 475 27–04
—— v. Bromley London Borough, ex p. Sievers (1980) 41 P. & C.R. 294; (1980) 255
  E.G. 359; sub nom. Sievers v. Bromley London Borough [1980] J.P.L. 520 42–02
—— v. Camden London Borough, ex p. Comyn Ching (1984) 47 P. & C.R. 417; [1984]
  J.P.L. 661 101–03
—— v. Carlisle City Council and Secretary of State for the Environment, ex p.
  Cumbrian Co-operative Society [1986] J.P.L. 206; (1985) 276 E.G. 1161 29–16,
  29–224
—— v. Castle Point District Council, ex p. Brooks [1985] J.P.L. 473 .... 25–21, 29–552
—— v. Chertsey JJ., ex p. Franks [1961] 2 Q.B. 152; [1961] 2 W.L.R. 442; 125 J.P. 305;
  105 S.J. 181; [1961] 1 All E.R. 825; 12 P. & C.R. 278; 59 L.G.R. 260 89–09
—— v. Chief Constable of Devon and Cornwall, ex p. Central Electricity Generating
  Board [1982] Q.B. 458; [1981] 3 W.L.R. 867; [1981] 3 All E.R. 826 .... 280/281–01
—— v. Derbyshire County Council, ex p. North East Derbyshire District Council
  (1979) 77 L.G.R. 389; [1980] J.P.L. 398 .... 22–674, 29–497
—— v. East Kesteven Rural District Council., ex p. Sleaford and District White City
  Sports Stadium Co. [1947] W.N. 58; 63 T.L.R. 112; 111 J.P. 192; [1947] 1 All
  E.R. 310 29–280
—— v. Edmundsbury Borough Council, ex p. Investors in Industry Commercial
  Properties Ltd. [1985] 3 All E.R. 234; (1985) 51 P. & C.R. 251 29–15
—— v. Endersby Properties (1975) 32 P. & C.R. 399 277–01
—— v. Hammersmith & Fulham Borough Council, ex p. People Before Profit Ltd.
  (1983) 45 P. & C.R. 364; (1982) 80 L.G.R. 322; [1981] J.P.L. 869 ...... 13–03, 29–44,
  29–548
—— v. Harrow Urban District Council, ex p. Joiner (1956) 6 P. & C.R. 151 29–540

xxxviii

R. v. Hillingdon London Borough Council, *ex p.* Royco Homes Ltd. [1974] 1 Q.B. 720; [1974] 2 W.L.R. 805; 118 S.J. 389; 72 L.G.R. 516; 28 P. & C.R. 251; *sub nom.* R. v. London Borough of Hillingdon, *ex p.* Royco Homes [1974] 2 All E.R. 643 .... 29–303, 29–354, 29–419, 29–542
—— v. Jenner [1983] 1 W.L.R. 873; (1983) 127 S.J. 324; [1983] 2 All E.R. 46; [1983] Crim.L.R. 398; [1983] J.P.L. 547; (1983) 147 J.P.N. 239 90–04
—— v. Lambeth London Borough Council, *ex p.* Sharp (1985) 50 P. & C.R. 284 .. 270–04
—— v. London Borough of Greenwich, *ex p.* Patel [1985] J.P.L. 851 .... 91–03, 243–08a
—— v. London Borough of Haringay, *ex p.* Norman Clifford Barrs [1983] J.P.L. 54 29–551
—— v. London County Quarter Sessions Appeals Committee, *ex p.* Rossi [1956] 1 Q.B. 682; [1956] 2 W.L.R. 800; 120 J.P. 239; 100 S.J. 225; [1956] 1 All E.R. 670 283–01
—— v. Melton & Belvoir Justices, *ex p.* Tynan (1977) 75 L.G.R. 544; (1977) 33 P. & C.R. 214 88–22
—— v. Minister of Fuel and Power, *ex p.* Warwickshire County Council [1957] 1 W.L.R. 861; 121 J.P. 491; 101 S.J. 555; [1957] 2 All E.R. 731; 55 L.G.R. 409; 8 P. & C.R. 305 222–01
—— v. Minister of Housing and Local Government, *ex p.* Chichester Rural District Council [1960] 1 W.L.R. 587; 124 J.P. 322; 104 S.J. 449; [1960] 2 All E.R. 407; 11 P. & C.R. 295; 58 L.G.R. 198 180–03
—— v. ——, *ex p.* Rank Organisation [1958] 1 W.L.R. 1093; 122 J.P. 485; 102 S.J. 811; [1958] 3 All E.R. 322; 10 P. & C.R. 9; 56 L.G.R. 403; [1959] J.P.L. 88 180–02
—— v. Minister of Town and Country Planning, *ex p.* Mantague Burton [1951] 1 K.B. 1; 66 T.L.R. (Pt. 2) 85; 114 J.P. 411; 94 S.J. 487; [1950] 2 All E.R. 282; 48 L.G.R. 461; 1 P. & C.R. 161; 155 E.G. 544, C.A.; affirming [1950] W.N. 38 292–01
—— v. North Hertfordshire District Council, *ex p.* Sullivan [1981] J.P.L. 752 55–02
—— v. Royal County of Berkshire, *ex p.* Mangall [1985] J.P.L. 258 29–220
—— v. St. Edmundsbury Borough Council, *ex p.* Investors in Industry Commercial Properties Ltd. [1985] 1 W.L.R. 1157; (1985) 129 S.J. 623; [1985] 3 All E.R. 234; [1985] J.P.L. 38; (1985) 82 L.S.Gaz. 2741 .... 29–330, 29–420, 31–02
—— v. Secretary of State for the Environment, *ex p.* Bilton (Percy) Industrial Properties (1975) 119 S.J. 794; (1975) 31 P. & C.R. 154; 74 L.G.R. 244; *sub nom.* Bilton (Percy) Industrial Properties v. Secretary of State for the Environment (1975) 237 E.G. 491 .... 25–12, 42–01
—— v. ——, *ex p.* Bulk Storage [1985] J.P.L. 35 292–07
—— v. ——, *ex p.* Centre 21 Ltd. [1985] J.P.L. 865 245–36
—— v. ——, *ex p.* Crossley [1985] J.P.L. 632 88–29
—— v. Secretary of State for the Environment and Others, *ex p.* Greater London Council [1985] J.P.L. 543 36–101
—— v. Secretary of State for the Environment, *ex p.* Hampshire County Council (1982) 44 P. & C.R. 343; [1981] J.P.L. 47 101–01
—— v. ——, *ex p.* Mistral Investments [1984] J.P.L. 516 36–49
—— v. ——, *ex p.* Newprop [1983] J.P.L. 386 35–02
—— v. ——, *ex p.* Ostler; *sub nom.* R. v. Secretary of State for Home Affairs, *ex p.* Ostler [1977] 1 Q.B. 122; (1976) 75 L.G.R. 45; (1976) 238 E.G. 971 242–01
—— v. ——, *ex p.* Panayi. *See* Panayi v. Secretary of State for the Environment.
—— v. Secretary of State for the Environment, *ex p.* Reinisch (1971) 22 P. & C.R. 1022; (1971) 70 L.G.R. 126 .... 29–489, 45–03, 282–03
—— v. ——, *ex p.* Three Rivers District Council [1983] J.P.L. 730 92–03
—— v. ——, *ex p.* Hillingdon Borough Council [1986] J.P.L. 363 87–08
—— v. Sevenoaks District Council, *ex p.* Terry (W.J.) [1985] 3 All E.R. 226; [1984] J.P.L. 420 .... 29–13, 29–15, 29–26
—— v. Sheffield City Council, *ex p.* Mansfield (1978) 77 L.G.R. 126; (1978) 37 P. & C.R. 1; [1978] J.P.L. 465; *sub nom.* Mansfield v. Sheffield City Council (1978) 247 E.G. 52 .... 29–08, 29–543
—— v. Smith (Thomas George) (1984) 48 P. & C.R. 392; [1985] J.P.L. 183; [1984] Crim.L.R. 630; (1984) 81 L.S.Gaz. 2775 .... 243–07, 243–09
—— v. Stroud District Council, *ex p.* Goodenough, Usborne and Tomlin (1982) 43 P. & C.R. 59; [1982] J.P.L. 246 .... 55–01, 101–02
—— v. Torfaen Borough Council (amended to Monmouth District Council), *ex p.* Jones [1986] J.P.L. 686 .... 29–16b

R. v. Wakefield Metropolitan District Council, *ex p.* Asquith [1986] J.P.L. 440 13–04
—— v. Wells Street Metropolitan Stipendiary Magistrates, *ex p.* Westminster City
    Council [1986] 1 W.L.R. 1046 .... 55–02a
—— v. West Oxfordshire D.C., *ex p.* Pearce Homes Ltd. [1986] J.P.L. 523 .... 29–16a
—— v. Worthing Borough Council and Secretary of State for the Environment, *ex p.*
    Burch (G.H.) (1983) 49 P. & C.R. 53; [1984] J.P.L. 261 .... 29–74, 266–04
—— v. Yeovil Borough Council, *ex p.* Trustees of Elim Pentecostal Church, Yeovil,
    116 S.J. 78; (1971) 70 L.G.R. 142; (1971) 23 P. & C.R. 39 29–06
R.K.T. Investments Ltd. v. Hackney London Borough Council (1978) 36 P. & C.R. 442;
    (1978) 246 E.G. 919; *sub nom.* R.T.K. Investments v. Hackney London Borough
    Council [1979] J.P.L. 234 29–05
Rael-Brook v. Minister of Housing and Local Government [1967] 2 Q.B. 65; [1967]
    2 W.L.R. 604; 111 S.J. 95; [1967] 1 All E.R. 262; 18 P. & C.R. 290; 65 L.G.R.
    239; *sub nom.* Rael-Brook v. Minister of Local Government (1966) 131 J.P.
    237 22–622
Ragsdale v. Creswick (1984) 148 J.P. 564; [1984] J.P.L. 883; (1984) 271 E.G. 1268 89–18
Rakusen Properties v. Leeds City Council. *See* Rakusen Properties; Rakusen Group;
    Rakusen (Lloyd) & Sons v. Leeds City Council.
Rakusen Properties; Rakusen Group; Rakusen (Lloyd) & Sons v. Leeds City Council
    (1978) 37 P. & C.R. 315; *sub nom.* Rakusen Properties v. Leeds City Council
    [1979] J.P.L. 37 .... 180–11, 181–05
Rann v. Secretary of State for the Environment (1980) 40 P. & C.R. 113; [1980] J.P.L.
    109; (1979) 254 E.G. 1095 .... 22–586, 22–665
Ransom & Luck Ltd. v. Surbiton Borough Council [1949] Ch. 180; [1949] L.J.R. 809; 65
    T.L.R. 57; 113 J.P. 95; 93 S.J. 41; [1941] 1 All E.R. 185; 47 L.G.R. 467 52–01
Radcliffe v. Secretary of State for the Environment (1975) 235 E.G. 901; [1975] J.P.L.
    728 22–428
Rawson v. Minister of Health (1965) 17 P. & C.R. 239 194–01
Reading Borough Council v. Secretary of State for the Environment and Commercial
    Union Properties (Investments) [1986] J.P.L. 115 36–135
Redbridge London Borough v. Perry (1976) 33 P. & C.R. 176; (1976) 75 L.G.R. 90;
    [1977] J.P.L. 247; (1976) 241 E.G. 457 .... 87–161, 89–16, 243–09
Red House Farms (Thorndon) Ltd. v. Mid-Suffolk District Council (1980) 40 P. & C.R.
    113; [1980] J.P.L. 748 105–01
Relton (W.G.) v. Minster of Housing and Local Government (1969) 67 L.G.R.
    469 29–487
Resdormel Borough Council v. Secretary of State for the Environment and Rabey
    (Patrick George and Susan Margaret) [1982] J.P.L. 785 22–120
Rhodes v. Minister of Housing and Local Government [1963] 1 W.L.R. 208; 127 J.P.
    179; 107 S.J. 57; [1963] 1 All E.R. 300; 14 P. & C.R. 122; 61 L.G.R. 194 ... 29–218
Rhymney Valley District Council v. Secretary of State for Wales and Isaac (G.) [1985]
    J.P.L. 27 .... 87–152, 246–13
Richmond, London Borough of v. Secretary of State for the Environment and
    Hutchinson & Locke & Monk [1984] J.P.L. 24 29–22
Richmond-upon-Thames Borough Council v. Secretary of State for the Environment
    (1972) 224 E.G. 1555 .... 88B–02
—— v. —— (1978) 37 P. & C.R. 151; (1978) 249 E.G. 244; [1979] J.P.L. 175 55–10
Ringroad Investments and Courtburn v. Secretary of State for the Environment (1979)
    49 P. & C.R. 99; [1979] J.P.L. 770 246–08
Roberts v. Vale Royal District Council and Secretary of State for the Environment
    (1977) 39 P. & C.R. 514; [1977] J.P.L. 369; (1977) 78 L.G.R. 368; (1977) 242
    E.G. 811 29–355
Rochdale Metropolitan Borough Council v. Simmonds (1980) 40 P. & C.R. 432; [1981]
    J.P.L. 191; (1980) 256 E.G. 607 .... 87–19, 87–83, 243–01
Rockhold Ltd. v. Secretary of State for the Environment and South Oxfordshire District
    Council [1986] J.P.L. 130 .... 28–64, 29–77
Rogelan Building Group Ltd. v. Secretary of State for the Environment and Kettering
    Borough Council [1981] J.P.L. 506 .... 36–121, 245–26
Rose v. Leeds Corporation [1964] 1 W.L.R. 1393; 129 J.P. 76; 108 S.J. 673; [1964] 3 All
    E.R. 618; 62 L.G.R. 637; 16 P. & C.R. 177 292–05
Routh v. Reading Corporation (1970) 217 E.G. 1337 242–03
Royal Borough of Kensington and Chelsea v. Elmton (1978) 256 E.G. 1011 109–01

Rugby School Governors v. Secretary of State for the Environment [1975] J.P.L. 97; (1974) 234 E.G. 371 29–37
Runnymede Borough Council v. Ball (D.M.) [1986] 1 W.L.R. 353; 130 S.J. 111; [1986] 1 All E.R. 629; [1986] J.P.L. 288 87–177
—— v. Smith [1986] J.P.L. 592 .... 87–177, 90–05
Russell (Robert) Developments v. Buckinghamshire County Council, 107 S.J. 515; 15 P. & C.R. 203; (1963) 61 L.G.R. 483; [1963] R.V.R. 757; 187 E.G. 453 29–478
Ryan v. Secretary of State for the Environment [1982] C.L.Y. 3178 36–124

S.J.D. Properties Ltd. v. Secretary of State for the Environment and Westminster City Council [1981] J.P.L. 673 .... 22–273, 88–44
Sabey & Sabey v. Hartlepool County Borough Council (1969) 21 P. & C.R. 448 ... 192–09, 195–07
Sabey (H.) & Co. Ltd. v. Secretary of State for the Environment [1978] 1 All E.R. 586; [1977] J.P.L. 661; (1977) 245 E.G. 397 .... 36–82, 245–17
Sainsbury (J.) Ltd. v. Secretary of State for the Environment and Colchester Borough Council [1978] J.P.L. 379 36–90
St. Albans District Council v. Harper (Norman) Autosales Ltd. (1977) 121 S.J. 851; (1977) 76 L.G.R. 300; (1977) 35 P. & C.R. 70; [1978] J.P.L. 552; (1977) 245 E.G. 1029 89–03
St. Edmundsbury Borough Council v. Secretary of State for the Environment [1985] J.P.L. 785 36–129
St. Herman's Estate Co. v. Havard & Waterloo Urban District Council (1971) 69 L.G.R. 286 22–107
St. Winfred, Welcomes Road, Kenley, Surrey, Re, British Paper and Board Industry Research Association v. Croydon Borough Council (1969) 113 S.J. 307; 20 P. & C.R. 583; sub nom. British Paper and Board Industry Research Association v. Croydon London Borough Council, 67 L.G.R. 491 22–593
Sainty v. Minister of Housing and Local Government (1964) 108 S.J. 118; (1964) 15 P. & C.R. 432; 62 L.G.R. 179; 189 E.G. 341 .... 22–475, 22–480
Saleem v. City of Bradford Metropolitan Council (1984) 25 R.V.R. 202; (1984) 271 E.G. 119 212–01
Salisbury (A.L.) Ltd. v. York Corporation (1960) 11 P. & C.R. 421 169–04
Salisbury District Council v. Secretary of State for the Environment and Parnwell (Gillian E.) [1982] J.P.L. 702 43–06
Sample (J. Warkworth) v. Alnwick District Council (1984) 48 P. & C.R. 474; [1984] J.P.L. 670; (1984) 271 E.G. 204; (1984) 24 R.V.R. 180 177–02
Sampson's Executors v. Nottinghamshire County Council [1949] 2 K.B. 439; 65 T.L.R. 376; 113 J.P. 328; [1949] 1 All E.R. 1051; (1950) 1 P. & C.R. 1; sub nom. Nottinghamshire County Council v. Sampson's Executors, 47 L.G.R. 425 22–494
Sand and Gravel Association Ltd. v. Buckinghamshire County Council [1984] J.P.L. 798 244–01
Sanders v. Secretary of State for the Environment and Epping Forest District Council [1981] J.P.L. 593 .... 87–133, 88A–18
Scarborough District Council v. Adams and Adams (1983) 147 J.P. 449; (1984) 47 P. & C.R. 133; [1983] J.P.L. 673 .... 87–50, 88–24, 89–17
Scott v. Secretary of State for the Environment and Bracknell District Council [1982] J.P.L. 108 .... 22–16, 87–84, 88A–19
Scott Markets Ltd. v. Waltham Forest London Borough Council (1979) 77 L.G.R. 565; (1979) 38 P. & C.R. 597; [1979] J.P.L. 392, C.A.; reversing (1978) 37 P. & C.R. 91 90–01
Scrivener v. Minister of Housing and Local Government (1966) 18 P. & C.R. 357; (1966) 64 L.G.R. 251 22–581
Scurlock v. Secretary of State for Wales (1977) 33 P. & C.R. 202; (1976) 238 E.G. 47 .... 24–09, 88A–11
Sears Blok v. Secretary of State for the Environment [1980] J.P.L. 523; (1980) 254 E.G. 1195 .... 29–72, 36–65, 36–118
Seddon Properties v. Secretary of State for the Environment and Macclesfield Borough Council (1981) 42 P. & C.R. 26; [1978] J.P.L. 835; sub nom. Seddon Properties and James Crosbie & Sons v. Secretary of State for the Environment (1978) 248 E.G. 951 .... 36–114, 245–20
Segal v. Manchester Corporation (1966) 18 P. & C..R. 112 203–02

TABLE OF CASES

Shanley (M.J.) (In Liquidation) Ltd. v. Secretary of State for the Environment and South Bedfordshire District Council [1982] J.P.L. 380 .... 29–362, 29–401, 36–10
Sheffield City Council v. Secretary of State for the Environment (1979) 251 E.G. 165 29–41
Shemara Ltd. v. Luton Corporation (1967) 18 P. & C.R. 520 25–08
Shephard v. Buckinghamshire County Council (1966) 18 P. & C.R. 419; (1966) 64 L.G.R. 422 22–614
—— v. Secretary of State for the Environment [1975] J.P.L. 352 ... 29–481, 184–02, 186–01
Shepperton Builders v. Secretary of State for the Environment [1979] J.P.L. 102 ... 36–116
Shop Properties v. Minister of Housing and Local Government (1969) 211 E.G. 161 55–08
Sievers v. Bromley London Borough. See R. v. Bromley London Borough, ex p. Sievers.
Simmonds v. Secretary of State for the Environment and Rochdale Metropolitan District Council [1981] J.P.L. 509 24–75
—— v. Secretary of State for the Environment [1985] J.P.L. 253 36–100
Simms (W.J.) Sons & Cooke v. Minister of Housing and Local Government (1969) 210 E.G. 705 14–03
Simpson v. Edinburgh Corporation, 1961 S.L.T. 17; 1960 S.C. 313 29–17
Sinclair-Lockhart's Trustees v. Central Land Board, 1 P. & C.R. 320; 1951 S.C. 258; 1951 S.L.T. 121; affirming (1950) 1 P. & C.R. 195; 1950 S.L.T. 283 . 22–492, 22–493
Skinner v. Secretary of State for the Environment [1978] J.P.L. 842; (1978) 247 E.G. 1173 .... 88A–47
Slough Estates v. Slough Borough Council (No. 2) [1971] A.C. 958; [1970] 2 W.L.R. 1187; 114 S.J. 435; [1970] 2 All E.R. 216; 21 P. & C.R. 573; sub nom. Slough Estates v. Slough Corporation (No. 2), 68 L.G.R. 669 .... 29–04, 29–485, 45–01
Small Pressure Castings Ltd. v. Secretary of State for the Environment (1973) 222 E.G. 1099 29–168
Smart & Courtenay Dale Ltd. v. Dover Rural District Council (1972) 23 P. & C.R. 408 180–10
Smith v. Central Land Board (1957) 8 P. & C.R. 357 137–02
—— v. East Elloe Rural District Council [1956] A.C. 736; [1956] 2 W.L.R. 888; 120 J.P. 263; 100 S.J. 282; [1956] 1 All E.R. 855; 54 L.G.R. 233; 6 P. & C.R. 102 242–01
—— v. King (1969) 21 P. & C.R. 560 .... 88–04, 243–09
—— v. Minister of Housing and Local Government (1966) 64 L.G.R. 235 23–04
—— v. Secretary of State for the Environment and Bristol City Council (1984) 47 P. & C.R. 194; [1983] J.P.L. 461 23–11
—— v. Somerset County Council (1965) 17 P. & C.R. 162 192–06
Smith and Snipes Hall Farm Ltd. v. River Douglas Catchment Board [1949] 2 K.B. 500; sub nom. Smith v. River Douglas Catchment Board, 65 T.L.R. 628; 113 J.P. 388; 93 S.J. 525; [1949] 2 All E.R. 179; 47 L.G.R. 627, C.A.; reversing [1948] W.N. 414 52–02
Snook v. Secretary of State for the Environment (1975) 33 P. & C.R. 1; [1976] J.P.L. 303; (1975) 237 E.G. 723 .... 22–09, 22–324
Snow v. Secretary of State for the Environment (1976) 33 P. & C.R. 81; (1976) 239 E.G. 655 36–37
Snowdon v. Secretary of State for the Environment and Bradford City Metropolitan Council [1980] J.P.L. 749 .... 29–174, 88–06
Solihull Metropolitan Borough Council v. Maxfern [1977] 1 W.L.R. 127; (1976) 120 S.J. 802; [1977] 2 All E.R. 177; (1976) 75 L.G.R. 327; [1977] J.P.L. 171 87–171
Solosigns v. Essex County Council [1956] J.P.L. 904 63–04
Somerset County Council v. Wall (1967) 243–01
Sorrell v. Maidstone Rural District Council (1961) 13 P. & C.R. 57 169–06
Sosmo Trust v. Secretary of State for the Environment, London Borough of Camden [1983] J.P.L. 806 29–156
South Cambridgeshire District Council v. Stokes [1981] Crim.L.R. 261; [1981] J.P.L. 594 89–05
South Glamorgan County Council v. Hobbs (Quarries) Ltd. [1980] J.P.L. 35; 253 E.G. 1014 .... 24–138, 24–154
South Oxfordshire District Council v. Secretary of State for the Environment [1981] 1 W.L.R. 1092 .... 29–70, 29–172, 29–176, 43–03
—— v. Secretary of State for the Environment and Keene [1986] J.P.L. 435 .... 22–21, 24–103, 24–130

Southend-on-Sea Corporation v. Hodgson (Wickford) [1962] 1 Q.B. 416; [1961] 2 W.L.R. 806; 125 J.P. 348; 105 S.J. 181; [1961] 2 All E.R. 46; 12 P. & C.R. 165; 59 L.G.R. 193 25–36
Southern Corporation v. Minister of Housing and Local Government (1963) 185 E.G. 605 36–01
Southern Olympia (Syndicate) Ltd. v. West Sussex County Council (1952) 3 P. & C.R. 60 164–04
Southwark London Borough v. Secretary of State for the Environment; Lambeth London Borough v. Same; Greater London Council v. Same; Spain v. Same [1984] J.P.L. 263, C.A.; affirming [1983] J.P.L. 793 .... 29–284, 36–127
Sovmots Investments v. Secretary of State for the Environment; Brampton Securities v. Same [1979] A.C. 144; [1977] 2 W.L.R. 951; [1977] 2 All E.R. 385; (1977) 75 L.G.R. 510; [1977] J.P.L. 443; (1977) 35 P. & C.R. 350; *sub nom.* Sovmots Investments and Brampton Securities v. Secretary of State for the Environment (1977) 243 E.G. 995, H.L.; reversing [1976] 3 W.L.R. 597 29–150
Spackman v. Secretary of State for the Environment [1977] 1 All E.R. 257; [1977] J.P.L. 174; *sub nom.* Spackman v. Wiltshire County Council; Spackman v. Secretary of State for the Environment (1976) 33 P. & C.R. 430 .... 29–170, 43–01
Sparkes v. Secretary of State for Wales (1973) 27 P. & C.R. 545 203–04
Spedeworth v. Secretary of State for the Environment (1972) 116 S.J. 729; (1972) 71 L.G.R. 123 24–03
Square Meals Frozen Foods Ltd. v. Dunstable Corporation [1974] 1 W.L.R. 59; 117 S.J. 875; [1974] 1 All E.R. 441; (1973) 26 P. & C.R. 560; (1973) 72 L.G.R. 180 . 243–03
Stafford Borough Council v. Elkenford Ltd. [1977] 1 W.L.R. 324; [1977] J.P.L. 170; (1976) 16 Man.L. 36; (1976) 75 L.G.R. 337 87–172
Stanger v. Hendon Borough Council [1948] 1 K.B. 571; [1948] L.J.R. 1008; 64 T.L.R. 164; 92 S.J. 153; *sub nom.* Hendon Borough Council v. Stanger, 112 J.P. 199; [1948] 1 All E.R. 377; 46 L.G.R. 129 22–620
Stanton v. Secretary of State for the Environment (1978) 248 E.G. 227 88–05
Steeples (J.J.) v. Derbyshire County Council [1985] 1 W.L.R. 256; [1984] 3 All E.R. 468; (1985) 82 L.S.Gaz. 358 .... 26–01, 29–11, 29–13, 29–15, 29–282, 29–545, 270–03, 283–07
—— v. —— [1981] J.P.L. 582 34–01
Steggles v. Basildon Urban Development Corporation (1976) 32 P. & C.R. 449; [1975] J.P.L. 96; (1976) 240 E.G. 139 29–491
Stephens v. Cuckfield Rural District Council [1960] 2 Q.B. 373; [1960] 3 W.L.R. 248; 124 J.P. 420; 104 S.J. 565; [1960] 2 All E.R. 716; 11 P. & C.R. 248; 58 L.G.R. 213, C.A.; affirming [1959] 1 Q.B. 516 .... 22–495, 65–01
Stephenson v. Secretary of State for the Environment (1985) 274 E.G. 1385 .... 36–129/132
Stevens v. Bromley London Borough Council [1972] Ch. 400; [1972] 2 W.L.R. 605; (1971) 116 S.J. 123; (1971) 23 P. & C.R. 142; 70 L.G.R. 170; *sub nom.* Stevens v. London Borough of Bromley [1972] 1 All E.R. 712, C.A.; affirming [1972] Ch. 39 87–49
—— v. Minister of Housing and Local Government (1966) 110 S.J. 567 36–55
Stock v. Wanstead and Woodfood Borough Council [1962] 2 Q.B. 479; [1961] 2 W.L.R. 868; 105 S.J. 426; [1961] 2 All E.R. 433; 12 P. & C.R. 336; 59 L.G.R. 399; [1961] R.V.R. 783 158–03
Stoke-on-Trent City Council v. B. & Q. (Retail); Wolverhampton Borough Council v. B. & Q.; Barking and Dagenham London Borough Council v. Home Charm Retail [1984] A.C. 754; [1984] 2 W.L.R. 929; (1984) 128 S.J. 364; [1984] 2 All E.R. 332; (1984) 82 L.G.R. 473; (1985) 4 Tr.L. 9, H.L.; affirming [1984] Ch. 1, C.A. 87–174
Strable v. Dartford Borough Council [1984] J.P.L. 329 29–554
Street v. Essex County Council (1965) 193 E.G. 537 22–476
Stringer v. Minister of Housing and Local Government [1970] 1 W.L.R. 1281; 114 S.J. 753; [1971] 1 All E.R. 65; 68 L.G.R. 788; [1971] J.P.L. 114; 22 P. & C.R. 255 .... 29–87, 29–103, 36–03
Stubbs v. West Hartlepool Corporation (1961) 12 P. & C.R. 365 193–01
Styler v. Central Land Board (1958) 9 P. & C.R. 329 158–01
Sunbell Properties v. Dorset County Council (1979) 253 E.G. 1123 270–02
Sunbury-on-Thames Urban District Council v. Mann (1958) 56 L.G.R. 235; (1958) P. & C.R. 309 .... 24–89, 29–473

Sutton London Borough Council v. Secretary of State for the Environment (1975) 119
S.J. 321; (1975) 29 P. & C.R. 350; 73 L.G.R. 349 .... 29–304, 29–490
Swallow & Pearson v. Middlesex County Council [1953] 1 W.L.R. 422; 97 S.J. 155;
[1959] 1 All E.R. 580; 3 P. & C.R. 314; 51 L.G.R. 253 .... 87–01, 87–159
Sykes v. Secretary of State for the Environment; South Oxfordshire District Council v.
Secretary of State for the Environment [1981] 1 W.L.R. 1092; 125 S.J. 444; [1981]
2 All E.R. 954; (1981) 42 P. & C.R. 19; [1981] J.P.L. 285; (1980) 257 E.G.
821 87–149
—— v. Underwood [1981] J.P.L. 285 22–563

T.L.G. Building Materials v. Secretary of State for the Environment (1980) 41 P. &
C.R. 243; [1981] J.P.L. 513 .... 22–387, 88–42, 88A–17
Tameside Metropolitan Borough Council v. Secretary of State for the Environment and
G.A. Myatt [1984] J.P.L. 180 29–205
Tandridge District Council v. Powers (1983) 45 P. & C.R. 408; (1982) 80 L.G.R. 453;
[1982] J.P.L. 645; [1982] Crim.L.R. 373 89–04
—— v. Secretary of State for the Environment and Nutley Print (Reigate) [1983] J.P.L.
667 22–122
Tarmac Properties v. Secretary of State for Wales (1976) 33 P. & C.R. 103; [1976] J.P.L.
576 .... 29–117, 245–16
Taylor (John) v. Secretary of State for Wales and Glydwr District Council [1985] J.P.L.
792 36–31
Tempo Discount Warehouses v. Enfield London Borough and the Secretary of State
for the Environment [1979] J.P.L. 79 .... 29–59, 29–227, 29–228
Tessier v. Secretary of State for the Environment (1975) 120 S.J. 8; (1975) 31 P. & C.R.
161; (1976) L.G.R. 279 .... 22–583, 22–591, 22–594
Test Valley Investments v. Tanner, 15 P. & C.R. 279; [1964] Crim.L.R. 62 89–10
Thackray v. Central Land Board [1952] W.N. 285; [1952] 1 All E.R. 1374; 3 P. & C.R.
75; sub nom. Thackray's Agreement, Re, 116 J.P. 353 52–04
Thames Water Authority v. Elmbridge Borough Council [1983] Q.B. 570; [1983] 2
W.L.R. 744; (1983) 127 S.J. 187; [1983] 1 All E.R. 836; [1983] J.P.L. 470; (1983)
81 L.G.R. 678 112–02
Thanet District Council v. Secretary of State for the Environment and Corpus Christi
College, Oxford [1978] J.P.L. 251; (1977) 246 E.G. 229 .... 36–88, 36–109
Third Greytown Properties v. Peterborough Corporation [1973] 3 All E.R. 731; 72
L.G.R. 238 121–01
Thirkwell (Lewis) Ltd. v. Secretary of State for the Environment [1978] J.P.L. 844;
(1978) 248 E.G. 685 .... 25–14, 29–91, 36–28
Thomas David (Porthcawl) Ltd. v. Penybont Rural District Council. See David
(Thomas) (Porthcawl) v. Penybont Rural District Council.
Thornville Properties Ltd. v. Secretary of State for the Environment [1981] J.P.L. 116;
(1980) 258 E.G. 172 .... 29–40, 29–60
Thrasyvoulou v. Secretary of State for the Environment and Hackney London Borough
Council [1984] J.P.L. 732 88–08
Tidswell v. Secretary of State for the Environment and Thurrock Borough Council
(1976) 34 P. & C.R. 152; [1977] J.P.L. 104; (1976) 241 E.G. 83 .... 24–90, 87–06
Tonbridge and Malling District Council v. Secretary of State for the Environment [1981]
J.P.L. 757 29–154
Toogood v. Bristol Corporation (1973) 26 P. & C.R. 132 181–04
Toomey (J.) Motors Ltd. v. Secretary of State for the Environment [1981] J.P.L.
418 .... 22–615, 87–21, 246–10
Tower Hamlets London Borough v. Secretary of State for the Environment and Lane
(Martin Stuart) [1983] J.P.L. 315 .... 29–203, 55–11
Tromans v. Secretary of State for the Environment and the Wyre Forest District Council
[1983] J.P.L. 474 29–23
Trentham (G. Percy) v. Gloucestershire County Council [1966] 1 W.L.R. 506; 130 J.P.
179; 110 S.J. 52; [1966] 1 All E.R. 701; 18 P. & C.R. 225; 64 L.G.R. 134, C.A.;
affirming (1965) 195 E.G. 211 .... 22–373, 22–644
Trevors Warehouses Ltd. v. Secretary of State for the Environment (1972) 23 P. & C.R.
215 .... 87–126, 87–146
Trinder v. Sevenoaks Rural District Council (1967) 204 E.G. 803 .... 29–484, 33–03

Trio Thames *v.* Secretary of State for the Environment and Reading Borough Council [1984] J.P.L. 183 29–510
Trustees of Castell-y-Mynach Estate *v.* Secretary of State for the Environment and Taff Ely Borough Council [1985] J.P.L. 40 22–432
Trustees of the Earl of Lichfield's Estate *v.* Secretary of State for the Environment and Stafford Borough Council [1985] J.P.L. 251 .... 22–481, 24–14
Trustees of Walton-on-Thames Charities *v.* Walton & Weybridge Urban District Council (1970) 68 L.G.R. 488; 21 P. & C.R. 411 29–488
Truvox *v.* Harrow Corporation (1959) 173 E.G. 627 29–475
Turner *v.* Secretary of State for the Environment (1973) 72 L.G.R. 380; (1973) 28 P. & C.R. 123; (1973) 228 E.G. 335 .... 245–02, 245–03, 245–04

United Refineries Ltd. *v.* Essex County Council [1978] J.P.L. 110; (1976) 241 E.G. 389 .... 22–11, 29–496
Upperton *v.* Hampshire County Council (1965) 16 P. & C.R. 333 164–09

Vale of Glamorgan Borough Council *v.* Palmer and Bowles [1984] J.P.L. 334; (1983) 81 L.G.R. 678; [1983] Crim.L.R. 334 60–07
—— *v.* Secretary of State for Wales and Sir Brandon Rhys Williams [1986] J.P.L. 198 29–222
Vale Estates Acton *v.* Secretary of State for the Environment (1971) 69 L.G.R. 543 36–72
Vallance and Jowitt *v.* Minister of Housing and Local Government [1968] R.V.R. 700; (1968) 207 E.G. 893 146–03
Vickers-Armstrong *v.* Central Land Board (1957) 9 P. & C.R. 33, C.A.; affirming (1957) 8 P. & C.R. 239; [1957] C.L.Y. 3475 22–371
Vyner (Frank) & Son *v.* Secretary of State for the Environment [1977] J.P.L. 795; (1977) 243 E.G. 597 22–383

Waddell *v.* Bhagwanani (1967) 202 E.G. 1225 22–496
—— *v.* Winter (1967) 65 L.G.R. 370; 18 P. & C.R. 497; 202 E.G. 1225 89–11
Wain *v.* Secretary of State for the Environment (1978) 39 P. & C.R. 82; [1979] J.P.L. 231 .... 88–23, 246–07
—— *v.* Secretary of State for the Environment and Wigan Metropolitan Borough Council (1982) 126 S.J. 79; (1982) 80 L.G.R. 438; (1982) 44 P. & C.R. 289; [1982] J.P.L. 244; (1982) E.G. 337 180–12
Wakelin *v.* Secretary of State for the Environment and St. Albans District Council (1978) 122 S.J. 507; (1978) 77 L.G.R. 101; (1983) 46 P. & C.R. 214; [1978] J.P.L. 769; (1978) 248 E.G. 867, C.A.; reversing [1977] J.P.L. 452 .... 22–123, 22–668
Walters *v.* Secretary of State for Wales (1978) 77 L.G.R. 529; (1978) 249 E.G. 245; *sub nom.* Walters *v.* Secretary of State for the Environment; (1978) 122 S.J. 826; [1979] J.P.L. 172 29–153
Warnock *v.* Secretary of State for the Environment and Dover District Council [1980] J.P.L. 690 .... 22–388, 22–561, 88–41
Washington Urban District Council *v.* Gray (1958) 10 P. & C.R. 264 22–311
Wass (W. & J.) Ltd. *v.* Secretary of State for the Environment and City of Stoke-on-Trent Council [1986] J.P.L. 120 88–45
Watford Borough Council *v.* Secretary of State for the Environment [1982] J.P.L. 518 29–504
Waverley District Council *v.* Secretary of State for the Environment and Miller and Davis [1982] J.P.L. 105 29–502
Wealden District Council *v.* Secretary of State for the Environment and Innocent [1983] J.P.L. 234; [1984] E.C.C. 203 .... 88A–20
Webb *v.* Secretary of State for the Environment (1972) 224 E.G. 889 36–73
—— *v.* Warwickshire County Council (1971) 23 P. & C.R. 63 203–03
Webber *v.* Minister of Housing and Local Government [1968] 1 W.L.R. 29; (1967) 132 J.P. 86; 111 S.J. 890; [1967] 3 All E.R. 981; 19 P. & C.R. 1, C.A.; reversing 18 P. & C.R. 491 .... 22–180, 22–420
Weitz and F.D.S. (Market Research) Ltd. *v.* Secretary of State for the Environment and Camden London Borough Council [1985] J.P.L. 171 29–180
Weitz (J.R.) F.D.S. (Market Research) *v.* Secretary of State for the Environment and Camden London Borough Council (1983) 43 P. & C.R. 150; [1983] J.P.L. 811 246–12

xlv

TABLE OF CASES

Wells v. Minister of Housing and Local Government [1967] 1 W.L.R. 1000; 131 J.P. 431; 111 S.J. 519; [1967] 2 All E.R. 1041; 65 L.G.R. 408; 18 P. & C.R. 401 .... 25–37, 25–40, 29–165, 55–03, 53–05

Welsh Aggregates v. Secretary of State for Wales [1983] J.P.L. 50; (1983) 265 E.G. 43 24–139

—— v. Secretary of State for the Environment and Clywd County Council. *See* Welsh Aggregates v. Secretary of State for Wales.

Wessex Regional Health Authority v. Salisbury District Council and Secretary of State for the Environment [1984] J.P.L. 344 29–328

West Bowers Farm Products v. Essex County Council [1985] J.P.L. 857 .... 22–20, 20–21

West Bromwich County Borough Council v. Minister of Housing and Local Government [1968] R.V.R. 349; (1968) 206 E.G. 1085 180–06

West Cheshire Caravan Co. v. Ellesmere Port Borough Council [1976] J.P.L. 235; (1975) 237 E.G. 573 22–381

Western Fish Products Ltd. v. Penrith District Council (1978) 122 S.J. 471; (1978) 77 L.G.R. 185; [1981] 2 All E.R. 204; (1978) 38 P. & C.R. 7; [1978] J.P.L. 623 .... 25–40, 25–49, 53–05, 53–24, 94–03

Westminster Bank Ltd. v. Minister of Housing and Local Government [1971] A.C. 508; [1970] 2 W.L.R. 645; 114 S.J. 190; [1970] 1 All E.R. 734; (1969) 21 P. & C.R. 379, H.L.; affirming *sub nom.* Westminster Bank v. Beverley Borough Council [1969] 1 Q.B. 499 29–89

Westminster City Council v. British Waterways Board [1985] A.C. 676; [1984] 3 W.L.R. 1047; (1984) 128 S.J. 783; [1984] 3 All E.R. 737; (1985) 49 P. & C.R. 117; [1985] J.P.L. 102; 272 E.G. 1279 29–112

—— v. Great Portland Estates [1985] A.C. 661; [1984] 3 W.L.R. 1035; 128 S.J. 784; [1984] 3 All E.R. 744; (1984) 49 P. & C.R. 34; [1985] J.P.L. 108, H.L.; reversing (1983) 49 P. & C.R. 20 .... 9–01, 11–01, 29–112, 29–113, 29–207

—— v. Jones (1982) 80 L.G.R. 241; [1981] J.P.L. 750 87–173

—— v. Secretary of State for the Environment, *The Times*, March 24, 1984 55–12

—— v. Secretary of State for the Environment and City Commercial Real Estates Investments [1984] J.P.L. 27 36–29

—— v. Secretary of State for the Environment [1984] J.P.L. 27 .... 29–24, 29–120, 242–07

Westminster Rensdale Ltd. v. Secretary of State for the Environment (1983) 127 S.J. 444; (1984) 48 P. & C.R. 255; [1983] J.P.L. 454 .... 29–119, 36–65

Wheatcroft (Bernard) Ltd. v. Secretary of State for the Environment (1982) 43 P. & C.R. 223 [1982] J.P.L. 37 .... 29–324, 29–326

Whistlecroft (G.A.) v. Secretary of State for the Environment and North Bedfordshire Borough Council [1983] J.P.L. 809 29–178

Whiteacre Estates U.K. Ltd. v. Secretary of State for the Environment and Tunbridge Wells Borough Council [1984] J.P.L. 177 245–33

Whitfield v. Gowling (1974) 118 S.J. 716; (1974) 72 L.G.R. 765; (1974) 28 P. & C.R. 386 89–02

Wholesale Mail Order Supplies v. Secretary of State for the Environment [1976] J.P.L. 163; (1975) 257 E.G. 185 36–60

Wilcock v. Secretary of State for the Environment [1975] J.P.L. 150; (1974) 232 E.G. 1385 121–02

Wild and A.G.M. Car Hire v. Secretary of State for the Environment [1976] J.P.L. 432 .. 88–39

William (Boyer) & Sons v. Minister of Housing and Local Government (1968) 20 P. & C.R. 176; 67 L.G.R. 374 .... 29–102, 245–09

Williams v. Cheadle and Gatley Urban District Council (1965) 17 P. & C.R. 153 ... 192–06

—— v. Minister of Housing and Local Government (1967) 111 S.J. 559; 65 L.G.R. 495; (1967) 18 P. & C.R. 514 .... 22–265, 22–375

Williams (Sir Brandon Meredith Rhys) v. Secretary of State for Wales and the Welsh Water Authority and Taff Ely Borough Council [1985] J.P.L. 29 .... 29–221, 35–03

Williamson & Stevens (Executors) v. Cambridgeshire County Council (1977) 34 P. & C.R. 117; [1977] J.P.L. 529; (1977) 232 E.G. 369 29–494

Wilson v. West Sussex County Council [1963] 2 Q.B. 764; [1963] 2 W.L.R. 669; 127 J.P. 243; 107 S.J. 114; [1963] 1 All E.R. 751; 14 P. & C.R. 301; 61 L.G.R. 287; [1963] R.V.R. 278, C.A.; affirming (1962) 13 P. & C.R. 310 .... 24–99, 29–479, 33–02, 87–15, 164–08

—— v. Secretary of State for the Environment [1973] 1 W.L.R. 1083; 117 S.J. 728; [1974] 1 All E.R. 428; (1973) 26 P. & C.R. 232; (1973) 71 L.G.R. 442 121–03

Wimpey (George) & Co. Ltd. *v.* New Forest District Council [1979] J.P.L. 314; (1979) 250 E.G. 249 30–02
—— *v.* Secretary of State for the Environment [1978] J.P.L. 776; (1978) 247 E.G. 470 .... 29–127, 29–128
Winchester City Council *v.* Secretary of State for the Environment and Eccles Winchester City Council *v.* Secretary of State for the Environment (1979) 77 L.G.R. 715; (1979) 39 P. & C.R. 1; (1979) 251 E.G. 259; [1979] J.P.L. 620, C.A.; affirming (1978) 36 P. & C.R. 455 .... 36–43, 36–91
Windsor and Maidenhead Rural Borough Council *v.* Brandrose Investments Ltd. [1983] 1 W.L.R. 509; [1983] 1 All E.R. 818; (1983) 45 P. & C.R. 349; [1983] J.P.L. 374; (1983) 266 E.G. 1195 52–12
Winmill *v.* Secretary of State for the Environment and Kingston-upon-Thames, Royal Borough [1982] J.P.L. 445 22–117
Winner Investments *v.* Hammersmith London Borough Council (1966) 64 L.G.R. 447 29–483
Winton *v.* Secretary of State for the Environment and Guildford Borough Council (1982) 46 P. & C.R. 205; [1984] J.P.L. 188 .... 22–124, 22–590
Wipperman & Buckingham *v.* Barking London Borough Council (1965) 17 P. & C.R. 225; 64 L.G.R. 97 22–99
Wivenhoe Port Ltd. *v.* Colchester Borough Council [1985] J.P.L. 396, C.A.; affirming [1985] J.P.L. 175 29–513
Wontner Smith & Co. *v.* Secretary of State for the Environment [1977] J.P.L. 103 36–86
Wood *v.* Secretary of State for the Environment [1973] 1 W.L.R. 707; 117 S.J. 430; [1973] 2 All E.R. 404; 25 P. & C.R. 303; 71 L.G.R. 339 ..... 22–268, 22–318, 22–378, 22–560, 24–07, 33–04
Wood's Application, *Re* [1952] C.P.C. 724 282–01
Woodspring District Council *v.* Secretary of State for the Environment and Goodall (Doreen Mary Winstone) [1982] J.P.L. 784 22–120
Wootton *v.* Central Land Board [1957] 1 W.L.R. 424; 121 J.P. 137; 101 S.J. 188; [1957] 1 All E.R. 441; 8 P. & C.R. 121; 55 L.G.R. 84, C.A.; reversing (1956) 6 P. & C.R. 177 282–02
Worthy Fuel Injection Ltd. *v.* Secretary of State for the Environment and Southampton City Council [1983] J.P.L. 173 .... 22–17, 87–31
Wright (W.S.) Ltd. *v.* Bromley Corporation (1950) 1 P. & C.R. 302 22–40

Ynys Môn-Isle of Anglesey Borough Council *v.* Secretary of State for Wales and Parry Bros. (Builders) Co. [1984] J.P.L. 646 29–206
Ynystawe, Ynyforgan and Glas Gypsy Side Action Group *v.* Secretary of State for Wales and West Glamorgan County Council [1981] J.P.L. 874 .... 29–20, 29–219
Young *v.* Secretary of State for the Environment [1983] 2 A.C. 662; [1983] 3 W.L.R. 382; (1983) 127 S.J. 537; [1983] 2 All E.R. 1105; (1984) 47 P. & C.R. 165; [1983] J.P.L. 667; (1983) 81 L.G.R. 779; (1984) 269 E.G. 219, H.L. 23–09, 23–12

TABLE OF STATUTES

1863	Harwich Harbour Act (26 & 27 Vict. c. 71) 29–281		1960	Caravan Sites and Control of Development Act—*cont.* Sched. 1, para. 9 24–155
1925	Law of Property Act (15 & 16 Geo. 5, c. 20)—			Pt. I 23–14
	s. 78 52–02		1961	Land Compensation Act (9 & 10 Eliz. 2, c. 33)—
	Land Charges Act (15 & 16 Geo. 5, c. 22)—			ss. 14–16 178–02
	s. 15 (7) (*b*) (ii) 292–05			s. 16 (7) 181–01
1932	Town and Country Planning Act (22 & 23 Geo. 5, c. 48) 27–01, 63–01, 63–02		1962	Town and Country Planning Act (10 & 11 Eliz. 2, c. 38)—
	s. 13 (4) 22–620			s. 12 (2) (*a*) 22–483
	s. 34 .... 52–01, 52–05			s. 13 (3) 23–04
	s. 192 192–01			s. 21 (2) 22–266
1937	National Trust Act—			s. 30 (3) 54–01
	s. 8 52–06			s. 31 (2) 54–01
1943	Town and Country Planning (Interim Development) Act (6 & 7 Geo. 6, c. 29) 292–05			s. 33 (2) 22–266
				s. 177 (1) 243–02
				s. 221 (1) 22–08
				Sched. 13, para. 7 292–06
	s. 4 29–491		1966	Selective Employment Payments Act (c. 32) 22–558
	s. 7 164–01			
1946	Building Restrictions (War-Time Contraventions) Act (9 & 10 Geo. 6, c. 35) 292–02		1967	Wireless Telegraphy Act (c. 72) 29–97
			1968	Caravan Sites Act (c. 52)—
				s. 13 29–538
	s. 4 (1) 292–04, 292–05		1972	Town and Country Planning (Amendment) Act (c. 42)—
	Acquisition of Land (Authorisation Procedure) Act (9 & 10 Geo. 6, c. 49) 121–03			
				s. 8 277–01
1947	Town and Country Planning Act (10 & 11 Geo. 6, c. 51) 63–02, 292–05			Local Government Act (c. 70)—
				s. 101 29–299
	s. 12 (2) 22–417			s. 222 .... 60–04, 87–171, 87–173
	(*e*) 22–559			(1) 87–174
	s. 23 .... 87–47, 292–04			s. 250 (5) 282–01
	(5) 245–01			Sched. 12, para. 39 195–04
	s. 25 52–07			para. 44 195–04
	s. 29 54–02			Sched. 15, para. 15 (2) 29–10
	s. 33 (1) 65–03			para. 32 (d) 29–10
	s. 76 (6) 292–03			para. 51 (1) 29–10
	s. 78 22–03		1973	Water Act (c. 37)—
	Pt. VI 146–01			s. 16 29–127
1949	Coast Protection Act (12, 13 & 14 Geo. 6, c. 74) 29–281		1977	Town and Country Planning (Amendment) Act (c. 29)—
1950	Shops Act (14 Geo. 6, c. 28) 87–172			
				s. 266 (1) (*b*) 266–05
1959	Town and Country Planning Act (7 & 8 Eliz. 2, c. 53)—		1981	Local Government and Planning (Amendment) Act (c. 41) 87–139, 243–01
	s. 31 54–02			Acquisition of Land Act (c. 67)—
	s. 39 (4) (*a*) 195–01			
1960	Caravan Sites and Control of Development Act (8 & 9 Eliz. 2, c. 62) 29–349			s. 16 238–01
				Town and Country Planning (Minerals) Act (c. 36) 22–60
	s. 5 29–396		1984	Town and Country Planning Act (c. 10) 29–74, 266–04, 266–05
	(1) 29–348			
	s. 13 52–07			

1985	Town and Country Planning Compensation Act (c. 19)—	1985	Town and Country Planning Compensation Act—*cont.*
	s. 169 169–09		s. 169 (3) 169–09
			Sched. 18, para. 1 169–09

TOWN AND COUNTRY PLANNING ACT 1971

PART II. DEVELOPMENT PLANS

SECTION 9. APPROVAL OR REJECTION OF STRUCTURE PLAN BY SECRETARY OF STATE

9–01 Edwin H. Bradley & Sons v. Sec. of State for Environment (1984) 47 P & C.R. 374. Section 9(8) required the giving of adequate and intelligible reasons but short reasons could suffice. Although the panel's reasoning had been defective, the Secretary of State had given intelligible reasons.

See also *Great Portland Estates* v. *Westminster C.C.* where Glidwell J.'s approach was adopted.

9–02 Barnham v. Sec. of State for Environment [1985] J.P.L. 861. Where there were substantial objections to alteration of the structure plan, there was a duty on the Secretary of State under s.9(8) to give some reasons, however brief, why he had approved, modified or rejected the alteration. Where the alteration was in conflict with policy guidance in a government circular, he should refer to that guidance in the statement of reasons for his decision.

SECTION 11. PREPARATION OF LOCAL PLANS

11–01 Great Portland Estates v. Westminster C.C. [1984] 3 W.L.R. 753.

(1) Planning policies were not concerned with the particular purposes of a particular occupier but personal circumstances could be the subject of specific exceptions to a general policy.

(2) An industrial policy encouraging a particular class of user could have a genuine planning purpose and so be valid even if it had the consequence of protecting existing occupiers.

(3) Proposals for the development and use of land could not be deliberately omitted from a local plan and so a policy in a local plan which left such policies to be set out in non–statutory guidelines was invalid. This part of the plan was quashed.

11–02 Buckinghamshire C.C. v. Hall Aggregates (Thames Valley) Ltd. and S.A.G.A. [1985] J.P.L. 634. A Minerals Subject Plan, which indicated preferred areas for the mining of gravel by the use of subjective constraints set out on maps, was within the powers of the Act and valid.

SECTION 13. INQUIRIES WITH RESPECT TO LOCAL PLANS

13–01 Fourth Investments v. Bury M.B.C. [1985] J.P.L. 185. Inspector incorrectly allocated in the local plan land to the green belt without considering future need for housing land. This part of the local plan was quashed.

13–02 Buckinghamshire C.C. v. Hall Aggregates (Thames Valley) Ltd. and S.A.G.A. [1985] J.P.L. 634. The duty of the inspector to allow and consider evidence by objectors which did not directly relate to the policies in the draft plan, was considered by the Court.
Held that the inspector had not acted in breach of natural justice.

13–03 R. v. Hammersmith and Fulham B.C. ex parte People Before Profit Ltd. [1981] J.P.L. 869. A local planning authority can reject the inspector's recommendations as long as the inspector's arguments are considered.

13–04 R. v. Wakefield M.D.C., ex p. Asquith [1986] J.P.L. 440. Three local plans prepared covering whole of District Planning Authority's area. Proposed to hold one inquiry into the policy aspects of all three plans and three separate inquiries into the specific sections of the plans.

S.13. INQUIRIES WITH RESPECT TO LOCAL PLANS

Held that no duty to consult objectors on the proposed procedure and that procedures could not be said to be a breach of natural justice.

SECTION 14. ADOPTION AND APPROVAL OF LOCAL PLANS

14–01 Kenwood v. Sec. of State forEnvironment [1984] J.P.L. 36. The Inspector was justified in reaching the conclusion that there was a conflict between the structure plan and local plan and in following the local plan in accordance with s.14(187).

Decisions on Old-style Development Plans

14–02 Easter Ross Land Use Committee v. Sec. of State for Scotland [1970] S.L.T. 317. The Town and Country Planning (Development Plans) (Scotland) Regulations, reg.5—need for consultation with agricultural executive committee before preparing development plan. Amendment of development plan approved without proper consultation.

W.J. Simms v. Min. of Housing & Local Govt. (1969) 210 E.G. 705. Inquiry as to amendment of development plan:
  (1) should not be inferred that because Minister had given no reasons, the reasons were in fact bad;
  (2) Minister or inspector under no duty to reach an express conclusion on every consideration advanced at the inquiry;
  (3) there is no burden of proof at such an inquiry, and complaint that inspector should not have considered that onus was on objectors to amendment was misconceived;
  (4) complaint that issue predetermined before inquiry because a great deal of work had been done on bills of quantities and selection of forms for tenders involving public expenditure was not sustainable.

Note

As to the relationship between local plan, decisions and development control, see decisions listed under Section 29.

PART III. GENERAL PLANNING CONTROL

SECTION 22. MEANING OF DEVELOPMENT

A. The General Concept of Development

22–01 Parkes v. Sec. of State for Environment [1979] 1 All E.R. 211, C.A. "Operations" are activities which result in some physical alteration to land which has some degree of permanence to the land itself. "Uses" are activities done in, alongside or on the land not interfering with the actual physical characteristics of the land. The storing and sorting of scrap did not alter the physical characteristics of the land, therefore it was a "use" for purposes of s.51.

B. Operational Development

22–02 Buckinghamshire C.C. v. Callingham [1952] 1 All E.R. 466. The erection of small or model buildings constituted development.

22–03 London C.C. v. Marks & Spencer [1953] A.C. 535. "Works for the erection of a building" contained in s.78 of the Town and Country Planning Act 1948 included the granting of permission to erect the building, the identification of the building by plans and demolition work which is necessary for the erection of the building.

22–04 Cheshire C.C. v. Woodward [1962] 2 W.L.R. 636. There was no one test to decide what operations altered the physical character of the land. All relevant circumstances had to be taken into consideration.

The concept turns on whether:
  (i) has the physical character of the land been changed by operations in or on it;
  (ii) has the physical character of what is under the land been changed by some operation under it;
  (iii) has the physical character of the air above the land been changed by operations over the land.

Although where structure was affixed to land it would usually constitute development, while if movable it would not, that was only one of the matters to be considered.

In referring to a building the Act is referring to any structure or erection which can be said to form part of the realty and to change the physical character of the land.

22–05 James v. Brecon C.C. (1963) 15 P. & C.R. 20. Building, structure or erection conveys an idea of permanency. The erection of swing boats capable of being removed by six men or dismantled in an hour were held not to amount to development by the Minister and his decision was upheld by the Divisional Court.

22–06 Howell v. Sunbury-on-Thames U.D.C. (1963) 15 P. & C.R. 26. Bare demolition of a building and storerooms could not constitute development but the laying of drains, the raising and concreting of an area and the erection of lamp standards and advertisements constituted building operations.

22–07 Coleshill and District Investment Co. Ltd. v. Min. of Housing & Local Govt. [1969] 1 W.L.R. 746, H.L. If an act of demolition came within one of the operations constituting development it would be development.

Blast walls and attendant embankments 4 ft from buildings were an integral part of the building.

Removal of 9 ft high and 10 ft wide embankment was an engineering operation.

Pulling down a blast wall was a structural alteration to the building and therefore a building operation which affected the external appearance of the building.

The meaning of "other operations" in the definition was considered together with the overall concept of operational development.

22–08 Barvis Ltd. v. S.O.S.E. (1971) 22 P. & C.R. 710. A crane 89 ft tall which ran on steel rails, and which was only installed on site until needed elsewhere, was capable of amounting to a "structure or erection" and therefore a "building" within s.221(1) of the Town and Country Planning Act 1962 (now see s.290(1) of the 1971 Act). Its erection was capable of being a building or other operation and so development. The test in *Cardiff Rating Authority* v. *Guest Keen Baldwins Iron and Steel Co.* [1949] 1 K.B. 385 as to what is a "building" was approved.

22–09 Thomas David (Porthcawl) Ltd. v. Penybont R.D.C. [1972] 1 W.L.R. 354, D.C. In an operational development such as mining, the planning unit had to be determined by looking at the whole of the area and where actual workings were in fact the beginning of the development of a larger area and were relative to that area the larger area was the planning unit. In mining operations every shovelful is a separate act of development.

22–10 Iddenden v. Sec. of State for Environment [1972] 1 W.L.R. 1433, C.A. Demolition of nissen huts and lean-to structure did not require planning permission.

22–11 United Refineries Ltd. v. Essex C.C. [1978] J.P.L. 110. Stripping of topsoil was a building operation and amounted to work being commenced to comply with the condition that building operations commence by a certain date.

S.22. MEANING OF DEVELOPMENT

22–12 Northavon D.C. v. Sec. of State for Environment (1980) 40 P. & C.R. 332. Where refuse and waste materials are to be deposited on agricultural land to raise the level of the land and facilitate drainage, and not to provide a last resting place for refuse, the proposed activity constitutes an operation for the purposes of s.22(1) and not a change of use.

22–13 Ewen Developments Ltd. v. Sec. of State for Environment [1980] J.P.L. 404. For embankments to constitute "engineering operations" they must be substantial.

22–14 Kensington & Chelsea R.L.B.C. v. C.G. Hotels (1980) 41 P. & C.R. 40. It was assumed but not determined that the installation of floodlights amounted to development.

22–15 City of Glasgow v. Sec. of State for Scotland [1982] J.P.L. 374. Partial demolition (for safety reasons) does not require permission if the works are ordered under statutory powers.

22–16 Scott v. Sec. of State for Environment [1983] J.P.L. 108. The Secretary of State did not err in law in finding that the placing of a portable office on land constituted operational development.

22–17 Worthy Fuel Injection Ltd. v. Sec. of State for Environment [1983] J.P.L. 173. In deciding whether the erection of a building consisted of one self-contained operation or two or more separate operations the appearance of the building may be decisive, but it would be difficult to determine the issue on the appearance of the building alone.

22–18 Fayrewood Fish Farms v. Sec. of State for Environment [1984] J.P.L. 267. Engineering operations were defined as operations of a kind usually undertaken by engineers but they did not require the participation of an engineer or the drawing-up of plans.

22–19 Bedfordshire C.C. v. Central Electricity Generating Board [1985] J.P.L. 43. Whether investigatory drilling amounted to operational development.

22–20 West Bowers Farm Products v. Essex C.C. [1985] J.P.L. 857. A proposal to erect a large reservoir would involve both mining and engineering operations. A single process might, for planning purposes, amount to two activities. However mining acts which were ancillary to engineering operations would not be treated as separate activities. It was all a question of fact and degree.

22–21 South Oxfordshire D.C. v. Sec. of State for Environment and Keene [1986] J.P.L. 435. Consideration of the Court of Appeal's decision in *West Bowers Farm Products* v. *Essex C.C.* above.

22–22 The construction of hardstanding and access on garden land used for the parking of motor coaches were engineering operations which were not incidental to the enjoyment of the house as a dwelling-house. [1966] J.P.L. 237.

22–23 The removal of soil embankments from the walls of magazine buildings constituted engineering operations. [1967] J.P.L. 486.

22–24 The fact that a structure is physically capable of being moved and is not affixed to the soil does not determine whether or not it is a building. Account must be taken of the degree of permanency of the structure on the land and all the circumstances of the matter. A car port on wheels, which would only be moved occasionally when works of maintenance were required on the house, is a building. [1967] J.P.L. 552.

22–25 The installation of a septic tank for a dwelling-house is probably a building rather than an engineering operation. [1967] J.P.L. 669.

22–26 The provision of car-parking space is an operation on land for which planning permission is required. [1967] J.P.L. 672.

22–27 The surfacing of land by dressing with hardcore is development requiring planning permission. [1968] J.P.L. 168.

22–28 The erection of a dwelling of timber construction within the curtilage of an existing dwelling-house and used as a separate dwelling is a building operation requiring planning permission. [1968] J.P.L. 352.

22–29 The installation of a paraffin vending machine on a concrete base fed by a pipe from a storage tank and connected to the electrical supply is a building or other operation constituting development. [1969] J.P.L. 415.

22–30 The erection of a tent intended for permanent storage purposes constituted operational development. [1969] J.P.L. 592.

22–31 Increase in width of access by only a few inches was insufficient to amount to development by an engineering operation. [1970] J.P.L. 542.

22–32 The erection of external window blinds constituted building operations. [1970] J.P.L. 710.

22–33 The tipping of earth to form a golf course constituted engineering operations. [1970] J.P.L. 713.

22–34 The installation of new stronger floodlights on existing poles was not a development requiring planning permission. The installation of a storage tank, catchpit and portable office was an operational development. [1972] J.P.L. 216.

22–35 The cutting of a mooring dyke and the erection of quay headings were engineering operations. [1973] J.P.L. 322.

22–37 The erection of new petrol pumps was an engineering or other operation. [1972] J.P.L. 577.

22–38 The erection of a balustrade on an extension was a building operation. [1973] J.P.L. 496.

22–39 The spreading of stone and hardcore on land to facilitate the parking of vehicles was a development requiring planning permission [1974] J.P.L. 159.

22–40 Portable cabins delivered to a site by low-load and which took one day to erect constituted buildings, and their erection a building operation. [1975] J.P.L. 368.

22–41 Drilling amounting to engineering operations. [1975] J.P.L. 609.

22–42 In general carrying out of works of demolition of a building does not constitute development. [1976] J.P.L. 53.

22–43 The erection of chicken verandahs constituted operational development. [1977] J.P.L. 47.

22–44 Twelve small metal pegs connected by a nylon rope around a site 170 ft by 100 ft was not sufficiently substantial to constitute a structure or erection and therefore did not amount to a building, engineering or other operation. [1977] J.P.L. 122.

22–45 The erection of a lean-to structure was a *de minimis* operation and of no material consequence in terms of development. [1978] J.P.L. 395.

22–46 An incinerator which had not been moved, which was surrounded by a fence, paving and fixed pipes indicating it would not normally be moved and which would need to be broken down to be moved was a "building." [1978] J.P.L. 487.

22–47 The provision of a "portakabin" building is a building operation rather than

S.22. MEANING OF DEVELOPMENT

a material change of use. The extension of an inspection pit is a building operation rather than an engineering operation. [1978] J.P.L. 571.

22–48 The raising of land to produce a particular contour in accordance with plans drawn up by a civil engineer is an "engineering operation" for the purposes of Class V1.1 of the General Development Order 1977. For these purposes the definition of the profession of a civil engineer by the Institution of Civil Engineers for their supplement Charter is not of assistance. [1979] J.P.L. 118.

22–49 The erection of a translucent roof supported by wooden posts over patio is a building operation requiring planning permission. [1979] J.P.L. 125.

22–50 The tipping of soil on land used for the business of a road haulage contractor in order to raise the level to form a parking area is an engineering or other operation, not a material change of use as alleged and therefore the notice was invalid. [1979] J.P.L. 489.

22–51 A slide taking 10 days to erect and 3 days to dismantle, secured to a pier by 64 bolts, was a building, and its erection a building operation. An inflatable whale which was inflated on most days between April and October and used as a type of enclosed trampoline, secured to a pier by guy ropes, was more in the nature of a piece of equipment than a building. [1979] J.P.L. 547.

22–52 The placing of a portable cabin for office use which was left on site for 9 months, with special equipment, prepared foundation and telephone and electricity connections, constituted operational development. [1979] J.P.L. 693.

22–53 Placing of a fuel tank on a lorry and the stationing of the lorry on land was not operational development and its use was ancillary to haulage business. [1980] J.P.L. 288.

22–54 Tipping to improve agricultural land was not an engineering or building operation. [1980] J.P.L. 348.

22–55 The excavation of land to form an artificial lake amounted to engineering operations. [1980] J.P.L. 418.

22–56 The deposition of material to raise the ground level is an engineering operation. The land was raised to a higher level than necessary to carry out site works and therefore it was unauthorised development. [1981] J.P.L. 132.

22–57 Engineering in the General Development Order would not cover the tipping of soil and similar excavated material for the purposes of raising the level of land to make it more suitable for agricultural use—that there was no specific plan for tipping and the fact that the managing director of the company was a chartered engineer was irrelevant. See also *Fayrewood Fish Farms* v. *Sec. of State of the Environment* [1981] J.P.L. 135.

22–58 Formation of a new access driveway involving excavation of material over a length of 100 ft to form a cutting 8 ft or more in width involves development. [1981] J.P.L. 378.

22–59 Removal of a removable section of fence installed by a landowner to allow access to the highway does not amount to "the formation of laying out" of a means of access and does not constitute any other form of engineering operation or any other operation and therefore is not development. [1981] J.P.L. 380.

22–60 Removal of shale from a former colliery tip would not amount to a mining or other operation because when extracted from land shale became of the nature of a chattel and deposit on land did not result in its reincorporation into land. [1981] J.P.L. 693; but see now Town and Country Planning (Minerals) Act 1981.

22–61 Removal of turf, even if it involved carrying away as little as one and a half inches of soil with it, could constitute an engineering operation amounting to development. [1981] J.P.L. 831.

22–62 Tipping in disused quarry of subsoil from building operations. Tipping can involve engineering or other operational development if the primary purpose is not merely the disposal of the materials tipped, but rather for the raising of the level of the land to render it suitable for some particular purpose. Disposal of subsoil must be considered as the disposal of waste materials and so not engineering operations. [1981] J.P.L. 911.

22–63 Provision of a door to a balcony and erection of a balustrade around the balcony was operational development. [1982] J.P.L. 199.

22–64 The siting of a lorry body in the garden of a dwelling-house was not a building or engineering operation. [1982] J.P.L. 202.

22–65 A proposal to tip material to produce a particular contour in accordance with plans previously drawn up by a Civil Engineer would be engineering operations for purposes of Class V1.1 of the General Development Order 1977. [1982] J.P.L. 262.

22–66 In deciding whether a deposit of refuse or waste material on land forming part of a dwelling-house in a rural area is operational or use development it is necessary to look at the primary intention of the persons responsible for the action alleged. In this case the person responsible was a tipper not the landowner. [1983] J.P.L. 756.

22–67 The laying of tarmac over an area measuring 53 ft by 149 ft where there had previously been hardcore surfacing would amount to operational development too extensive to be *de minimis*. [1982] J.P.L. 800.

22–68 A radio aerial mast two inches in diameter extending above the roof of a house. As mast wires were embedded in and secured by guy ropes to the ground as well as being clamped to the wall it was fixed in such a way as to be permanent and immobile and its re-erection amounted to a building operation. [1983] J.P.L. 75.

22–69 (1) An agreement between a purchaser of land and British Rail that a disused railway bridge be demolished was immaterial as to whether planning permission was necessary. (2) Removal of part of an embankment supporting a bridge involved taking away considerable quantities of material and constituted an engineering operation. (3) Demolition of the arch of a bridge involved alterations materially affecting the appearance of the structure and constituted a building operation. [1983] J.P.L. 616.

22–70 The placing of weaner box on land used as a pig farm was operational development as it was intended to form a permanent and important feature of a pig-rearing system despite the fact that boxes delivered to the site were already assembled, were freestanding on concrete blocks and had only minimal connection with the ground through water, gas and drainage pipes. [1983] J.P.L. 621.

22–71 The stationing of a barge securely on mud flats so that it did not float, and which had substantial electrical cables supplying power to it, was a building operation requiring planning permission. [1984] J.P.L. 57.

22–72 The raising of the level of agricultural land by excavation, filling and replacement of topsoil was an engineering operation. [1984] J.P.L. 196.

22–73 The placing of an already-built portakabin on land was not a building operation. Use ancillary to garage use. [1984] J.P.L. 450.

22–74 A permanent fixture to land is not the decisive consideration as to whether a structure is a "building." Where it is intended that the structure should remain per-

S.22. MEANING OF DEVELOPMENT

manently in one location and function as a horse-shelter and fodder-store it amounted to a building. [1985] J.P.L. 63.

22–75 The meaning of the phrase "other operations" depends upon its context and it does not only have the meaning associated with building which it bears in the definition of building operations in s.290(1) of the Act. The installation of a protective grille over a shop window and door was an operation within s. 22(1) of the Act. [1985] J.P.L. 129.

22–76 Strictly speaking all television aerials constitute development although they are usually regarded as *de minimus* and no specific permission is required for their erection. All other erections such as radio masts/aerials in excess of 3 metres in height fall to be considered on their individual merits as development requiring planning permission. [1985] J.P.L. 211.

22–77 The stationing of three freezer units on land was not operational development as the units were simply placed on the land and were capable of being stationed anywhere provided there was access to an electricity supply. [1985] J.P.L. 342.

22–78 Assembly and erection of pre-fabricated stable/shelter and fodder store for horses building operations even though not fixed to ground because intention that they should remain permanently in place. [1985] J.P.L. 63.

22–79 Formation and construction of a road by excavating soil and laying bricks an engineering operation. [1985] J.P.L. 658.

22–80 Removal of soil from derelict land development requiring planning permission. [1985] J.P.L. 893.

22–81 Erection of a wooden horse shelter held to be a building operation as the shelter amounted to a building and not a chattel but the placing of a free-standing aluminium van was held not to be a building operation. [1986] J.P.L. 55.

22–82 Placing of box-van on land amounted to operational development as it had the permanence to alter the state of the land. [1986] J.P.L. 462.

22–83 The fixing of blinds or canopies can amount to "other operations" because they are intended to be permanent fixtures which can materially affect the appearance of the building. Important factor that although in this case blinds could be retracted this was a laborious process. [1986] J.P.L. 545.

22–84 Erection of a plastic "herbie" tree amounted to a building or engineering operation as it was intended to be a permanent structure. [1986] J.P.L. 637.

22–85 Installation of jet car wash at service station amounted to building or engineering operations. [1986] J.P.L. 615.

22–86 Installation of "Dutch" blinds amounted to development as the installation materially affected the appearance of the building because of their bulk and appearance. [1986] J.P.L. 540.

C. Material Change of Use

1. What Amounts to a Material Change of Use

22–90 Eastbourne B.C. v. Anon. [1958] J.P.L. 738. The parking of a van used to carry goods in the drive of a private house was a material change of use constituting development.

22–91 Washington U.D.C. v. Gray (1958) 10 P. & C.R. 264. Waste land used as a fairground for seven to nine weeks a year. Its use as fairground was its only use and therefore its use as a fairground for the greater part of the year did not involve a material change of use.

22–92 East Barnet U.D.C. v. British Transport Commission [1962] 2 Q.B. 484. What is to be considered is the character of the use of the land not the particular purpose of a particular occupier.

22–93 Marshall v. Nottingham Corpn. [1960] 1 W.L.R. 707. A change in the type of goods dealt with in the course of a business does not necessarily involve a change of use, still less a material change. It is a question of fact and degree.

22–94 Hidderley v. Warwickshire C.C. (1963) 61 L.G.R. 266.

(1) Although there is a distinction between a change in use and a change in the method by which a use is carried out, the change of method might nevertheless be of such a kind and degree as in itself to amount to a material change of use.

(2) A change from selling eggs from a farm to passers-by who called in, to the introduction of an egg-vending machine next to the road was a material change of use.

22–95 Devonshire C.C. v. Horton (1962) 61 L.G.R. 60.

(1) The storage of caravans off-season may be incidental to their use for habitation during the season and so be permitted as incidental to that occasional use.

(2) Whether or not a general or a particular use must be considered to see if there has been a change of use depends on all of the circumstances and is almost entirely a question of fact and degree.

22–96 Gray v. Oxfordshire C.C. (1963) 15 P. & C.R. 1.

(1) It is not possible to make a distinction between kind of use and method of use.

(2) In any event change from lock-up garages, stables and dwelling-house to use of a site for the storage, servicing and maintenance of a coach fleet was a case of material change in kind of use.

22–97 Ben Jay Auto Sales v. Min. of Housing & Local Govt. (1964) 62 L.G.R. 360. The sale of petrol from a repairs garage and motor salerooms where some oil had been sold with the cars constituted a material change of use.

22–98 Birmingham Corpn. v. Habib Ullah [1964] 1 Q.B. 178. The question of whether a material change of use is one of fact and degree for the Minister.

Change from a single dwelling to a "house let in lodgings" could be a material change of use.

Note

For other cases concerning multiple paying occupation, see *Duffy* v. *Pilling* (1976) 33 P. & C.R. 85; *Lipson* v. *Sec. of State for Environment* (1976) 33 P. & C.R. 95.

22–99 Wipperman v. Barking L.B.C. (1965) 17 P. & C.R. 225. The cessation of one of two component dissimilar activities was not of itself a material change of use, but it could be if one component use increased at the expense of the other. It is immaterial whether two uses were carried on over different areas of a planning unit or intermingled. You looked at use of land as a whole.

22–100 Brooks v. Gloucestershire C.C. (1967) 19 P. & C.R. 90. Where there are two concurrent uses and one use absorbs the whole site to the exclusion of the other, there may be a material change of use. It is a matter of fact and degree.

22–101 Marshallsay v. Min. of Housing & Local Govt. (1967) 204 E.G. 695. Five and a half acres of land used for agricultural purposes in winter, and in summer for approximately twelve tents. No material change of use in summer amounting to development.

S.22. MEANING OF DEVELOPMENT

22–102 Clarke v. Min. of Housing & Local Govt. (1968) 18 P. & C.R. 82. Residential property. The change from single family unit occupation to staff accommodation hostel was a material change of use.

The relevant consideration is the use of premises not the relationship of the occupant to other people.

22–103 Frith v. Min. of Housing & Local Govt. (1969) 210 E.G. 213. In considering whether a material change of use has occurred you should look at the whole of area used, including any part of the area incidental or ancillary to the achievement of that purpose, and not simply analyse activities carried on at each part of the site.

22–104 Cook v. Sec. of State for Wales (1970) 220 E.G. 1433. A taxi business with three taxis run from home. The firm's paperwork was done at home and the home address and telephone number appeared in the telephone book under the name of the taxi business. The taxi operated from a rank in town and there was no other sign of the business use of the house. There was evidence on which the Minister could find a material change of use.

22–105 Lewis v. Sec. of State for Environment (1971) 23 P. & C.R. 125. The change in identity of a person carrying out the same activity did not result in a material change of use. Similarly, a change from the repair of a site-owner's vehicles to vehicles belonging to the general public did not result in a material change of use.

22–106 Cheshire C.C. v. Sec. of State for Environment (1971) 222 E.G. 35. Where a change of use is gradual, you compare the pre-1964 position with the present position to see if there is a material change of use.

22–107 St. Herman's Estate Co. v. Havant & Waterloo U.D.C. (1971) 69 L.G.R. 286. The superimposition of a new activity does not automatically constitute a material change in the use of land.

22–108 Jones v. Sec. of State for Environment (1974) 28 P. & C.R. 362. Where an ancillary user of premises becomes the principal user there may be a material change of user such as to justify an enforcement notice, which would prevent even the previously acceptable ancillary user.

22–109 Snook v. Sec. of State for Environment (1975) 33 P. & C.R. 1. Material change of use depended on the character of the use of land not the purpose of the occupier.

No material change of use occurred where materials stored in a builder's yard were destined for use by the purchaser rather than the builder. There might have been a material change of use if the proportion of on-site sales increased.

22–110 Mayflower Cambridge Ltd. v. Sec. of State for Environment (1975) 30 P. & C.R. 28. A hotel took transient passengers; a bed-sitting room was used as a house. Therefore, in a seven-storey building comprising 110 bed-sitting room units the letting of the top three storeys on nightly terms was a hotel category use and amounted to a material change of use of the building as a whole.

22–111 Hammersmith L.B.C. v. Sec. of State for Environment (1975) 30 P. & C.R. 19. Altering a house to sleep 16 students could be a material change of use.

22–112 Chrysanthou v. Sec. of State for Environment [1976] J.P.L. 371. The change from a retail baker's shop to the baking of bread was a material change of use. It amounted to new industrial use.

22–113 Braddon v. Sec. of State for Environment [1976] J.P.L. 508. Premises used originally as a wheelwrights and then as a garage for private cars with limited ancillary repairs. The change to a car repair business was a material change of use.

S.22. MEANING OF DEVELOPMENT

22–114 Hilliard v. Sec. of State for Environment (1979) 37 P. & C.R. 129, C.A. The Secretary of State is not entitled to reach a conclusion that a material change of use has occurred, where there is insufficient evidence to support it and the inspector has made no such finding.

22–115 Maddern v. Sec. of State for Environment [1980] J.P.L. 676. Four buildings used for mushroom farming. The change of use of one to the storage of coffee-grinding and vending machines was capable of being a material change of use.

22–116 Blackpool B.C. v. Sec. of State for the Environment [1980] J.P.L. 527. Residential property used as a holiday home by the owner, his friends and staff on a non-paying basis and by other single households for rent. Although not every residential use was necessarily use as a private house, there was no material change of use in this case.

22–117 Winmill v. Sec. of State for Environment [1982] J.P.L. 445. In finding that there had been a material change of use from bed-sitting rooms and flats to a guesthouse, the Secretary of State had failed to take into account relevant considerations such as length of stay and provision of services. Multiple occupation was not relevant.

22–118 Phillip Farrington Properties v. Sec. of State for Environment [1982] J.P.L. 638. Insufficient evidence to support inspector's finding that there had been a material change of use, when there had been no change in the character of the use of the site.

22–119 Cook v. Sec. of State for Environment [1982] J.P.L. 644. It was agreed that the cessation of one of two uses could not by itself amount to a material change of use.

22–120 Restormel B.C. v. Sec. of State for Environment [1982] J.P.L. 785. To decide whether the stationing of six caravans on a piece of land amounts to a material change of use one must look at the purpose for which it is used and the planning unit. One cannot look at the stationing of the caravan in isolation.
See also *Woodspring D.C. v. Sec. of State for Environment* [1982] J.P.L. 784.

22–121 Backer v. Sec. of State for Environment (1982) 264 E.G. 535. Mere conversion of a building, without occupation, is capable of constituting a material change to use as a dwelling-house.

22–122 Tanbridge D.C. v. Sec. of State for Environment [1983] J.P.L. 667. The Secretary of State's decision that the use of a village store for retail stationery and offset duplication would not constitute a change of use was upheld.

22–123 Wakelin v. Sec. of State for Environment (1983) 46 P. & C.R. 214. The division of a house used as a single planning unit into two separate planning units can involve a material change of use for which planning permission is required.

22–124 Winton v. Sec. of State for Environment (1983) 46 P. & C.R. 205.
(1) If the subdivision of a planning unit has no planning consequences, it does not amount to development.
(2) Whether the subdivision of a planning unit amounts to a material change of use is a matter of fact and degree for the Secretary of State and the proper test is to compare the permitted use of a building with its actual use following subdivision.

22–125 Impey v. Sec. of State for Environment (1984) 47 P. & C.R. 157. (*Sub. nom. Lake District Special Planning Board v. Sec. of State for the Environment* [1981] J.P.L. 363). Change of use to a residential use may commence prior to actual use as such. Both the physical state of the premises and the actual, intended or attempted use of them are important, but neither is decisive.

S.22. MEANING OF DEVELOPMENT

21–126 Burkmar v. Sec. of State for Environment (1984) 271 E.G. 377. Change from a yacht club to a diving club. There was ample material for the inspector to hold that a material change of use had taken place.

22–127 Philglow v. Sec. of State for Environment and London Borough of Hillingdon [1985] J.P.L. 318. The mere cessation of a use does not amount to a material change of use. Where one of two uses ceases, there must be evidence of positive intensification of the remaining use to warrant a conclusion that a material change of use has occurred.
Wipperman v. *Min. of Housing & Local Govt.* explained.

22–128 Panayi v. Sec. of State for Environment and Hackney L.B.C. [1985] J.P.L. 783. Enforcement alleging breach of planning control by change to "Hostel" use: examination of the meaning of the word "hostel" in planning law. Held to be capable of being a material change of use.

CATEGORIES OF MINISTERIAL DECISIONS AS TO WHAT AMOUNTS TO A MATERIAL CHANGE OF USE

(a) Changes relating to residential type uses

22–129 Change in a house from single to multiple occupation was a material change of use even though both uses were residential. [1966] J.P.L. 481. Upheld by D.C.; see *Clark* v. *Caterham and Warlingham U.D.C.*

22–130 A single house changed to two separate dwellings or a house in multiple paying occupation constituted a material change of use. [1966] J.P.L. 665.

22–131 A material change of use from a single dwelling to multiple paying occupation. [1968] J.P.L. 173.

22–132 Mere occupation by a number of tenants is insufficient to change a dwelling-house into a boarding-house. [1968] J.P.L. 527.

22–133 The change from two flats to four flats was a material change of use. [1968] J.P.L. 529.

22–134 The use of a house to house 31 students or staff of one college could properly be described as a hostel. The change from four self-contained flats to a hostel was a material change of use. [1968] J.P.L. 583.

22–135 The garden to a dwelling-house used for commercial purposes when an aviary was opened to the public, who were invited to make voluntary financial contributions, was no longer incidental to dwelling-house use. A subsequent change to an admission charge rather than voluntary contributions was not a further change of use.[1969] J.P.L. 217.

22–136 Use partly as an old people's home and partly as a dwelling-house was materially different from use for multiple paying occupation (individual bed-sitting rooms). [1969] J.P.L. 349.

22–137 Use of living accommodation attached to a dwelling-house as a staff cottage—separate dwelling—a material change of use. [1969] J.P.L. 534.

22–138 Change of use of a building from a miscellany of uses including some overnight accommodation to a hotel use was a material change. [1969] J.P.L. 656.

22–139 Two separate buildings occupied as one dwelling. Occupation as two separate dwellings was a material change of use. [1969] J.P.L. 600.

22–140 Change of use from residential with ancillary dental practice (one surgery) to dental surgeries (two surgeries) with ancillary residential accommodation was a material change. [1970] J.P.L. 95.

S.22. MEANING OF DEVELOPMENT

22–141 Premises let to a single tenant but used by four unconnected adults each occupying a single bedroom and sharing the lounge, dining-room, kitchen and bathroom amounted to multiple paying occupation of premises. [1970] J.P.L. 271.

22–142 Extension to dwelling-house used full time for the business of printing and processing with no domestic use amounts to a material change of use. [1971] J.P.L. 287.

22–143 Display of settees and chairs used as the furniture of a house to obtain orders for similar furniture was a change from residential to mixer use, but not a material change of use. [1971] J.P.L. 529.

22–144 Change of use from single dwelling-house (one-family occupation) to multiple occupation was a material change of use. [1976] J.P.L. 55.

22–145 Change from a hotel to a hostel for convalescents and elderly persons was a material change of use. [1976] J.P.L. 522.

22–146 Use of a dwelling-house for multiple paying occupation for six people was a material change of use. [1977] J.P.L. 535.

22–147 Use of a dwelling-house for accommodation of hotel staff (hostel) was not a material change of use. [1978] J.P.L. 399.

22–148 A dwelling-house in multiple-paying occupation—change of use of the garage from storage ancillary to dwelling-house to use as a bed-sitting room, increasing number of tenancies from five to six was not a material change. [1978] J.P.L. 578.

22–148a Two cottages built within the same walls and under the same roof which from outside could be mistaken for one dwelling. Use as one dwelling would not amount to a material change of use. [1982] J.P.L. 119.

22–149 Ten people living in a dwelling-house, paying money into pooled account for expenses and renting unfurnished from owner—lounge/television room, kitchen, bathroom and toilet facilities shared. Still essentially single occupation and therefore no material change of use. [1979] J.P.L. 123.

22–150 Change of use of a house from use as six flats with shared facilities to a hostel was a material change of use. [1979] J.P.L. 338.

22–151 Use of flats for holiday lettings instead of long-term lettings was not a material change of use. [1980] J.P.L. 342.

22–152 Use of one room of a dwelling-house for a commercial food preparation business as well as for domestic use and employing of three women part-time was a material change of use. [1980] J.P.L. 854.

22–153 Change of use from a house to holiday flats was a material change of use. [1981] J.P.L. 612.

22–154 Use of roof extension to a residential dwelling as a balcony or open amenity area amounted to material change of use because of the effects of use on neighbours. [1982] J.P.L. 199.

22–155 House used for housing college students under the control of a lodging housekeeper changed to housing students under direct control of the college did not require planning permission as the system of supervision and management did not go to planning status of the land, which was that of a University lodging house. [1983] J.P.L. 485.

22–156 Dwelling-house used for limited business purposes—business mail addressed there and sorted for one hour each morning, some business phone calls made and received, scaffolding stored there and one or two commercial vans parked nearby—was not a material change of use. [1983] J.P.L. 496.

22–157 Change from dwelling-house use to a refuge for battered women and their children was development requiring planning permission. [1984] J.P.L. 822.

22–158 Use of part of a house as a doctor's surgery can constitute a material change of use, but an average of three patients visiting per week insufficient to amount to a material change of use. [1985] J.P.L. 339.

22–159 Proposal to change the use of house from that of single family dwelling-house to use as a shared house for four single people with one resident staff member, each having their own bedroom but sharing all other facilities, would constitute or involve development of land. [1986] J.P.L. 376.

(b) Changes relating to shop/restaurant/type uses

22–160 Day-time cafe–restaurant with ancillary fried fish shop. Change to use as a fried fish shop in the late evening was a material change of use. [1960] J.P.L. 171.

22–161 Introduction of egg-vending machine to a garage forecourt involved a material change of use. (1962) 13 P. & C.R. 453.

22–162 Installation of a milk-vending machine on agricultural land constituted development. (1962) 13 P. & C.R. 353.

22–163 Where premises are used for serving food their use is as a restaurant and it is not altered by the means of transport used by customers. [1969] J.P.L. 38.

22–164 A forecourt can be used in connection with the purposes to which a building is put without a material change of use being involved—but the stationing of a mobile shop on the forecourt of an industrial building is a material change of use. [1968] J.P.L. 42.

22–165 Change from a licensed restaurant to licensed premises with restaurant facilities is a material change of use. [1969] J.P.L. 52.

22–166 Use of a previously existing shop as two shops does not amount to a material change of use. [1969] J.P.L. 483.

22–167 Change from packing and dispatch to "cash and carry" retail sales is a material change of use. [1970] J.P.L. 461.

22–168 Change from a car-park ancillary to business use to sale of boats ancillary to the same use does not involve a material change of use. Identification of the area on which a particular activity is carried out. [1972] J.P.L. 37.

22–169 Change from a wholesale warehouse with some retail sales to a retail supermarket is a material change of use. [1972] J.P.L. 273.

22–170 Independent retail sales carried out on the forecourt of a shop is development requiring planning permission. [1972] J.P.L. 393.

22–171 Change from dual use with predominant use for the retail sales of building materials to use for sales of builder's and household materials was not a material change of use. [1973] J.P.L. 261.

22–172 Use for sale of less than 12 cars per year *de minimus*. [1974] J.P.L. 300.

22–173 Bar use ancillary to hotel and restaurant use. Use of a bar with full on-licence for the general public would be necessarily limited by the nature of the facilities and the needs of the guests and diners and would not as a matter of fact and degree amount to a material change of use. [1979] J.P.L. 185.

22–174 Conversion of a single shop into two shops does not involve development. [1979] J.P.L. 705.

22–175 Use of shop premises for the showing of films in booths in addition to normal shop use a material change of use, even though it provided a relatively small part of the weekly takings of the premises, and the films shown could be bought in the shop. Film viewing took up half the floor area. [1980] J.P.L. 58.

22–176 Caravan stationed on a trunk road lay-by near to a motorway, supported by jacks rather than wheels—in place almost continuously for three years, and used as a mobile snack bar/cafe. Whether or not the caravan was capable of or had been moved from the site, it was intended to be regularly stationed on the site and amounted to a material change of use. [1982] J.P.L. 405.

22–177 Cafe with a take-away business amounting to 20–30 per cent. of total sales changed to a cafe with a hot take-away food shop amounting to 70–83 per cent. of total sales. Change of use from cafe to mixed cafe and shop. Material change because of extended trading period, substantial alteration in ratio of in to out sales, larger catering equipment and greater intensity of cooking smells, rise in level of litter, noise and disturbance to residents. [1983] J.P.L. 400.

22–178 Display of horse-boxes for sale on garage premises with an area where sales of motor vehicles permitted—a material change of use. [1984] J.P.L. 826.

22–179 Availability and use of three video amusement machines in a small take-away food shop constituted a change in use from take-away food to a mixed use for take-away food and video machines.

(c) Changes relating to agricultural type uses

22–180 Alternating summer and winter uses for car parking and agricultural purposes respectively resulted in two material changes of use per year, albeit agricultural use did not involve development. [1967] J.P.L. 233; but see *Webber* v. *Min. of Housing and Local Government*.

22–181 Change of use from keeping and breeding pigs (agricultural use) to keeping and breeding greyhounds was a material change of use. [1967] J.P.L. 662.

22–182 Repair of a farm's own agricultural implements and vehicles was ancillary to agricultural use. Change to log-sawing and the manufacture of fire-lighters was a material change of use to industrial use. Further change to storage was a material change of use. Further change to the repair of vehicles was a material change of use. [1972] J.P.L. 388.

22–183 Importation of any produce for sale on an agricultural holding constitutes a material change of use. [1973] J.P.L. 386.

22–184 Agricultural land still in agricultural use, used also for flying model aircraft with radio control, was a change of use to composite use. [1975] J.P.L. 40.

22–185 Sale of meat from a farm—preparation and packaging constituting development. [1976] J.P.L. 369.

22–186 Laying-out of a formal garden on rough grassland previously in agricultural and occasional recreational use was a material change of use. [1979] J.P.L. 189.

22–187 Storage of two caravans in a farmyard was not a material change of use from agricultural use, but storage of 12 was. [1982] J.P.L. 268.

(d) Changes relating to haulage uses

22–188 Change from a haulage depot to a staging depot in the transportation of goods in containers was a material change of use. [1970] J.P.L. 717.

22–189 Material change of use from the excavation of sand and gravel with ancillary haulage to independent haulage use. [1973] J.P.L. 666.

S.22. MEANING OF DEVELOPMENT

22–190 Material change of use from a builder's yard to the parking of vehicles for a haulage business. [1974] J.P.L. 159.

22–191 Change from the sale and display of agricultural machinery to a parking depot for haulage business was a material change of use. [1976] J.P.L. 766.

22–192 Road haulage depot—use for recovery of broken-down vehicles on average on no more than one occasion per week was *de minimis* and disregarded. [1978] J.P.L. 646.

22–193 Haulage depot—use of part of a site for the sale of motor cars and private garaging, and the statement never to have a haulier again, was evidence that haulage use was abandoned. Change from use of a site for vans delivering parcels with some parking of heavy vehicles to use as a road haulage depot was a material change of use. [1980] J.P.L. 205.

(e) Changes relating to office type uses

22–194 Office use. Change in the identity of the occupier immaterial (even if change from a statutory body to a non-statutory body). Terms of planning permission for present use were not relevant to whether change of use involves development. [1967] J.P.L. 173.

22–195 Change from a commercial training college to office use was a material change of use. [1969] J.P.L. 351.

22–196 Use of former offices with incidental parking as a taxi, car-hire and coach business was a material change of use. [1971] J.P.L. 583.

22–197 Change from a shop to a car-hire office for a car-hire business was a material change of use. [1972] J.P.L. 458.

22–198 Change from a police station to an office was a material change of use even though the majority of rooms may have been used as offices. [1980] J.P.L. 47.

22–199 Building comprising offices and residential accommodation. Use of access to the residential part in connection with the office use was a material change of use. [1981] J.P.L. 533.

(f) Changes relating to industrial type uses

22–200 Change of use from the manufacture of wooden crates and the sale of firewood to the display and sale of garden machinery and accessories and the storage of material used for landscape gardening was a material change. [1970] J.P.L. 465.

22–201 Change from the sale of cars and minor repairs and servicing to the sale and fitting of new exhaust systems to motor cars was a material change of use. [1970] J.P.L. 591.

22–202 Change from the joint use of a haulage business with the ancillary repair of vehicles and an industrial-use firewood business to a single industrial use (motor repairs) was a material change of use. [1971] J.P.L. 236.

22–203 Concrete batching plant. Change in the source of materials does not result in a material change of use. [1973] J.P.L. 552.

22–204 Subdivision of premises used for light industrial purposes into several units for light industrial use was not a material change of use. [1984] J.P.L. 892.

(g) Changes relating to social/recreational type uses

22–205 Use of a holiday club arena as a greyhound track involves development, because although sporting activities in which visitors take part for their own enjoyment are part of a holiday club use, the running of dogs is materially different as it does not involve the participation of the owners and is not a normal holiday club use. [1967] J.P.L. 557.

22–206 Material change of use from greyhound racing to greyhound racing and car racing. [1972] J.P.L. 219.

22–207 In deciding whether there has been a change of use regard must be had to the previous operative use, not to a use permitted by an unimplemented planning permission. Change of use from a music room for dancing classes to a music studio and dancing classes. [1975] J.P.L. 616.

22–208 Use of school premises, outside school hours, for social functions not connected with education purposes was a material change of use. [1978] J.P.L. 51.

22–209 A change in the categories of persons using a club does not thereby establish that there has been a material change in the character of the use. [1978] J.P.L. 401.

22–210/211 Change of use of a greyhound-racing stadium to include a speedway was a material change of use. [1979] J.P.L. 633.

22–212 Change from a social club to a cinema club showing uncensored films was a material change of use even though both were recreational uses. [1983] J.P.L. 626.

22–213 Public house—ancillary entertainment with music, disc jockey and flashing lights but no dancing was not a material change of use. The effect on the neighbourhood is not the only criterion for determining whether there has been a material change of use. [1984] J.P.L. 122.

22–214 Change from full time military and commercial operations on airfield to use for a limited number of microlight aircraft for recreational purposes on relatively few days in the year a material change of use. [1985] J.P.L. 426.

(h) Changes relating to storage/parking type uses

22–215 Storage of vehicles and parts. Established storage use incidental to agricultural use did not allow independent storage use. Storage or dumping of one old car did not establish use for storage of vehicles. Creation of a rubbish dump in a disused pit does not amount to material use of land for storage. [1966] J.P.L. 115.

22–216 Stationing of caravans was a use distinct from use as a play area for caravans on another field. [1966] J.P.L. 418.

22–217 Planning permission for storage of timber, coal and coke. Change from the storage and cutting of logs to the storage of hardcore, bricks and old iron was not a material change of use. [1966] J.P.L. 663.

22–218 Use of land for parking vehicles is not affected by the reason for which they are parked or the business of the owners during the time parked, therefore there was no material change of use when use changed from the private parking and garaging of vehicles to the parking of vehicles in connection with a business. [1967] J.P.L. 294.

22–219 Change from the garaging of motor vehicles in connection with a driving school to a motor vehicle workshop and garage was a material change of use. [1967] J.P.L. 415.

22–220 Material change of use from the storage and delivery of domestic fuel oil, with incidental vehicle parking and maintenance, to the parking and maintenance of tanker vehicles. [1969] J.P.L. 40.

22–221 Use of land for the repair and reconditioning of motor vehicles for resale was materially different from the use of land for the business of a soil and manure contractor with incidental maintenance and repair of vehicles. [1969] J.P.L. 153.

S.22. MEANING OF DEVELOPMENT

22–222 Use for the preparation of vegetables was an industrial use and materially different from the storage and distribution of fruit and vegetables. The cleaning and repair of carpets and the storage, cleaning and general preparation of motor cars for sale were both industrial uses. [1969] J.P.L. 411.

22–223 Land formerly used for vehicle parking and storage of spare parts. A change to use as a garden resulted in a change to residential use and a resumption of use for the storage of vehicles and parts was a material change of use. [1969] J.P.L. 707.

22–224 Change from playing fields to a car park was a material change of use. [1970] J.P.L. 43.

22–225 Change of use from a gypsy encampment with small piles of domestic scrap metal and an occasional scrap car, to use for the storage and sale of scrap motor vehicles was a material change of use. [1970] J.P.L. 158.

22–226 Change from the storage of laundry, machinery and vehicles in connection with adjacent laundry premises to recovery of copper was not a material change of use. [1970] J.P.L. 221.

22–227 Change from parking motor cars for car-hire business to parking motor coaches was a material change of use. [1971] J.P.L. 173.

22–228 Stationing of a caravan on land incidental to sale, repair or breaking of caravans. Change to the seasonal storage of caravans of a travelling showman was a material change of use. [1971] J.P.L. 356.

22–229 Change from use for railway undertaking to the storage of engineering plant, machinery and vehicles was a material change of use. [1971] J.P.L. 457.

22–230 Change of use from ancillary car parking to independent car parking was a material change. [1974] J.P.L. 426.

22–231 Use of an existing building in a rural area for storage when it was previously only used for occasional storage was a material change of use. [1975] J.P.L. 162.

22–232 Change from the storage of coal and coke for a gas works to the storage of cars was a material change of use. [1976] J.P.L. 248.

22–233 Use of land as a public highway is a separate and distinguishable use—a change to use for parking vehicles is a material change of use. [1978] J.P.L. 274.

22–234 Use of land for storage independent of established haulage business amounted to a material change of use. [1980] J.P.L. 288.

(i) Changes relating to uses concerned with motor vehicles

22–235 Display and sale of motor cars, amounting to 56 per cent. of turnover, where previously a small proportion of the business, was a material change of use. [1966] J.P.L. 118.

22–236 Premises used for a motoring school and car hire. There was a material change of use when 15 per cent. of the business consisted of car repairs and the sale of motor accessories—mixed use. An increase in car repairs and the sale of motor accessories to 30 per cent. of the business was not a further material change of use. The sale of one motor vehicle in six months was insufficient to amount to a material change of use, but the sale of 15 cars in one year would be sufficient. [1968] J.P.L. 354.

22–237 Builder's yard with ancillary servicing, maintenance and repair of its own vehicles. The introduction of the repair and maintenance of other vehicles on a commercial basis was a material change of use. The use of a builder's yard for a plant-hire business was a material change of use. Evidence of alleged uses. [1974] J.P.L. 614.

22–238 Use of former lock-up garages for the repair of motor vehicles was a material change of use. [1974] J.P.L. 677.

22–239 Change from a builder's yard to a workshop for vehicle repairs was a material change of use. [1975] J.P.L. 614.

22–240 Change of use of a building from the repair of motor cars as a part-time occupation to the business of motor-car repairs was not a material change of use. [1976] J.P.L. 530.

22–241 A commercial vehicle depot involves a basic activity which does not alter with the alteration in the kind of vehicle involved unless the alteration is so significant as to change the basic activity of the use itself—a change from goods vehicles to coaches was immaterial. [1979] J.P.L. 701.

22–242 Change from a motor showroom and repair garage to use for the retail sale and storage of furniture in pre-packed kits was a material change of use. Employment of 17 out of 34 staff and the use of an area 80 ft by 120 ft for repairs and servicing was inconsistent with the contention that the sale of cars was the main use of the premises. [1980] J.P.L. 693.

22–243 Change of use from the storage of a motor car to the manufacture and assembly, wholesale and retailing, of car components was a material change of use. [1982] J.P.L. 657.

(j) Changes relating to tipping/dumping uses

22–244 Dumping of empty bottles and the occasional discarding of unwanted articles on land attached to a public house was not sufficient to amount to a change of use or a use for the deposit of waste material. Even if excavated spoil is not "waste material," brick, concrete, rubble and timber are, and their subsequent dumping amounts to a material change of use. [1967] J.P.L. 46.

22–245 Use of a quarry as a refuse tip. A substantial increase in the superficial area of deposit was a material change of use. [1968] J.P.L. 474.

(k) Changes relating to the mooring and other use of boats

22–246 Mooring of a vessel, otherwise than in the course of navigation, involves a material change of use of the land over which it is so moored, whether that land is covered at all times by water or not. [1969] J.P.L. 221 & 521.

22–247 Use of land for sailing and fishing on a commercial basis requires planning permission. [1972] J.P.L. 395.

22–248 Introduction of the mooring of a boat on land covered by water is a material change of use. [1973] J.P.L. 322.

22–249 The mooring of a boat otherwise than in the normal course of navigation involves a material change of use of the land over which it is moored. [1975] J.P.L. 234.

22–250 Mooring and use for residential purposes of a floating mobile home in a boatyard is a material change of use. [1975] J.P.L. 486.

22–251 Permanent mooring of a houseboat is a material change of use. [1981] J.P.L. 833.

22–252 Storage of fish and shellfish in a barge stationed on mud flats was a material change of use requiring planning permission. [1984] J.P.L. 57.

S.22. MEANING OF DEVELOPMENT

(l) Changes relating to general commercial uses

22–253 Use of a wood yard as a coal yard was not a material change of use. [1966] J.P.L. 542.

22–254 Change from a builder's yard to a plant-hire and haulage depot was a material change of use. [1968] J.P.L. 639.

22–255 Change from a builder's yard to a general printing works was a material change of use. The primary purpose determines the character of the use. [1968] J.P.L. 712.

22–256 Use of a slaughterhouse for the business of a meat processor's agent was not a material change of use. [1969] J.P.L. 595.

22–257 Building used for the sale of builder's materials to the building trade and to the public. Change to use for the distribution through agents of plant manufactured elsewhere was a material change of use. [1973] J.P.L. 391.

22–258 Use of a former knacker's yard for the collection, storage and distribution of animal bones and fat was a material change of use. [1977] J.P.L. 118.

22–259 Change from a coal merchant's yard to a builders merchant's yard was a material change of use. [1978] J.P.L. 343.

22–260 Change from a builder's yard to a shopfitter's workshop was not a material change of use. [1978] J.P.L. 721.

22–261 Use of an established sand pit for the mixing of sand with gravel brought to the premises was a material change of use. [1978] J.P.L. 785.

22–262 Material change of use from a slaughterhouse with ancillary storage of carcasses to the storage of carcasses of animals not slaughtered on the premises. Twenty-six deliveries a year was not *de minimis*. [1980] J.P.L. 343.

2. The Distinction Between Primary and Ancillary or Incidental Uses

22–263 Logue v. L.C.C. (1964) 192 E.G. 281. Use of premises as an arcade where stall-holders displayed goods for sale was a shop use and was not incidental or ancillary to a storage use.

22–264 Lloyd Jones v. Min. of Health & Local Govt. (1967) 204 E.G. 49. Sale of produce.

22–265 Williams v. Min. of Housing & Local Govt. (1967) 18 P. & C.R. 514. Agricultural use necessarily includes the selling of products but the selling of "imported" products is not ancillary to such use.

22–266 Peake v. Sec. of State for Wales (1971) 22 P. & C.R. 859. Garage designed as a private garage, but never used as such, used for paid maintenance and repair. By virtue of s.21(2) of the Town and Country Planning Act 1962 (now see s.33(2)), as the garage was designed as a private garage that was its primary use. It could have an ancillary use of paid repair and maintenance as a part-time hobby, but not as a full-time business.

22–267 Hussain v. Sec. of State for Environment (1971) 23 P. & C.R. 330. In deciding whether a use is ordinarily incidental to a retail shop it must be considered whether it is ordinarily incidental to the retail trade generally. In so deciding it is not proper to consider the special requirements of particular localities, areas and customers.

The keeping of chickens for slaughter in a Muslim area was not incidental.

S.22. MEANING OF DEVELOPMENT

22–268 Wood v. Sec. of State for Environment. [1973] 1 W.L.R. 707. Sale of home-produced produce on a holding was incidental to agricultural activity. The bringing-in and selling of somebody else's produce was a separate use from agricultural use.

22–269 Bromley L.B. v. George Haeltschi & Son (1977) 244 E.G. 49. There is a change of use as soon as produce is imported for retail sale into a shop ancillary to agricultural use. When such change occurs it is a question of fact and degree—20 per cent. imported was held by the Minister not to be ancillary to agricultural use.

22–270 Pollock v. Sec. of State for Environment (1979) 40 P. & C.R. 94. Character of use of land is determined by its primary use and not by parts of its use.

22–271 Emma Hotels Ltd. v. Sec. of State for Environment (1980) 41 P. & C.R. 255. Hotel bar where 70–80 per cent. of the customers were non-residents. The bar was ancillary to hotel use.
See also [1979] J.P.L. 390.

22–272 David W. Barling v. Sec. of State for Environment [1980] J.P.L. 594. Storage of building materials for construction of a bungalow was an incidental use but when fenced off and materials stored for use on other buildings this created a new planning unit and was no longer incidental.

22–273 S.J.D. Properties Ltd. v. Sec. of State for Environment [1981] J.P.L. 673. There was a real distinction between allowing a person to view a film for the purposes of seeing whether he wished to purchase the film and allowing a person to view a film at a charge in such circumstances that, if he wanted to do so, he could purchase the film thereafter and get a refund of the charge — the latter would not be ancillary to a shop use.

22–274 Jillings v. Sec. of State for Environment [1984] J.P.L. 32. Change of use from a hire business with ancillary manufacture of boats to primary use of boat hire and manufacture was a material change of use.

22–275 Lydcare v. Sec. of State for Environment [1984] J.P.L. 810, C.A. Viewing of films in cubicles by feeding coins into machines amounted to a primary use and was not incidental to a shop use.

22–276 Sale, or display of cars for sale, is not incidental to the fuelling, repair and servicing of vehicles nor can such uses carry with them any implied right to use premises for the sale or display of cars for sale. [1966] J.P.L. 485.

22–277 Use of the forecourt of a pet shop for motor-car sales. The forecourt of a shop is an ancillary part of shop. Use of the forecourt was entirely unconnected with the use of shop therefore was a material change of use not within the General Development Order and needed planning permission. [1966] J.P.L. 688.

22–278 Repair works on cars garaged in a lock-up garage is ancillary to use as a lock-up garage, but general repair work on cars for sale in a showroom is not. [1968] J.P.L. 357.

22–279 Storage and display of garden sheds and ornaments is not ancillary to agricultural use, but the storage and display of plant pots and gardener's materials is. [1968] J.P.L. 364.

22–280 Carrying-out of routine maintenance and minor repairs arising therefrom is ancillary to petrol station use, but carrying out of major repairs is not. [1968] J.P.L. 585.

22–281 Bakehouse use was not ancillary to an adjacent shop where only a small proportion of the produce was sold. [1968] J.P.L. 589.

22–282 Use of the front room of a dwelling-house for piano-teaching and another room as a waiting-room for students and office purposes in connection with piano-

S.22. MEANING OF DEVELOPMENT

teaching was not an independent office use; premises were used as a dwelling-house with minor use for piano-teaching. [1969] J.P.L. 94.

22–283 Fitting of tyres and batteries is ancillary to shop use. [1969] J.P.L. 417.

22–284 Occasional use of premises as ancillary to main dwelling-house did not prevent continuation of established independent residential use of premises. [1972] J.P.L. 165.

22–285 Storage of bodies pending internment is ancillary to an undertaker's business (shop) use. [1972] J.P.L. 456.

22–286 Cutting-room used for the cutting and making-up of garments elsewhere, as well as on the premises, was not ancillary to clothes-shop use. [1973] J.P.L. 62.

22–287 Bricks intended for building development (with planning permission) left on site over a long period of time amounted to independent storage use. [1973] J.P.L. 179.

22–288 Slaughtering, jointing, packaging and sale of meat is not ancillary to agricultural use. [1974] J.P.L. 165.

22–289 Use of a farm for an agricultural contractor's business (hire of machinery) was not ancillary to the agricultural use of the farm. [1974] J.P.L. 734.

22–290 Sale of food and household goods from petrol-filling station is not ancillary to use as a petrol filling station. [1975] J.P.L. 687.

22–291 Garage building used in conjunction with adjoining laundry building. Change to a use ancillary to the permitted use of the adjoining building for warehousing. Subsequent change of use to independent use for the repairs and servicing of vehicles. [1976] J.P.L. 196.

22–292 Change of use when a builder's yard used for the production of joinery items for other companies within a group of companies—no longer ancillary to builder's yard. Former offices used in connection with a builder's yard used as a group area office—change of use no longer ancillary to the builder's yard. [1977] J.P.L. 45.

22–293 Shop not ancillary to a petrol-filling station and garage. [1977] J.P.L. 190.

22–294 Use of a basement flat by the caretaker of a five-storey building was ancillary to the office use of the remainder of the building. [1977] J.P.L. 464.

22–295 Sales of meat were not ancillary to a slaughterhouse business. [1977] J.P.L. 817.

22–296 Storage and sale of furniture and other goods in a church building for the benefit of the church and other charities is not ancillary to church use. [1978] J.P.L. 126.

22–297 Use of a building within the curtilage of a dwelling-house to stable the owner's horse was a material change of use. [1978] J.P.L. 128.

22–298 Holding of auctions and sales is not ancillary to hotel use. [1978] J.P.L. 279.

22–299 Occupation of the first floor of a bank/building society by the manager as a residence was ancillary to the bank (office) use and therefore the use of the first floor as offices did not involve development. [1978] J.P.L. 333.

22–300 Keeping of 43 cats and 3 dogs as pets was ancillary to dwelling-house use. [1978] J.P.L. 335.

22–301 Use for recovery of broken-down vehicles on average between 29 and 39 times per week was not ancillary to haulage use. [1978] J.P.L. 646.

22–302 Processing and sale of meat from livestock reared on a farm is not ancillary to agricultural use. [1978] J.P.L. 792.

22–303 Shop with living accommodation. The living accommodation was always closely related to the shop, and the shop had always been the dominant use. Change of use of the living accommodation to an office and storage ancillary to shop use was not a material change of use. [1979] J.P.L. 54.

22–304 Stationing of a caravan for storing tools and shelter on land used for agriculture was ancillary to the agricultural use. The determining factor in deciding whether a caravan is used for human habitation is its actual use rather than its potential use. [1981] J.P.L. 536.

22–305 Function room in a hotel let between June and September for the retail sales of various items taking place seven days a week at times differing from normal shopping hours attracting non-residents to hotel who then used other hotel facilities. Use not ancillary to the hotel amounted to an identifiable independent use as a retail shop. [1983] J.P.L. 132.

22–306 Caravan used for storage and as a canteen ancillary to the use of land as a nursery. [1983] J.P.L. 274.

22–307 Retail sale of meat from animals slaughtered in an abbattoir, when in active operation, is not ancillary to the slaughtering of animals as retailing of the product on the premises not a part of, nor did it contribute to, the processes which were the primary use of the land and buildings. [1983] J.P.L. 396.

22–308 Use of eight amusement machines was not ancillary to an ice-cream parlour—mixed use of retail sales and the provision and playing of amusement machines. [1983] J.P.L. 499.

22–309 Some recreational and/or amusement element may fairly be introduced on to the premises of any club, whatever its basic concept, but the introduction of seven pool tables and three video machines taking up half of the space of a boxing club results in a change to part boxing-club and part pool-room and amusement centre use. [1983] J.P.L. 623.

3. Intensification as Material Change of Use

JUDICIAL DECISIONS ON INTENSIFICATION

22–310 Guildford R.D.C. v. Fortescue [1959] 2 Q.B. 112, C.A. An increase or intensification of the use of land might amount to a material change of use. Whether or not it did was a question of fact—there was no ground to interfere with a decision that an increase from 8 caravans to 21 and then to 27 on a $1\frac{1}{2}$ acre piece of land was not a material change of use.

22–311 Washington U.D.C. v. Gray (1958) 10 P. & C.R. 264, D.C. Waste land used for seven to nine weeks per year as a fairground. Its only use was a fairground and therefore when used for the greater part of the year as a fairground there was no material change of use.

22–312 Dyble v. Min. of Health & Local Govt. (1966) 197 E.G. 457, D.C. Change from the part-time repairing of vehicles to a full-time business was a material change of use.

22–313 Glamorgan C.C. v. Carter [1963] 1 W.L.R. 1, D.C. *Quaere per* Salmon J. Once it is established that the whole site is used as a caravan site there would be no material change of use by bringing a larger number of caravans upon the site.

22–314 Esdell Caravan Parks Ltd. v. Hemel Hempstead R.D.C. [1966] 1 Q.B. 895, C.A. *Per* Lord Denning M.R.: An increase from 24 to 78 caravans on a 4.8 acre field may amount to a material change of use.

S.22. MEANING OF DEVELOPMENT

22–315 James v. Min. of Housing & Local Government [1966] 1 W.L.R. 135, C.A. Whether intensification amounted to a material change of use was a question of fact and degree.

22–316 Brooks v. Gloucestershire C.C. (1967) 19 P. & C.R. 90. *Per curiam*: Intensification normally concerns a situation where an area of land is used throughout the relevant time for the same purpose but the intensity of activity varies.

22–317 Lewis v. Sec. of State for Environment (1971) 23 P. & C.R. 125. *See* section on primary and ancillary uses.

22–318 Wood v. Sec. of State for Environment [1973] J.P.L. 429, D.C. When looking at intensification the planning unit as a whole must be looked at.

22–319 Cheshire C.C. v. Sec. of State for Environment (1971) 222 E.G. 35, D.C. Increase from four tippers, one breakdown lorry and one articulated vehicle to 11 articulated lorries, more than 20 trailers and three fixed-chassis vehicles was not a material change of use.

22–320 Peake v. Sec. of State for Wales (1972) 22 P. & C.R. 889. A change in activity from part-time to full-time could not of itself amount to a material change of use.

22–321 De Mulder v. Sec. of State for Environment (1974) Q.B. 792, D.C. An intensification as a material change of use occurs at a point where the landowner has already exercised every right under the Planning Acts by which time any latitude of the kind mentioned in *Mansi* v. *Elstree R.D.C.* has already been absorbed and enjoyed. One can fix on a particular date when intensification results in a material change of use.

22–322 Johnston v. Sec. of State for Environment (1974) 28 P. & C.R. 424, D.C. Garages—change from composite use for garaging and repair to sole use for repair is a material change of use.

22–323 Brooks & Burton Ltd. v. Sec. of State for Environment [1977] 1 W.L.R. 1294, C.A. Where an intensified use falls within the same class for the purposes of the Town and Country Planning Use Classes Order 1972 as the earlier use, then by virtue of s.22(2)(f) of the Town and Country Planning Act 1971 such intensified use cannot be taken to involve development.

22–324 Snook v. Sec. of State for Environment (1977) 33 P. & C.R. 1. Decision quashed as no evidence before the Minister that there had been an intensification.

22–325 Hilliard v. Sec. of State for Environment (1979) 37 P. & C.R. 129, C.A. The Secretary of State is not entitled to reach a conclusion that there has been a material change of use, where there is insufficient evidence to support it and the inspector has made no such finding. Not sufficient evidence to support a finding of a material change of use by intensification.

22–326 R.B. of Kensington & Chelsea v. Sec. of State for Environment [1981] J.P.L. 50, C.A. *Per Donaldson LJ*: In planning language intensification meant a change to something different. It would be better if the word were not used. If the planners were incapable of formulating what was the use after "intensification" and what was the use before "intensification"then there had been no material change of use.

22–327 Hipsey v. Sec. of State for Environment [1984] J.P.L. 806. Intensification of use. Intensification had occurred by the time an established use certificate application had been made and the Secretary of State was not entitled to certify that a lesser use had been established.

22–328 Philglow v. Sec. of State for Environment [1985] J.P.L. 318, C.A. Mere cessation of one of the elements of a composite use is not of itself a material change of use. There must be positive evidence that the remaining use has intensified to such an extent as to amount to a change in character; though it need not have extended over the whole of the planning unit.

MINISTERIAL DECISIONS ON INTENSIFICATION

(a) Intensification resulting in a material change of use

22–328a Increase from the intermittent use of part of a site incidental to its use as a repair garage to a substantial part of the site with sale as the primary use of the land. [1961] 13 P. & C.R. 97.

22–329 Change from casual use of land for dog-boarding to substantial use. [1962] J.P.L. 341.

22–330 Change from land with predominant agricultural use with subsidiary, slight and intermittent use for car-breaking to full-time use for car-breaking. [1965] J.P.L. 629.

22–331 Storage and hire of equipment and vehicles. Change from casual to recognisably continuous use. [1965] J.P.L. 307.

22–332 Large house — multiple paying occupation. Change from three separate dwellings to 21 apartments. [1964] J.P.L. 569.

22–333 Change from parking one or two lorries to parking 35 or 40. [1967] J.P.L. 292.

22–334 Use of land for a caravan site was an intensification of use. [1967] J.P.L. 296.

22–335 0.55 acres—increase from the storage of two caravans and sporadic storage of another five to storage of 40 caravans. [1969] J.P.L. 705.

22–336 Increase from five vehicles including one articulated lorry and the occasional use of containers to seven articulated vehicles, one platform vehicle, two pick-up vans, two cars, three trailers and containers. [1970] J.P.L. 717.

22–337 Introduction of the sale of fried fish to take away representing between 22 per cent. and 35 per cent. of total turnover resulted in a change of use from a shop to a fried-fish shop. [1971] J.P.L. 61.

22–338 Garage repairs—change from a spare-time activity to a full-time occupation. [1971] J.P.L. 176.

22–339 Repair of vehicles—change from a small-scale *de minimis* operation to a significant full-time operation. [1971] J.P.L. 346.

22–340 Change from the extensive breeding and occasional boarding of dogs as a hobby to the extensive boarding of dogs as a business. [1971] J.P.L. 647.

22–341 Repair and storage of motor-vehicles—change from a hobby to a business. [1972] J.P.L. 213.

22–342 Repair of cars as a hobby was so substantial that it could not be regarded as incidental to the enjoyment of a dwelling-house. [1972] J.P.L. 339.

22–343 Coal depot—change from little open stacking to over 20 stacks. [1974] J.P.L. 100.

22–344 Storage of caravans on 3.2 acre site—increase from 4 to between 24 and 41. [1974] J.P.L. 733.

22–345/346 Use of land for agricultural purposes with ancillary storage and wholesale distribution of indigenous and non-indigenous produce. Storage and wholesale distribution of non-indigenous produce amounted to intensification. [1977] J.P.L. 123.

S.22. MEANING OF DEVELOPMENT

(b) Intensification not involving a material change of use

22–347 Increase in use for renovating caravans but still only a subsidiary use. [1963] J.P.L. 349.

22–348 Parking vehicles—increase from 6 to 25. [1963] J.P.L. 617.

22–349 Gradual intensification of storage and maintenance of vehicles. [1965] J.P.L. 633.

22–350 Increase from 11 to 16 caravans. [1967] J.P.L. 421.

22–351 Parking of transport vehicles and dumping of derelict vehicles. [1967] J.P.L. 292.

22–352 Use of lounge of private hotel for non-residential functions. Increase in functions from 39 in March to December 1962 to 97 in 1965. [1967] J.P.L. 355.

22–353 Change from use as a school of music in the afternoon and evening to include general kindergarten school in the mornings and afternoons. No increase in the number of rooms used. [1967] J.P.L. 672.

22–354 Roadside cafe—increase in the number of vehicles by 90 per cent. and a change in custom from predominantly private vehicles with a small proportion of commercial vehicles to 50 per cent. commercial. [1969] J.P.L. 38.

22–355 Increase from three to nine lorries with an attendant increase in the number of men employed and the amount of repair work carried out. [1969] J.P.L. 526.

22–356 Marked intensification of use but the character of the use remained the same. [1970] J.P.L. 542.

22–357 Haulage depot—increase from 6 to 18 vehicles. [1970] J.P.L. 653.

22–358 Storage of caravans—increase from 10 to 35. [1970] J.P.L. 714.

22–359 Change to full-time use from a part-time use which was not *de minimis*. [1971] J.P.L. 348.

22–360 40–feet square piece of land—increase from one to two caravans used exclusively by the owner and his family in connection with the management of a neighbouring cafe. [1971] J.P.L. 405.

22–361 Transport yard—change in the type and number of vehicles. [1972] J.P.L. 216.

22–362 Haulage business—increase from five articulated trucks and five trailers to 12 articulated tractor units over 20 trailers and three fixed-chassis vehicles. [1972] J.P.L. 270.

22–363 Evidence of business use. Part-time business involving 30 hours work a week and invoices for motor-car parts was a substantial business use. A subsequent increase to full-time working was not an intensification amounting to a material change of use. [1972] J.P.L. 653.

22–364 Storage of civil engineering and contractors' materials—marked intensification from intermittent and minor basis but always one of the main users of the site. [1973] J.P.L. 264.

22–365 Change from manual to mechanical operations—no development by intensification of use. [1976] J.P.L. 652.

22–366 Storage of caravans increasing from between 4 to 10 to 35 was not a material change of use. [1976] J.P.L. 714.

22–367 Increase in proportion of retail sales from 10 per cent. to 34 per cent. [1977] J.P.L. 817.

Terraced house equipped to take five people under public health legislation—increase from occupation by owner and two paying guests to owner and three paying guests did not amount to a material change. [1978] J.P.L. 270.

22–368 Distribution depot for dairy produce and eggs—increase from two motor vans and two private cars serving 1,200 customers to 13 vehicles serving 9,000 customers with attendant increase in staff and delivery to premises. [1978] J.P.L. 395.

22–369 Increase in size of vehicles since 1948 in common with all haulage vehicles was not an intensification of use. [1979] J.P.L. 701.

22–370 Whether change in the type of material tipped could amount to a material change of use by intensification. Held in the circumstances not to be material change. [1980] J.P.L. 77.

4. The Identification of the Correct Planning Unit

22–371 Vickers-Armstrong v. Central Land Board (1957) 8 P. & C.R. 33, C.A. Unreal to look at part rather than building or works as a whole.

22–372 Bendles Motors Ltd. v. Bristol Corpn. [1963] 1 W.L.R. 247, D.C. Egg-vending machine on free-standing base of 2 feet 7 inches square on a garage forecourt 120 feet by 15 feet. The planning unit was the whole of the forecourt.

22–373 G. Percy Trentham Ltd. v. Gloucester C.C. [1966] 1 W.L.R. 506, C.A. One should look at the whole area on which a particular activity is carried on, including uses which are ordinarily incidental to or included in the activity.
Per Harman J.: The unit with which you are concerned is the unit which the vendor had.

22–374 Brazil (Concrete) Ltd. v. Amersham R.D.C. (1967) 18 P. & C.R. 396, C.A. The unit is the whole area on which a particular activity is carried on.

22–375 Williams v. Min. of Housing & Local Govt. (1967) 18 P. & C.R. 514, D.C. Three acre nursery with a building in the centre. The planning unit was the whole nursery not the separate building.

22–376 Brooks v. Gloucestershire C.C. (1967) 19 P. & C.R. 90, D.C. Where two different uses are carried out concurrently on the same premises and one is extended to absorb the whole site to the exclusion of the other, the appropriate planning unit is the whole of the premises.

22–377 Burdle v. Sec. of State for Environment [1972] 1 W.L.R. 1209, D.C. Criteria for determining a planning unit:
   (i) where the occupier uses land for a single main purpose to which secondary activities are incidental or ancillary, the whole unit of occupation should be considered;
   (ii) where the occupier carries on a variety of activities and it is not possible to say one is incidental or ancillary to another, it may be apt to consider the entire unit of occupation, especially where different activities are not confined within separate and physically distinct areas of land;
   (iii) where within a single unit of occupation two or more physically separate and distinct areas are occupied for substantially different and unrelated purposes each area used for a different main purpose ought to be considered as a separate planning unit.

22–378 Wood v. Sec. of State for Environment [1973] 1 W.L.R. 707, D.C. Sale of produce in a conservatory attached to a farmhouse—permitted uses of the conser-

S.22. MEANING OF DEVELOPMENT

vatory are the same as those of the farmhouse and accordingly the conservatory could not be regarded in isolation as a separate planning unit.

Per curiam: It is rarely if ever right to dissect a single dwelling house and regard one room in isolation as a planning unit.

22–379 De Mulder v. Sec. of State for Environment [1974] Q.B. 792, D.C. The planning unit was the whole site and any question of a material change of use had to be considered in relation to that site.

22–380 Johnston v. Sec. of State for Environment (1974) 28 P. & C.R. 424 D.C. What was the appropriate planning unit was a question of fact and degree in each case. The unit of occupation is of great, if not predominant, importance and prima facie the planning unit is the area occupied as a single holding by a single occupier. Forty-four garages originally occupied as a whole but then occupied singly or in groups—the Secretary of State could not be criticised for treating individual garages and groups of garages in the same occupation as the appropriate planning units.

Per curiam: In the case of a block of flats in single ownership but let to separate and different tenants the planning unit will normally be the individual flat in question.

22–381 West Cheshire Caravan Co. v. Ellesmere Port B.C. [1976] J.P.L. 235, D.C. Where a plot of land was divided into four for planning applications the Secretary of State could not be expected to discover that it constituted one planning unit when it was not suggested to him that it might be one unit.

22–382 Joyce Shopfitters v. Sec. of State for Environment [1976] J.P.L. 236, D.C. Correct planning unit is the unit of occupation. Therefore where extensions to buildings demolished, the area formerly covered by the extensions would have the same industrial use as the rest of the site.

22–383 Frank Vyner & Son v. Sec. of State for Environment (1977) 243 E.G. 597, D.C. Flat adjoining factory premises did not form a single planning unit as it was occupied for separate residential purpose even though in the gift of the occupiers of the factory.

22–384 Bromsgrove B.C. v. Sec. of State for Environment [1977] J.P.L. 797. Industrial use moving from one building to another on a site containing three buildings— the correct planning unit is the whole site.

22–385 Kwik Save Discount Group Ltd. v. Sec. of State for Wales (1978) 37 P. & C.R. 170, D.C. Planning unit primarily a matter of activity not title therefore severance of title did not automatically create a new planning unit.

22–386 Camden L.B.C. v. Sec. of State for Environment [1979] J.P.L. 311, C.A. Spread of sauna use from part of ground floor to all of ground floor. The Secretary of State had assumed one planning unit of the whole ground floor not two planning units.

22–387 TLG Building Materials v. Sec. of State for Environment (1980) 31 P. & C.R. 243, D.C. Removal of a boundary to incorporate an area into a larger site— the larger site became the planning unit.

22–388 Warnock v. Sec. of State for Environment [1980] J.P.L. 590, D.C. Lairage on a 417 acre farm constituted a separate planning unit as it was not incidental or ancillary to the agricultural use of the adjoining land.

22–389 Newbury D.C. v. Sec. of State for Environment [1981] A.C. 578, H.L. Where the grant of planning permission, whether to build or for a change of use, was of such a character that the implementation of the permission led to the creation of a new planning unit the existing use rights attaching to the former planning unit were extinguished.

S.22. MEANING OF DEVELOPMENT

22–390 Duffy v. Sec. of State for Environment [1981] J.P.L. 811, D.C. Geographical separation must be a major and may be the main factor in deciding the correct planning unit.

22–391 Aston v. Sec. of State for Environment (1982) 43 P. & C.R. 331, D.C. Erection of a new building creates a new planning unit with no permitted planning uses other than those derived from s.33 (2). But see now *Jennings Motors Ltd.* v. *Sec. of State for Environment*.

22–392 Jennings Motors Ltd. v. Sec. of State for Environment [1982] 2 W.L.R. 131, C.A. Erection of a new building on part of a site did not by itself automatically constitute a new planning unit, which extinguished existing use rights.

Note

See Hawkey v. *Sec. of State for Environment* (1971) 22 P. & C.R. 610, D.C.; *De Mulder* v. *Sec. of State for Environment* [1974] Q.B. 792, D.C.; *Morris* v. *Sec. of State for Environment* (1975) 31 P. & C.R. 216, D.C.; *LG Buildings Materials* v. *Sec. of State for Environment* (1980) 41 P. & C.R. 243, D.C. for judicial decisions on enforcement notices and the planning unit.

22–393/394 Sports ground separated from a factory by a security fence but in the same ownership was a different planning unit from the factory. Zoning of an area in the development plan was irrelevant as to the issue of what comprised the planning unit. [1970] J.P.L. 43.

22–395/396 Planning unit consisting of various adjoining premises making up composite use for a motor-car business. [1972] J.P.L. 730.

22–397 Planning unit was a whole field even though the main use was of a small mown strip. [1975] J.P.L. 40.

22–398 Part of an office building in residential use as a caretaker's flat—the planning unit was the whole building. [1975] J.P.L. 686.

22–399 Planning unit—was the house and land use for dual use as a residential unit and smallholding. [1976] J.P.L. 124.

22–400 Mixed use of farm land adjoining a river for (1) agriculture, and (2) mooring and storage of boats. The planning unit was the whole farm. [1976] J.P.L. 590.

22–401 Established use certificate. House and curtilage was used for mixed residential use and the business of a builder, decorator and plumber. The relevant planning unit was the whole curtilage. [1977] J.P.L. 188.

22–402 Planning unit was the whole premises in ownership. It was not essential for an enforcement notice to relate to the whole unit. [1976] J.P.L. 120.

22–403 Original planning unit was a 5-acre field used for agricultural purposes. The siting of a caravan in the field did not alter the planning unit, but subsequent fencing-off of the area surrounding the caravan created a new separate planning unit. [1978] J.P.L. 58.

22–404 Three-storey building—the ground floor was a bank and the first floor was a self-contained flat occupied by the Manager as a term of his employment. The relevant planning unit was the whole building as the bank manager's residential occupation was ancillary to the use of the building as a bank. [1978] J.P.L. 333.

22–405 Original planning unit used for TV and radio repairs. The incorporation into a larger planning unit used for the manufacture of woodwork and joinery was a material change of use. [1979] J.P.L. 50.

22–406 Composite use of a site comprising repair garage and sales of motor vehicles. The planning unit was the whole area. [1980] J.P.L. 693.

S.22. MEANING OF DEVELOPMENT

22–407 Claim that parts of the whole area were kept separate administratively. There were no separate business letterheads, employees were transferred between areas and there was no physical demarcation of areas, therefore the planning unit was the whole area. [1982] J.P.L. 115.

22–408 Building with planning permission for retail use on the ground floor and office/storage on the first and second floors. The building was occupied primarily for retail sales and other uses of building were entirely in support of that purpose, therefore it was a single planning unit and use of first floor for retail sales did not amount to a material change of use. [1982] J.P.L. 534.

22–409 Parking bays provided as ancillary to residential development. The planning unit was each individual parking bay. Commercial letting of a parking bay to non-residents for the storage of a caravan was a material change of use. [1982] J.P.L. 537.

22–410 A dwelling spread over four separate buildings in one-family occupation was still one planning unit and therefore all four buildings were within the one curtilage. The redeployment of different parts of a residential curtilage so that one part is used more and another less intensively cannot amount to a material change of use while there is one residential use of one residential planning unit. [1983] J.P.L. 68.

22–411 Although within a planning unit with mixed use, uses can be changed around from building to building without involving development, in this case there were two separate planning units within one unit of occupation. [1983] J.P.L. 634.

22–412 Farm building severed from dwelling and therefore agricultural use was the sole permitted use. The building was two-thirds full of furniture and domestic equipment, therefore private storage—and a material change of use. [1984] J.P.L. 59.

22–413 Identification of a planning unit (or units) where more than one use is carried on on land in one occupation. Rock drilling not ancillary to quarrying operations and so two separate main uses being carried on in two different planning units. [1985] J.P.L. 194.

22–414 Airfield—no flying use between 1970 and 1979, most of the buildings demolished and, apart from metalled surfaces of the main runways and part of the perimeter track, airfield used for agriculture and various temporary uses—lack of intent ever to return land to operational flying role—use abandoned. Use of just part of one runway and an associated stretch of perimeter track for flying of microlights involve creation of a new planning unit in former airfield. [1985] J.P.L. 426.

22–415 In defining the planning unit held necessary in the circumstances to look at the whole area which was used for a particular purpose: *Morris* v. *Sec. of State for the Environment* applied. [1986] J.P.L. 62.

22–416 Where staircase removed from terraced house with the result that the upper part could only be reached from the adjoining house, the upper part and the adjoining house formed one separate planning unit. Therefore where two enforcement notices served which got the correct planning units wrong, the notices had to be quashed as this could have created difficulties. [1986] J.P.L. 382.

5. Material Change of Use due to Loss of Established Use

(a) Loss of existing use rights by change to another use

22–417 Erroll v. Essex C.C. (1962) 185 E.G. 15, D.C. Even though use of land for agricultural purposes did not constitute development by reason of s.12(2) of the Town and Country Planning Act 1947, where use of land as a paint shop was superseded by use as pig farm, the former industrial use had ceased and could not be resumed without planning permission.

22–418 McKellan v. Min. of Housing & Local Government (1966) 198 E.G. 683. Although change of use to agricultural use does not involve development, a change back to non-agricultural use does involve development.

22–419 Hawes v. Thornton Cleveleys U.D.C. (1965) 17 P. & C.R. 22. Necessary to distinguish between cessation of a use and temporary suspension of activities which constitute the use. Where use by its nature involved intermittent activity with temporary suspension of that activity, neither suspension nor resumption could by itself amount to a material change of use.

22–420 Webber v. Min. of Housing & Local Government [1968] 1 W.L.R. 29. Seasonal land uses—camping in summer, agriculture in winter. Normal use of the land could only be ascertained after comparing its manner of use from year to year. The changeover within each year was not a material change of use.

22–421 Grillo v. Min. of Housing & Local Government (1968) 208 E.G. 1201, D.C. Not open to an occupier to claim that a use had been kept notionally alive in his mind when he had used land for a different purpose.

22–422 When land formerly used as a railway undertaking and coal yard was not used at all for a period of six years and then subdivided into plots and used for activities other than the loading, unloading and storage of goods, then a material change of use had occurred, requiring planning permission. [1977] C.L.Y. 2934.

22–423 Where there was an unauthorised change of use but no enforcement action had been taken reversion to the former authorised use is a material change of use requiring planning permission. [1982] J.P.L. 798.

(b) Loss by abandonment

22–424 Fyson v. Buckinghamshire C.C. [1958] 1 W.L.R. 634. Long interruption in use. Seven years with only a four-month interval. No other use. Resumption of former use was not a change of use.

22–425 Hamblett v. Flintshire C.C. (1960) 11 P. & C.R. 284. Where a use ceases from time to time, the correct question in deciding whether there has been development, is not whether the use has been discontinued but whether resumption amounts to a material change of use.

22–426 Hartley v. Min. of Housing & Local Govt. [1970] 2 W.L.R. 1, C.A. If land remains unused for a considerable time in such circumstances that a reasonable man might conclude that the previous use had been abandoned, it may be found to be abandoned. Where use ceases with no view to resumption it is abandoned. Use ceased for four years and therefore abandoned.

22–427 Draco v. Oxfordshire C.C. (1972) 224 E.G. 1037. Filling station had ceased for seven years to be licensed for storage of petrol, petrol sales had ceased and tanks had been rendered useless. Ample evidence for Secretary of State to hold that petrol selling had been abandoned even though he had held residential use of cottage had not been abandoned.

22–428 Ratcliffe v. Sec. of State for Environment (1975) 235 E.G. 901, D.C. Use of quarry as a tip abandoned even though subsequently used sporadically as a tip by trespassers.

22–429 Hale v. Lichfield D.C. [1979] J.P.L. 425. Cottage used only occasionally between 1961 and 1968 and not at all thereafter. Furniture was removed and no rates paid. "Occupier" in hospital. Residential use not abandoned.

22–430 Nicholls v. Sec. of State for Environment [1981] J.P.L. 890, D.C. Use of site declined to such an extent as not to be material in planning terms. Situation continued for six years. Despite evidence that no intention to abandon use, there was evidence for a reasonable man to decide that use had been abandoned.

S.22. MEANING OF DEVELOPMENT

22-431 Balco Transport Services Ltd. v. Sec. of State for Environment [1982] J.P.L. 177, D.C. If there is a change of use from a lawful use and an enforcement notice is then served, it could not be said that previous lawful use was abandoned. Combinations of periods of nil use and other uses are sufficient as a matter of law to show abandonment. Whether the facts showed abandonment was a question for the inspector.

22-432 Trustees of Castell-y-Mynach Estate v. Sec. of State for Wales [1985] J.P.L. 40. Whether residential use of dwelling-house had been abandoned. Tests applied by the inspector approved.

Note

As to the abandonment of a planning permission, see judicial decisions on section 45.

22-433 Discontinuance and subsequent resumption of industrial use—held that the use of the land for agricultural purposes constituted abandonment of industrial use. [1967] J.P.L. 110.

22-434 Foundry use not abandoned even though the premises had been completely unused for seven or eight years. Equipment had been removed and buildings had been allowed to deteriorate and were now derelict. [1968] J.P.L. 478.

22-435 Application for planning permission for an alternative use does not necessarily show an intention to abandon present use. Cessation in use because tenant vacated property does not necessarily show an intention to abandon present use. [1971] J.P.L. 244.

22-436 Closure of a railway line and vacating of station manager's house resulted in the abandonment of railway use of the land. [1971] J.P.L. 457.

22-437 Premises unoccupied for eight or nine years. No abandonment of use. [1971] J.P.L. 583.

22-438 Office building vacant but no abandonment of use. [1971] J.P.L. 653.

22-439 Former petrol-filling station use abandoned on the removal of pumps and the rendering useless of petrol storage tanks together with an application that the land be rated for residential occupation. [1972] J.P.L. 577.

22-440 Use abandoned where it was ended consequent upon a discontinuance notice. [1973] J.P.L. 48.

22-441 Use of land as railway operational land was not abandoned on the closure and subsequent demolition of a railway station. [1974] J.P.L. 245.

22-442 Use for garaging and storage ancillary to retail stores ending when the stores were demolished. Subsequent use for storage, repairs and servicing of vehicles and storage in connection with business use was not an established use. [1976] J.P.L. 323.

22-443 Abandonment of residential use of a cottage by disuse and works rendering it uninhabitable. [1977] J.P.L. 326.

22-444 Dwelling-house use not abandoned even though unoccupied for 23 years. [1978] J.P.L. 653.

22-445 Farmhouse, uninhabited for approximately 35 years. Recognisable as a former dwelling but presently uninhabitable. Occasionally used for hay and cattle. No evidence of intention to reoccupy as a dwelling. Residential use abandoned. [1979] J.P.L. 551.

S.22. MEANING OF DEVELOPMENT

22–446 Cottage uninhabited for approximately 10 years. In good structural condition, but internal walls and floor removed to prevent use by squatters although it was not intended to abandon residential use. Intention was to make it uninhabitable and therefore residential use abandoned. [1977] J.P.L. 326.

22–447 Change from a haulage business with ancillary vehicle repairs to the repair and renovation of motor vehicles amounted to the abandonment of haulage use. [1978] J.P.L. 571.

22–448 In the case of a dwelling-house evidence was needed of positive actions to abandon use. Cottage uninhabited for approximately 35 years, for 12 years of which the owner did not intend to use it as a dwelling-house. It was not in a habitable state, but the building was still recognisable as a dwelling-house and most of the roof and exterior walls were intact. No abandonment. [1978] J.P.L. 651.

22–449 Cottage, uninhabited for approximately 23 years. Revocation order. No appeal against earlier s.53 determination that resumption of residential use needed planning permission. Neglect and non-use, but no evidence of a permanent intention to abandon residential use. [1978] J.P.L. 653.

22–450 Fifteen years of "non-use" and derelict condition led to the conclusion that residential use was abandoned, so Class 1 of Sched. 1 to the General Development Order 1977 was not applicable. [1979] J.P.L. 177.

22–451 Buildings unoccupied from 1963 to 1980 and not maintained during that period. Owner gave evidence he did not intend to abandon use. This accepted and therefore use not abandoned. [1980] J.P.L. 49.

22–452 Dwelling-house vacant from 1958 to 1973. At that time it was surplus to the requirements of the owner, but there was no evidence that the owner intended residential use to be abandoned. Residential use not lost. [1982] J.P.L. 194.

22–453 Dwelling-house not occupied for 14 years. Uninhabitable for six years. Use not abandoned. [1980] J.P.L. 759.

22–454 Land used by Direct Labour Organisation of the railways for 30 years had builder's yard use. Not used for eight years. No abandonment of use. [1981] J.P.L. 375.

22–455 Cottage no longer recognisable as a former dwelling and uninhabitable. Not used for 16 years. Use abandoned. [1981] J.P.L. 914.

22–456 Although cottages uninhabitable for 15 years after closing orders made they had not been used for any non–residential purposes. No part had been deliberately demolished and a planning application had demonstrated a continuing intention to resume residential use. No abandonment. [1982] J.P.L. 119.

22–457 Manufacture of cardboard boxes is an industrial-type use. A haulage business is a transport undertaking, the main purpose of which is to operate a fleet of commercial vehicles either owned, on contract or on hire for the carriage of goods. No manufacturing process is undertaken. Materials do not enter site to undergo an industrial process. Change from a haulage business to an industrial use entailed abandonment of haulage use. [1982] J.P.L. 121.

22–458 Dwelling-house vacant from 1958 to 1973 at that time surplus to the requirements of the owner, but no evidence that the owner intended residential use to be abandoned. Residential use not lost. [1982] J.P.L. 194.

22–459 House not used for 30 years and so abandonment of dwelling-use. [1982] J.P.L. 794.

22–460 Whether former use as a fish and chip shop abandoned or merely discontinued with the right to resume it. Last used as fish and chip shop 9 years earlier.

S.22. MEANING OF DEVELOPMENT

Conduct since then—sale of some of the equipment. Fish-and-chip use was held to have been abandoned and resumption was a material change. [1983] J.P.L. 488.

22–461 Derelict dwellings unoccupied for 30 years. Residential use remained. [1984] J.P.L. 207.

22–462 Airfield use. Cessation of use with no intention to resume it at a particular time. Use abandoned. [1985] J.P.L. 426.

22–463 War-time use of requisitioned land as an aerodrome abandoned when reverted to agricultural use and handed back to the owners. [1984] J.P.L. 451.

(c) Loss by radical change in planning history

22–464 Gray v. Min. of Housing & Local Government (1970) 68 L.G.R. 15, C.A. Application for planning permission and its later implementation may prevent the later reliance of "existing user rights" under the four-year rule: but see now *Newbury District Council v. Sec. of State for Environment* and *Jennings Motors Ltd v. Sec. of State for Environment*.

22–465 Aston v. Sec. of State for Environment (1982) 43 P. & C.R. 331. Erection of a new building creates a new planning unit with no permitted planning uses other than those derived from s.33 (2). But see now *Jennings Motors Ltd. v. Sec. of State for Environment*.

22–466 Petticoat Lane Rentals Ltd. v. Sec. of State for Environment [1971] 1 W.L.R. 1112. Where land is merged in a new building the previous planning unit ceases to exist and a new unit starts with a nil use. Former uses are automatically extinguished and there is no need for an express condition. Land is merged with a building even though the ground floor is open. But see now *Jenning Motors Ltd. v. Sec. of State for Environment*.

22–467 Jennings Motors Ltd. v. Sec. of State for the Environment [1982] 2 W.L.R. 131, C.A. A new building does not *per se* create a new planning unit, but it is one of the factors to be taken into account in considering whether the land has undergone a change of so radical a nature as to constitute a "break in the planning history" or a "new planning unit." Whether an alteration is of such a character is a question of fact and degree.

22–468 Newbury D.C. v. Sec. of State for Environment [1980] 2 W.L.R. 379. The grant and subsequent implementation of a planning permission could be of such a character as to create a new planning unit with the consequence of extinguishing previous user rights.

Note

As to judicial decisions on conditions restricting existing user rights, see cases listed under planning conditions.

22–469 Use of a building does not confer the right to use the land on which the building stood for the same purpose after the building has been demolished. [1968] J.P.L. 296.

22–470 A newly erected building does not acquire any use rights from the land on which it is built or from any building which previously stood on the site, and if erected without planning permission it has no use on completion, so that the first use after completion is a material change of use. [1971] J.P.L. 716.

22–471 Replacement of a former brickworks by concrete, brick and block works. Loss of existing use rights on the demolition of a building. [1976] J.P.L. 59.

22–472 Stationing of a residential caravan. Bungalow demolished in 1974 or 1975 at which point land in use for no purpose. Conditional planning permission for dwelling granted January 24, 1978 followed by detailed permission May 30, 1978. Stationing of caravans in November 1977 a material change of use without planning permission. [1979] J.P.L. 45.

22–473 Extinguishment of established use on demolition of a building. Storage use in residential area. [1980] J.P.L. 761.

D. Operations and Uses not Involving Development: section 22(2)

1. Maintenance, Improvement or Other Alteration of a Building: section 22(2)(a)

22–474 National Provincial Bank v. Portsmouth Corpn. (1959) 11 P. & C.R. 6. Redevelopment of bank premises of which two top floors had been destroyed by enemy action was not an enlargement, improvement or other alteration.

22–475 Sainty v. Min. of Housing & Local Government (1964) 15 P. & C.R. 452, D.C. A dwelling-house after demolition is no longer capable of being enlarged, improved or altered. Demolition of two cottages replaced by two differently designed houses on slightly different foundations not within "enlargement, improvement or other alteration."

22–476 Street v. Essex C.C. (1965) 193 E.G. 537. Whether or not constructional works amount to "maintenance" or "rebuilding" is a question of fact and degree. Where all that remains of the original house is two walls which enclosed the original kitchen, so little remained of the original structure that development had taken place.

22–477 Bradford M.D.C. v. Sec. of State for Environment (1977) 35 P. & C.R. 387. Stone-cladding of the front elevation of a building did not come within s.22(2)(*a*).

22–478 C.W. Larking v. Basildon D.C. [1980] J.P.L. 407. Open to the Secretary of State to find that where two external walls of a house had been rebuilt and then later the other two rebuilt, the works were not an improvement of a dwelling-house.

22–479 Kensington & Chelsea R.L.B.C. v. C.G. Hotels (1980) 41 P. & C.R. 40. External appearance of a building was materially affected by running electricity through cables to floodlights, but not by the actual installation of floodlights.

22–480 Hewlitt v. Sec. of State for Environment and Brentwood D.C. [1985] J.P.L 404, C.A. The fact that rebuilding works done in stages did not mean that works amounted to improvements rather than rebuilding works. *Sainty* v. *Min. of Housing & Local Govt.* applied.

22–481 Trustees of Earl of Lichfield's Estate v. Sec. of State for Environment [1985] J.P.L. 251. Whether ruined building still capable of being considered to be a "dwelling-house." Approach in various Ministerial Decisions approved and importance placed on whether dwelling-house use had been abandoned.

22–482 Works to a building which retained the original main frame, roof and two walls amounted to alterations and improvements not the erection of a new building. Conversion of a dilapidated shed with double doors into a closed building with two large windows and a small entrance door, having the appearance of a shop, involved development because it materially affected the external appearance. [1967] J.P.L. 42.

22–483 Construction of a new building occupying three times the area of a previous demolished building and made of different materials with an altered external appearance constituted development and was not within s. 12(2)(*a*) of the 1962 Act (now s. 22(2)(*a*).) [1969] J.P.L. 408.

22–484 Building with no slates on the roof and no windows or doors. Slating of the

S.22. MEANING OF DEVELOPMENT

roof and the installation of doors and windows would materially affect the external appearance of the building therefore development was involved. [1979] J.P.L. 117.

22–485 Erection of a glass screen enclosing a balcony would convert an open recessed balcony into an internal enclosed space within the building, making the present external window and partition an internal partition, and would materially affect the external appearance of the building. [1979] J.P.L. 326.

22–486 Demolition and subsequent rebuilding in new material of all external walls except part of rear wall; demolition and rebuilding in part of internal walls; roof frame needed propping. Although carried out in stages, so little of the fabric of the original dwelling-house remaining that work amounted to the rebuilding of the dwelling-house rather than enlargement or improvement.

22–487 "Restored" building was so different from the original building that there remained no identity between the two. "Restored" building constituted the erection of a new building, not renovation and enlargement of an existing dwelling-house. [1982] J.P.L. 794.

22–488 Two radio masts located in a garden and one mounted on a detached garage. None would be attached to or form part of the structure of the dwelling and therefore would not fall within the "enlargement improvement or other alteration of a dwelling house." [1983] J.P.L. 77.

22–489 Conversion of the garage of a dwelling-house to a study by the replacement of a door with a window would materially affect the external appearance of the building and therefore it was development, but permitted by Class 1(1) of General Development Order 1977. [1983] J.P.L. 258.

22–490 Enlargement and reopening of the former entrance to an industrial laundry premises materially affected the external appearance of the building. [1983] J.P.L. 557.

22–491 Rebuilding of a fire-damaged building materially affecting the external appearance of the building. Planning permission required. In the case of a fire-damaged building, in determining whether the external appearance of the building is materially affected, one must compare the appearance of the building once works have been carried out to it with its appearance immediately before those works were started. [1984] J.P.L. 531.

22–491a Replacement of window with door did not materially affect external appearance as it would rarely be opened. [1984] J.P.L. 674.

2. Uses Incidental to a Dwelling-house within its Curtilage: section 22(2)(d)

22–492 Sinclair-Lockhart's Trustees v. C.L.B. (1950) 1 P. & C.R. 195. *Per* Lord Mackintosh: Land does not have to be marked off or enclosed to be within the curtilage of a house or building. It is enough if it served the purposes of house or building in some necessary or reasonably useful way.

22–493 Sinclair-Lockhart's Trustees v. C.L.B. (1950) 1 P. & C.R. 320, 335. *Per* Lord Keith: Agriculture is an industrial or business operation. Cultivation of a garden attached to a dwelling, not cultivated for profit, is not an agricultural use.

22–494 Sampson's Executors v. Nottinghamshire C.C. (1950) 1 P. & C.R. 1, 8, D.C. *Per* Lord Goddard C.J.: An alteration is made in the use of the land if agricultural land is brought within the curtilage of a dwelling-house.

22–495 Stephens v. Cuckfield R.D.C. [1959] 1 Q.B. 516. Definition of curtilage of a building.

22–496 Waddell v. Bhagwanani (1967) 202 E.G. 1225. For a caravan to be incidental to the enjoyment of the house within the curtilage of which the caravan stands

S.22. MEANING OF DEVELOPMENT

there has to be a dwelling-house used as such. A house which is unfit for human habitation does not qualify.

22–497 Change from use as a garage and store by a builder with a small business parking two cars, and occasionally a lorry, to the parking of motor coaches was a material change of use. Former use so small as to be ancillary to dwelling-house use. [1966] J.P.L. 237.

22–498 Use of the garden and one room in a home for a nursery play-group carried on three hours daily as a business was not incidental to dwelling-house use. [1966] J.P.L. 493.

22–499 Broken concrete tipped to form a terraced rock garden near to a house. Use incidental to use as dwelling-house. [1967] J.P.L. 46.

22–500 Breeding and boarding of dogs with erection of six dog kennels, although mainly a hobby, was not reasonably incidental to dwelling-house use and involved development. [1967] J.P.L. 176.

22–501 Use of a dwelling-house on a small part-time scale for the sale and repair of motor vehicles was incidental to residential use. Subsequent full-time use was a material change of use. [1967] J.P.L. 612.

22–502 Parking of a commercial vehicle, used for carrier's business, within curtilage of dwelling-house, was a material change of use. [1967] J.P.L. 728.

22–503 Stationing of caravans with a charge for the occupation of the same was not incidental to dwelling-house use. [1968] J.P.L. 239.

22–504 Use of part of a house for a child-minding group was not incidental to dwelling-house use. [1968] J.P.L. 539.

22–505 Use of a front room for the occupier's business as a tailor was not ancillary to dwelling-house use. [1968] J.P.L. 637.

22–506 Use of premises for three paying guests who provided and prepared their own meals was use for multiple paying occupation. Not ancillary to dwelling-house use. [1968] J.P.L. 700.

22–507 Garden to a dwelling-house used for commercial purposes when an aviary opened to the public who were invited to make voluntary financial contributions. No longer incidental to dwelling-house use. [1969] J.P.L. 217.

22–508 Use of a paddock adjoining a dwelling-house for the storage of old military vehicles which were displayed at exhibitions as a hobby was incidental to dwelling-house use. [1969] J.P.L. 413.

22–509 Use of a room for the religious devotions of the occupant was ancillary to dwelling-house use, but use as a meeting-place for co-religionists was not. [1969] J.P.L. 539.

22–510 Stationing of a residential caravan within the curtilage of a dwelling-house to be occupied by the owner's parents was incidental to dwelling-house use. [1970] J.P.L. 223.

22–511 Stationing of a mobile home within the curtilage of a dwelling-house to provide accommodation for the occupier's parents was not ancillary to dwelling-house use as it was to be used as a separate residence. [1971] J.P.L. 187.

22–512 Change from a henhouse to a store for plastics was a material change of use and not ancillary to dwelling-house. [1971] J.P.L. 233.

22–513 The use of part of residential premises for the carrying-on of a trade for

S.22. MEANING OF DEVELOPMENT

commercial or industrial purposes cannot be regarded as ancillary to dwelling-house use. [1971] J.P.L. 287.

22–514 Parking and electrical charging of two ice-cream vans and storage of stock was not incidental to dwelling-house use. [1971] J.P.L. 646.

22–515 Boarding and breeding of up to 60 dogs and puppies as a hobby was incidental to dwelling-house use. [1971] J.P.L. 642.

22–516 Storage and sale of motor vehicles was not reasonably incidental to dwelling-house use. [1971] J.P.L. 641.

22–517 Radio control of taxis from a dwelling-house three nights a week. Taxis otherwise controlled from a separate office. Not incidental to dwelling-house use. [1971] J.P.L. 533.

22–518 Storage of three cars with the sale of approximately one car per month within the curtilage of a dwelling-house was not ancillary to dwelling-house use. [1971] J.P.L. 546.

22–519 Parking of a commercial vehicle in domestic curtilage to keep it safe and to have it conveniently nearby for business use was not ancillary to dwelling-house use. [1972] J.P.L. 390.

22–520 Repair of 35 to 40 cars annually on a non-commercial basis was not ancillary to dwelling-house use. [1972] J.P.L. 339.

22–521 Use of a dwelling-house partly for the accommodation of paying guests to whom advice and treatment was given in naturopathy, osteopathy and yoga was not ancillary to dwelling-house use. [1973] J.P.L. 109.

22–522 Running of a business partly from a house was not ancillary to dwelling-house use. [1973] J.P.L. 55.

22–523 The placing on land within the curtilage of a dwelling-house of caravans for residential use by a caretaker was not ancillary to dwelling-house use. [1973] J.P.L. 381.

22–524 Caravan used by paying guests was not ancillary to dwelling-house use. Change of use of a private swimming pool to a public swimming pool was not ancillary to dwelling-house use. [1974] J.P.L. 241.

22–525 Use of premises in connection with an ice-cream business was not ancillary to dwelling-house use. [1974] J.P.L. 672.

22–526 Parking, storage and maintenance of lorries in connection with a haulage business was not ancillary to dwelling-house use. [1974] J.P.L. 610.

22–527 Use of a room in a dwelling-house as a nursing agency was not ancillary to residential use. [1974] J.P.L. 554.

22–528 Caravan used as a separate residential unit was not ancillary to dwelling-house use. [1974] J.P.L. 43.

22–529 Use of two rooms of a dwelling-house by the occupier for the practice of a veterinary surgeon was not ancillary to dwelling-house use. [1976] J.P.L. 328.

22–530 Parking of a commercial van in the curtilage of a dwelling-house, whilst convenient, was not incidental to use as a dwelling-house even if it was used to get to work. [1976] J.P.L. 529.

22–531 Stationing of a caravan to be used as an extra bedroom was incidental to use of dwelling-house. [1976] J.P.L. 586.

22–532 Use of the curtilage of a dwelling-house in connection with a hobby of stock-car racing was not ancillary to dwelling-house use. [1976] J.P.L. 588.

S.22. MEANING OF DEVELOPMENT

22–533 Use of a domestic garage and shed for the purposes of the owner's profession of a veterinary surgeon was not ancillary to dwelling-house use. [1976] J.P.L. 768.

22–534 Because an activity is carried on as a hobby it does not automatically follow that it is incidental to the enjoyment of a dwelling-house. The nature and scale of use must be considered and whether it could reasonably be expected to be carried out in or around the house for the domestic needs of or incidental to the personal enjoyment of the dwelling-house by the occupants. It was a matter of fact and degree. The maintenance and repair of hang gliders involved the use of metal-working equipment, and so taking into account the nature and scale, it was akin to an industrial activity. [1977] J.P.L. 116.

22–535 Dogs kept and bred as a hobby. Use ancillary to dwelling-house. [1977] J.P.L. 192.

22–536 Whether the parking of a vehicle incidental to use as a dwelling-house depends on the facts of particular case. Taking into account the size of the lorry, the size of the parking area and the nature of the premises, it was not incidental even if used as a means of transport to and from work. [1977] J.P.L. 397.

22–537 Repair and maintenance of four cars used for stock-car racing exceeded that necessary for private cars used in the normal way and was not incidental to use of dwelling-house. [1978] J.P.L. 201.

22–538 Use of two rooms exclusively for business purposes was not ancillary to dwelling-house use. [1978] J.P.L. 338.

22–539 Caravan capable of use as an independent residential unit and no evidence to show that the occupants of the caravan have been or would be dependent in any vital way on dwelling-house — not ancillary to dwelling-house use. [1978] J.P.L. 489.

22–540 Parking within the curtilage of a dwelling-house of a vehicle primarily used for business purposes or commercial purposes (a lorry) was not incidental use. [1978] J.P.L. 789.

22–541 Caravan in the garden of dwelling-house, used for sleeping purposes only. Ancillary to use as dwelling-house. [1979] J.P.L. 124.

22–542 Parking a commercial vehicle (ice-cream van) in a garage adjacent to a house was a commercial use, and not an ancillary residential use. [1980] J.P.L. 209.

22–543 Car repairs within the curtilage of a dwelling-house. Reasonable to repair one's own car and as enthusiast to acquire three Jaguar cars for repair and restoration and also for the son to acquire experience on his own car, but repair of cars for neighbours and friends, even if payment was only made for parts, exceeded dwelling-house use. [1980] J.P.L. 472.

22–544 Boat owned and occupied by persons who are only friends of owners of house and mooring point. Use cannot be said to be incidental to the enjoyment of the dwelling-house. [1981] J.P.L. 833.

22–545 Erection in the back garden of a bungalow of kennels for up to eight dogs kept as household pets and for showing, where no profit was made from showing, and the occasional sale of puppies, was incidental to use of dwelling-house. [1982] J.P.L. 60.

22–546 Use of balcony as open amenity did not come within s.22(2)(*d*) as the balcony was not part of the curtilage but part of the dwelling itself. [1982] J.P.L. 199.

22–547 Use of a lorry body as a garden workshop incidental to use of dwelling-house. [1982] J.P.L. 202.

22–548 Three cars and one four-wheeled trailer/car transporter in driveway. Garage big enough for four cars had three cars in it all on jacks apparently undergoing extensive repair or renovation. Two motor cycles in garage and seven motor cycles in a conservatory at rear of the house. Tools and repair accessories in garage. Material change of use—vehicles not incidental to use of the dwelling. [1983] J.P.L. 74.

22–549 There is a threshold in the scale and nature of an activity beyond which, as a matter of fact and degree it can no longer be reasonably regarded as incidental to the personal enjoyment of a dwelling-house by its occupants. Effect upon the neighbourhood must be considered. Storage of two hulls of a boat (catamaran) pursuant to a boat-building hobby was not incidental to dwelling-house use. [1984] J.P.L. 288.

22–550 Use of a residential property in connection with a hobby need not necessarily be considered as incidental to the use of a dwelling-house. Nature of a use and its general impact on the environment can be a planning factor. Use of the curtilage of a dwelling-house for the construction, repair and storage of motor vehicles for use by the occupiers in the hobby of a motor sport was not incidental to dwelling-house use. [1984] J.P.L. 291.

22–551 As to whether a balcony is part of the dwelling-house or its curtilage, the Secretary of State would incline to the view that in this case the dwelling-house was a building within its own curtilage. [1984] J.P.L. 674.

22–552 The keeping of 45 dogs is an operation on a commercial scale whether or not a profit is made and it is not incidental to a dwelling-house use. [1985] J.P.L. 201.

22–553 Use of a room in a dwelling-house as an optician's consulting room was a material change of use. [1984] J.P.L. 599.

22–554 Use of a small part of a house as a "doctor's surgery" was not a material change of use when only three patients a week attended at the house. [1985] J.P.L. 339.

22–555 Parking of a commercial vehicle which is an integral factor of an employer's business is not ancillary to dwelling-house use. [1985] J.P.L. 416.

22–556 Curtilage of farmhouse only covered the land immediately surrounding and associated with the dwelling and not other agricultural land. So private flying activities outside curtilage did not come within s.22(2)(*d*). [1986] J.P.L. 455.

3. Use of Land for Agricultural and Forestry Purposes: section 22(2)(e)

22–556 Belmont Farm Ltd. v. Min. of Housing & Local Govt. (1962) 13 P. & C.R. 417, D.C.
 (1) "Livestock" in s.290 does not include any animal whatsoever.
 (2) The breeding and keeping of horses is only an agricultural use if the horses are used in farming the land.

22–557 McKellan v. Min. of Housing & Local Govt. (1966) 198 E.G. 683. Although a change of use to agricultural use does not involve development, a change back to non-agricultural use does involve development.

22–558 Min. of Agriculture, Fisheries and Food v. Appleton [1969] 3 All E.R. 1051. Selective Employment Payments Act 1966. "Agriculture" did not include the breeding of cats and dogs for research purposes.

22–559 Hidderley v. Warwickshire C.C. (1963) 61 L.G.R. 266. "For the purposes of agriculture" in s.12(2)(*e*) of the Town and Country Planning Act 1947 refers to

S.22. MEANING OF DEVELOPMENT

the production processes of agriculture and not to the buying and selling of agricultural products.

22–560 Wood v. Sec. of State for Environment [1973] 1 W.L.R. 707. Sale of home-produced produce on a holding is incidental to agricultural use, but the bringing in and selling of somebody else's produce is not.

22–561 Warnock v. Sec. of State for Environment [1980] J.P.L. 590. Fact that buildings were occupied together with land in use for the purposes of agriculture or forestry could not be sufficient to convey that use to buildings.

Lairage is not an agricultural use, even if animals come from an adjoining farm.

22–562 Crowborough P.C. v. Sec. of State for Environment [1981] J.P.L. 281. Allotments are an agricultural use as activities on an allotment fall within the definition of "agricultural" in s.290.

22–563 Sykes v. Underwood [1981] J.P.L. 285, D.C. Use of land for grazing horses is agricultural, but use of land to keep horses where they incidentally graze is not. Must consider what is *the purpose* the land is used for.

22–564 North Warwickshire B.C. v. Sec. of State for Environment [1984] J.P.L. 434, D.C. Buildings used for the purposes of agriculture are included within the term "land" in s.22(2).

22–565 Gill v. Sec. of State for Environment and North Warwickshire D.C. [1985] J.P.L. 710, D.C. The slaughtering of animals in any large numbers did not come within the definition of agriculture in s.290.

22–566 Land used for the display and sale of plants grown elsewhere was not an agricultural use. [1966] J.P.L. 178.

22–567 Use of agricultural land for gardens of cottages assumed to need planning permission. [1967] J.P.L. 620.

22–568 Sale of meat even from animals reared on a farm is not ancillary to agricultural use, especially if animals are slaughtered elsewhere. [1977] J.P.L. 196.

22–569 Sale of produce grown on land ancillary to agricultural use includes the sale of eggs and live poultry. Adaptation for sale of that produce on the holding is not ancillary, but amounts to a separate use for retail sales. Sale of 100 chickens at Christmas 1963 and the odd joint of pork in 1963 was *de minimis* and to be disregarded. [1977] J.P.L. 741.

22–570 Sale of beef produced on farm. Slaughter, jointing, packaging and freezing is processing involving adaptation of an article for sale not ancillary to agricultural use or use ancillary to an independent shop use. [1978] J.P.L. 792.

22–571 Use as a fish farm for food is an agricultural use, but a fish farm producing stock for fishing clubs and pet shops is not an agricultural use. [1980] J.P.L. 480.

22–572 Slaughterhouse essentially entails the preparation of food and is akin to an industrial use rather than an agricultural use. Permission refused for the erection of a slaughterhouse and cold store on agricultural land within the green belt. [1981] J.P.L. 67.

22–573 Land used solely for the grazing of horses for recreational purposes is not agricultural land when severed from other agricultural land. [1985] J.P.L. 63.

22–574 Breeding and keeping of ponies not used in farming the land is not an agricultural use of the land. [1985] J.P.L. 198.

22–575 Breeding of dogs for show is not an agricultural use. [1985] J.P.L. 201.

S.22. MEANING OF DEVELOPMENT

22–576 Neither a farmhouse nor a garden constitute agricultural land. [1985] J.P.L. 336.

22–577 Building intended for accommodation of horses together with the storage of their food is not used for agricultural purposes.

Building with appearance of a dwelling rather than a barn not a structure primarily designed for agriculture even though it is used for the storage of hay. [1985] J.P.L. 656.

22–578 Use of land for keeping of horses and ponies maintained for recreational purposes, any grazing merely incidental thereto and not a main use of the land—not an agricultural use.

Schooling and exercising horses a non-agricultural use. [1985] J.P.L. 731.

22–579 Processing and bottling milk produced on farm is not ancillary to agricultural use. [1985] J.P.L. 889.

22–580 The stationing of ex-railway box van for the storage of hay, on land used for keeping and grazing of horses for pleasure did not come within s.22(2)(*e*). [1986] J.P.L. 462.

4. Use Classes: section 22(2)(f)

(a) General approach to use classes

22–581 Scrivener v. Min. of Housing & Local Govt. (1966) 64 L.G.R. 251, D.C. In interpreting use classes attention must be given to the process to be used, as affecting the degree of disturbance of the neighbourhood, as well as the ultimate purpose. Therefore use of a building for coach-building involving the spraying with cellulose lacquers of a large proportion of the bodies dealt with, was use for purpose of the employment of such lacquers within Use Class VIII of the Town and Country Planning (Use Classes) Order 1963.

A subsidiary use is not permitted by art.3(3) of the Use Classes Order unless it is "ordinarily" incidental to the class as a whole, such as an office which is ordinarily incidental to any general industrial use. It is not sufficient that the subsidiary use is incidental to the particular manufacture carried on in a general industrial building.

22–582 City of London Corpn. v. Sec. of State for Environment (1971) 23 P. & C.R. 169, D.C. A condition in a planning permission may restrict the operation of the Use Classes Order, provided it is reasonable and is fairly and reasonably related to the permitted development.

22–583 Tessier v. Sec. of State for Environment (1975) 31 P. & C.R. 161, D.C. It is desirable that the Use Classes Order should not be stretched to embrace activities which do not clearly fall within it, because it is better that unusual activities should be treated as *sui generis* for Use Classes Order purposes. But see *Forkhurst* v. *Sec. of State for Environment*.

22–584 Brooks & Burton v. Sec. of State for Environment [1977] 1 W.L.R. 1294, C.A. Activities keeping within a use class are authorised even if they amount to a material change of use by intensification.

For the purposes of art.2(3) of the Use Classes Order whether land occupied with a building had acquired industrial rights depended on the use to which the land had been put. If land is used for same purpose as the building it is to be regarded planning-wise as one unit with the building, but if not so used, could not be so regarded.

22–585 Emma Hotels v. Sec. of State for Environment [1979] J.P.L. 390, D.C. Change of use to another use within the same class in the Use Classes Order did not constitute development.

22–586 Rann v. Sec. of State for Environment (1980) 40 P. & C.R. 113. D.C. A change from one class to another did not necessarily involve development.

S.22. MEANING OF DEVELOPMENT

22–587 Carpet Decor (Guildford) Ltd. v. Sec. of State for Environment [1981] J.P.L. 806, D.C. Change of one use to another within the same class of the Use Classes Order, no matter how material, is not development.

22–588 Day & Mid-Warwickshire Motors Ltd. v. Sec. of State for Environment [1979] J.P.L. 538, D.C. Use Classes Order only applied if the primary use of the site as a whole before and after the change came within their scope.

22–589 Kwik Save Discount Group Ltd. v. Sec. of State for Environment [1981] J.P.L. 198, C.A. More than purely minimal implementation is required before an order can be exploited.

22–590 Winton v. Sec. of State for Environment (1982) 46 P. & C.R. 205, D.C. Section 22(2)(*e*) and Use Classes Order 1972, para.3(1) require comparison to be made between different uses carried on in different planning units and could therefore have no application in this case even though the use of buildings prior to subdivision and the use of two parts following subdivision all fell within Class IV.

22–591 Forkhurst v. Sec. of State for Environment (1982) 46 P. & C.R. 89, D.C. Inspector misdirected himself in deciding that earlier use as a scrapyard was *sui generis* and as to whether post-1972 use was a general industrial use within Class IV. Approach of Lord Widgery C.J. to the interpretation of the Use Classes Order in *Tessier* v. *Sec. of State for Environment* disapproved.

22–592 The primary purpose determines the character of the use. A builder's yard is not a use within the Use Classes Order. The fact that a builder's yard should not be permitted in residential areas does not, of itself, place a use in an industrial class in the Use Classes Order. A change of use from a use not within Use Classes Order to one within the Order is not *ipso facto* material. Change from a builder's yard to a general printing works was a material change of use. [1968] J.P.L. 712.

(b) Uses which are sui generis

22–593 British Paper & Board Industry Research Association v. L.B. of Croydon (1969) 210 E.G. 461. Industrial research establishment involving elements of laboratory work and office work as distinct from office or laboratory use alone and did not fall within any of the classes in the Use Classes Order.

22–594 Tessier v. Sec. of State for Environment (1975) 31 P. & C.R. 161, D.C. The making of articles by an artist expressing his art form was *sui generis* and should not be regarded as a process carried on in the course of trade or business within the Use Classes Order 1972 merely because articles made in that way are from time to time sold.

22–595 Farm Facilities and Prunadand Investments v. Sec. of State for Environment [1981] J.P.L. 42, D.C. Car-hire business use *sui generis*.

22–596 In particular circumstances a motor-driving school is neither an office nor a shop use. [1966] J.P.L. 733.

22–597 A commercial training college does not come within any of the classes in the Use Classes Order. [1969] J.P.L. 351.

22–598 Storage of gas in gas holders was not a use within the Use Classes Order and did not establish use rights for other forms of storage. [1969] J.P.L. 532.

22–599 Use of a site as a milk distribution depot, involving the maintenance and storage of milk delivery vehicles and the storage of goods in connection therewith, was a use *sui generis* and not within any class in the Use Classes Order. [1979] J.P.L. 408.

22–600 Use for the purposes of an agricultural contractor's yard and use for the purposes of a building and civil engineering contractor's yard are both *sui generis*

S.22. MEANING OF DEVELOPMENT

and materially different by reason of the potential difference in character and because one might be appropriate in a location in which the other was not. [1980] J.P.L. 282.

22–601 Change of use from storage ancillary to operational railway undertaking *sui generis* to independent storage use was a material change of use. [1980] J.P.L. 285.

22–602 Use as a composite use for purposes of a building contractor's business not falling within any particular Use Class. Use of part as separate industrial workshops and offices independent of builder's yard would involve a change of use. [1982] J.P.L. 115.

22–603 Garden centre a *sui generis* use and does not fall within Class I. It does not include the sale of the products of horticulture imported from elsewhere. [1985] J.P.L. 884.

(c) The specific classes

Class I: Shops

22–604 C.L.B. v. Saxone Shoe Co. [1955] 3 W.L.R. 614, C.A. Licensed premises on which light refreshments are served are not a shop for the purposes of the Use Classes Order.

22–605 Howell v. Sunbury-on-Thames U.D.C. (1963) 62 L.G.R. 119, C.A.
(1) It was impossible to define the limited area to which the existing shop use attached.
(2) A car mart was not a "shop" within art.2(2) of the Use Classes Order 1950.
Per Willmer and Upjohn L.JJ.: Use of a car mart as an office prevented it from being a shop.

22–606 Hussain v. Sec. of State for Environment (1971) 23 P. & C.R. 330, D.C. In judging whether a use is incidental to the use as a shop, you look at the shop as an activity as a whole and consideration should not be given to particular localities or areas or customers. Slaughtering chickens is not incidental.

22–607 Lydcare v. Sec. of State for Environment (1984) 272 E.G. 175, C.A. For premises to qualify as "shops" within art.2(2) of the Use Classes Order 1972 it was necessary both for them to be used for the carrying on of a retail trade or retail business, and for the primary purpose of such use to be the selling of goods by retail. Showing films in coin-operated cubicles did not come within this definition and, even if subsidiary to shop use, took site out of the class of "shop".

22–608 Sales of agricultural supplies to farmers was different from the retail sale of goods. Storage of items to be sold by travelling salesmen was not use for the retail sale of goods. [1972] J.P.L. 720.

22–609 Premises from which petrol was sold from pumps and on which body repairs were carried out on motor vehicles and on which a company's administrative offices were situated cannot be said to have a shop use. [1972] J.P.L. 730.

22–610 Distinction between wholesale and retail sales. [1977] J.P.L. 817.

22–611 Installation of a dry-cleaning unit in premises used for the purposes of the reception of goods to be washed, cleaned or repaired took the premises out of shop use as they ceased to be used for reception and became used for general or light industrial operations. [1981] J.P.L. 439.

22–612 One-off sale of surplus stock was not sufficient to amount to a shop use in order to take advantage of art. 3 of the Use Classes Order. [1983] J.P.L. 400.

22–613 D.I.Y. retail shop use within Class I—criteria is not that the purchaser is obtaining the goods for his own use or benefit but the type and quantity of goods supplied.

The supply of generally small items and quantities to the trade can fall within the D.I.Y. bracket but bulk supplies whether to private individuals or professional builders become the product of a builder's merchant's yard.

Skip hire and heavy plant operation and hire is not ancillary to a D.I.Y. shop or a builder's merchant's yard.

A builder's yard use is use as a support base for building operations carried out elsewhere by the occupier and does not include the sale of building materials and the storage of skips, vehicles and plant for hire as well as repair facilities for heavy vehicles and plant. [1985] J.P.L. 274.

Class II: Offices

22–614 Shephard v. Buckinghamshire C.C. (1966) 64 L.G.R. 422, D.C. Office use by the services, including the United States Air Force in England, is "use as an office for any purpose" within Class II in the Schedule to the (Use Classes) Order 1963 and accordingly any other office use is permitted by the Order.

22–615 J. Toomey Motors Ltd. v. Sec. of State for Environment [1981] J.P.L. 418, D.C. A radio-controlled car-hire business is not an "office" use within meaning of the Use Classes Order 1972.

22–616 Estate agent is an office rather than a shop use. [1973] J.P.L. 383.

22–617 Definition of "office purposes" in s.73(5) is relevant only to s.73 and does not define "office" for the purposes of the Use Classes Order. Sending and receiving radio messages and attendance at an office of customers and employers of a radio taxi business comes within office use. [1980] J.P.L. 346.

22–618 Office use is "a place for the transaction of business . . . applied to the room or department in which the clerical work of an establishment is done, also to that in which the business of any department of a large concern is conducted." A taxi and car-hire firm operated from a room by radio control is office use. [1985] J.P.L. 127.

22–619 Use of premises as a Government job centre is use as an employment agency within Class II of the Use Classes Order. [1985] J.P.L. 331.

Classes III and IV: Light and general industrial buildings

22–620 Stanger v. Hendon B.C. [1948] 1 K.B. 571, C.A. Meaning of an "industrial building" under s. 13(4) of the Town and Country Planning Act 1932.

22–621 Horwitz v. Rowson [1960] 1 W.L.R. 803, D.C.
(1) Use of a basement for the storing, sorting, dispatching and repairing of goods sold or used in a horticultural shop opposite the basement and its subsequent use as a workshop in connection with a printer's and engraver's business. Both uses are industrial within art.2(2) of the Use Classes Order 1950.
(2) Basement not used as a "shop" within art.2(2) of the Use Classes Order 1950.
(3) Basement not used as a "repository" within Class X of the Schedule to the Order.

22–622 Rael-Brook v. Min. of Housing and Local Government [1967] 2 Q.B. 65, D.C. In determining whether a process was carried on in the course of a trade or business, for the purposes of coming within the definition of "industrial building" in art.2(2) of the Use Classes Order 1950 neither the making of profit nor any commercial activity is essential.

22–623 Brazil (Concrete) v. Amersham R.D.C. (1967) 65 L.G.R. 365, C.A. Builder's shed is not an industrial building as its primary purpose is its use with the builder's yard.

S.22. MEANING OF DEVELOPMENT

22–624 Walter Chadburn & Son v. Leeds Corpn. (1969) 20 P. & C.R. 241, C.A. The use of premises for the business of a duly licensed rag flock manufacturer who complies with British Standards is included in Class IV in the Schedule to the Use Classes Order 1963 and not in Class IX.

22–625 Essex C.C. v. Sec. of State for Environment [1974] J.P.L. 286, D.C. Classification of a builder's yard with joinery and metal fabrication. Test—if use is detrimental to the amenities of residents if carried on in a residential area, it cannot be "light industrial use." In this case it was general industrial use.

22–626 W.T. Lamb Properties v. Sec. of State for Environment [1983] J.P.L. 303, D.C. In deciding whether a building's use is as a "light industrial building" under the Use Classes Order 1972 you must consider the question of noise and other nuisances in the context of any residential area, not just the area in question. The fact that a particular area was near to a noisy airport was irrelevant. The question of how you test the emissions from an industrial building was considered.

22–627 Use of a mill for the grinding of corn was not ancillary to the use of other buildings for the storage of animal foodstuffs and other articles sold in the owners' shops. Grinding of grain into flour or meal for the purpose of selling it by retail is a process of adaptation of an article for sale, and within the definition of "industrial building" in the Use Classes Order. Such a use was not carried on in the course of agriculture and was a general industrial use. [1967] J.P.L. 364.

22–628 Steam laundry a light industrial use. [1967] J.P.L. 559.

22–629 Use of land for the storage and repair of boxes for horticultural purposes not associated with agricultural land was a Class IV use and there was no material change of use on a change to use for the storage, repair and paint-spraying of motor coaches. [1968] J.P.L. 181.

22–630 Use of a building by an aircraft corporation for the servicing and repair of vehicles was an industrial use. [1968] J.P.L. 251.

22–631 Bakehouse with a shop and van round was an industrial use not ancillary to the shop. [1968] J.P.L. 301.

22–632 General industrial use did not become a light industrial use by effective sound-proofing. [1968] J.P.L. 367.

22–633 Bakehouse was a light industrial use. Motor vehicle repairs involving the use of a compressor, welding apparatus and electrical drilling and grinding equipment was a light industrial use. [1968] J.P.L. 589.

22–634 Breaking-up or dismantling of copper articles to recover copper was an industrial use. As use was carried out in the open it was not a Class III use, as that related to the use of a building. [1970] J.P.L. 221.

22–635 Dressmaker's business a mixed use for light industry and shop. [1972] J.P.L. 279.

22–636 Processing of chickens a general industrial use. Motor vehicle repairs a general industrial use. Change from one general industrial use to another required planning permission where the original general industrial use commenced without planning permission. Brief use disregarded as *de minimis*. [1972] J.P.L. 341.

22–637 Blacksmith's forge and workshop, and scrap-metal merchant's business, both general industrial uses. [1973] J.P.L. 669.

22–638 Manufacture of organs was a Class IV use because of the noise. [1977] J.P.L. 811.

22–639 Change of use from a laundry (light industrial use) to use for the manufacture and moulding of fibreglass sheeting (general industrial use). [1975] J.P.L. 484.

22–640 Laundry premises originally a Class IV use, but subsequently became a Class III use, therefore change to metal fabrication (Class IV use) a material change of use. [1978] J.P.L. 781.

22–641 Chicken-packing station a general industrial use—Class IV. Furniture manufacture a general industrial use—Class IV. [1970] J.P.L. 722.

22–642 Use of site as an egg-packing station held to be *sui generis* and did not fall within Class IV. [1986] J.P.L. 62.

Class V: Special industrial buildings

22–643 George Cohen 600 Group v. Min. of Housing & Local Govt. [1961] 1 W.L.R. 944, D.C. "Recovering of metal from scrap" in Class V(iv) of the Use Classes Order 1950 means the recovering of metal other than scrap metal from scrap.

Class X: Wholesale warehouses and repositories

22–644 G. Percy Trentham v. Gloucestershire C.C. [1966] 1 W.L.R. 506, C.A. An agricultural building on a farm used for storing farm machinery and equipment is not "a wholesale warehouse or repository" which means a building used as part of a storage business, not as part of a farming business.

22–645 Decorative & Caravan Paints Ltd. v. Min. of Housing & Local Govt. [1970] 214 E.G. 1355, D.C. Use of premises as a warehouse does not include use as a shop.

22–646 LTSS Print & Supply Services Ltd. v. Hackney L.B. [1976] 2 W.L.R. 253, C.A. The word "warehouse" is an ordinary English word and its meaning is not a matter of law. The Secretary of State's decision that a cash-and-carry establishment was not a "warehouse" within Class X was upheld.

22–647 Monomart (Warehouses) v. Sec. of State for Environment (1977) 34 P. & C.R. 305. A "warehouse" means a place at which goods are stored. Premises used primarily for the sale by retail of goods are not being used as a warehouse.

22–648 Hooper v. Slater [1978] J.P.L. 252, D.C. "Warehouse" use implied covered storage and not any kind of storage. It did not cover the storage of caravans in the open.

22–649 Newbury D.C. v. Sec. of State for Environment [1980] 1 All E.R. 731, H.L. Under class X of the Uses Classes Order 1950, a "repository" was not restricted to a building where goods were kept or stored in the course of a trade or business but extended to any place the principal use of which was storage. Hangars were used as a repository when used by the Crown to store civil defence vehicles.

22–650 Meadows v. Sec. of State for Environment [1983] J.P.L. 538, D.C. The Class X word "store" was not synonymous with either the word "repository" or "wholesale warehouse" but store use likely to be classifiable as that of repository or as wholesale warehouse.

22–651 "Wholesale warehouse" denotes a building to be used mainly for the storage of goods prior to distribution and sale elsewhere and any wholesale sales that do take place must be ancillary to use as a warehouse. Selling of goods to the general public in larger quantities than are usual in a retail shop, or at a discount, does not constitute wholesale sales. [1972] J.P.L. 35.

22–652 Use as a "wholesale warehouse or repository for any purpose" covered storage of things prior to sale of those things. [1973] J.P.L. 391.

S.22. MEANING OF DEVELOPMENT

22–653 Building used partly for the storage of corn and partly for the storage of cardboard boxes and trays was not incidental to the use of adjoining arable land. Use as a repository. Change to storage of agricultural products and machinery, both agricultural and non-agricultural, could involve a material change of use, but would still be a repository and therefore within Class X of the Use Classes Order. [1982] J.P.L. 459.

22–654 A building incorporating a retail collection counter area is one not used, or at least not in its entirety, for Class X. [1985] J.P.L. 817.

Class XI: Boarding and guest houses and hotels

22–655 Mornford Investments Ltd. v. Min. of Housing & Local Govt. [1970] 2 All E.R. 253, D.C. Whether use as a students' hostel *sui generis* or within Class XI of the Use Classes Order.

22–656 May Flower Cambridge Ltd. v. Sec. of State for Environment (1975) 30 P. & C.R. 28 D.C. Use as a hotel distinguished from use as bed-sitting rooms. Essence of hotel that it took in transient visitors.

22–657 English-Speaking Union v. Westminster L.B.C. (1975) 26 P. & C.R. 575, Ch. In general use as a residential club would be materially different from use as an hotel.

22–658 Emma Hotels v. Sec. of State for Environment [1979] J.P.L. 390, D.C. A hotel does not fall outside Class XI merely because it provides a bar open to non-residents as one of the incidents of hotel use.

22–659 Commercial and Residential Property Development Co. Ltd. v. Sec. of State for Environment [1982] J.P.L. 513, D.C. Meaning of the term "hostel."

22–660 Breachberry v. Sec. of State for Environment. [1985] J.P.L. 180, D.C. Change from hotel use to a house in multiple occupation. Whether use remained within Class XI of the Use Classes Order. Crucial date is the date of the service of the enforcement order, though later behaviour can be looked at as evidence that a material change had taken place.

22–661 Use of premises for the communal accommodation of a number of persons in a particular category, all of whom are employed by the organisation controlling the premises (nurses home), is a materially different use from use as an hotel. [1971] J.P.L. 595.

22–662 A hostel for transients is likely to differ materially from a guest-house or hotel in respect of number of guests per room, size of rooms, facilities and services provided, rules and control of guests, ratio of staff to guests and in other ways. Not a Class XI use. [1977] J.P.L. 42.

22–663 "Guest-house" generally describes accommodation provided on a short-term basis, akin to hotel use. [1977] J.P.L. 328.

22–664 Introduction of a non-residential use of a present dining-room would be incidental to hotel use and within Class XI of the Use Classes Order [1983] J.P.L. 199.

Class XIV: Use as home or institution

22–665 Rann v. Sec. of State for Environment (1979) 40 P. & C.R. 113, D.C. To come within a Class XIV use the "care and maintenance" must be of a special nature actually provided by the home or institution.

22–666 Use of a house as a "boarding-house" for the care of the elderly and children in need of a home is Class XIV use. [1968] J.P.L. 531.

S.22. MEANING OF DEVELOPMENT

22–667 Holiday home for mentally handicapped persons and a permanent residential home for discharged mental after-care patients are both within Class XIV of the Use Classes Order 1972. [1978] J.P.L. 566.

E. Changes of Use which are Development: section 22(3)

1. Use as Two or More Separate Dwelling-houses: section 22(3)(a)

22–668 Wakelin v. Sec. of State for Environment (1978) 77 L.G.R. 101. By analogy with s. 22(3)(*a*), use of a site for two or more dwelling-houses, which had previously been used as a single dwelling-house, can amount to development.

22–669 Ealing Corpn. v. Ryan [1965] 2 Q.B. 486, D.C. For a building to be used as two or more dwelling-houses for the purposes of a material change of use, it is necessary to have physically separate dwellings which are self-contained and independent of other parts of the same property. Multiple occupation alone is insufficient.

Note

Also see *R.* v. *Min. of Housing & Local Govt., ex p. Habid Ullah* [1964] 1 Q.B. 178, *Clarke* v. *Caterham and Warlingham U.D.C.* (1966) 18 P. & C.R. 82 for decisions on multiple paying occupation which fall short of being separate dwelling-houses.

2. Extension of Refuse Tips

22–670 W.S. Wright Ltd. v. Bromley Corpn. (1950) 1 P. & C.R. 302. Controlled tipping of refuse and waste materials in an excavated gravel pit is not an agricultural use.

Quaere—whether, where deposit does not exceed the natural level of adjoining land but does exceed the level of an adjoining excavated area, the height of the deposit exceeds "the level of the land adjoining the site."

22–671 Macdonald v. Glasgow Corpn. (1960) 11 P. & C.R. 318, Sheriff Ct. Reason for the deposit of materials is important, *e.g.* the deposit for the object of road-building would not be a deposit of refuse or waste material.

Per curiam: "Adjoining land" means the varying contours of the immediately adjoining land.

22–672 Alexandra Transport v. Sec. of State for Scotland (1973) 27 P. & C.R. 352, Ct. of Sess. Use of a quarry as a tip for refuse brought in from outside constitutes a material change of use from the infilling of mineral excavations.

22–673 Duckworth v. Haslingdon U.D.C. [1973] J.P.L. 196, D.C. Quarry of 7.8 acres. The whole quarry was the planning unit therefore tipping in any part of it which resulted in an increase in height exceeding adjoining land involved a material change of use of the whole site.

22–674 R. v. Derbyshire C.C., ex p. North East Derbyshire D.C. (1979) 77 L.G.R. 389, D.C. Disposal of waste is treated by planning legislation as involving a use of land rather than an engineering operation.

22–675 Bilboe v. Sec. of State for Environment (1980) 39 P. & C.R. 495, 505, C.A. Tipping constitutes a material change of use, not operations, therefore the four-year rule is inapplicable but if tipping commenced before 1964 an enforcement notice could not be served.

22–676 Tipping of materials for the express purpose of rendering them fit for use for some other purpose is not tipping of refuse or waste materials for the purpose of disposing of them. It is the carrying out of operations on the land. Section 22(3)(*b*)

S.22. MEANING OF DEVELOPMENT

only applies where waste materials are tipped for the purpose of disposing of them. [1976] J.P.L. 655.

22–677 Meaning of "dumping" of materials, soil and waste—nature of use when in connection with a business. [1977] J.P.L. 264.

22–678 Whether planning permission required following changes in material tipped. The Act does not distinguish between types of waste. No distinction is to be drawn between solid and liquid waste. Whether the superficial area of deposit had been extended. [1980] J.P.L. 771.

22–679 Tipping of soil to improve agricultural land, but not pursuant to a detailed plan, constitutes "other operations." Section 22(3)(*b*) is inapplicable as the soil tipped was neither refuse nor waste material. [1981] J.P.L. 135.

22–680 Material change of use by the deposit of waste materials above the surrounding level despite the previous established use certificate.

SECTION 23. DEVELOPMENT REQUIRING PLANNING PERMISSION

A. Planning Permission is Required for the Carrying Out of Development: section 23(1)

23–01 Minister of Agriculture, Fisheries and Food v. Jenkins [1963] 2 W.L.R. 906, C.A. The Crown does not need planning permission as it is not expressly or implicitly included in the legislation.

23–02 Argyll & Bute D.C. v. Sec. of State for Environment, 1977 SLT 33. Planning jurisdiction does not extend below tide-mark.

B. Rights to Revert to Former Uses of Land: section 23(2)–(10)

23–03 Glamorgan C.C. v Carter (1963) 14 P. & C.R. 88, D.C. User rights cannot be acquired by virtue of an illegal use of land.

23–04 Smith v. Min. of Housing & Local Govt. (1966) 64 L.G.R. 235, D.C. Land normally used for one purpose but "on occasions" used for another purpose before the appointed day, will give rise to existing use rights under s.13(3) of the Town and Country Planning Act 1962 for the occasional use, if it is so used on an unspecified number of days not preponderant in any year and not so great as to amount to continuous or normal use, whether or not on any particular day or for any particular event. In such a case there is an existing use right for a similar number of days only.

23–05 Kingdon v. Min. of Housing & Local Govt. [1967] 3 W.L.R. 990, D.C. Resumption of normal use from temporary use involves two things:
  (i) there must be no intervention of any other use,
  (ii) there must be resumption at a time when both normal and temporary use still exist; if circumstances show that temporary use has become normal use there cannot be a reversion back to the former normal use.

23–06 W.T. Lamb & Sons v. Sec. of State for Environment (1975) 30 P. & C.R. 371, D.C. Use for storage interrupted for 13 months by use for the maintaining and repairing of motor vehicles. New use was not *de minimis* and reversion to storage use needed planning permission.

Under s.23(9) "use of land for the purpose for which . . . it could lawfully have been used if that development had not been carried out" included a use which was not immune from enforcement proceedings but in respect of which enforcement proceedings had not been taken. But see now *L.T.S.S. Print and Supply Services Ltd.* v. *Hackney L.B.C.*

23–07 L.T.S.S. Print and Supply Services Ltd. v. Hackney L.B.C. [1976] Q.B. 663, C.A. An established use of land is not a lawful use under s.23(9) to which owners could revert, as such a use merely provided immunity from enforcement proceedings. Once an established use is discontinued in favour of a fresh use involving development the owners have no right to revert to the previous established use.

23–08 Mid-Warwickshire Motors Ltd. v. Sec. of State for Environment [1979] J.P.L. 538. An enforcement notice should be drafted so as to safeguard possible rights of reversion under s.23(9).

23–09 Balco Transport Services Ltd. v. Sec. of State for Environment [1982] J.P.L. 177, D.C. Possible to revert to a use under s.23(9) even though not an immediate preceding use: but see *Young* v. *Sec. of State for Environment*.

23–10 Clwyd C.C. v. Sec. of State for Wales [1982] J.P.L. 696, D.C. Failure to comply with a condition, other than a condition precedent, does not render unlawful a use which is otherwise authorised by a permission.

23–11 Smith v. Sec. of State for Environment (1983) J.P.L. 461, D.C. Enforcement notice served on expiration of time-limited permission. The inspector had erred in law as, in deciding not to grant permission for continuance of the use, he had been under the misapprehension that there was no right to revert to normal use to which site had been put before grant of limited permission. Under subsections (5) and (6) the right to revert to normal use should be exercised as soon as under limited permission ceased even if time under the permission had not elapsed. To get to the normal use you could go back in time through a series of limited permissions. However you could not revert to a use which had commenced unlawfully but which had become established.

23–12 Young v. Sec. of State for Environment [1983] 2 All E.R. 1105, H.L. A person on whom an enforcement notice is served under s.23(9) alleging change of user, may revert to the use immediately preceding the present user only if it was lawful—he may not go back beyond that use to an earlier lawful use.

Approach in *L.T.S.S. and Print and Supply Services Ltd.* v. *Hackney L.B.C.* as to what constitutes a lawful use approved.

23–13 Cynon Valley B.C. v. Sec. of State for Wales [1986] J.P.L. 283. Meaning of s.23(8). Held, reversing High Court, that the limits on permitted development set out in Class III(d)(i) Schedule to the General Development Order, are of the "limitations" within the meaning of that word in the General Development Order and in s.23(8). However an express grant of permission to implement a material change of use did not authorise reversion to that use if it had been previously implemented.

23–14 Continuance after 1948 of an established caravan site did not constitute development requiring planning permission, but planning permission was granted to enable the owners to obtain a site licence under Part I of the Caravan Sites and Control of Development Act 1960. (1962) 13 P. & C.R. 449.

23–15 For a use to be lawful it must either have planning permission or have been carried out since before July 1, 1948 without being abandoned or replaced by a materially different use. [1978] J.P.L. 571.

23–16 Although there must come a time when the right to resume a lawful use in accordance with s.23(9) lapses, it is reasonable to conclude that the right to assume that use has not lapsed even though it has not been so used for the previous 16 years and an enforcement notice was served 10 years previously.

SECTION 24. DEVELOPMENT ORDERS

A. General Approach to Development Orders

24–01 Essex City Council v. Min. of Housing & Local Govt. (1967) 18 P. & C.R. 531, C.A. The Minister's power to make a development order is a purely administrative legislative power answerable only to Parliament. There is no need to comply with the rules of natural justice.

24-02 Cole v. Somerset C.C. [1957] 1 Q.B. 23, D.C. Permission under the General Development Order may not be withdrawn under Art. 4 after it has been implemented.

24-03 Spedeworth v. Sec. of State for Environment (1972) 71 L.G.R. 123, C.A. A direction that development of specified land shall not be carried out otherwise than as a caravan site is a general direction falling under Art. 4(1)(a) of the General Development Order and publication of the direction in a newspaper is sufficient.

24-04 Garland v. Min. of Housing & Local Govt. (1968) 20 P. & C.R. 93, C.A. The limit of cubic capacity set out in the General Development Order is part of the definition of the permitted development. Therefore a development which exceeds that limit is totally unauthorised and an enforcement notice may require the whole of the development to be removed not just the part exceeding the limit. It would be a different matter if the excess were trifling.

24-05 Jurisdiction of the Minister where development within a Landscape Areas Special Development Order 1950. [1966] J.P.L. 550.

24-06 Where a building exceeds the size limits in a General Development Order permission, no part of the building can be permitted development. [1971] J.P.L. 169.

B. Particular Categories of Permitted Development under the General Development Order

1. Class I: Development within the Curtilage of a Dwelling-house

24-07 Wood v. Sec. of State for Environment [1973] 1 W.L.R. 707. D.C. An extension to a building under Class 1 of the General Development Order takes on the characteristics of the original building and can be used for the same purposes as the original building. Section 33(2) is not applicable.

24-08 Scurlock v. Sec. State for Wales [1976] J.P.L. 431 D.C. Building used as a residence and for business had a dual purpose and could not be a "dwelling-house" within Class 1.

24-09 Bradford M.D.C. v. Sec. of State for Environment (1977) 35 P. & C.R. 387. Permitted development under para. (c) of Class 1(1) was not limited to structural as opposed to cosmetic features—the two concepts are not mutually exclusive. Where proposed stone-cladding will not project beyond the window sills of the front wall of a house, it was open to the Secretary of State to hold that it did not project beyond the front wall, and planning permission was not required.

24-10 Dawson v. Sec. of State for Environment [1983] J.P.L. 544, D.C. Roof extension and second-floor balcony exceeded permitted development under Class 1(1). By virtue of the 1981 amendment to the Order the extension was permitted as the words "or otherwise" brought into account extensions which were put up without the benefit of planning permission.

24-11 L.B. Havering v. Sec. of State for Environment [1983] J.P.L. 665, D.C. Provisions (i) and (ii) of Class 1(1)(e) are not mutually exclusive.

24-12 North Western Leicestershire D.C. v. Sec. of State for Environment (1983) 46 P. & C.R. 154, D.C. Reference in Class 1(1)(c) to "the forwardmost part of any wall" presupposes that a wall might be one other than in a straight line and it is a question of fact and degree in each case what constitutes a wall. Two walls of an L-shaped house could be treated as one wall.

S.24. DEVELOPMENT ORDERS

24–13 Gravesham B.C. v. Sec. of State for Environment (1984) 47 P. & C.R. 142, D.C. One of the main considerations as to whether premises are a "dwelling-house" under the Order is that there should be a building which provides facilities for daily private domestic existence. The use to which a building is put is not necessarily conclusive nor is the frequency of user always relevant.

A holiday chalet does not cease to be a dwelling-house merely because there are restrictions on the duration and frequency of its use.

24–14 Trustees of Earl of Lichfield's Estate v. Sec. of State for Environment [1985] J.P.L. 251. Whether a ruined building still capable of being considered to be a "dwelling-house"—approach in various Ministerial Decisions approved and importance placed on whether dwelling-house use had been abandoned.

24–15/16 Enclosure of the verandah of a house to form a sun lounge. Whether the "front" of a house is where the main entrance is, or on the most publicly exposed side of the house. [1966] J.P.L. 352.

24–17 Partial demolition and rebuilding of a cottage—so little left of the original structure that it amounted to rebuilding not maintenance, improvement or alteration. Original cottage was not a dwelling-house capable of benefiting from the Order. [1966] J.P.L. 601.

24–18 Cannot have permitted extension or alteration of a building where use has been abandoned. [1967] J.P.L. 110.

24–19 Conversion of a room of a dwelling-house to a garage amounted to permitted development. [1967] J.P.L. 116.

24–20 Restoration of the ruins of a cottage to substantially its former appearance. As a matter of fact and degree the works amounted to rebuilding of the cottage not maintenance improvement, or other alteration. As what has remained of cottage had not been a dwelling-house capable of benefiting from the Order, it did not apply. When considering the former state of the cottage, its state immediately before the relevant works began, should be considered. As works amounted to rebuilding the whole building should be removed under an enforcement notice. [1967] J.P.L. 351.

24–21 Installation of a septic tank for a dwelling-house involves construction (underground) of a building for a purpose incidental to the enjoyment of a dwelling-house and comes within Class 1(2) of the Order. [1967] J.P.L. 669.

24–22 Installation of a septic tank for purposes incidental to a dwelling-house is construction of a building within Class I(2). [1968] J.P.L. 46.

24–23 Septic tank and ancillary works comprise a building required for a purpose incidental to the enjoyment of the dwelling-house and are permitted development within Class I. [1969] J.P.L. 50.

24–24 Removal and reconstruction of the roof, rebuilding and extension of one wall and alteration of the other three walls amounted to improvement and enlargement of a dwelling within Class I rather than to its rebuilding. [1969] J.P.L. 92.

24–25 An individual flat is not a dwelling-house for the purposes of Class I. A window cannot be regarded as part of the facing of a building. [1969] J.P.L. 151.

24–26 Works on a dwelling-house can only be constituted an "enlargement improvement or other alteration" if sufficient of the existing fabric of the building remains for the identity of the original dwelling-house not to be lost. Replacement of the roof, demolition and replacement of the west gable wall and construction of new exterior walls above the levels of the ceilings of the ground floor amounts to rebuilding. [1970] J.P.L. 165.

S.24. DEVELOPMENT ORDERS

24-27 Works involving construction of a new west wall and double doorway and a new south wall and flat roof amounted to erection of a new building and required planning permission. [1970] J.P.L. 268.

24-28 For the purposes of Class I the cubic capacity of the "original dwelling-house" is calculated as at July 1, 1948 and does not include additions which have become immune from enforcement proceedings. [1970] J.P.L. 351.

24-29 Formation of a balcony to a dwelling-house by the erection of a balustrade on a permitted extension was a building operation, but it was an improvement or other alteration within Class I. [1970] J.P.L. 589.

24-30 Where all that remained above ground level was part of three of the original external walls the works consisted of rebuilding of the dwelling-house. Works which have received express planning permission must be included in the tolerance calculation. [1970] J.P.L. 706.

24-31 A car port is a garage for the purposes of the General Development Order. Whilst the enlargement of a dwelling with express planning permission counted against the allowance in Class I(1), the erection of a separate garage with express planning permission did not. [1971] J.P.L. 290.

24-32 Where only a small portion of one wall of the original building remains before rebuilding is commenced works cannot be considered as the maintenance, improvement or other alteration of a building even if the new building appears to be the same as the old, and the old materials are used. [1971] J.P.L. 230.

24-33 After demolition of two walls, the first floor and roof of a former cottage it was no longer a dwelling-house capable of benefiting from the provisions of the General Development Order. [1971] J.P.L. 584.

24-34 An integral garage is to be treated as part of a dwelling-house for the purposes of Class I so that its conversion into living accommodation is not an enlargement of the original dwelling-house to be debited against Class I tolerance. [1971] J.P.L. 720.

24-35 Works on a dwelling-house which would result in stripping external walls down to the bare wooden framework would amount to rebuilding as the original building would lose its identity. [1972] J.P.L. 345.

24-36 Erection of a screen or parapet on the flat roof of a dwelling-house was permitted development within Class I(1). [1972] J.P.L. 719.

24-37 Erection of a skin of brickwork and breeze blocks around a dwelling-house was not permitted development. In calculating cubic capacity the reduction in actual volume of the building by the construction of a new raised floor must be disregarded as the original floor forms part of the original building. [1973] J.P.L. 107.

24-38 To be a dwelling-house a building must, *inter alia*, be capable of supporting the major activities of life, *i.e.* cooking, feeding and sleeping. [1976] J.P.L. 326.

24-39 In calculating the permissible volume of any extension of a dwelling-house any previous extensions must be included even if made under an express grant of planning permission. [1977] J.P.L. 113 and 115.

24-40 Stone-cladding which will not project beyond existing walls or window surrounds is permitted development within Class 1. [1978] J.P.L. 61.

24-41 L-shaped bungalow. Two sections of wall facing the highway were regarded as the same wall for the purposes of the General Development Order. A garage which replaced an earlier garage had been erected after the bungalow was completed and was counted against tolerance for Class I(1) of the General Development Order. [1978] J.P.L. 271.

24–42 Where only one gable and wall and a partition wall with a chimney stack, and six upright RSJ's with possibly a roof frame above remained, works would amount to rebuilding. [1978] J.P.L. 491.

24–43 Pergola on a terrace was a "building" even though it lacked a roof and was not fully enclosed at the sides. Pergola did not amount to an enlargement, improvement or other alteration of a dwelling-house within Class I(1) but could come within Class I(3).

24–44 A dwelling-house does not cease to be a dwelling-house merely because renovation works make it for the time being uninhabitable. Where a house was reduced to the original roof timbers, three fully-erected walls and the underpinned foundations of the fourth external wall, it was still recognisable as a dwelling-house under renovation. [1979] J.P.L. 332.

24–45 "Forwardmost part of any wall of the original dwelling-house" does not include a wall of a building or structure detached from a dwelling-house. [1979] J.P.L. 336.

24–46 Removal of the front and rear walls and floor of a bungalow would not result in its loss of identity as a dwelling-house and was permitted development. Replacement of the front and rear walls and roof of a bungalow and the erection of a rear single storey extension would deprive it of its identity as a dwelling-house and require planning permission. [1979] J.P.L. 630.

24–47 Underground cellar wall being invisible is not a wall fronting on to highway under Class 1(3). [1980] J.P.L. 196.

24–48 In calculating whether the limit of development has been exceeded under Class I(1) you take into account any enlargement carried out under express permission as well as development carried out under the Order. [1981] J.P.L. 373.

24–49 Stationing of a caravan in curtilage of a building and used for recreational purposes and the occasional sleeping of guests. Premises had a dual restaurant and residential purpose and therefore stationing of the caravan could not come within Class I(3) and constituted development. [1981] J.P.L. 441.

24–50 Even the rear wall of a house can "front" on to a road, but whether a wall fronts a road is a question of fact and degree. The fact that a plot abuts a highway does not mean that at least one wall of the house must front on to the highway—the distance from the highway and the presence of other buildings is relevant. A wall 33 metres downhill from a highway behind the line of the rear boundaries of neighbouring curtilages did not front on to the highway. [1982] J.P.L. 53.

24–51 It is a matter of fact and degree whether a house fronts on to a street and the existence of an intervening strip of land which is not within the ownership of the householder is not of itself a determining factor. [1983] J.P.L. 405.

24–52 Dwelling-house fronting a highway. Wall fronting the highway was in two sections, one nearer to the highway than the other. The section of wall nearer to the highway was the forwardmost part of the wall. "Forwardmost part of the wall" was the sill of the bow window. [1982] J.P.L. 531.

24–53 To benefit from Class I(1) there must be a dwelling-house in existence when the operations are being carried out. While building need not necessarily be a dwelling-house actually in habitation at the time, there must at all times remain on the land a structure sufficiently intact as reasonably to support the description of a dwelling-house and not the ruins of a dwelling. [1982] J.P.L. 806.

24–54 Provision of a dormer window in the roof of a semi-dedached dwelling was development within Class I(1). [1982] J.P.L. 809.

S.24. DEVELOPMENT ORDERS

24–55 Erection of a first-floor extension to a dwelling-house supported by four brick piers. Ground-floor space underneath unenclosed. For the purposes of the Order the cubic capacity of the extension included the volume of space covered by the proposed extension at ground-floor level even though unwalled and unenclosed. [1983] J.P.L. 67.

24–56 To qualify under Class 1(3) development should not include any accommodation which could be regarded as adding to or extending the normal living accommodation of the dwelling-house and therefore a cocktail bar, bedroom, bathroom and study do not come within it whilst a swimming pool, with playroom, sauna, shower, changing and filter room can come within it. [1983] J.P.L. 683.

24–57 Class I(1)(c). For a wall to front on to the highway it does not have to run parallel or roughly parallel to the highway. The forwardmost part of wall must be considered by reference to the line of the wall and not by the fact that a particular point on the wall would be closer to the highway because it is at an angle to the highway. [1983] J.P.L. 750.

24–58 Three self-contained flats and one separate bed-sitting room did not constitute a dwelling-house. [1983] J.P.L. 831.

24–59 Alterations to a dwelling-house to provide rooms in the roof space. Alterations to roof too substantial to come within Class I(1)(e) relationship between (e)(i) and (e)(ii) considered. [1984] J.P.L. 50.

24–60/61 To benefit from Class I(1) there must be a structure which can be regarded as a dwelling-house. For a structure to be regarded as a dwelling-house there must be a building in existence and capable of being used—if need be, after essential repairs and refurbishment—for ordinary residential purposes. A dilapidated building, entirely uninhabitable, which had been uninhabited for a considerable period of time, and which grazing animals may have used for shelter cannot be regarded as a dwelling-house for the purposes of Class I(1). [1984] J.P.L. 282.

24–62 Garage constructed with a dwelling-house and sharing an integral party wall with it must be regarded as part of the original dwelling-house for the purposes of Class I. [1985] J.P.L. 199.

24–63 Whether a structure is a dwelling-house is a matter to be determined by reference to all the relevant factors which may indicate whether a building ordinarily affords the facilities required for day-to-day private domestic existence. Rating records are not necessarily conclusive for planning control purposes. A building designed in the form of a boathouse, but used as such only intermittently, continuously equipped and intended for residential purposes, was a dwelling-house for the purposes of the General Development Order. [1985] J.P.L. 411.

24–64 Dwelling-house with a forward-projecting integral garage. The front of the garage constituted the forwardmost part of the wall and therefore an extension in front of the main part of the house but behind the front of the garage was within Class I of the General Development Order. [1985] J.P.L. 501.

24–65 Planning permission required for stone cladding on home for elderly people as building in commercial use and so did not come within Class I. [1985] J.P.L. 736.

24–66 Stone cladding projecting beyond forwardmost part of any wall of original dwelling-house not permitted development under Class 1 and it requires planning permission. [1985] J.P.L. 739.

24–67 Complete renovation of ruined remains of a dwelling-house development requiring planning permission and is not within Class I. [1985] J.P.L. 807.

24–68 The insertion of dormer windows and other alterations to building did not come within proviso (*e*)(i) to Class I.1. [1986] J.P.L. 37.

24–69 The erection of a new roof which was higher than original does not come within Class I.1. In deciding whether a wall "fronts" a highway, it does not follow that because a curtilage or plot of dwelling-house abuts a highway that the corresponding wall of the dwelling-house "fronts" that highway. Other matters are relevant such as the distance between and the circumstances of the intervening land. [1986] J.P.L. 143.

24–70 The erection of a single storey building containing swimming pool with a spa, two garden rooms, boiler/plant room, store changing room, sauna and shower, came within Class I.3. Although, the works could be said to be engineering operations, looked at in their entirety, they were ancillary to, *i.e.* part of the building. [1986] J.P.L. 306.

24–71 The creation of dormer windows and the raising of front and rear eaves of a dwelling were on too large a scale to be described as the insertion of windows within the proviso (*e*)(1) to Class I.1 but they did come within the scope of alterations as they neither totally absorbed or replaced existing roof, and so fell within Class I(1)(*a*). [1986] J.P.L. 378.

24–72 The erection of a shelter to provide for domestic leisure equipment, which shelter was attached to the existing dwelling-house, came within Class I.3. There was nothing in Class I.3 which requires physical separation of the development from the main building of the dwelling-house except in the case of a garage or coach house. This was not an extension of the normal living accommodation as access could not be reached from within the dwelling-house. [1986] J.P.L. 449.

2. Class II: Sundry Minor Operations

24–73 Prengate Properties v. Sec. of State for Environment (1973) 25 P. & C.R. 311, D.C. Class II(1) does not authorise the building of a wall unless it has some function of enclosure; but a wall that is prima facie authorised does not lose its authority because some time in the future the landowner intends to incorporate it into some larger engineering operation.

24–74 Ewen Development Ltd. v. Sec. of State for Environment [1980] J.P.L. 404, D.C. The creation of embankments was outside Class II as the inspector had concluded that they were not a means of enclosure. Held that this conclusion was a question of fact and degree and would not be upset.

24–75 Simmond v. Sec. of State for Environment [1981] J.P.L. 509, D.C. Fence 0.55 metres and 0.70 metres back from a stone wall boundary on land abutting boundary. Inspector's conclusion as a matter of fact and degree that the fence abutted the highway was not manifestly wrong.

24–76 Class I(1) of the 1963 G.D.O. covered the formation of access to an unclassified road. [1967] J.P.L. 116.

24–77 When measuring the height of a fence the height is the height above natural ground level and therefore where a fence is erected on a raised patio the height of the patio must be added to the height of the fence. [1979] J.P.L. 491.

24–78 Fence separated from a highway only by a hedge "abutted" the highway. [1969] J.P.L. 526.

24–79 To "abut" a highway a fence does not need to be actually situated on its boundary. [1976] J.P.L. 190.

24–80 "Abut" does not necessarily import contiguity: a 6 foot fence within 4 inches of the edge of the highway abuts the highway in planning terms. [1981] J.P.L. 70.

24–81 Planning permission for a dwelling-house did not implicitly permit the construction of ornamental gates and flank walls. Gateway and walls do not need to be

S.24. DEVELOPMENT ORDERS

actually situated on the boundary of a highway for them to be "abutting on" the highway for the purposes of Class II. The Road is still a highway used by vehicular traffic even though not a public right of way and not maintained by the Council. [1982] J.P.L. 129.

24–82 Where fence erected so that it was supported by existing wall, the height of wall must be taken into account in measuring the height of the fence. [1982] J.P.L. 197.

24–83 Front and side walls abutted highway as only minimally separated from footway. [1984] J.P.L. 295.

24–84 Forwardmost part of forward-projecting integral garage is forwardmost part of main wall for Class II. [1985] J.P.L. 501.

3. Class III

24–85 Cyon Valley B.C. v. Sec. of State for Wales [1986] J.P.L. 283. Class III(a) only covered change from a *lawful* general industrial to a light industrial use and did not apply when the general industrial use was itself unauthorised.

24–86 Change of use from a shop for the sale of motor vehicles to any other shop is permitted development within Class III. The fitting of tyres and batteries is ancillary to shop use. [1969] J.P.L. 417.

24–92 General vehicle repairs, rebuilding and conversion of motor vehicles and bodywork repairs are all general industrial uses within Class IV. [1969] J.P.L. 707.

24–87 Change from a milk-bottling plant (general industrial building) to the manufacture of packaging materials (light industrial building) is permitted development. [1976] J.P.L. 520.

4. Class V: Temporary Buildings and Uses

24–88 Brown v. Hayes & Harlington U.D.C. (1963) 62 L.G.R. 66, D.C. General Development Order 1950, Sched. 1, Class IV(1) permitted erection or construction incidental to the main building operation, but not to the use of land for parking of vehicles and equipment.

24–89 Sunbury-on-Thames U.D.C. v. Mann (1958) 9 P. & C.R. 309, D.C. Buildings cannot be erected under Class IV(1) where permission for a use only has been granted.

24–90 Tidswell v. Sec. of State for Environment (1976) 34 P. & C.R. 152, D.C. Enforcement notice served on a market held at a football ground on nine successive Sundays. A distinction has to be drawn between a general and temporary casual use and the beginning of a permanent use. By the time of the inquiry there was ample evidence to show that the market use was not a temporary 14-day use, and it was irrelevant that only nine markets been held at the time of the service of the enforcement notice.

Note

For the complexities raised by the 28 days with regard to enforcement notices, see *Postill* v. *East Riding C.C.* [1956] 2 Q.B. 386; *Francis* v. *Yiewsley & West Drayton U.D.C.* [1958] 1 Q.B. 478; *Cater* v. *Essex C.C.* [1959] 2 W.L.R. 739; *Miller-Mead* v. *Min. of Housing & Local Govt.* [1963] 2 W.L.R. 225.

24–91 Permission in Class IV(1) relates to building and other operations temporarily needed in connection with operational development for which there is planning permission, not to a temporary change in the use of land in connection with such development.

24–92 General vehicle repairs, rebuilding and conversion of motor vehicles and body work repairs are all general industrial uses within Class IV. [1969] J.P.L. 707.

24-93 Use of a football ground for a Sunday market on nine consecutive Sundays. Whether a temporary use. [1976] J.P.L. 113.

24-94 Necessity to remove a temporary building and works in connection with a permitted operation. [1976] J.P.L. 456.

5. Class VI: Agricultural Buildings, Works and Uses

24-95 Belmont Farm Ltd. v. Min. of Housing & Local Govt. (1962) 13 P. & C.R. 417, D.C. A building is "designed" for the purpose for which its physical layout and appearance fit it.

24-96 North Avon D.C. v. Sec. of State for Environment (1980) 40 P. & C.R. 332. To come within Class VI tipping must be for the purpose of improving the land for agriculture not to provide a last resting place for refuse.

24-97 Fayrewood Fish Farms v. Sec. of State for Environment [1984] J.P.L. 267. Development not within Class VI(1) as part of works within 25 metres of a classified road.

24-98 Jones v. Stockport M.B.C. (1984) 269 E.G. 408, C.A.
(1) The words "requisite for the use of that land for the purposes of agriculture" in Class VI mean that a building must be requisite for the use of the land as an agriculture unit, including the building and the operation carried on inside it; it is not necessary for the remainder of the land to have an independent agricultural existence to which the building is ancillary.
(2) The words of Class VI require an existing use for agriculture.

24-99 Harding v. Sec. of State for Environment [1984] J.P.L. 503, D.C. Whether a building was "designed for the purposes of agriculture" was to be determined by looking at its physical appearance and layout not by intentions.
Belmont v. *Min. of Health & Local Govt.* followed in preference to *Wilson* v. *West Suffolk C.C.*

24-100 Green v. Sec. of State for Environment [1985] J.P.L. 323, D.C. Building in the course of erection. Inspector concluded that the building was going to be a dwelling-house and so was not within Class VI. Inspector's view upheld.

24-101 Macpherson v. Sec. of State for Scotland [1985] J.P.L. 788. Whether tipping "requisite" for the use of land for the purposes of agriculture to come within Class VI. Reporter held that because of the scale of the tipping it was not requisite. Held that the reporter had acted correctly and that "requisite" should be interpreted as meaning "reasonably necessary."

24-102 West Bowers Farm Products v. Essex C.C. [1985] J.P.L. 857. Where construction of reservoir on a farm included the extraction of huge quantities of gravel then both mining and engineering operations involved and each required to be covered by planning permission. Test was whether the mining operations ancillary to the engineering operations.

24-103 South Oxfordshire D.C. v. Sec. of State for the Environment [1986] J.P.L. 435. Whether construction of reservoir on farm within Class VI. 1. Even if operations were engineering operations they could result in buildings and so have to keep within the restrictions on buildings. 2. Whether or not an embankment was a building was a question of fact and degree and the meaning of "means of enclosure had to be interpreted *eusdem generis* with fences walls and gates. 3. Class VI 3 did not cover mining for the purposes of getting materials to construct buildings.

24-104 Ten ex-road-railway goods containers standing on agricultural land, slightly modified and used for pig-breeding were not structures designed for agricultural purposes under Class VI(1). [1966] J.P.L. 5440.

S.24. DEVELOPMENT ORDERS

24-105 Preparation of horticultural compost was not an agricultural use of the land. [1968] J.P.L. 416.

24-106 A building for livestock which does not depend upon the land is not requisite for the use of agricultural land for agricultural purposes within Class VI. [1971] J.P.L. 169.

24-107 Storage of railway sleepers and timber on agricultural land is not an agricultural use even though mainly sold to farmers. [1971] J.P.L. 125.

24-108 Building with the appearance of a bungalow not designed for the purposes of agriculture. [1972] J.P.L. 512.

24-109 Building such as a mushroom-growing shed is not a building requisite to the use of land for the purposes of agriculture. [1972] J.P.L. 520.

24-110 Land used for the sale of produce from nearby agricultural land:
 (i) whether it comprised an agricultural unit,
 (ii) whether use by a weighbridge is ancillary to agricultural use.
[1973] J.P.L. 609.

24-111 Erection of chicken verandahs is an operational development. Pullets and food brought in from outside do not depend on the surrounding land for support, therefore are not incidental to the agricultural use of the land and so are not within Class VI. [1977] J.P.L. 47.

24-112 A building erected in connection with other building operations could not be retained for agricultural purposes as permitted development under Class VI(I). [1978] J.P.L. 61.

24-113 In the absence of a full definition of "engineering operations" the word "engineering" in the General Development Orders would not cover the tipping of refuse on land or even the tipping of soil and similar excavated material for the purpose of raising level of land to render it more suitable for agricultural use. [1978] J.P.L. 494.

24-114 Erection of a mini-pit laying-house on agricultural land. None of the poultry were fed with food grown on the holding and only 10 per cent. of poultry manure was used on the holding, therefore there was no conclusive evidence that the buildings were requisite for agricultural purposes and so were not permitted under Class VI(1). [1978] J.P.L. 795.

24-115 To come within Class VI land must be in use for agriculture for the purposes of a trade or business at the time the buildings are erected, although land could be used for agriculture in the future without constituting development not in use for agriculture at present. To come within the provisions any building erected would need as a matter of fact and degree to be requisite to the use of land in relation to the situation as it was when the buildings were erected. Although the keeping and breeding of rabbits for food is an agricultural activity it is not requisite to the use of surrounding land for growing vegetables to be used as one-third of the daily food requirement of the rabbits. Although the internal design of the building was suitable for keeping rabbits, its external appearance was that of a residential prefabricated bungalow, for which purpose it was formerly used, and therefore it was not designed for the purposes of agriculture. [1981] J.P.L. 129.

24-116 Fish-farming for food is agriculture within the meaning of s.290(1). Building and engineering operations for such fish-farming fall within Class VI. [1981] J.P.L. 766.

24-117 Erection of a building said to be for agricultural use with subsequent modification to include features indicating its use as a bungalow—the building was not designed for the purposes of agriculture. [1982] J.P.L. 55.

S.24. DEVELOPMENT ORDERS

24–118 Works are requisite for the use of land for the purposes of agriculture provided that they are for a purpose forming part of the overall use of land for the purposes of agriculture. If it relates to livestock, the livestock do not need to be dependent upon the land. Building and concrete drive needed for agriculture purposes. [1982] J.P.L. 126.

24–119 Class VI is not limited to looking at current agriculture use and must be interpreted as looking to the future (and therefore intention). An agricultural dwelling can normally be justified only in connection with some change in the enterprise, and it is then necessary to consider whether the enterprise after the change or the new enterprise has a good prospect of long-term viability. [1982] J.P.L. 584.

24–120 Limited grazing of cattle not carried out for the purposes of a trade or business and therefore not an agricultural use within Class VI. [1983] J.P.L. 178.

24–121 Excavation of ponds for fish-farming. Excavation to a greater depth than required for the breeding of carp. Excavation was not for agricultural purposes. [1983] J.P.L. 256.

24–122 Tipping. Whether requisite for the use of the land for the purposes of agriculture. "Requisite" defined as "reasonably necessary." [1983] J.P.L. 561.

24–123 For the deposit of soil on agricultural land to come within Class VI evidence is necessary that engineering operations are involved requisite for the use of the land for agriculture. Inadequate plans and provision to show that works were engineering operations that would benefit the land. [1983] J.P.L. 618.

24–124 Grain bin, weaner boxes and slurry tank placed on land. They were reasonably necessary for the continuation of the established agricultural activity on the surrounding land and came within Class VI. [1983] J.P.L. 621.

24–125 Extension of a trout farm by the construction of further tanks did not come within Class VI because although land to be used was land adjacent to agricultural land it was not agricultural land. Use of goats grazing to tidy up the land was not an agricultural use. The fact that food for fish would have to be imported was irrelevant to question of agricultural use. [1983] J.P.L. 687.

24–126 Whether tipping was permitted development. [1983] J.P.L. 826.

24–127 Erection of building—Held not requisite for the use of the land for agriculture as little agricultural activity and because of buildings appearance and size. [1984] J.P.L. 535.

24–128 Land used only for grazing of horses used for recreational purposes is not agricultural land within Class VI. [1985] J.P.L. 63.

24–129 Tipping of waste materials was not permitted development within Class VI as the land was not agricultural land, and works did not amount to engineering operations. [1985] J.P.L. 131.

24–130 Class VI—"engineering operations" may reasonably include works which involve the application or exercise of engineering skills. Construction of a farm irrigation reservoir was permitted development within Class VI, but see now South Oxfordshire D.C. v. Keene [1985] J.P.L. 270.

24–131 A farmhouse and its garden do not constitute agricultural land. When two areas of agricultural land are separated by a substantial feature, such as a made-up public road, which is clearly not in itself agricultural land, the land on either side cannot be regarded as a single piece of land for the purpose of Class VI. [1985] J.P.L. 336.

24–132 In determining for the purposes of Class VI whether building "requisite" for agriculture, the only matters to be considered are those which stem from the inter-relationship between the land and the building and wider planning implications are excluded. Erection of calf-rearing building was not requisite as building of its size and height not needed. [1986] J.P.L. 230.

24–133 In calculating whether site of more than one acre comes within Class VI land which was divided by four metre public road did not prevent it from being one site and not two. It would have been different if the two parts of the land had been a long distance apart. [1986] J.P.L.

24–134 Stables and building which were erected on land which was used for growing of hay and grazing, did not come within Class VI(1) as probably not "agricultural land" and in any case construction of the buildings not requisite for the purposes of agriculture because of shape and size of buildings. [1986] J.P.L. 462.

6. Class VII

24–135 A building capable of providing overnight accommodation is more in the nature of a dwelling than a shelter and is not needed as such for the purposes of carrying on forestry, so is not within Class VII. [1971] J.P.L. 598.

24–136 Erection of a workshop building to replace one destroyed by fire is not an extension or alteration of a building within Class VIII(1)(iv). [1972] J.P.L. 582.

7. Class VIII: Development for Industrial Purposes

34–137 Brooks and Burton v. Sec. of State for Environment [1977] 1 W.L.R. 1294, C.A. Class VIII does not apply when a use is not carried on under a planning permission, even though the use is immune from attack because of the four-year rule.

24–138 South Glamorgan C.C. v. Hobbs (Quarries) [1980] J.P.L. 35. Development of a plant for the development of ready-mixed concrete was not within Classes VIII and XIX(2).

24–139 Welsh Aggregates v. Sec. of State for Environment (1983) 265 E.G. 43, C.A. Access road forming part of the planning unit of a quarry was incidental or ancillary to the achievement of the purpose of operations of quarry. Construction of an access road was an industrial process permitted in the absence of specific planning permission under Class VIII.

24–140 Erection of a permanent gantry (overhead crane) amounts to development, but comes within Class VIII(1)(i) as a private conveyor. [1971] J.P.L. 285.

24–141 Extension and alteration of an industrial building—Class VIII(1)(iv). Where a proposal involves the total demolition and replacement of the original building or the remaining original building the permission contained in Class VIII(1) is not available. Once a building is erected either by express planning permission or as permitted development it does not become an original building for the purposes of calculating future permitted development but counts towards exhausting the permitted tolerance. [1982] J.P.L. 457.

24–142 Extension of an existing industrial building. Limits of permitted development are not affected by any extension carried out under specific planning permission, unless a condition of the permission so requires. Extension materially affecting the external appearance of an existing building is not within permission for industrial development. [1984] J.P.L. 199.

8. Class IX: Repairs to Unadopted Streets and Private Ways

24–143 Maintenance—works to a private roadway are within Class IX. [1966] J.P.L. 728.

9. Class X

24-144 Premises can be used as a wholesale warehouse by an undertaking which is carrying on a retail sales business. Storage of cars on a site which would be moved to showroom on a separate site when members of the public wished to view them was use as a wholesale warehouse or a repository and came within Class X. [1969] J.P.L. 419.

10. Class XII: Development under Local Private Acts

24-145 Pyx Granite Co. v. Min. of Housing & Local Govt. [1960] A.C. 260, H.L. The Malvern Hills Act 1924 authorised quarrying operations.

24-146 Class XII (development authorised by private or local Act)—refusal on ground of amenity restricted to actual or apprehended injury to visual amenity by virtue of reference to "design or external appearance." [1972] J.P.L. 529.

11. Class XV

24-147 Retail sales within a limited range of products necessary for the treatment of illness or injury were incidental to the Class XV use of premises as a pharmaceutical dispensary. *De minimis* sales outside the Class ignored. [1969] J.P.L. 99.

12. Class XVII

24-148 Buildings or plant needed for the handling of traffic at terminals and the necessary storage of goods before and after movement by rail comes within the Class. The carrying-out of industrial processes on railway operational land by virtue only of the fact that the materials used in the process have been brought to the site and that it is more convenient and more economic to carry out the manufacture there than to transfer the material to another site does not come within the class. [1971] J.P.L. 412.

13. Class XVIII: Development by Statutory Undertakers

24-149 East Barnet U.D.C. v. British Transport Commission [1962] 2 W.L.R. 134, D.C. Use of land for the handling and storage of motor vehicles was in connection with the movement of traffic by rail over operational land and so came within Class XVIII.

24-150 Where development is required solely for the purpose of unloading goods from railway trucks on to the vehicles in which they will continue their journey (whether by rail or otherwise), the development can properly be considered as being required in connection with the movement of goods by rail. Erection of hoppers and elevators and the temporary storage of sand and gravel in transit was permitted development. [1967] J.P.L. 49.

24-151 Extent of Class XVIII. A permission for development of railway operational land required in connection with the movement of traffic by rail. [1976] J.P.L. 652.

24-152 Class XVIII was not applicable to the removal of a bridge where the movement of rail traffic had ceased and only defined statutory undertakers could benefit from it. [1983] J.P.L. 616.

14. Class XIX: Development by Mineral Undertakers

24-153 English Clays Lovering Pochin & Co. v. Plymouth Corpn. [1974] 1 W.L.R. 742, C.A. The words "adjacent to" in class XVIII(2) are to be construed as meaning close to or nearby or lying by, so that any development would not appear to be other than a growth of a site.

Per curiam: The words "and belonging to" indicate that the land on which the building is to be erected is, or is to be, dedicated to the service of the mine in, or adjacent to which it is, and not to the service of some distant mine.

24–154 South Glamorgan C.C. v. Hobbs (Quarries) Ltd. [1980] J.P.L. 35. The erection of a ready-mixed concrete batching plant not within para. 2 of Class XIX as not reasonably required in connection with the winning and working or treatment or disposal of minerals.

15. Class XXII: Use as a Caravan Site

24–155 Stationing of a caravan for residential occupation by a person carrying out building operations on a self-help or "do-it-yourself" basis came within Class XXII and para. 9 Sched. 1 to the Caravan Sites Act 1960. [1982] J.P.L. 724.

SECTION 25. FORM AND CONTENT OF APPLICATIONS

A. General

25–01 Pilkington v. Sec. of State for Environment [1973] 1 W.L.R. 1527, D.C. Landowner can make as many mutually inconsistent applications for planning permission on the same piece of land as he wishes, but once he implements one he cannot then implement another.

Per curiam: It is the duty of the planning authority to deal with each application on its individual merits, it does not have to relate one to another.

25–02 Kent C.C. v. Sec. of State for Environment [1976] 33 P. & C.R. 70. Where an application consists of a number of separate and divisible elements it is lawful for them to be separately dealt with. You can have part permission and part refusal.

25–03 Britannia (Cheltenham) Ltd. v. Sec. of State for Environment [1978] J.P.L. 554. An applicant and a planning authority can agree to a variation of an application at any time up to the determination of the application.

25–04 Edmunds v. Sec. of State for Environment [1981] J.P.L. 52, D.C. Plan for a planning application modified by an accompanying letter stating it was impossible to provide a perfectly accurate plan.

25–05 Definition of the area of a planning application is a matter for the applicant, the planning authority cannot require an amended plan. [1971] J.P.L. 125.

25–06 A decision cannot be given on an application to change the use of a building which has not been erected. [1970] J.P.L. 348.

B. Outline Applications

25–07 Hamilton v. West Sussex C.C. [1958] 2 W.L.R. 873. Outline permission to build a cottage on a farm of 40 acres. Application for approval of reserved matters showed the cottage at a different location within the site. Held not to be a fresh application and that the change of access on a private road was immaterial.

25–08 Shermara Ltd. v. Luton Corp. (1967) 18 P. & C.R. 520. *Hamilton v. West Sussex C.C.* doubted.

Outline permission for three five-storey blocks of flats on a north-south axis with 64 garages. New plan proposed for four four-storey blocks of flats arranged diagonally. Planning authority was entitled to refuse permission on the grounds that it would prejudice the development of adjoining sites, did not provide adequate parking and did not provide adequate vehicular access. It was a radical departure from the planning principles in the outline permission.

25–09 Cardiff Corpn. v. Sec. of State for Wales (1971) 22 P. & C.R. 718. An application for full planning permission for a development already authorised by outline planning permission can be construed as an application for the approval of reserved matters. A local planning authority cannot eliminate an outline planning permission merely by failing to consider and approve detailed plans which are submitted in time for an appeal to be entered to the Minister either against a refusal or a mere failure to approve.

25–10 Chelmsford Corp. v. Sec. of State for Environment (1971) 22 P. & C.R. 880.

(1) Outline planning permission granted with conditions as to "lay-out" will not necessarily reserve to the local planning authority the power to decide whether walls or fences for decorative purposes and to protect privacy should be provided and if so where.

(2) "Lay-out" meant the arrangement of the various parts of the development, and not the methods by which its boundaries were to be enclosed.

25–11 Calcaria Construction Co. (York) Ltd. v. Sec. of State for Environment (1974) 27 P. & C.R. 435. Outline permission for the "erection of a warehouse for wholesale and retail distribution of foodstuffs and household goods" gave permission for a building whose primary purpose was the storage of goods not the retail of goods. Therefore it was correct to refuse detailed permission where the primary purpose was retail. It may be different if permission is obtained for a "discount warehouse" or "wholesale warehouse."

25–12 R. v. Sec. of State for Environment, ex p. Percy Bilton (1975) 31 P. & C.R. 154. Where outline permission is made subject to the approval of siting details, that approval can be given in stages. In the case of a 22-acre site, where outline permission was subject to the approval of siting details, it was impossible to argue that outline permission had been a collection of separate agreements, and there was nothing in the course of dealings to suggest any variation of permission. Therefore, as parts of the site been developed, outline permission had not time-expired.

25–13 Chalgray Ltd. v. Sec. of State for Environment (1976) 33 P. & C.R. 10. Application for approval of reserved matters may not include matters not reserved by the outline permission.

25–14 Lewis Thirkwell Ltd. v. Sec. of State for Environment [1978] J.P.L. 844. Where outline permission for residenial development resulted in the urbanisation of a bridle path, that urbanisation could not be relied on as a reason for dismissing a detailed application.

A proposed layout cannot be rejected because of disagreement on the line of the public right of way as that involves different legal procedures.

25–15 Heron Ltd. v. Manchester Council [1978] 1 W.L.R. 937, C.A. It is possible to make more than one application for the approval of reserved matters covering the same ground. Application for the approval of reserved matters need not cover all matters of detail reserved in the outline planning permission although it is permitted to refuse to deal with one of a number of interrelated matters in isolation on planning grounds.

Per Lord Denning M.R.: If an applicant wishes to depart from outline permission or its conditions in any significant respect, he must apply for a new planning permission.

25–16 Hammersmith & Fulham L.B.C. v. Sec. of State for Environment [1980] J.P.L. 750, D.C. Where a council detailed plans on an outline application, on subsequent appeal the Inspector was entitled to treat an application as one for full planning permission.

25–17 Centre Hotels (Cranston) Ltd. v. Sec. of State for Environment [1982] J.P.L. 108, D.C. Reserved matters may not be used to alter the nature of the development for which outline permission has been granted.

S.25. FORM AND CONTENT OF APPLICATIONS

25–18 Inverclyde D.C. v. The Lord Advocate (1982) 43 P. & C.R. 375.
(1) Part of an application can be abandoned without invalidating all of the application.
(2) The requirements of s.6(1) of the Town and Country Planning (General Development) (Scotland) Order 1975 are directory not mandatory.
(3) The application was not one in which technical rules are appropriate and the Secretary of State could call for further details in order to deal fairly with the application.

25–19 Etheridge v. Sec. of State for Environment [1984] J.P.L. 340, D.C. Grant of an application for full planning permission is effectively the same as an approval of details reserved in the outline planning permission.

25–20 Lobb v. Sec. of State for Environment [1984] J.P.L. 336, D.C. Approval of reserved matters in respect of a plot subject to two outline planning permissions.— The Secretary of State had failed to consider whether the approval of reserved matters could be taken to relate to more than one of the extant outline permissions. Implementation of the later outline permission materially affected implementation of the original outline permission.

25–21 R. v. Castle Point D.C., ex p. Brooks [1985] J.P.L. D.C. 473. Outline permission for a "bungalow" does not empower a local planning authority to approve detailed plans for a large house.

25–21a R. v. Hammersmith and Fulham L.B.C., ex p. Greater London Council [1986] J.P.L. 528. Outline planning permission granted for major development including bus garage application for approval of reserved matters omitted bus garage. Held applying *Heron Corp.* v. *Manchester City Corp.* that planning authority entitled to treat application as still within the ambit of outline permission.

25–22 Outline application for planning permission with detailed plans was effectively a detailed application and dismissed because of objections to details without prejudice to the submission of a revised application. [1966] J.P.L. 292.

25–23 Application for detailed approval was inconsistent with outline planning permission. [1966] J.P.L. 671.

25–24 Detailed approval following outline planning permission. Incorporation of plans and drawings into permission. [1967] J.P.L. 114.

25–25 Application for approval of details following outline planning permission. Whether properly made in accordance with outline permission. [1967] J.P.L. 237.

25–26 On an application for approval of reserved matters, the approval of details only can be dealt with and account cannot be taken of any objections which do not relate to those details. [1967] J.P.L. 555.

25–27 Permission for application expressed to be outline, but accompanied by plans with details of siting design, external appearance and access. [1967] J.P.L. 666.

25–28 Sketches submitted with an outline application treated as illustrative only. [1968] J.P.L. 111.

25–29 On an application for approval of details a local planning authority are confined to considering the details put before them and may not consider whether the development is appropriate. A plan with planning application marking a shop as "Ironmonger-shop" does not restrict the shop to an ironmonger's shop. [1969] J.P.L. 156.

25–30 Where no conditions relating to screen walls and fences were reserved on an outline planning application, they could not be imposed on the approval of reserved matters. [1970] J.P.L. 350.

S.25. FORM AND CONTENT OF APPLICATIONS

25–31 Application following an outline permission to be construed as an application for approval of reserved matters. [1970] J.P.L. 545.

25–32 Whether application is for approval of details following outline permission or for full planning permission. [1974] J.P.L. 45.

25–33 Once reserved matters have been approved following a grant of outline planning permission, they cannot be revised or varied by a further submission of reserved matters under the same outline consent. [1975] J.P.L. 555.

25–34 Unable to grant planning permission specifying a means of access other than that specified in outline application. [1975] J.P.L. 749.

25–35 Conditions of detailed permission following outline permission must be related to the submitted details and be consistent with the outline permission. [1980] J.P.L. 354.

C. Informal Applications and Estoppel

25–36 Southend-on-Sea Corp v. Hodgson [1961] 2 W.L.R. 806, D.C. Estoppel cannot be raised so as to hinder a local authority in the exercise of a discretion conferred on it by statute.

25–37 Wells v. Min. of Housing & Local Govt. [1967] 1 W.L.R. 1000, C.A. A local planning authority are entitled to make a determination under s.53 of the 1971 Act without the necessity of a fomal written application and an application for planning permission contains an implicit invitation to do so.

25–38 Lever Finances Ltd. v. Westminster (City) L.B.C. [1971] W.L.R. 732, C.A. Proved practice of local authority to allow its planning officers to tell applicants whether a variation was material. As applicants had acted upon it, it bound the local authority.

Per Lord Denning M.R.: Planning permission includes immaterial variations. If a planning officer tells a developer that a variation is immaterial and the developer acts upon it, the authority are bound by it.

A public authority may be bound by a representation made by one of its officers within the scope of his ostensible authority on which another acts. A person dealing with a local authority is entitled to assume that all necessary internal resolutions concerning delegation have been passed.

Per Sachs L.J.: In some circumstances the formalities of an application could be dispensed with.

25–39 Brooks and Burton Ltd. v. Sec. of State for Environment (1976) 35 P. & C.R. 27, D.C. Any attempt to expand the doctrine of estoppel as applied to local planning authorities is to be deprecated. It is necessary to strike a balance between the ability to give general and imprecise advice and the total drying-up of all advice from planning authorities.

25–40 Western Fish Products Ltd. v. Penwith D.C. [1981] 2 All E.R., C.A. The principle of proprietary estoppel only applies where the plaintiff, encouraged by the defendant, acts to his detriment in relation to his own land in the expectation of acquiring a right over the defendant's land and therefore it has no application to representations made by a planning authority or its officers as to the need for planning permission.

An estoppel cannot be raised to prevent a statutory body exercising its statutory discretion or performing its statutory duty, and therefore even if a council's officers, while acting in the apparent scope of their authority, purport to determine a planning application in advance, it is not binding on the council because it alone has power under the 1971 Act to determine planning applications. Furthermore, although a planning authority might be bound by the decisions of an officer if the power to decide the particular matter had been, or appeared to be, delegated to the

S.25. FORM AND CONTENT OF APPLICATIONS

officer, for an estoppel to arise in such circumstances there had to be some evidence, over and above the mere fact of the officer's position, on which the applicant was justified in thinking that the officer's statement would bind the council.

Ratio of *Wells* v. *Min. of Housing & Local Govt.* was that it was unnecessary for a person to make a formal application for a written determination under s.53 that planning permission was not required if an application for planning permission had already been submitted, since the application for permission impliedly invites the authority to determine that permission is not required, but this principle does not extend to cases where no application for permission has been made: in those cases a formal written application is still required.

25–41 Bedfordia Plant Ltd. v. Sec. of State for Environment [1981] J.P.L. 122, D.C. Whether estoppel applied was a question of fact and degree for the Secretary of State. No authority to grant established use certificate and little evidence that the local authority had stated that use established.

25–42 Failure to establish estoppel. [1975] J.P.L. 609.

25–43 Failure to make out an alleged statement to found an estoppel. [1976] J.P.L. 766.

25–44 Alleged estoppel was no evidence of detriment. [1976] J.P.L. 527.

25–45 Letter from an officer of the Council stating an opinion that planning permission was not required was held to be binding on the Council. [1976] J.P.L. 587.

25–46 Estoppel of a local planning authority in respect of a letter from the Environmental Health Officer as to permitted use. [1977] J.P.L. 118.

25–47 Appellants not prejudiced by earlier statements made by the planning authority that development was not involved so that estoppel could not arise. [1978] J.P.L. 200.

25–48 The Secretary of State thought it unlikely that the doctrine of estoppel applies at all to statements made or undertakings given by applicants for planning permission. [1982] J.P.L. 733.

25–49 Following informal inquiry, officer wrote letter stating that proposed works constituted permitted development. It was held, applying *Western Fish Products* v. *Penwith D.C.* that this did not estop the council, as it was an informal inquiry the answer to which was not binding on the elected members of the planning authority. [1986] J.P.L. 386.

SECTION 26. PUBLICATION OF NOTICES OF APPLICATION

26–01 J.J. Steeples v. Derbyshire C.C. [1984] 3 All E.R. 468. Sections 26 and 27 do not apply to developments by or on land of local planning authorities: s.270(1).

26–02 "Amusement arcade" and "funfair" are not synonymous for the purposes of the General Development Order. Items commonly associated with a "funfair" include roundabouts, "dodgem" cars and shooting machines. Refusal of permission for the use of shop premises as an amusement arcade (in a listed building) as less attractive than a shop. [1979] J.P.L. 56.

26–03 Planning application for the use of land as a caravan site. It was necessary to advertise the application under s.26 because the subsequent issue of a site licence would normally entail a requirement for foul drainage which, if permission were granted, would be permitted development under Class XXIII of the General Development Order thus by-passing s.26. [1983] J.P.L. 138.

26–04 Application to create artificial lakes for fish production. Whether s.26 and Art. 8(1)(b) of the General Development Order applied. Held that the creation of the lakes would not amount to "use of land for the disposal of refuse and waste materials." [1983] J.P.L. 147.

SECTION 27. NOTIFICATION OF APPLICATIONS TO OWNERS AND AGRICULTURAL TENANTS

27–01 Ayles v. Romsey & Stockbridge R.D.C. [1944] 42 L.G.R. 210. Case under the Town and Country Planning Act 1932. A builder with no present or prospective interest in land, who had been refused a planning application, had not sufficient interest to challenge the refusal.

27–02 Hanily v. Min. of Housing & Local Govt. [1952] 2 Q.B. 444, D.C.

(1) Anyone who genuinely hopes to acquire the interest in a piece of land can properly apply for planning permission.

(2) Although proceedings before a planning authority may be in the nature of judicial proceedings that does not mean that the procedure followed in the courts of law must be adopted and there was no ground for saying that any particular notice should be given to an owner or that the owner should be given an opportunity of being heard.

27–03 Frescati v. Walker [1975] I.R. 177. Case under the Eire legislation (Local Government (Planning and Development) Act 1963). Applicant for planning permission needed the approval of the owner so that he would be able to carry out the proposed development.

27–04 R. v. Bradford-on-Avon U.D.C., ex p. Boulton [1964] 1 W.L.R. 1136, D.C. Planning authority had jurisdiction to entertain an application for planning permission if it was accompanied by a genuine certificate in the approved terms signed by the actual applicant, and a factual error in the certificate did not deprive the authority of jurisdiction.

Where an application for outline permission is followed by an application for approval of details, the outline application is the "application for planning permission" and only that application need be accompanied by a certificate.

Per curiam: No prejudice that mistake of ownership of a party wall—planning authority can approve a proposal even though there may be some difficulty in carrying it out.

Now see *Main* v. *Swansea C.C.*

27–05 English v. Dedham Vale Properties Ltd. [1978] 1 W.L.R. 93, Ch. Where a purchaser obtains planning permission by purporting to act as agent for the vendor, but in fact without his knowledge or approval, he may be liable to account to the vendor for any additional value accruing thereby to the land over and above the agreed purchase price.

27–06 Main v. Swansea C.C. (1985) 49 P. & C.R. 26. A certificate under s.27 that the applicant was the sole owner was incorrect as a small part was owned by someone else unknown. Held that such a factual error made the subsequent grant of planning permission invalid but that the court had a discretion to decide whether to declare the grant invalid.

Failure to give notice under Art. 11 of the General Development Order (land within 67 metres of a highway), meant that the court had the discretion to hold a grant of planning permission invalid on the request of anyone with sufficient interest.

27–07 Notice of refusal was invalid where no certificate of notice had been given to any landowner as agricultural tenant and there was therefore no power for the Minister to hear an appeal. [1966] J.P.L. 492.

27–08 Applicant for planning permission is not required to show a legal right to proposed access. [1967] J.P.L. 615.

27–09 Failure by an applicant to serve a statutory notice on the owner of a footpath and the fact that certificates were inaccurate did not invalidate the application or affect the Minister's jurisdiction to determine the appeal. [1970] J.P.L. 48.

27–10 Planning application and appeal were invalidated where there was non-compliance with the requirements of s.27 as to the certificate of ownership or notification. [1973] J.P.L. 612.

27–11 Planning application made in the landowner's name but without his knowledge and authority was void as was the permission granted on it. [1978] J.P.L. 568.

SECTION 29. DETERMINATION OF APPLICATIONS

A. The Procedures for Determining a Planning Application.

29–01 Brayhead (Ascot) Ltd. v. Berkshire C.C. [1964] 2 W.L.R. 507. Under article 5(9) of the Town and Country Planning General Development Order 1950 the planning authority had a mandatory duty to give reasons for granting a conditional planning permission. However, failure to give reasons did not render the condition void nor was an enforcement notice alleging non-compliance with the conditions invalid. "Final determination" means a determination which disposes of the application as between the local authority and the applicant by the receipt by the latter of an effective notice of decision.

29–02 London Ballast Co. Ltd. v. Bucks C.C. (1966) 18 P. & C.R. 446. Where applicant amended his application after the expiry of time limit for planning authority's decision, he could not thereafter allege that the authority was precluded in law from giving a decision on an amended application. His actions were meaningless unless the authority was still competent to decide and he had represented by his conduct that he still wanted a decision. The time limit did not necessarily start afresh on submission of an amended application; the authority's duty was to give its decision in a reasonable time. Eight months was reasonable in this case.

Per curiam: An excess of permitted time may or may not have effect of making a decision voidable depending on all the circumstances.

29–03 James v. Min. of Housing & Local Govt. [1966] 1 W.L.R. 135. Provisions of the General Development Order and Development Charge Applications Regulations 1950 as to the time for determining planning application are directory only. A grant or refusal of planning permission outside time is not void but at most voidable. At any rate if it is accepted and acted upon it is too late to avoid it.

Approved by House of Lords in *James* v. *Sec. of State for Wales* [1966] 3 All E.R. 964.

Dictum of Salmon J. in *Edwick* v. *Sunbury on Thames U.D.C.* (*No. 2*) [1962] 1 Q.B. 229 disapproved.

29–04 Slough Estates v. Slough B.C. [1969] 2 W.L.R. 1157, C.A. *Per* Lord Denning M.R.: The grant of planning permission is not validly made until it is formally issued in writing to the applicant.

29–05 RKT Investments Ltd. v. Hackney L.B.C. (1978) 36 P. & C.R. 442, D.C. Where reasons are given for a condition attaching to a planning permission a court should not go behind them unless their bona fides are challenged or it is alleged that there could be no evidence to support them. Where by omission no reasons are given for the condition the reasons may be obtained by extrinsic evidence and the court is entitled to look at all the surrounding circumstances in which the permission was granted in so far as they assist in discerning the reasons. If the purpose or motive is to coerce the applicant into changing the use of other premises that would be *ultra vires*.

29–06 R. v. Yeovil B.C., ex p. Trustees of Elim Pentecostal Church (1971) 23 P. & C.R. 39, D.C. Resolution of a planning committee to grant permission does not constitute a valid permission until notice in writing has been issued to the applicant.

29–07 Norfolk C.C. v. Sec. of State for Environment [1973] 1 W.L.R. 1400, D.C. Where no planning permission was granted the planning authority was entitled to go behind a document purporting to be a planning permission and to refer to an actual resolution amongst other things.

Where a planning officer was only authorised to notify the result of the decision of the local planning authority, there was no planning permission if he mistakenly said that permission was granted.

If an applicant had not acted to his detriment the planning authority could not be estopped from denying the validity of a notice of planning permission.

29–08 R. v. Sheffield C.C., ex p. Mansfield (1978) 37 P. & C.R. 1, D.C. There is no general obligation in planning law to have organised consultations with small and highly independent bodies of persons different from the rest of the community, such as the gypsy community.

29–09 Co-operative Retail Services Ltd. v. Taff-Ely B.C. (1978) 38 P. & C.R. 156. Although provisions of the 1971 Act are not conclusive, taken as a whole they point in favour of the written notice constituting planning permission rather than the resolution of the planning authority, because it would be unjust for time to run against an applicant without knowledge or the means of knowledge and some of the provisions are difficult to reconcile with a grant by resolution.

29–10 Co-operative Retail Services Ltd. v. Taff-Ely B.C. (1979) 39 P. & C.R. 223, C.A. Purported grant of planning permission was invalid and a nullity as on a true construction of the meeting of the district council adopting the report of their sub-committee, there had not been a resolution to grant permission. The clerk to the district council therefore had no authority to issue a grant of planning permission which was therefore *ultra vires* and void and could not be relied upon by bona fide holders of it.

Per curiam: Where the issue is whether a planning permission was ever granted, or whether it was within the power of the local planning authority to grant it, the court is entitled to go behind the purported grant and ascertain the true facts.

A declaration would be granted that purported grant of planning permission was invalid and a nullity.

Per Ormrod L.J.: If a planning permission is valid on its face, it can and must be acted on until it is declared to be void by a competent court. Such orders can be said to be voidable, but the option to avoid lies with the court, not the parties.

Per curiam: Paragraph 51(1) of Sched. 16 to the Local Government Act 1972 has no application where neither authority has power to grant planning permission or (*per* Lord Denning M.R.) where the grant was entirely unauthorised *ultra vires* and of no effect. Whether or not an application "appears to relate to a county matter" (1972 Act, Sched. 16, paras. 15(2) and 32(d)) is a matter for the opinion of the district planning authority; (*per* Browne L.J.) it is not appropriate for review by the courts.

Affirmed by House of Lords see (1980) 42 P. & C.R. 1.

29–11 Steeples v. Derbyshire C.C. [1984] 3 All E.R. 468. Grant of planning permission by a county council after it had entered into a legally enforceable contract to use its best endeavours to obtain planning permission was in breach of natural justice and either voidable or void.

29–12 Bovis Homes (Scotland) Ltd. v. Inverclyde D.C. [1982] S.L.T. 473 [1983] J.P.L. 171. Duty of a local planning authority to issue its notice of determination extends beyond the eight-week period specified in the General Development Order.

S.29. DETERMINATION OF APPLICATIONS

29–13 R. v. Sevenoaks D.C. ex p. Terry [1984] J.P.L. 420. Grant of planning permission where it appeared that the local planning authority were committed to granting planning permission. Permission would only be invalid if the circumstances made it impossible for the planning authority to exercise its discretion properly. It did not matter if a reasonable man might have thought otherwise. The test propounded in *Steeples* v. *Derbyshire C.C.* rejected.

29–14 R. v. Amber Valley D.C., ex p. Jackson [1984] 3 All E.R. 501, D.C. The fact that the majority of a planning authority are politically predisposed as result of council policy in relation to an application for planning permission does not disqualify them from adjudicating, so long as they act fairly and take into account all material considerations.

29–15 R. v. St. Edmundsbury B.C. ex p. Investors in Industry Commercial Properties Ltd. [1985] 3 All E.R. 234. The grant of planning permission by a local planning authority which had a corporate interest in the grant was only invalid if the local planning authority had not genuinely and impartially exercised its discretion. The approach of Glidewell J. in *R.* v. *Sevenoaks D.C., ex p. Terry* preferred to that of Webster J. in *Steeples* v. *Derbyshire C.C.*

29–16 R. v. Carlisle City Council and Sec. of State for Environment, ex p. Cumbrian Co-operative Society [1986] J.P.L. 206. Reg. 4(4) of the Development Plans Directions 1981 directory and not mandatory and so failure to comply did not invalidate a grant of permission. Article 11 of the General Development Order was similarly directory.

29–16a R. v. West Oxfordshire D.C., ex p. Pearce Homes Ltd. [1986] J.P.L. 523. Resolution of planning committee that permission be granted subject to the execution of s.52 agreement but no written notification of grant issued. Held that resolution did not amount to a final decision and in any case grant not complete until written notification according to art. 7(7) of the General Development Order.

29–16b R. v. Torfaen B.C. (amended to Monmouth D.C.), ex p. Jones [1986] J.P.L. 686. Local planning authority under a duty to consider a planning application fairly and this involved treating objectors fairly. Decision quashed because objectors had been unable to make representations as misled by statements of the local planning authority.

B. The Factors to be Considered in Determining the Planning Application: section 29(1).

1. The Development Plan

29–17 Simpson v. Edinburgh Corpn. [1961] S.L.T. 17. Duty to "have regard" to the development plan does not mean "slavishly adhere" and planning permission can be granted which departs from policies in the plan.

29–18 Enfield L.B.C. v. Sec. of State for Environment [1975] J.P.L. 155, D.C. Requirement in s.29 to "have regard to" the development plan does not make adherence to the plan mandatory.

29–19 Niarchos (London) Ltd. v. Sec. of State for Environment (1977) 35 P. & C.R. 259, D.C. In misdirecting himself as to the provisions of the development plan the Secretary of State exceeded his powers.

29–20 Ynystawe Ynyforgan and Glas Gypsy Site Action Group v. Sec. of State for Wales [1981] J.P.L. 874, D.C. Decision letter did not make it clear whether there had been regard to the fact that the development conflicted with the development plan. Decision quashed.

29–21 Holmes and Trustees of the Kingston Meeting Rooms Trust v. Sec. of State for Environment [1983] J.P.L. 476. Failure to take into account whether a proposed development would preserve or improve the open nature of the area within the meaning of para. 9(16)(iii) of the Greater London Development Plan was a failure to take into account a material consideration.

29–22 L.B. Richmond-upon-Thames v. Sec. of State for Environment [1984] J.P.L. 24. Inspector was wrong in considering that the Property Advisory Group's report "Planning Gain" overrode the provision of the local plan.

29–23 Tromans v. Sec. of State for Environment [1983] J.P.L. 474, D.C. Inspector had correctly interpreted the structure plan reference to "Development in the Green Belt, whether new construction or the change of use of an existing building will not normally be allowed . . . " as applying to extensions to existing buildings.

29–24 Westminster C.C. v. Sec. of State for Environment [1984] J.P.L. 27, D.C. Local planning authority was not entitled to rely upon the provisions of the Greater London Development Plan dealing with new offices, given the previous history of the building.

29–25 Kenwood v. Sec. of State for Environment [1984] J.P.L. 36. Inspector was justified in reaching the conclusion that there was a conflict between the structure plan and the local plan and in following the local plan, as laid down by s.14(8).

29–26 R. v. Sevenoaks D.C., ex p. Terry [1984] J.P.L. 420. Planning authority had failed to have regard to the structure plan as required by s.29(1) as the policies had not been referred to the planning committee by the planning officer. The court refused to quash the grant as it was confident that the failure had not affected the outcome.

29–27 Chelmsford B.C. v. Sec. of State for Environment and E.R. Alexander Ltd. [1986] J.P.L. 112. Meaning of the policies contained in the Essex Structure Plan considered.

29–28 Where Structure Plan is approved it is the principal policy document to be considered on residential development rather than the guide-lines in Circulars 10/70 and 122/73. [1980] J.P.L. 200: but see now later decisions.

29–29 Residential development—unit for assessment of a five-year supply of house-building land (Circular 9/80). Excess of demand over supply was not in itself a sufficient reason to outweigh valid planning objections unless it was reflected in an insufficient rate of land release as indicated by the structure plan. [1983] J.P.L. 572.

29–30 Where the district plan differs from Circular 22/80 the Circular must be accorded the greater weight. [1983] J.P.L. 79.

29–31 Erection of a large D.I.Y. store ("retail warehouse")—application of structure plan polices. [1984] J.P.L. 608.

29–32 An informal planning study cannot have the same weight as the approved structure plan. [1985] J.P.L. 136.

29–33 Erection of large "car-based convenience" stores—application of structure plan policies. [1984] J.P.L. 610.

29–34 Where development plan conflicts with non-statutory supplement, it is inappropriate to give much weight to the supplement. [1986] J.P.L. 66.

2. Development Plans in Preparation and Non-statutory Plans

29–35 Myton v. Min. of Housing & Local Govt. (1963) 61 L.G.R. 556, D.C. A planning decision taken by the Minister on appeal based on a sketch plan showing

S.29. DETERMINATION OF APPLICATIONS

proposed changes to the development plan is unobjectionable. Such a decision does not prejudice any public inquiry to be held later on the amendment.

29–36 Marrable Estates v. Sec. of State for Environment (1973) 229 E.G. 967. Boundary of the green belt could be affected by the position of a road. As a secure line had not been fixed, it was valid to refuse on the basis of the green belt.

29–37 Rugby School Governors v. Sec. of State for Environment [1975] J.P.L. 97, D.C. Minister's decision to uphold the policy of the local planning authority not to grant applications prior to the preparation of a master plan was not a failure to exercise his duty on appeal where he had considered the fairness of the policy.

29–38 Link Homes v. Sec. of State for Environment [1976] J.P.L. 430. Preparation of a plan cannot be used as a rubber-stamp objection to the consideration of a planning application but after considering the merits it may be decided that deviation from the proposed plan or policy is not justified.

29–39 Charles Church v. Sec. of State for Environment (1979) 251 E.G. 674, D.C. Decision based on the green belt and not on possible changes in the proposed structure plan upheld.

29–40 Thornville Properties Ltd. v. Sec. of State for Environment [1981] J.P.L. 116, D.C. The fact that a local plan had not been adopted could not be conclusive. The decision must specify what in the plan would nullify the assumption that permission should be granted. It was not enough just to reject on the grounds of prematurity.

29–41 Sheffield C.C. v. Sec. of State for Environment (1979) 251 E.G. 165. Where it was clear that he had given due consideration to all relevant matters, the Secretary of State's failure to mention the draft district plan did not invalidate his decision.

29–42 Allen v. Corpn. of the City of London (1981) 79 L.G.R. 273. A local planning authority is not bound by the provisions of the development plan. An inquiry into a draft local plan could not prevent the local planning authority from exercising its function of determining a planning application.

29–43 Davies v. L.B. of Hammersmith & Fulham [1981] J.P.L. 682. So long as the effect on the draft plan is considered and permission is granted for proper reasons (and not simply to pre-empt the draft plan) it does not matter that permission will pre-empt the plan.

29–44 R. v. Hammersmith & Fulham B.C., ex p. People Before Profit Ltd. [1981] J.P.L. 869. Objections to the plan upheld by the Inspector. So long as the inspector's report was considered permission could be granted even though this went against objections which had been upheld by the inspector.

29–45 Chelmsford B.C. v. Sec. of State for Environment [1985] J.P.L. 554. Interpretation of the draft Chelmsford Town Centre Local Plan—policy to restrict uses other than Class 1 of the Use Classes Order.

29–46 An "improvement line" not formally adopted by the local authority is an inadequate ground for refusing planning permission. [1968] J.P.L. 111.

29–47 Non-statutory town centre map was a material consideration on a planning application. [1972] J.P.L. 344.

29–48 Regard given primarily to an interim development plan where the development plan was not approved. [1972] J.P.L. 733.

29–49 Office and residential developments in Central London. The possibility of the modification of the Initial Development Plan was not a ground for departing from it. [1973] J.P.L. 333.

29–50 Divergence between policy in the present Initial Development Plan and the proposed Greater London Development Plan—reliance placed primarily upon the Initial Development Plan. [1973] J.P.L. 615.

29–51 Local authority's informal non-statutory documents were a material consideration on a planning application. [1974] J.P.L. 44.

29–52 Proposed large office development—relevance of county policy to secure improvement in the local housing situation to permit the growth of established industry and commerce before admitting new firms to the area. [1976] J.P.L. 657.

29–53 Assessment of housing need pending a decision on a county structure plan—permission granted for large-scale residential and ancillary development. [1978] J.P.L. 276.

29–54 The emergence of a local plan is not reason enough to withhold planning permission. While strong local opposition to a proposal must be considered it is not the sole determining factor. It is necessary to take into account the interests of the community as a whole. [1981] J.P.L. 65.

29–55 Permission refused for residential development—as it would be premature pending the local plan Grant of permission prior to the local plan would cause resentment in the village. [1981] J.P.L. 541.

29–56 Grant of planning permission for part only of the land and development included in the application where not altering the substance of the development for which permission was sought in the application, even though contrary to the provision of the subsequently deposited local plan. [1981] J.P.L. 837.

29–57 Indications given in a previous appeal decision overridden by proposals in a draft plan which were firmer than previously, reflected the results of public participation and had been adopted by resolution of the borough councils as a basis for development control. [1984] J.P.L. 125.

29–58 Refusal of permission for a change of use from a single private dwelling to a residential care home because it was contrary to a non-statutory local planning policy. [1985] J.P.L. 432.

3. The Policy of a Presumption in Favour of Granting Permission

29–59 Tempo Discount Warehouse v. Sec. of State for Environment [1979] J.P.L. 98, D.C. There is no burden of proof issue in a planning appeal, despite the guidelines issued by circular that sound and clear-cut reasons should be given for refusing permission. The exercise was on known facts to reach a planning judgment in the light of Ministerial policies.

29–60 Thornville Properties Ltd. v. Sec. of State for Environment [1981] J.P.L. 116. Planning permission should never be refused unless there were positive reasons against it.

29–61 Pye (Oxford) Estates Ltd. v. West Oxfordshire D.C. [1982] J.P.L. 577. The term "burden of proof" was not appropriate in planning appeals but planning authorities have to consider whether there are any sound and clear-cut reasons for the refusal of planning permission.

29–62 Federated Estates Ltd. v. Sec. of State for Environment [1983] J.P.L. 812. Breach of a structure plan policy is a sound and clear-cut reason for refusal of planning permission but in applying those policies there was an initial duty on the local planning authority to inform themselves sufficiently to decide the application and what were reasonable steps would depend on all the circumstances of the case.

29–63 Arlington Securities Ltd. v. Sec. of State for Environment [1985] J.P.L. 550. Inspector's decision was quashed as it failed to spell out in sufficient clarity the sound and clear-cut objections necessary to justify a refusal.

29–64 Rockhold Ltd. v. Sec. of State for Environment and South Oxfordshire D.C. [1986] J.P.L. 130. Meaning of the policies contained in Circular 22/80 considered and the statement of Glidewell J. in *J.A. Pye (Oxford) Estates Limited* v. *Wychavon D.C.* not followed.

4. Government Policies

29–65 Hodgkinson (Ringway) Ltd. v. Bucklow R.D.C. (1972) 225 E.G. 2105. The status of "interim green belt."

29–66 Kent C.C. v. Sec. of State for Environment (1976) 33 P. & C.R. 70. The policy of other Government departments is relevant.

29–67 Link Homes Ltd. v. Basildon D.C. [1977] J.P.L. 310. Circular 122/73 was a relevant consideration and had been properly applied by the inspector.

29–68 French Kier Developments Ltd. v. Sec. of State for Environment [1977] J.P.L. 311. Decision quashed as there were no real reasons given for rejecting the strong presumption in favour of housing development expressed in policy circulars.

29–69 Hope v. Sec. of State for Environment [1979] J.P.L. 104. Consideration of Circular 122/73.

29–70 Peak Park Joint Planning Board v. Sec. of State for Environment [1979] J.P.L. 618. Circular 17/69 (considerations on application for renewal of a planning permission) was not a planning policy consideration. If anything it was some form of administrative policy unrelated to planning and therefore *ultra vires*: but see South Oxfordshire D.C. v. S.O.S.E.

29–71 Bradford M.B.C. v. Sec. of State for Environment [1980] J.P.L. 752. Application for the demolition and the erection of a new building was classified by the inspector as being a "rebuilding" within the meaning of the term in the Development Control Policy Notes. Held that the inspector had acted correctly.

29–72 Sears Blok v. Sec. of State for Environment [1982] J.P.L. 248. The power of inspectors to make or change policy considered.

29–73 J.A. Pye (Oxford) Estates Ltd. v. West Oxfordshire D.C. [1982] J.P.L. 577. A draft circular was not a relevant consideration for a planning decision, but if a relevant circular came into existence between the hearing and the decision it was a material factor of which account must be taken. There was no reference to Circular 22/80 and so it was presumed that the Secretary of State had wrongly failed to consider it.

29–74 R. v. Worthing B.C., ex p. Burch [1984] J.P.L. 261, D.C. Ministry of Housing and Local Government Circular 49/63 setting out the procedure whereby the Secretary of State could express an opinion that on an appeal he would give permission for the development of certain Crown lands which a Government department might wish to sell was unlawful because it constrained the planning authority to grant any subsequent application for planning permission thereby depriving local people of their right to be heard and make representations.

Now see Town and Country Planning Act 1984.

29–75 Comben Homes (Midlands) Ltd. v. Sec. of State for Environment [1985] J.P.L. 321. Interpretation of Circular 22/80.

29–76 Chelmsford B.C. v. Sec. of State for Environment [1985] J.P.L. 316. Inspectors had no powers to lay down general policy or give decisions which would be regarded as precedents.

29–77 Rockhold Ltd. v. Sec. of State for Environment and South Oxfordshire D.C. [1986] J.P.L. 130. Inspectors in determining planning appeals are free to disagree with the decisions of other inspectors. However, if previous decision was drawn to the attention of an inspector, he should state if he disagreed with it and give his reasons.

29–78 Dimsdale Developments (South East) Ltd. v. Sec. of State for Environment and Hounslow L.B.C. [1986] J.P.L. 276. Court reluctantly took into account after dinner speech by Minister in determining what were the content of Government policies. Although such policies had to be taken into account by inspector, they were not to be given the force of law.

29–79 Penwith D.C. v. Sec. of State for Environment and Main Street Marketing Ltd. [1986] J.P.L. 432. Decision letter of the inspector failed to deal with argument based on Development Policy Note No. 11 on amusement centres. This had been specifically raised by the applicant and so decision invalid either because it had not had regard to this consideration or had failed to give adequate reasons.

29–79a E.C. Gransden v. Sec. of State for the Environment [1986] J.P.L. 519. Policy statements in Circulars cannot make what would otherwise be a material planning consideration an irrelevant consideration.

29–80 Application to extract sand and gravel—policies in Circular 21/84 applied. [1984] J.P.L. 465.

29–81 Not the intention of Circular 22/80 that a new purpose-built industrial estate should be built, on permission granted under its aegis, in a countryside location. [1985] J.P.L. 349.

29–82 Lengthy analysis of all submitted material on issue as to whether an adequate five-year supply of housing land inappropriate where site only involves 15 dwellings. [1985] J.P.L. 418.

29–83 Conflict between Ministry Circular and Structure Plan—appeal decided on basis of Ministry Circular. [1985] J.P.L. 898.

29–84 Residential development in rural coastal areas. Restrictive policies in development plan sufficient to rebut presumption in favour of development because of shortfall in five-year supply of building land. [1986] J.P.L. 555.

29–85 Example of the application of the policies regarding five-year supply of building land in Circulars 22/80 and 14/85. [1986] J.P.L. 551.

5. *Other Material Considerations*

(a) The general approach to what are planning considerations

29–86 Esdell Caravan Parks Ltd. v. Hemel Hempstead R.D.C. [1965] 3 W.L.R. 1238, C.A. [Caravan Site Licence case]. Conditions imposed on caravans site licence must be fairly and reasonably relevant to the use of land as a caravan site and not be pure planning considerations. Green Belt a pure planning consideration. Statement by Lord Denning MR as to what are planning considerations.

29–87 Stringer v. Min. of Housing & Local Govt. [1970] 1 W.L.R. 1281. Material considerations are not confined to matters relating to an amenity. Any consideration relating to the use and development of land is capable of being a planning consideration and whether it is material depends on the circumstances of each case. It is possible to have a particular policy for an area around the appeal site provided that policy is not pursued in disregard of other relevant considerations. There is an entitlement to consider whether the proposed development is compatible with the proper and desirable use of other land in the area.

S.29. DETERMINATION OF APPLICATIONS

29–88 Bradwell Industrial Aggregates v. Sec. of State for Environment [1981] J.P.L. 276. The Secretary of State and his inspector had failed to take into account several relevant considerations, including economic and social factors.

(b) Matters regulated by other statutes

29–89 Westminster Bank Ltd. v. Min. of Housing and Local Govt. [1970] 2 W.L.R. 645, H.L. Planning authority could refuse permission because development might prejudice future road-widening, even though no improvement line drawn, and no compensation payable. The fact that powers were available under the Highways legislation, which provided for compensation, did not prevent the use of planning powers.

29–90 Hoveringham Gravels v. Sec. of State for Environment [1975] 2 W.L.R. 897. Archaeological considerations are material, and so you can take into account the effect of a proposal on a local monument. Ancient monuments by their inclusion in the Ancient Monuments Acts are not taken out of the ambit of planning.

29–91 Lewis Thirkwell Ltd. v. Sec. of State for Environment [1978] J.P.L. 844. Proposed layout cannot be rejected because of a disagreement on the line of a public right of way as that involves different legal procedures.

29–92 Ladbroke (Rentals) Ltd. v. Sec. of State for Environment [1981] J.P.L. 427. Disturbance or annoyance caused by a casino to other occupiers in the vicinity was a relevant planning consideration. It was irrelevant that similar considerations might apply in Gaming Act powers.

29–93 London Borough of Newham v. Sec. of State for the Environment [1986] J.P.L. 607. The question of whether the powers to take action against noise nuisance under the Control of Pollution Act 1974 precluded planning conditions requiring noise insulation considered but not decided.

29–94 Whether or not premises are capable of providing satisfactorily the type of accommodation for which permission is sought is a proper planning consideration even if the proposal complies with housing and public health requirements. Occupancy and facilities should not be left entirely to housing and public health requirements. Division of premises into flats or to permit multi-occupation has an effect on the neighbourhood if it is composed of houses in single occupation. [1967] J.P.L. 417.

29–95 Permission for an increase in the number of caravans at caravan site—internal site matters should be left to the site licensing authority. [1972] J.P.L. 407.

29–96 Planning permission for a yacht marina granted without regard for the possible detrimental effect by obstruction and danger to navigation, in view of other legislation more specifically controlling such matters. [1973] J.P.L. 112.

29–97 Radio and television interference is a matter for British Telecom under the Wireless Telegraphy Act. [1983] J.P.L. 75.

29–98 Planning development controls should not be used for the purposes of health planning. Whether the possible adverse effects of development on local health services and the general employment situation are material considerations. [1983] J.P.L. 142.

29–99 Normally it is preferable not to use planning powers to restrict or control development when specific regulatory powers exist under other legislation, therefore in the majority of cases the control of operations on a waste disposal site should be left to the site licensing stage. (See Circular 5/68). [1983] J.P.L. 695.

29–100 Radio mast and aerial in the garden of a dwelling-house. Interference with neighbours' television appliances was a relevant planning consideration. As the only method of control open to the planning authority was to issue temporary planning permission so that it could monitor the use of the radio mast, there was nothing wrong with time-limited permission. [1983] J.P.L. 760.

29–101 Imposition of a time-limit on planning permission to ensure the proper maintenance of a building is improper. The durability of materials of construction is a matter for Building Regulations control and is not a planning issue. [1985] J.P.L. 70.

(c) Protection of private interests

29–102 William Boyer & Sons v. Min. of Housing & Local Govt. (1968) 20 P. & C.R. 176. Where an application is made for permission to extract gravel from a part of gravel-bearing land, it is not irrelevant to consider the effect of the granting of permission on the rest of the land and on nearby gravel-bearing land.

29–103 Stringer v. Min. of Housing & Local Govt. [1970] 1 W.L.R. 1281. Entitled to consider whether proposed development is compatible with the proper and desirable use of other land in the area.

The protection of the interests of the individual occupier is an important aspect of public interest as a whole.

Interference with a radio telescope was a material consideration.

29–104 J.R.M.C. Management Services Ltd. v. Sec. of State for Environment (1972) 222 E.G. 1593. Protection of adjoining occupiers' special interests in clear air was a material planning consideration. It is irrelevant that it gave them a benefit beyond their common-law rights.

29–105 Barrat Developments (Eastern) Ltd. v. Sec. of State for Environment [1982] J.P.L. 648. Private interests of an individual householder are a planning consideration.

29–106 Refusal of permission for the extension of a dwelling-house because of the effect on neighbours. [1972] J.P.L. 660.

29–107 Refusal of permission for a residential development which would cause other land with development potential to be landlocked. [1977] J.P.L. 685.

29–108 Any dwelling adjacent to a farmyard must reasonably expect to experience the smells and activity normally associated with a farmyard, but a silage clamp only 22 feet from the walls of an adjacent dwelling impinges unacceptably upon residential amenities. [1985] J.P.L. 336.

(d) Desirability of retaining existing use or promoting different use

29–109 Granada Theatres v. Sec. of State for Environment [1976] J.P.L. 96, D.C. Consideration that refusal of permission would mean the retention of cinema use was an irrelevant consideration. But see *Clyde & Co. v. Sec. of State for Environment.*

29–110 Clyde & Co. v. Sec. of State for Environment [1977] 1 W.L.R. 926. "Material considerations" had to be planning considerations material to the application. The need to preserve existing use was a material consideration. The fact that a housing shortage would be intensified by a change of use to offices was a material consideration.

29–111 Granada Theatres Ltd. v. Sec. of State for Environment [1981] J.P.L. 278. Desirability of retaining an existing use is always a material consideration but where there is no possibility that refusal of permission would result in its retention it is unnecessary to consider it.

The Secretary of State had to consider whether there was a reasonable possibility that the existing use would be preserved if permission was refused, albeit the exist-

S.29. DETERMINATION OF APPLICATIONS

ing use might be a part of a new multiple proposal. The Secretary of State was entitled to consider whether all the possibilities for retention had been considered.

29–112 City of Westminster v. British Waterways Board (1984). The desirability of preserving an existing use is a valid planning consideration, if on the balance of probability the refusal of planning permission for one use will lead to the land being used for the desired use. In contrast, the desirability of protecting the occupation of a particular occupier is not a valid planning consideration. But see *Great Portland Estates* v. *City of Westminster.*

29–113 Great Portland Estates v. City of Westminster (1984). Planning policy to protect certain industrial activities was valid as having a genuine planning purpose.

29–114 Permission for a change of use where a proposed use was unobjectionable, but there were objections to the loss of the existing use. [1976] J.P.L. 463.

29–115 Permission refused for the replacement of the existing non-conforming use by another less objectionable non-conforming use. [1976] J.P.L. 713.

29–116 Refusal of permission to change the use of a theatre/cinema to a bingo and social club where there was the prospect of continuance of its use as a live theatre. [1984] J.P.L. 537.

(e) Section 52 agreements

29–117 Tarmac Properties v. Sec. of State for Wales (1976) 33 P. & C.R. 103. The Secretary of State, when considering an appeal, need not take into account section 52 agreements which have not yet been made.

29–118 McLaren v. Sec. of State for Environment [1981] J.P.L. 423. The Secretary of State was entitled in an appropriate case to take into account the fact that the parties were contemplating entering into a section 52 agreement and were prepared to enter into one if planning permission were granted, but the Secretary of State was not bound to take into account in all cases that there had been discussion of a proposed section 52 agreement.

(f) The need for "planning gain"

29–119 Westminster Renslade Ltd. v. Sec. of State for Environment [1983] J.P.L. 454. A planning application could not be refused because it did not contain provision for the increase in the proportion of parking space subject to public control as to impose such a condition would be *ultra vires* and you cannot get around that by making it clear that planning permission will be refused unless and until a developer makes voluntary provision.

29–120 Westminster C.C. v. Sec. of State for Environment [1984] J.P.L. 27. Views of the Property Advisory Group on planning gain were a relevant consideration.

29–121 Use of residential accommodation for bank offices. Propriety of the suggestion that the appellant should make a financial contribution to the cost of car parks. The fact that it would be advantageous to the bank to have room for any subsequent expansion was not a material consideration. [1967] J.P.L. 493.

29–122 Permission for use of a house in a residential area for residential accommodation and offices because this would lead to the restoration of a listed building. [1975] J.P.L. 239.

29–123 In the absence of any statutory requirement for a developer to contribute financially towards social infrastructure, payments cannot be demanded by the local planning authority even though the need for infrastructure may have arisen in part from the proposed development. Provision of infrastructure should be

S.29. DETERMINATION OF APPLICATIONS

resolved by the local plan and applications conforming with the local plan should be approved. [1980] J.P.L. 841.

29–124 Provision of car-parking for new offices. Possibility of the offer of commuted payment for additional public car parking in place of on-site facilities. Permission could be refused because the proposal did not provide adequate parking facilities but a developer cannot be required to offer a sum towards the cost of public parking. [1982] J.P.L. 463.

29–125 Planning permission for an office building—requirement to make a commuted payment for car parking spaces. Refusal upheld by the Secretary of State. [1982] J.P.L. 665.

29–126 Planning gain—whether provision for some residential or small office units in an office development was appropriate. Wrong to argue that a particular aspect cannot be construed as a planning advantage because it would be achieved in some other development. "Planning advantages" have to be considered in the context of the particular site under consideration. [1983] J.P.L. 265.

(g) Water and sewerage problems

29–127 George Wimpey & Co. v. Sec. of State for Environment [1978] J.P.L. 773. Duty of the Water Authority under s.16 of the Water Act 1973 to provide sewers does not arise until planning permission is granted and therefore the Secretary of State does not have to consider it on a planning application.

29–128 George Wimpey v. Sec. of State for Environment [1978] J.P.L. 776. Flooding problems—the effects of considering proposed improvements upon an application for planning permission for two adjoining sites.

29–129 Erection of dwelling-house—inadequacy of existing sewage disposal works. [1966] J.P.L. 677.

29–130 Refusal of permission for the erection of a dwelling-house in an area where the main sewerage system was overloaded.

29–131 Refusal of permission for residential development in Green Belt area—sewage disposal works inadequate.

29–132 Permission for the extension of a dwelling-house in an area liable to flooding where an extension was unlikely to cause harm in times of flood. [1971] J.P.L. 295.

29–133 Permission for the erection of a dwelling-house refused where the main sewage disposal works were inadequate. [1972] J.P.L. 170.

29–134 Permission for the erection of bungalows where there was an agricultural need for them, but the main drainage system was overburdened. [1973] J.P.L. 119.

29–135 Residential development—refused because of need for special requirement as to drainage. [1974] J.P.L. 108.

29–136 Effect of a proposed development on the water supply in an area was a material consideration. [1974] J.P.L. 307.

29–137 Caravan site—unlimited planning permission was premature where the sewerage facilities were inadequate, notwithstanding that the site had been established for more than 20 years. [1974] J.P.L. 433.

29–138 Refusal of permission for residential development until the developers were able to give adequate assurance of their ability to carry out the construction of sewers through neighbouring land. [1975] J.P.L. 558.

29–139 Possible effect of the disposal of farm-yard manure on water supplies was

S.29. DETERMINATION OF APPLICATIONS

not a relevant consideration on a planning appeal. It was a matter for effective operational management. [1980] J.P.L. 850.

(h) Housing standards

29–140 Refusal of permission for the conversion of a dwelling-house into flatlets because of inadequate lavatory accommodation. [1968] J.P.L. 246.

29–141 Planning authority was justified in refusing permission for the erection of a dwelling-house on account of its design after having sought the advice of a panel of architects. [1971] J.P.L. 293.

29–142 Whilst it was desirable to maintain high internal design standards for residential development, the choice of design was a commercial judgment for the individual developer. [1979] J.P.L. 191.

29–143 Not a function of development control to ensure compliance with housing standards. Parker Norris standards are not applicable to private-sector housing. Requirement of the provision of lifts for four-storey flats was unreasonable. [1980] J.P.L. 704.

29–144 Housing standards were not the province of planning control but planning is concerned with the way in which land and buildings are used and in some cases absence of a lift could significantly impede the use of a building for its intended purpose in which case it might be a proper planning consideration. [1981] J.P.L. 138.

29–145 Internal space in flats is a matter for developers and their customers, if dwellings suitable, and is not a reason for the refusal of planning permission. [1983] J.P.L. 407.

29–146 Housing development—over-provision of a particular type of dwelling is a relevant consideration. Internal space standards are more a matter for the developer and his clients. [1983] J.P.L. 694.

29–147 Planning should primarily be concerned with internal arrangements when they have an influence upon the immediate locality. Use of a house as a hostel. Kitchen arrangements had no impact on the immediate locality. [1984] J.P.L. 458.

(i) Economic considerations

29–148 J. Murphy & Sons v. Sec. of State for Environment [1973] 1 W.L.R. 560. In determining, under s.29(1) whether planning permission should be granted, the Secretary of State is not entitled to have regard to the cost of development as a factor to be considered.

29–149 Hambledon & Chidding Ford P.C. v. Sec. of State for Environment [1976] J.P.L. 502. General proposition in the *Murphy* case that economic considerations are not material may have been stated too widely.

29–150 Sovmot Investments Ltd. v. Sec. of State for Environment [1977] 1 Q.B. 411. Planning authority must be entitled to bear in mind the likelihood of the proposed development being carried out.

29–151 Niarchos (London) Ltd. v. Sec. of State for Environment (1977) 35 P. & C.R. 259. Where a development plan prohibited the extension of time for office permission on premises which could "reasonably be used or adapted for use for residential occupation" it was impossible to decide whether an exception applied without taking into account the cost of adaptation.

29–152 Brighton B.C. v. Sec. of State for Environment [1979] J.P.L. 173. Application to develop part of school land. Profits to be spent on school buildings.

Proper to take into account the possibility that granting permission would result in planning benefit elsewhere.

29–153 Walters v. Sec. of State for Wales [1979] J.P.L. 170. Proper to take into account the financial consequences of planning permission but the grant of planning permission did not depend on the resources and intentions of the applicant. It was not material to consider whether development was economically possible. Sterile permissions are prevented by time-limits.

29–154 Tonbridge & Malling D.C. v. Sec. of State for Environment [1981] J.P.L. 757. Relevant to take into account the waste of resources involved in demolition and the costs incurred in building.

29–155 Calflane Ltd. v. Sec. of State for Environment [1981] J.P.L. 897. The Secretary of State was entitled to bear in mind the question of cost upon the likelihood of a proposed development being carried out and also the prospect of a preferred alternative development being carried into effect.

29–156 Sosmo Trust v. Sec. of State for Environment [1983] J.P.L. 806. Financial effects of a proposed development are a material consideration.

29–157 Finn (Co.) v. Sec. of State for Environment [1984] J.P.L. 734. Planning permission for continued office use refused as contrary to the Greater London Development plan in that it resulted in the loss of residential accommodation. The Secretary of State failed to consider whether refusal of planning permission would result in the reversion of premises to residential use. Status of economic considerations considered.

29–158 R. v. Beverley B.C. ex p. Wilson [1983] C.L.Y. 3721, D.C. Financial position of an applicant for planning permission is a relevant and material consideration under s.29.

29–159 Desirability of profitable use to ensure maintenance of building is a material consideration. [1971] J.P.L. 185.

29–160 Planning permission for oil refinery—importance to local and national economy was a material consideration. [1971] J.P.L. 475.

29–161 The conferring of financial benefits on, or the avoidance of financial disadvantage to, the local planning authority cannot be a material consideration in dealing with a planning application. [1975] J.P.L. 424.

29–162 Viability of an airport irrelevant save as a pointer to indicate the level of public need or demand in the absence of any better evidence. [1975] J.P.L. 695.

29–163 Refusal of permission for the erection of a dwelling for an agricultural worker where there was insufficient evidence that an economically viable agricultural enterprise would be achieved in the foreseeable future. [1977] J.P.L. 537.

29–164 The fact that the refusal of permission for storage use was unlikely to lead to the provision of extra living accommodation because of difficulties of security and uneconomic expenditure was a material consideration. [1979] J.P.L. 54.

(j) Planning rights and general planning background

29–165 Wells v. Min. of Housing & Local Govt. [1967] 1 W.L.R. 1000, C.A. The fact that there was permitted development to erect a 27 feet 6 inches plant was a relevant factor in determining whether to grant permission for a 48 feet plant.

29–166 Walter Hermans & Sons v. Sec. of State for Environment [1975] J.P.L. 351. Application for building in connection with established business—should not consider the case as if there was no existing business and should consider the appli-

S.29. DETERMINATION OF APPLICATIONS

cation in the context of ameliorating conditions. It was irrelevant that applications to expand might be encouraged if the appeal was allowed.

29–167 North Surrey Water Co. v. Sec. of State for Environment (1976) 34 P. & C.R. 140. In holding that the existing planning rights could not be a material consideration the Secretary of State had misdirected himself.

29–168 Small Pressure Castings Ltd. v. Sec. of State for Environment (1973) 222 E.G. 1099. Duty to consider what the applicant could do even if he was not granted permission.

29–169 Spackman v. Sec. of State for Environment [1977] 1 All E.R. 257. Decision quashed as in considering an application for a revised plan the inspector failed to take into account the existence of a valid planning permission which was a material consideration.

29–170 Magoa Services v. Sec. of State for Environment [1978] J.P.L. 383.
(1) Demolition of an existing building gives no ground for granting planning permission for rebuilding.
(2) Inspector is entitled to look at the state of affairs after the development has been carried out.

29–171 Millard v. Sec. of State for Environment (1979) 254 E.G. 733. The consequences of the appellant taking up existing planning permission must be considered when considering whether to grant permission for different development.

29–172 Peak Park Joint Planning Board v. Sec. of State for Environment [1979] J.P.L. 618. Expired planning permission is not a material consideration. But see *South Oxfordshire D.C. v. Sec. of State for Environment.*

29–173 Chris Fashionware (West End) v Sec. of State for Environment [1980] J.P.L. 678. The Secretary of State did not err in disregarding the fact that development had taken place when considering an application for planning permission for development.

29–174 Snowdon v. Sec. of State for Environment [1980] J.P.L. 749, C.A. Inspector has a duty to compare alternative lawful uses on an enforcement notice appeal, where there is a real likelihood that an alternative lawful use will be taken up.

29–175 Enticott & Fullite v. Sec. of State for Environment [1981] J.P.L. 759. Inspector's report quashed as it failed to make clear whether he had considered the question of whether established use rights applied to all, or only part, of the site.

29–176 South Oxfordshire D.C. v. Sec. of State for Environment [1981] 1 W.L.R. 1092. A pre-existing planning permission might be a relevant or material circumstance which a planning authority was permitted to take into account, though it had to do it properly, and, as it was unlikely to be of great moment, not give it more weight than appropriate. There was no reason why general policy in Circular 17/69 should be *ultra vires.*

29–177 Newbury D.C. v. Sec. of State for Environment [1983] J.P.L. 381. In considering an application to remove a condition restricting the use of extensions to a building to local government purposes only, it could properly be taken into account that 75 per cent. of the whole building was used for local government even though there was no restriction upon it.

29–178 Whistlecraft v. Sec. of State for Environment [1983] J.P.L. 809. Past established user rights were not material in a planning application determination where those rights were lost through failure to appeal against an enforcement notice.

29–179 Lewstar v. Sec. of State for Environment [1984] J.P.L. 116.
(1) As the inspector had recited the parties' arguments regarding the comparison of alternative uses, it could not be said that he had failed to consider the matter.

(2) As the inspector had found that the present use was the worst possible use of the premises he was not obliged to compare the present use to any other worse use that the premises might revert to.

29–180 Weitz and F.D.S. (Market Research) Ltd. v. Sec. of State for Environment and Camden L.B.C. [1985] J.P.L. 171. The fact that a use might have been established in the planning past even though such established user rights were now lost, might just be relevant but was of very minor importance.

29–181 Nash v. Sec. of State for Environment and Epping D.C. [1986] J.P.L. 128. On planning application it could not be argued that land had established user rights, if enforcement notice had been served requiring such uses to cease and there had been no appeal. However the Court assumed, though it was not decided, that question of personal hardship relating to the loss of alleged established user rights could be considered.

29–182 Permission for the extension of a long-established industrial development in the green belt area. [1968] J.P.L. 54.

29–183 Wrong to regularise development carried out in defiance of planning control by granting permission where it is clear that such permission would have been unlikely to have been granted if applied for in the first place. [1968] J.P.L. 104.

29–184 Permission for the development of houses for sale, where permission had previously been granted for local authority houses. [1969] J.P.L. 662.

29–185 Permission for the erection of broiler houses in agricultural countryside of great landscape value next to existing broiler houses. [1970] J.P.L. 171.

29–186 Existing use rights are a material, but not a paramount, consideration on an application for planning permission for that use. Permission given for use because of existing use rights, even though it would otherwise have been refused on planning grounds. [1970] J.P.L. 597.

29–187 Planning authority may grant a time-limited permission for a use notwithstanding fact that that use has become immune from enforcement, where the use is in fact illegal because of failure to appeal against an enforcement notice requiring use to cease. [1971] J.P.L. 350.
See also [1971] J.P.L. 353.

29–188 Applications for the erection of dwelling-houses—relation to existing development and planning permission. [1972] J.P.L. 468.

29–189 Application for a warehouse and ancillary development—possible existing planning permission for industrial development is a material consideration. [1973] J.P.L. 63.

29–190 Permission for permanent buildings to service an occasional activity permitted under the General Development Order "Jalopy racing" in a rural area. [1973] J.P.L. 125.

29–191 Permission for a detached dwelling in the Green Belt, to replace a pair of old semi-detached cottages. [1974] J.P.L. 49.

29–192 Permission for the rebuilding of house after the commencement of works of renovation granted because of special circumstances. [1975] J.P.L. 418.

29–193 Siting and size of a new dwelling-house to replace a dwelling damaged by fire. [1974] J.P.L. 558.

29–194 Permission for the erection of a bungalow to replace a previous dwelling where there was no material change in circumstances since the previous grant of permission which had expired. [1975] J.P.L. 302.

S.29. DETERMINATION OF APPLICATIONS

29–195 Refusal of permission for the erection of a dwelling-house on land formerly part of the curtilage of an existing dwelling-house. [1975] J.P.L. 361.

29–196 Refusal of permission even though there had been a previous outline permission and no change in planning circumstances. [1979] J.P.L. 416.

29–197 Refusal of permission despite previous outline permission. [1979] J.P.L. 418.

29–198 Refusal to renew time—expired planning permission for the erection of dwelling-house after a material change of circumstances. [1979] J.P.L. 419.

29–199 Refusal of permission for development notwithstanding the former grant of permission for similar development 15 years before. Permission had lapsed and there had been a material change in planning circumstances. [1981] J.P.L. 297.

29–200 Refusal of permission for residential development despite former permissions and development plan allocation—re-evaluation of the relevant planning policies. [1981] J.P.L. 298.

29–201 Plastic dome over a swimming pool in the garden of a bungalow—0.2 metres higher than permitted under the General Development Order. The difference between the actual structure and that which would have been permitted was so small that permission was granted for the actual structure. [1984] J.P.L. 205.

29–202 Distinction between the erection of permanent residential units and chalet bungalows for seasonal occupation was insufficient to warrant the refusal of planning permission where buildings had existed on a holiday camp site for 40 years. [1985] J.P.L. 138.

(k) Hardship and other exceptional circumstances

29–203 L.B. Tower Hamlets v. Sec. of State for Environment [1983] J.P.L. 315, D.C. Listed building application for a change from residential to office use. The inspector was entitled to regard as exceptional circumstances justifying grant of permission the facts that (1) the applicant had restored the property, (2) at the time of the inspector's decision the applicant had the right to change the use and would have done so had his fresh application been refused.

29–204 New Forest D.C. v. Sec. of State for Environment [1984] J.P.L. 178. Personal circumstances were a peripheral material consideration.

29–205 Thameside M.B.C. v. Sec. of State for Environment [1984] J.P.L. 180. On appeal against the refusal of permission for the continued use of land, the inspector is entitled to take into account matters of personal hardship.

29–206 Ynys Mon-Isle of Anglesey B.C. v. Sec. of State for Wales [1984] J.P.L. 646. Where necessary to achieve fairness the history of a planning application can properly be taken into account.

29–207 Great Portland Estates v. City of Westminster (1984). Personal circumtances such as hardship were not to be ignored in the administration of planning control and could be given direct effect as an exception to a general rule.

29–208 Permission to resume use of cottage as a dwelling-house because of hardship to family. [1971] J.P.L. 233.

29–209 Personal permission to station a residential caravan in an isolated position because of the applicant's medical condition. [1971] J.P.L. 469.

29–210 Permission for the continuance of a caravan site in metropolitan green belt. Exceptional circumstances:
   (i) site existed for 20 years without causing complaint from local residents;
   (ii) hardship to families if forced to move;

(iii) not unduly noticeable in the landscape;
(iv) highway problems relatively minor;
(v) local authority proposing to acquire land and run down site over a period of time;
(vi) necessary facilities reasonably proximate.
[1972] J.P.L. 453.

29–211 Refusal of permission for a seasonal caravan site for showmen in green belt area. Personal hardship was insufficient to outweigh the planning merits. [1972] J.P.L. 727.

29–212 Permission for a new dwelling-house within green belt to replace one to be demolished due to a new road. [1973] J.P.L. 123.

29–213 Permission for the extension of a dwelling-house subject to an agricultural occupancy condition. The dwelling-house was larger than normal for an agricultural worker but the applicant had a large family. [1978] J.P.L. 131.

29–214 Permission for the redevelopment of premises for an existing non-conforming use for furniture removal and storage—long-established family business which had been operated without causing problems. [1978] J.P.L. 132.

29–215 Planning permission for a bungalow where permission previously granted had expired through the oversight of the owner. Equity overrode planning considerations. [1979] J.P.L. 565.

29–216 Limited five-year permission for a gypsy caravan site in the green belt despite an earlier refusal on appeal because in the absence of firm evidence that alternative accommodation was available or likely to be available on an authorised site in the district for the appellant and his family an enforced move was likely to cause hardship and to result in the use of some other unauthorised site which could be much less suitable and also because of evidence of a change in the attitude of the local residents. [1983] J.P.L. 563.

29–217 Although personal matters particular to the present owner have to be viewed sympathetically, events which are not unexpected or unseen cannot affect planning considerations. [1985] J.P.L. 279.

(l) Alternative sites for the proposed development

29–218 Rhodes v. Min. of Housing & Local Govt. [1963] 1 W.L.R. 208. The availability of an alternative site for a proposed airport is a material consideration, but the Minister is not bound to consider any evidence not adduced at the inquiry and does not himself have to rout-around for alternative sites. [1963] 1 W.L.R. 208.

29–219 Ynystawe Ynyforgan and Glas Gypsy Site Action Group v. Sec. of State for Wales [1981] J.P.L. 874. Appeal against permission for a gypsy caravan site allowed because:
(1) the inspector had failed to consider alternative sites and the possibility of debate;
(2) the Secretary of State was wrong to allow conventional planning criteria to be overridden by the consideration of urgency.

29–220 R. v. Berkshire C.C., ex p. Mangall [1985] J.P.L. 258. Where there are two alternative sites for proposed sand pit it is the duty of the authority when considering whether to grant the planning permission sought to have proper regard to the second site, although their comparative evaluation need not be carried out equally.

29–221 Sir Brandon Meredith Rhys Williams v. Sec. of State for Wales [1985] J.P.L. The extent to which an alternative site had to be considered depended on many factors and it would not always be decisive.

S.29. DETERMINATION OF APPLICATIONS

29–222 **Vale of Glamorgan B.C. v. Sec. of State for Wales and Sir Brandon Rhys-Williams** [1986] J.P.L. 198. Whether the existence of an alternative site was a relevant consideration was a matter for the local planning authority or the Secretary of State respectively and the courts could only interfere if their judgment was unreasonable.

29–223 **Greater London Council v. Sec. of State for Environment and London Docklands Development Corporation** (1986) J.P.L. 193. An alternative site was a relevant consideration in the following circumstances:
1. there was a clear public convenience in the proposal;
2. the proposal would have inevitable adverse effects or disadvantages to the public;
3. the alternative site would not have those effects or to the same extent;
4. it was a proposal for which only one or at the least only a limited number of permissions could be granted.

29–224 **R. v. Carlisle City Council and Sec. of State for Environment, ex p. Cumbrian Co-operative Society** [1986] J.P.L. 206. Alternative site was only relevant when the proposed development would have serious environmental disadvantage; this did not apply to an application for a superstore.

29–225 Two rival applications for superstores—each individually acceptable but accumulatively unacceptable—permission granted for the store making best land-use. [1985] J.P.L. 741.

(m) Fear of precedent

29–226 **Collis Radio Ltd. v. Sec. of State for Environment** (1975) 29 P. & C.R. 390, D.C. Although granting one particular permission might not be harmful, relevant consideration that the grant could lead to the proliferation of similar applications the granting of which would be harmful.

29–227 **Tempo Discount Warehouse v. Sec. of State for Environment** [1979] J.P.L. 98. Possible consequences on other sites of a grant of permission is a material planning consideration.

29–228 **Anglia Building Society v. Sec. of State for Environment** [1984] J.P.L. 175. Proper to refuse planning permission because the fear of setting a precedent. Decisions in *Collis Radio* and *Tempo Discount Warehouses* considered.

29–229 Permission for the conversion of a house into two flats—unlikely to set a precedent. [1968] J.P.L. 651.

29–230 Where any further development would require further planning permissions the effects of that further development was not a material consideration on a planning application. [1971] J.P.L. 242.

29–231/232 Refusal of planning permission for the construction of a prison in an area of restraint within the Green Belt because of the possibility of alternative sites not having been sufficiently explored to make out a case for the use of this site. [1983] J.P.L. 403.

(n) Moral considerations

29–233 **Finlay v. Sec. of State for Environment** [1983] J.P.L. 802. A decision that a sex-cinema was unsuitable because the clientele may have a detrimental effect upon neighbourhood is an environmental decision not a moral one.

29–234 Moral objections to bingo are not a relevant planning consideration. The desire to keep open the town's only public cinema, even though running at a loss, was not a relevant planning consideration on an application to convert it into a bingo hall and indoor games centre. [1967] J.P.L. 556.

29–235 Objections on moral grounds are not material planning considerations—a betting shop in a holiday camp. [1968] J.P.L. 108.

29–236 Moral or civic considerations regarding the local distribution of amusement centres are not a relevant planning consideration. [1969] J.P.L. 605.

(o) **Educational considerations**

29–237 The fact that an education authority has formulated proposals to use a site for educational purposes was a material consideration. [1969] J.P.L. 484.

29–238 Shortage of educational facilities cannot be a reason for deferring the building of much-needed houses. [1973] J.P.L. 272.

(p) **Shopping policies**

29–239 It is not a proper function of planning control to regulate the number of shops within a local planning authority's area which may carry on a particular trade or business, although it can regulate specific shop uses which would be out of place in a particular locality. [1968] J.P.L. 710.

29–240 Refusal of permission for a shop with living accomodation over to replace an existing house and shop in an area of scattered shopping development was appropriate to encourage the concentration of shops and prevent the perpetuation of scattered shops. [1971] J.P.L. 478.

29–241 Protection of in-town shopping facilities is a material consideration on an application for an out-of-town retail shopping centre. [1972] J.P.L. 720.

29–242 Permission for out-of town shopping facilities despite the effect on the town shopping centre. Although competition is not a material consideration the effects of competition upon the community is. [1972] J.P.L. 403.

29–243 Refusal of permission for the erection of a retail superstore on the periphery of a large built-up area. [1974] J.P.L. 435.

29–244 Refusal of permission for a large retail store outside the existing shopping centres. [1975] J.P.L. 430.

29–245 Refusal of permission for a hypermarket situated outside the existing shopping centres. [1975] J.P.L. 427.

29–246 Superstore—its effect on the neighbouring existing town and local shopping centres. [1976] J.P.L. 198.

29–247 Wholesale and retail sales of furniture and furnishings in an area allocated to warehouse/industrial use—its effect on other shops in the district. [1977] J.P.L. 49.

29–248 Large retail shop (superstore or hypermarket)—its effect on existing nearby shopping centres and towns. [1977] J.P.L. 475.

29–249 Refusal of permission for a change of use from a shop (launderette) to a betting office in a small neighbourhood shopping centre with a general shortage of shops. [1984] J.P.L. 130.

(q) **Public development needs.**

29–250 Possible conflict with undefined and nebulous future public development is insufficient reason to refuse planning permission. [1971] J.P.L. 180.

29–251 Wrong to refuse permission for a housing development merely because required by Council for such a development. [1974] J.P.L. 167.

S.29. DETERMINATION OF APPLICATIONS

29–252 Intention to construct a highway over a site of proposed development is a material consideration, but not an overriding one. [1973] J.P.L. 389.

29–253 Residential development—whether necessary to reserve the site for highway purposes. [1975] J.P.L. 491.

(r) Noise and pollution

29–254 London Borough of Newham v. Sec. of State for Environment [1986] J.P.L. 607. Where single dwelling-house divided into two separate dwelling-houses the increased noise nuisance to the occupants of the new dwellings a material consideration.

29–255 Refusal of permission for the conversion of maisonettes into flats—problem of noise through the party wall. [1968] J.P.L.308.

29–256 Refusal of permission for the use of land as a kart-racing track—noise disturbance. [1970] J.P.L. 115.

29–257 Refusal of permission for a permanent caravan site for gypsies because of smoke pollution. [1970] J.P.L. 169.

29–258 Refusal of permission for "banger racing" near a village—noise, eyesore, highway problem. [1973] J.P.L. 110.

29–259 Refusal of permission for a residential development where the site was subject to noise from road traffic on the main road. [1973] J.P.L. 436.

29–260 Refusal of permission for a residential development near to the motorway because of noise. [1975] J.P.L. 110 & 111.

29–261 Potential noise nuisance is a planning consideration. [1985] J.P.L.567.

(s) Car-parking needs

29–262 Change of use of an existing bingo club to a bingo club licensed for the sale of liquor. Local authority's car-parking standards. [1964] J.P.L. 563.

29–263 Refusal of permission for the conversion of a house to offices because of inadequate car-parking provision. [1968] J.P.L. 50.

29–264 Refusal of permission for a betting office in a shopping street because of lack of car-parking for clients. [1968] J.P.L. 304.

29–265 Permission for conversion of a house into two flats despite the lack of garage and parking space. [1968] J.P.L. 362.

29–266 Refusal of permission for a betting office because of the lack of car-parking for clients. [1968] J.P.L. 364.

29–267 Conversion of a house to flats—application of the standard for the provision for car-parking. [1974] J.P.L. 48.

(t) Traffic and safety problems

29–268 Refusal of permission for the construction of a shop-front at the rear of shop premises to face a back service road as it would detract from service facilities. [1968] J.P.L. 50.

29–269 Permission for development refused because there was no access to the highway and the adjacent landowner was not prepared to allow access. [1969] J.P.L. 484.

29–270 Refusal of permission for the use of a dwelling-house in a residential area in connection with a car-hire business and driving school—increase in vehicular activity. [1969] J.P.L. 486.

29–271 Refusal of permission for the erection of lock-up garages 2 feet back from the foot-path of a road in a residential area—traffic hazard. 1970] J.P.L. 112.

29–272 Refusal of permission for shop use in an area allocated for industrial use and which encouraged pedestrian crossing of a busy road and prohibited parking. [1970] J.P.L. 162.

29–273 Refusal of permission for the erection of a private garage where the access road was sub–standard. [1972] J.P.L. 175.

29–274 Permission for a small boat-building and repair yard in open countryside refused because of poor access. [1972] J.P.L. 400.

29–275 Refusal of permission for a residential development where access was required over land not under the applicant's control. [1973] J.P.L. 435.

29–276 Residential development—the need for satisfactory access arrangements. [1974] J.P.L. 106.

29–277 Development with access to a trunk road—the need for turning space. [1974[J.P.L. 110.

29–278 Development near a gas works—public safety paramount. [1975] J.P.L. 751.

29–279 On application for planning permission for residential development must take into consideration the fact that a satisfactory means of access can only be provided over land which the owner has made clear will not be made available. [1984] J.P.L. 125.

(u) Miscellaneous

29–280 R. v. Kesteven R.D.C., ex p. Sleaford & District White City Sports Stadium Co. [1947] All E.R. 310. Planning permission can be refused for sports stadium on the grounds of the over-riding need to preserve the land for agricultural use, even though agricultural quality may not be high.

29–281 Harwich Harbour. Conservancy Board v. Sec. of State for Environment [1974] 118 S.J. 755. The Harwich Harbour Acts 1863 and 1865 and the Coast Protection Act 1949 did not give controls over the effect of an additional user of a harbour on the use of the harbour by vessels. The generation of extra traffic which would be caused by the development of a marina and the extent to which this traffic would cause interference and have a detrimental effect on the commercial operation of the port, was a planning matter and should have been considered by the Minister on appeal.

29–282 Steeples v. Derbyshire C.C. [1981] J.P.L. 582. The fact that council had decided to seek planning permission was not a material consideration within s. 29(1).

29–283 Hatfield Construction v. Sec. of State for Environment [1983] J.P.L. 605. It is perfectly proper to compare residential densities within and without a site to test the effect of a proposed development.

29–284 Greater London Council and Others v. Sec of State for Environment [1983] J.P.L. 793. Policy as to the mix of housing and offices in a proposed development upheld.

29–285 Anglia Building Society v. Sec. of State for Environment [1984] J.P.L. 175. Inspector had properly taken into account that it was appropriate to uphold the planning policy of restricting non-retail trade.

29–286 Refusal of permission for the use of a dwelling-house in a residential area for a dentist's surgery and professional offices. Whether any need for further office accomodation was a consideration relevant to the appeal. [1966] J.P.L. 674.

29–287 Refusal of permission for the erection of a building which would intensify the use for storage of agricultural tractors or machinery close to a residential estate. [1968] J.P.L. 49.

29–288 Application for access to a proposed house for which planning permission had not been granted was premature. [1968] J.P.L. 302.

29–289 Refusal of permission for development likely to intensify existing non-conforming use. [1968] J.P.L. 303.

29–290 Refusal of permission for the erection of semi-detached dwellings as prejudicial to the redevelopment of an area of obsolete lay-out. [1970] J.P.L. 102.

29–291 Refusal of permission for the extension of a dwelling-house and its conversion to flats in an area where family houses were needed as smaller units. [1973] J.P.L. 268.

29–292 Permission for residential development refused where the need for land was insufficiently urgent to override the local planning authority's programme for phased development. [1972] J.P.L. 396.

29–293 Permission for the conversion of residential premises to estate agent's offices in a shopping/residential area—making the best use of the premises. [1973] J.P.L. 442.

29–294 Refusal of permission for a detached house on a narrow plot. [1974] J.P.L. 112.

29–295 Refusal of permission for a solicitor's office in a residential area. Although neighbours had not objected, possible changes in occupancy must be taken into account. A Dentist's surgery in a residential area can be justified as more frequently used by neighbours than a solicitor's office. [1981] J.P.L. 371.

29–296 Refusal of permission for the erection of a welfare shelter for 1,000 people on land. Views on the merits of the use were not relevant to planning. The application was refused as the site was reserved for obtrusive industrial uses and there was a shortage of alternative sites for such uses. [1984] J.P.L. 909.

C. Conditional Planning Permission

1. General Approach

29–297 Newbury D.C. v. Sec. of State for Environment [1980] 1 All E.R. 731, H.L. A local planning authority can only impose conditions to a planning permission if:
  (i) they are imposed for a "planning" purpose and not for any ulterior purpose; and
  (ii) they fairly and reasonably relate to the development permitted by the planning permission; and
  (iii) they are not so unreasonable that no reasonable planning authority could impose them.

29–298/299 Fawcett Properties v. Buckingham C.C. [1961] A.C. 674, H.L. A planning authority may impose a condition on a planning permission restricting use of land to the circumstances of the person using it so long as the condition can fairly and reasonably be said to relate to any policy under the Town and Country Planning Act and is sufficiently certain.

29–300 Extension of a cafe and the provision of a car park and access. Condition reserving approval of a detail of the development which is included in the application is improper. [1966] J.P.L. 736.

S.29. DETERMINATION OF APPLICATIONS

2. Conditions must be Imposed for a Planning Purpose

29–301 Fawcett v. Buckinghamshire C.C. [1959] C.H. 543. *Per* Pearce L.J.: Restrictions based upon housing or public health or social considerations other than town planning would be taking a wrong matter into account and the restrictions would be invalid.

29–302 East Suffolk C.C. v. Sec. of State for Environment [1972] 70 L.G.R. 595, D.C. A planning authority can restrict a dwelling-house to agricultural workers by imposing a condition to that effect, but not by granting a restricted planning permission, because subsequent occupation by some other kind of person is not a change of use and cannot lead to enforcement.

29–303 R. v. Hillingdon L.B.C., ex p. Royco Homes Ltd. [1974] 1 Q.B. 720. Conditions imposed for an ulterior housing purpose invalid.

29–304 Sutton L.B.C. v. Sec. of State for Environment (1975) 29 P.&C.R. 350, D.C. Planning in general is not concerned with the quality of the work. Condition that the type and treatment of materials be approved by the local planning authority was questioned.

29–305 Condition requiring a building to be set back was valid as there were sound planning reasons for imposing it. Condition as to the nature and construction of the building and its drainage was unnecessary as they were matters within the scope of the building by-laws. [1966] J.P.L. 290.

29–306 Condition restricting or prohibiting the display of advertisements on premises on the grant of permission for development was unnecessary as this was covered by special controls over advertisements. [1966] J.P.L. 670.

29–307 Condition restricting the display of advertisements was inappropriate given the control available in advertisement regulations. [1971] J.P.L. 716.

29–308 Outline planning permission for a large industrial (ammonia) plant. Conditions as to noise and fumes were inappropriate as they were duplicating the powers of the Alkali and Clean Air Inspectorate. [1977] J.P.L. 820.

29–309 The time-limit condition and the recording and notifying of emissions condition on planning permission for an emergency vent stack were discharged as attempts to use planning control where other statutory controls were more appropriate and the application was clearly intended to be for a permanent development. [1982] J.P.L. 335.

29–310 Condition restricting advertisements to be dealt with under the control of Advertisment Regulations and not by a planning condition. [1982] J.P.L. 733.

29–311 Use of part of a dwelling in a rural area for an office and laboratory: conditions forbidding the outside use of sound-emitting plant and equipment, and restricting hours of use. This could be done under planning legislation notwithstanding possible powers of control under other legislation. [1983] J.P.L. 697.

29–312 Two different sorts of development on the same site can be acceptable, particularly where there are no clear planning objections to either form of development. An informal planning study cannot have the same weight as the approved structure plan where the council do not intend to adopt it as a statutory local plan. It would be wrong to give planning permission for a private hospital on a site which was required to remedy a shortage of housing land. [1985] J.P.L. 136.

29–313 Refusal of permission for change of use from single private dwelling to residential care home because would lead to over-concentration of rest home establishments in the locality. [1985] J.P.L. 432.

29–314 Where deterioration of a building occurs, even through default, the practi-

S.29. DETERMINATION OF APPLICATIONS

cability and likelihood of reinstatement are material considerations. [1985] J.P.L. 745.

29–315 Policy to refuse permission for rest homes to correct age imbalance in the local population probably not a valid planning policy as not concerned with the use of land but the identity of the occupiers of land. Loss of income from rates not a planning matter. Equally doubtful if strain on services a planning matter. [1986] J.P.L. 621.

3. Conditions must Fairly and Reasonably Relate to the Proposed Development

29–316 Pyx Granite Co. Ltd. v. Min. of Housing & Local Govt. [1958] 2 W.L.R. 371. *Per* Lord Denning: Conditions to be valid must fairly and reasonably relate to the permitted development. Planning authorities cannot use their powers for an ulterior object, however desirable it may seem in the public interest.

29–317 Richmond-upon-Thames v. Sec. of State for Environment [1974] 1 All E.R. 193. Condition relating to off-street car-parking upheld.

29–318 Kent C.C. v. Sec. of State for Environment (1976) 33 P.&C.R. 70. It is a question of fact and degree whether a particular condition is such as to take away the substance of a permission in which case it will be invalid. An oil refinery condition prohibiting deliveries did not make it unworkable.

29–319 A.I. & P. (Stratford) v. L.B. of Tower Hamlets [1976] J.P.L. 234. Planning permission for the erection of warehouse and industrial units granted subject to a condition that the existing office accomodation on-site should only be used as ancillary to non-office uses on-site. Reasons for the condition were partly to prevent parts of the new units being used for offices by future occupiers, resulting in a net increase in office floor space contrary to the council's policy and therefore the condition did not relate to permitted development.

29–320 Penwith D.C. v. Sec. of State for Environment (1977) 34 P.&C.R. 269. Extension to a factory would enable the factory to be used more effectively and therefore conditions could be attached restricting the existing use of the factory in the interest of amenity as they related to development.

29–321 Brittania (Cheltenham) Ltd. v. Sec. of State for Environment [1978] J.P.L. 554. Although the Secretary of State cannot give permission for a development other than that applied for, an application was deemed to include any development ancillary or incidental to a proposed development so applications for residential developments for 250 and 1,000 people could contain conditions relating to shopping facilities and open space.

On an outline application an area to be preserved for an ancillary purpose can be identified and does not result in granting permission for development of an area materially different from that in the application.

29–322 Peak Park J.P.B. v. Sec. of State for Environment [1980] J.P.L. 114. Condition in planning permission may limit rights on a geographically separate site if related to a proposed development. It is a question of fact whether a condition fairly and reasonably relates to permitted development.

29–323 Newbury D.C. v. Sec. of State for Environment [1980] 1 All E.R. 731, H.L. Condition requiring the eventual demolition of buildings imposed on a planning application to use buildings will rarely be valid.

29–324 Bernard Wheatcroft Ltd. v. Sec. of State for Environment [1982] J.P.L. 37. The power to impose conditions which reduce the scope of the development does not depend on whether the applications is severable. The true test is whether the effect of the conditional planning permission is to allow development which is in substance not that which was applied for.

29–325 Robert Frederick Kember v. Sec. of State for Environment [1982] J.P.L. 383. Condition that a cottage, not the subject of an application, be limited to persons solely or mainly employed in agriculture imposed because the planning authorities wanted the dwelling kept as part of the agricultural stock was invalid as it did not relate to the development authorised.

29–326 Clwyd C.C. v. Sec. of State for Environment [1982] J.P.L. 696. Consideration of the principle set out in *Wheatcroft* v. *Sec. of State for Environment*

29–327 Inverclyde D.C. v. Inverkip Building Co. [1983] J.P.L. 118. Conditions which related fairly and reasonably to a proposed development were not *ultra vires* even though they were not strictly within the definition of reserved matters in the General Development Order.

29–328 Wessex Regional Health Authority v. Salisbury D.C. [1984] J.P.L. 344. On an application for outline planning permission for 48 houses where 37 would be acceptable it would be wrong to grant permission subject to a condition that only 37 be built.

29–329 Gill v. Sec. of State for Environment & North Warwickshire D.C. [1985] J.P.L. 710. Conditions imposed by the Secretary of State to a grant of permission for the retention of fences and structures for a fox farm.

Condition requiring that no further buildings be erected without express permission (and so restricting normal rights under the General Development Order) was held fairly and reasonably to relate to the permitted development.

Condition requiring no slaughtering of animals was too wide as it did not relate to the development which was intended for foxes not any animals, but a condition requiring no slaughtering of foxes in the pens would have been valid.

29–330 R. v. St. Edmundsbury B.C., ex p. Investors in Industry Commercial Properties Ltd. [1985] 3 All E.R. 234. Condition attached to permission for a supermarket requiring three independent retail units fairly and reasonably related to the development granted and was not clearly unreasonable.

Note

Also see judicial decision 5 on section 30,(1)(a).

29–331 Condition insufficiently related to the development permitted. [1966] J.P.L. 418.

29–332 Condition imposed on planning permission for an extension which required the demolition not only of the extension but also of the existing buildings after a period of time was held to be *ultra vires*. [1967] J.P.L. 239.

29–333 Condition limiting the hours of use for an industrial purpose where there was a previous established industrial use which was invalid. [1967] J.P.L. 411.

29–334 Where space is available for on-site car-parking in urban areas, arising from a change of use to offices, it is reasonable that provision should be made, but it should be related to increased office floor space, taking into account the fact that it is not new separate development and should not involve an attempt to remedy existing deficiencies relating to existing office floor space. [1967] J.P.L. 495.

29–335 On a detailed application for a building with a dormer window it is not open to the Council to grant permission for the development subject to a condition stipulating that the dormer window be excluded. [1969] J.P.L. 105.

29–336 Condition requiring the construction of an estate road up to the boundary of the estate was not necessary for development and was invalid. [1979] J.P.L. 485.

29–337 Conditions on planning permission for additions and alteration at a petrol filling station. Conditions for controlling the illumination of a canopy and of advertisments, and detriment to amenity from the use. Whether condition related to the development. [1974] J.P.L. 486.

29–338 Discharge of a condition requiring a residential unit (bungalow) to be used only in connection with the residential use of other property. Condition was no longer relevant or reasonable after physical separation by way of the erection of a fence. [1981] J.P.L. 700.

29–339 Agricultural occupancy condition attached to an existing dwelling-house by a condition of planning permission for a second dwelling-house fairly relates to permission because the second house creates the possibility that the first house may cease to be used as a farmhouse. [1982] J.P.L. 208.

29–340 Condition requiring the erection of pavement bollards to restrict vehicular access on planning permission for shop fronts and a canopy was invalid as the development permitted only affected the external appearance and the condition did not relate to that. [1983] J.P.L. 259.

29–341 Planning permission for the extension of industrial storage premises. Validity of conditions relating to the whole of the premises. [1983] J.P.L. 833.

29–342 Conditions relating to premises not within the bounds of the planning application were invalid. [1984] J.P.L. 199.

29–343 Condition requiring the replacement of development permitted by a "permanent structure employing traditional materials" was not relevant to the development permitted and was probably unenforceable. [1985] J.P.L. 70.

4. Conditions must not be Totally Unreasonable

29–344 Birnie v. Banff C.C. [1954] S.L.T. 90. No power to impose a condition to planning permission requiring work to be carried out on land not belonging to the applicant.

29–345 Alan Markovits v. Hove B.C. [1958] 9 P.&C.R. 292. Conditions requiring that property should not be used for any other purpose and that no detriment to the amenities of the area by reason of noise vibration, smell, smoke, fumes or dust were proper conditions.

29–346 Hall & Co. Ltd. v. Shoreham-by-Sea U.D.C. [1964] 1 W.L.R. 240. Condition requiring the construction of an ancillary road and effectively dedication of the road to the public without any compensation was unreasonable and *ultra vires*. There was a more regular course available under the Highways Act 1959.

Per Harman L.J.: Condition requiring an applicant to grant his neighbour a right of way over his land may be *intra vires*.

29–347 Allnat London Properties v. Middlesex (1964) 62 L.G.R. 304. Conditions on planning permission affecting the existing use rights are unreasonable and void—but see later decisions.

29–348 Mixnam Properties v. Chertsey U.D.C. [1964] 2 W.L.R. 1210, H.L. (Caravan site licence case.) Conditions which a planning authority can impose on a caravan site license under s.5(1) Caravan Sites and Control of Development Act 1960 are limited to conditions relating to the use of the site not to the use of the licensee's legal powers of letting or licensing caravan spaces.

29–349 Hartnell v. Min. of Housing & Local Govt. [1965] 2 W.L.R. 474. (Caravan site licence case.) Where under the Caravan Sites and Control of Development Act 1960 a site owner had to apply for planning permission to obtain a licence, that permission could not contain conditions materially reducing pre-existing rights without paying compensation.

29–350 Kingsway Investments v. Kent C.C. [1970] 2 W.L.R. 397, H.L. Time conditions could validly be annexed to a grant of outline planning permission.

29–351 City of London Corp. v. Sec. of State for Environment (1971) 23 P.&C.R. 169. Provided a planning authority had regard to all material considerations and the condition was reasonable and it fairly and reasonably related to the permitted development, a planning authority may impose restrictions beyond those laid down specifically in the legislation even if that meant a restriction of a use which would not amount to development.

Condition that premises should be used only as an employment agency upheld.

29–352 Kingston L.B.C. v. Sec. of State for Environment [1973] 1 W.L.R. 1549. A condition in a planning permission restricting existing use rights without payment of compensation is valid.

29–353 Leighton & Newman Ltd. v. Sec. of State for Environment (1976) 32 P.&C.R. 1, 10. Where a permission is acted upon and it has an express condition prohibiting a previous established use, that use is extinguished.

29–354 R. v. Hillingdon L.B.C., ex p. Royco Homes Ltd. [1974] 2 W.L.R. 805, D.C. Condition that houses when built should be occupied by people on a local authority waiting list with security of tenure of 10 years required the applicants to assume the authority's duties as the housing authority, a fundamental departure from the rights of ownership and so unreasonable that no local planning authority properly directing itself could impose them, therefore *ultra vires* as they were fundamental to the grant of planning permission.

29–355 Roberts v. Vale Royal D.C. (1977) 39 P.&C.R. 514, D.C. Although the Act makes no specific provision for "reserved matters" in respect of a "material change of use" development, no inference is to be drawn that a condition attached to a planning permission, which postpones administrative decisions about such developments is void. Condition upheld which required approval of the materials to be tipped.

29–356 Brittania (Cheltenham) Ltd. v. Sec. of State for Environment [1978] J.P.L. 554. There was nothing wrong with requiring an area to be set aside for shopping facilities or open land. There was nothing in the condition which said that open land must be dedicated to public, therefore it was distinguishable from *Hall* v. *Shoreham* U.D.C.

29–357 Augier v. Sec. of State for Environment *Sub nom.* **Hildenborough Village Preservation Association v. Sec. of State for Environment** [1978] J.P.L. 708. Where an applicant for planning permission gives an undertaking and, in reliance upon that, planning permission is granted subject to a condition in terms broad enough to embrace the undertaking, the applicant cannot later be heard to say that there is no power to require compliance with the undertaking.

29–358 B.A.A. v. Sec. of State for Scotland [1980] J.P.L. 260. Condition restricting the flight path of planes was *ultra vires* as a flight path is controlled by the Civil Aviation Authority and the developer had no power to ensure compliance.

Condition restricting the time of flights was *ultra vires* as the developer did not occupy the ground from which the helicopter flew and he therefore had no control over the timing of flights.

Quaere whether the grant of conditional permission overrode rights under the General Development Order. Condition restricting the operator's use to control aircraft noise was *ultra vires* as this was already achieved by imposing a condition upon the B.A.A. who controlled the runway.

29–359 Peak Park J.P.B. v. Sec. of State for Environment [1980] J.P.L. 114. A condition in a planning permission may detract from an existing planning permission.

S.29. DETERMINATION OF APPLICATIONS

29–360 Carpet Decor (Guildford) v. Sec. of State for Environment [1981] J.P.L. 806. If a planning authority wants to exclude a General Development Order or Use Classes Order by condition it must be unequivocal.

29–361 Irlam Brick Co. v. Warrington B.C. [1982] J.P.L. 709. Condition reserving power to stop tipping if after 10 years works had not been reinstated was valid. Permission to tip was always subject to a planning authority's right to determine it after 10 years of the working having ceased and therefore termination was not a derogation from what had been granted.

29–362 M.J.Shanley Ltd. v. Sec. of State for Environment [1982] J.P.L. 380. A condition requiring the provision of 40 acres of open space for public use on the development of 10 acres of residential property was invalid.

29–363 Commercial and Residential Property Development Co. v. Sec. of State for Environment (1982) 80 L.G.R. 443. Planning permission for a hostel. Condition limiting the length of stay of visitors was reasonable and valid.

29–364 Property Investment Holdings v. Sec. of State for Environment [1984] J.P.L. 587. Restrictive conditions as to hours of work at a factory upheld.

29–365 Atkinson v. Sec. of State for Environment [1983] J.P.L. 599. Condition of planning permission for seven houses that a farmhouse be demolished was upheld even though it had been sold to somebody else. There was no need to rely on s.30 when the application included the land which was the subject of the condition. Such a condition was not invalid, even though it might cause hardship in special circumstances.

29–366 Grampian Regional Council v. City of Aberdeen D.C. [1984] S.L.T. 197, H.L. Difference between a negative condition which prohibited development until something outside the applicant's power was done, and a positive condition which required him to do it—the negative condition can be enforced by the courts. Power to impose a condition that development should not start until a road was closed, even though the road was not under the total control of the applicants.

29–367 Bradford City Metropolitan Council v. Sec. of State for Environment (1986) 278 E.G. 1473, C.A. Condition requiring a highway to be widened was ultra vires as being manifestly unreasonable even if the applicant has suggested or consented to the terms of the condition; quaere whether condition would have been valid if it had been drafted negatively to read that the development should not be carried out until the road had been widened.

29–368 Conditions restricting the sale of commodities and the installation and use of cooking apparatus on premises used as a tea garden upheld. Conditions were not too remote from planning or unreasonable. [1961] 12 P &C.R. 406.

29–369 Cannot require an applicant to carry out road works on land not within the application site or not within the applicant's control. [1967] J.P.L. 114.

29–370 Condition on the approval of a detailed application (after outline approval) purporting to exclude General Development Order permission was invalid. The fact that the applicant agreed to the condition in negotiations did not affect its legal position. [1967] J.P.L. 726.

29–371 Condition requiring an applicant to satisfy the local planning authority as to the existence of a right of way was inappropriate. Condition requiring works on land outside the applicant's control was improper. [1968] J.P.L. 306.

29–372 Condition attached to planning permission for the extension of buildings requiring the closing of the existing access to the site was valid and capable of enforcement. [1969] J.P.L. 287.

S.29. DETERMINATION OF APPLICATIONS

29–373 Discharge of a condition on permission for the erection of a bungalow that the existing building must cease to be used as dwelling-house. [1970] J.P.L. 415.

29–374 In granting permission for the retention of a building existing use rights cannot be limited. [1970] J.P.L. 542.

29–375 Condition restricting established use rights was improper. [1973] J.P.L. 261.

29–376 Residential development—condition requiring an estate road to be built up to the boundary was unnecessary. [1974] J.P.L. 680.

29–377 Removal of a condition allowing human habitation of a tower on limited days only. [1974] J.P.L. 683.

29–378 Improper to make planning permission conditional upon a financial contribution to a communal car park. [1975] J.P.L. 620.

29–379 Conditions of planning permission removing General Development Order rights can only be justified on strong grounds. [1977] J.P.L. 127.

29–380 Permission for the mixing of soil and peat for compost. Condition prohibiting any storage of waste whatsoever was wider than necessary. [1977] C.L.Y. 2977, Ref. No. 118/77.

29–381 Appeal allowed against a condition requiring a farm shop to sell only produce grown on farms within a specified county. [1977] J.P.L. 742.

29–382 Planning permission for a complex of development—condition requiring the whole of the development to be commenced simultaneously and completed as a whole was invalid. [1979] J.P.L. 549.

29–383 Conditions limiting the occupation of a dwelling-house to an owner or employee of the adjoining premises and limiting permission to ensure it was for the benefit of the applicant only was no longer reasonable. [1980] J.P.L. 845.

29–384 Unreasonable for a condition to be imposed giving a local planning authority the power to vet the prospective occupant of a building. [1981] J.P.L. 918.

29–385 Residential development—condition requiring the prior completion of drainage works on land not owned by the applicant or the water authority imposed by the Secretary of State for the Environment. [1982] J.P.L. 541.

29–386 Condition requiring the provision in all dwellings for communal television services in a non-conservation area discharged. [1982] J.P.L. 658.

29–387 Condition of outline planning permission for dwellings specifying the type of materials to be used for external walls and roofs was *intra vires* and reasonable. [1983] J.P.L. 413.

29–388 Permission subject to a condition prohibiting the occupation of dwellings prior to the completion of a sewage treatment works on land not under the control of the applicant imposed by Secretary of State. [1983] J.P.L. 415.

29–389 Condition of permission for extending stables requiring the roof of existing stables to be painted in an agreed colour was invalid. [1983] J.P.L. 762.

29–390 Condition requiring the provision of access to a different planning unit in separate ownership, albeit formerly in the same planning unit was invalid as being unreasonable. [1983] J.P.L. 764.

29–391 Permission for industrial and warehousing development where road access substandard. Requirement that the developer contribute to the cost of a new road before planning permission granted was wrong in law. [1983] J.P.L. 769.

29–392 Condition limiting residential occupancy to employment in a Children's

S.29. DETERMINATION OF APPLICATIONS

Home so limited freedom to dispose of property as to be unreasonable. [1985] J.P.L. 72.

29–393 A condition in a planning permission for the use of gaming machines in an existing cafe, which limited the hours of use of the cafe was *ultra vires* as it took away existing use rights. [1985] J.P.L. 507.

29–394 Condition prohibiting use of power tools and machinery unreasonable because it would provide no additional protection to local residents and it would seriously hamper the flexible use of the units involved. [1985] J.P.L. 668.

29–395 Condition that rear garden area of public house should not be open to customers held to be reasonable. [1986] J.P.L. 633.

5. *Conditions must not be Hopelessly Uncertain*

29–396 Mixnam's Porperties Ltd. v. Chertsey U.D.C. [1964] 2 W.L.R. 1210, H.L. If a condition is uncertain it is invalid.

29–397 Bizony v. Sec. of State for Environment [1976] J.P.L. 306. Difficulties in enforcing a condition will not render it void if it is not unintelligible.

29–398 Hall & Co. Ltd. v. Shoreham-by-Sea U.D.C. [1964] 1 W.L.R. 240. *Per* Willmer L.J.:Uncertainty test in whether the language of the conditions makes sense, not whether the applicant is left uncertain as to how the conditions will operate, that is relevant to considering reasonableness.

29–399 Carnall v. Jones (1966) 65 L.G.R. 217, D.C. (Caravan Site Licence case.) Condition in a caravan site licence that the "site shall be kept free of unauthorised tents and structures" was not so uncertain that a breach could not be prosecuted and the prosecution was not bound to disprove existing use rights.

29–400 Brittania (Cheltenham) Ltd. v. Sec. of State for Environment [1978] J.P.L. 554. Condition that land be reserved for open space or shopping facilities was not uncertain.

29–401 M.J. Shanley Ltd. v. Sec. of State for Environment [1982] J.P.L. 380. Condition that the first opportunity to buy houses should be given to local people was invalid for uncertainty.

29–402 Alderson v. Sec. of State for Environment [1984] J.P.L. 429, C.A. A planning condition is only void for uncertainty if it can be given no meaning or no sensible or intelligible meaning—"locally" has a perfectly intelligible meaning. First instance decision reversed; see [1984] J.P.L. 185.

29–403 Penwith D.C. v. Sec. of State for Environment and Mainstreet Marketing Ltd. [1986] J.P.L. 432. Condition requiring a scheme to be agreed by local planning authority on opening hours invalid as it required matters to be read in by implication which could lead to arguments if subsequent enforcement.

29–404 Condition requiring maintenance to a specified standard of repair is void for uncertainty or unreasonableness as imposing a continuing obligation to keep site up to a particular standard of repair. [1966] J.P.L. 663.

29–405 Refusal to impose a condition which would be unenforceable in practice. [1969] J.P.L. 486.

29–406 Condition as to "smell" is too vague and the matter is more appropriately dealt with under other legislation. A condition requiring the reinstatement of land in the event of a future abandonment of use is not appropriate in a permission for permanent buildings. [1971] J.P.L. 475.

S.29. DETERMINATION OF APPLICATIONS

29–407 Condition requiring yard to be kept clean and tidy is unenforceable. [1971] J.P.L. 716.

29–408 Condition requiring the future maintenance of a silo is too vague. [1976] J.P.L. 324.

29–409 Condition of planning permission that no nuisance be caused to residential properties in the area by reason of the emission of noise, vibration, smoke, smell, fumes, soot, ash, dust or grit is not too vague. [1977] J.P.L. 677.

29–410 Condition requiring a site to be kept tidy is imprecise and unacceptable. [1979] J.P.L. 414.

29–411 A condition limiting the occupancy of a building should be sufficiently precise both to indicate to the developer what he must do to comply with it and to enable a prospective occupant to ascertain from the outset from the terms of the condition whether or not he is covered by it. [1981] J.P.L. 918.

29–412 Licensed club-house—condition of planning permission limiting its use to the occupants of caravans on nearby sites was held to be necessary, reasonable and enforceable. [1985] J.P.L. 429.

29–413 Condition in planning permission for use of gaming machine in cafe restricting previously unrestricted opening hours of cafe is *ultra vires*. Any condition which sought to control the use of the gaming machines within the premises independantly of the cafe use would be unenforceable.

Use of gaming machines in cafe unacceptable without a condition restricting that use but no such condition can properly be imposed, therefore permission refused on an appeal against conditional planning permission. [1985] J.P.L. 507.

29–414 Licensed club-house—condition of planning permission limiting use to occupants of caravans on nearby sites. Impossible to frame a condition relating to noise levels outside the building with sufficient precision. [1985] J.P.L. 429.

6. Severence of Invalid Conditions

29–415 Pyx Grantie Ltd. v. Min. of Housing & Local Govt. [1958] 1 Q.B. 554, C.A. *Per* Hodson L.J.: the court has no power to alter the nature of planning permission by severance.

29–416 Kingsway Investment (Kent) Ltd. v. Kent C.C. [1969] 2 W.L.R. 249, C.A. *Per* Davies L.J.: If an invalid condition relates not to a development but to matters introductory to permission or its final form it is severable.

29–417 Kingsway Investments (Kent) Ltd. v. Kent C.C. [1970] 2 W.L.R. 397, H.L. An *ultra vires* condition can only be severed from planning permission if it is unimportant or incidental or superimposed.

Per Lord Reid: If a condition has nothing to do with planning considerations but is only calculated to achieve some ulterior object thought to be in the public interest it should be severed from permission which should stand. But an *ultra vires* or unreasonable condition which limits the manner in which land can be developed is not severable.

29–418 Allnatt London Properties v. Middlesex (1964) 62 L.G.R. 304. As no reasonable planning authority, in the circumstances, would have refused application for planning permission, it should stand free of conditions.

29–419 R. v. Hillingdon L.B.C., ex p. Royco Homes Ltd. [1974] 1 Q.B. 720. Condition which was fundamentally unreasonable could not be severed.

29–420 R. v. Edmundsbury B.C., *ex p.* **Investors in Industry Commercial Properties Ltd.** [1985] 3 All E.R. 234. Condition requiring three independent retail units, even if invalid, could be severed from permission for a supermarket.

S.29. DETERMINATION OF APPLICATIONS

7. Examples of Ministerial Policies towards Conditions

(a) General

29–421 Conditions on brickworks. [1977] C.L.Y. 2968.

29–422 Erection of a dwelling-house in a Conservation Area—relevant conditions. [1980] J.P.L. 768.

29–423 Extraction of sand and gravel—planning conditions. [1983] J.P.L. 701.

29–424 Appropriate conditions on permission for the drying and storage of grain in the Green Belt. [1985] J.P.L. 212.

29–425 Conditions attached to permission for the extraction of silica sand by surface working. [1985] J.P.L. 584.

29–426 Conditions providing for the adequate restoration and after-care on the recovery of coal from a disused colliery spoil heap. [1985] J.P.L. 502.

(b) Conditions relating to section 52 agreements.

29–427 Contributions by developers towards the cost of public car-parking facilities are only appropriate where:
  (a) the developer would be able to provide parking space on the site (or nearby land under his control);
  (b) the local planning authority decides (in the light of relevant considerations) that the imposition of a planning condition requiring parking spaces to be provided on or near the site could be justified;
  (c) the developer is prepares to make, and the local planning authority to receive, a voluntary contribution in lieu. [1968] J.P.L. 423.

29–428 Unlawful to grant planning permission subject to a requirement that the developer shall enter into an agreement under s.52 of the Town and Country Planning Act 1971. [1980] J.P.L. 841.

29–429 Condition requiring the developer to enter into Scottish equivalent of a section 52 agreement. [1981] J.P.L. 301.

29–430 Matters covered by section 52 agreement but a standard condition concerning reserved matters was still added. It was not appropriate to amend a section 52 agreement by way of a condition to planning permission. [1982] J.P.L. 326.

29–431 Planning permission conditional upon a prior section 52 agreement. [1983] J.P.L. 704.

(c) Personal conditions

29–432 Removal of a condition limiting planning permission to the applicant or other person approved by the planning authority. [1970] J.P.L. 599.

29–433 Permission for the use of part of a dwelling-house by the owner for professional purposes limited to the owner. [1970] J.P.L. 664.

29–434 A personal permission for the erection of permanent buildings will scarcely ever be justified. [1971] J.P.L. 190.

29–435 Personal permission for a ladies' hairdressing business in a bungalow in a primarily residential area. [1972] J.P.L. 663.

29–436 Personal permission to use part of a dwelling-house as an architect's drawing-office. [1973] J.P.L. 188.

29–437 Personal permission for a limited period for the stationing of a mobile home on a small agricultural unit. [1974] J.P.L. 496.

29–438 Personal permission for a limited period for a change of use of the bay of a retail furniture warehouse from a customer car park to the display and storage of furniture. [1974] J.P.L. 626.

29–439 Condition limiting the benefit of permission to the applicant was held to be unreasonable. [1982] J.P.L. 265.

29–440 Conditions limiting sales from a farm shop, including a personal condition. [1984] J.P.L. 835.

(d) Occupancy conditions

29–441 Condition of permission for the erection of a village hall with a flat over that the flat be occupied by a full-time caretaker—condition was discharged. [1966] J.P.L. 298.

29–442 Site of a single caravan in a rural area—existing caravan site in 1960—condition limiting occupation to specified persons. [1966] J.P.L. 611.

29–443 Condition limiting the occupation of cottages to service cottages to a mansion house discontinued. [1966] J.P.L. 738.

29–444 Condition restricting the occupation of a dwelling-house to a member of the agricultural population. [1967] J.P.L. 178 & 179.

29–445 Condition restricting the use of a warehouse to firms already occupying premises in the county could not reasonably be imposed where such a policy was not included in the development plan or any other formally adopted policy. [1967] J.P.L. 737.

29–446 Part-time employment in agriculture (450 hours per year between the family) was sufficient to comply with an agricultural occupancy condition on a dwelling-house. [1969] J.P.L. 590.

29–447 Removal of a condition limiting occupation of a cottage in the Green Belt to occupation as a service cottage. [1970] J.P.L. 472.

29–448 Form of condition restricting occupancy to a local firm. [1975] J.P.L. 556.

29–449 A condition restricting the use of a factory to firms and companies of specified categories must relate to development plan provisions. [1972] J.P.L. 50.

29–450 Leisure-time working on a holding fulfilling agricultural occupancy condition. [1972] J.P.L. 106.

29–451 Condition limiting occupation of a bungalow to a disabled person. [1973] J.P.L. 671.

29–452 Permission for the erection of a storeroom in a residential area. Condition restricting permission to the applicant, or to a local firm. [1975] J.P.L. 301.

29–453 Condition as to agricultural occupancy replacing a condition linked to employment at a specified farm. [1975] J.P.L. 46.

29–454 Occupancy condition was unreasonable where discretion was left with the local planning authority as to size of an acceptable firm. Occupancy condition based on a development plan policy was not acceptable for a period beyond the period of the plan. [1977] J.P.L. 398.

29–455 As to the size below which it may be difficult to qualify an occupancy condition on permission for offices. [1979] J.P.L. 412 & [1979] J.P.L. 414.

29–456 Office development conditions requiring occupiers to be approved by the local planning authority, and to be an established business or related to the needs of the local community—speculative development. Difficult to formulate a condition which was apposite, reasonable and enforceable. [1980] J.P.L. 212.

S.29. DETERMINATION OF APPLICATIONS

29–457 Rebuilding of offices in central London—condition restricting occupancy designed to secure retention of small offices was discharged. [1980] J.P.L. 848.

29–458 Agricultural occupancy condition varied to comply with the terms of Circular 24/73. [1981] J.P.L. 701.

29–459 Removal of a condition limiting planning permission to one named occupier. [1982] J.P.L. 464.

29–460 Condition restricting the use of a building to office use by a named Government Department only removed. [1982] J.P.L. 543.

29–461 Warehouse storage development situated in Surrey two miles from the Berkshire and Hampshire borders with good access to Heathrow Airport. Condition restricting occupancy to a business already established in the county of Surrey was unduly harsh given the sites particular location and the access condition was relaxed. Condition requiring that prospective tenants should obtain written approval from the Council before occupying a building introduced an undesirable and burdensome additional approval process. [1983] J.P.L. 260.

29–462 Continued waiver of an agricultural occupancy was justified only if every effort to find a suitable agricultural occupant had been made and had been unsuccessful. [1971] J.P.L. 657.

29–463 Discharge of a condition restricting occupation to persons with local connection. [1983] J.P.L. 837.

29–464 Occupancy condition restricting the occupation of a dwelling-house to a person employed in a neighbouring children's home was no longer reasonable on the disposal of the children's home. [1985] J.P.L. 72.

29–465 To justify the discharge of an agricultural occupancy condition it was necessary to show:
 (i) that existing development is surplus to the original agricultural requirements which justified the original grant;
 (ii) to date every reasonable effort has been made to ensure a continued occupancy by a person associated with an agricultural activity and that failing discharge of the condition there are no long-term prospects for use of the premises.
[1985] J.P.L. 279.

29–466 Agricultural occupancy condition was discharged where appeal site was incapable of providing a viable living for one person and the property was unsold despite considerable efforts. [1985] J.P.L. 282.

29–467 Person self-employed as an agricultural haulage contractor, with occasional keeping of animals, not employed locally in agriculture. [1985] J.P.L. 494.

29–468 Need for a full time porter/caretaker in block of flats not a material planning consideration. Application to remove condition restricting occupation of a bungalow to a porter for flats allowed on appeal. [1985] J.P.L. 510.

29–469 Condition restricting occupation of dwelling-house to person with local connection; permission granted to continue occupation in breach of the condition, on the grounds that such a condition concerned social rather than planning effects and if no need for dwelling then permission should be refused outright. [1986] J.P.L. 388.

29–470 Condition restricting occupation to person with local business connection; permission granted to continue occupation in breach of the condition on the grounds that not sufficient exceptional circumstances to justify an occupancy condition. [1986] J.P.L. 390.

S.29. DETERMINATION OF APPLICATIONS

Note

For other examples of Ministerial decisions on occupancy conditions see [1967] J.P.L. 673; [1968] J.P.L. 535; [1971] J.P.L. 656; [1972] J.P.L. 113 & 114; [1972] J.P.L. 349; [1975] J.P.L. 47; [1975] J.P.L. 48; [1975] J.P.L. 232; [1977] J.P.L. 402; [1979] J.P.L. 706; [1984] J.P.L. 374; [1984] J.P.L. 368.

D. The Interpretation of Planning Permissions

29–471 Crisp from the Fens Ltd. v. Rutland C.C. (1950) 1 P. & C.R. 48, C.A. Permission to manufacture potato crisps subject to a condition that the use of the building shall be confined to the manufacture of potato crisps or any use within Class 3. Therefore permission to manufacture potato crisps was given subject to their manufacture being within Class 3.

Per Singleton L.J.: It would be wrong to construe permission against a planning authority as it was their duty to protect public amenities.

29–472 Creighton Estates v. London C.C. [1958] C.L.Y. 3319. Permission for the use of premises "as offices and a hostel by the BBC" allowed use either as offices or a hostel and was not restricted to use by the BBC.

29–473 Sunbury–on–Thames U.D.C. v. Mann (1958) 56 L.G.R. 235, D.C. A planning permission for the continued use of a building does not give permission for building operations.

29–474 Kent v. Guildford R.D.C. (1959) 11 P. & C.R. 255, D.C. Plan accompanying an application incorporated in the permission—permission was construed by reference to the plan and the plan construed by reference to the background and surrounding circumstances at the time of the application.

29–475 Truvox v. Harrow Corpn. (1959) 173 E.G. 627. Planning permission subject to a condition that permission to expire on a certain date meant authorised use was to be discontinued on that date.

29–476 Dorking & Horley R.D.C. v. Fry (1960) 11 P. & C.R. 289, D.C. A person who continues to use land in a way for which temporary planning permission was given after it expires is in breach of a condition of that permission.

29–477 Ellis v. Worcestershire C.C. (1961) 12 P. & C.R. 178. Two separate permissions for two different farmhouses on different sites on the same farm. Once one permission was used and the farmhouse built the other permission ceased to be practically effective (except to build a farmhouse if the other destroyed) as the use of the word "farmhouse" limited the occupation of the building as effectively as if a specific condition had been imposed and did not permit the erection of a private dwelling-house severed from the farm.

29–478 Robert Russell Developments v. Buckinghamshire C.C. (1963) 61 L.G.R. 483. Conditions of planning permission requiring a cul-de-sac to be built to certain specifications. Cul-de-sac built so that there was a slight gap between the edge of the footway and the adjacent land. It was held that the plans were inconclusive and so the condition did not require strict coincidence between the footway and the neighbouring land.

29–479 Wilson v. West Sussex [1963] 2 Q.B. 764, C.A.

(1) Where planning permission specifically incorporates the terms of an application for permission it was necessary to refer to the terms of the application in construing planning permission.

(2) The word "agricultural" in planning permission had a functional significance and was to be construed as limiting the proposed building to one intended to be occupied by an agricultural worker or one engaged in agriculture.

Quaere—whether permission to erect an "agricultural cottage" which limited the

S.29. DETERMINATION OF APPLICATIONS

first occupants of the cottage to agricultural occupants imposed a similar limitation on the class of subsequent occupants.

Per Willmer J.: It was a very unfortunate practice to incorporate correspondence into planning permission.

29–480 Pardes House School Trustees v. Hendon B.C. (1964) 15 P. & C.R. 326. A condition enforceable by an enforcement notice cannot be implied from the terms of a planning permission.

29–481 F. Lucas & Sons v. Dorking & Horley R.D.C. (1964) 62 L.G.R. 481. Although a planning authority may have as its object in granting planning permission for a contemplated housing estate the development of the whole estate, it does not follow that the permission is conditional and that development conforming to that layout is permitted only if the layout is completed. What is not permitted is the erection of any of the houses other than that in accordance with the permission.

See also *Shepherd* v. *Sec. of State for Environment* [1975] J.P.L. 352.

29–482 Hall & Co. Ltd. v. Shoreham-by-Sea U.D.C. [1964] 1 W.L.R. 240 at 245. *Per* Willmer L.J.: Condition imposed by a local authority should be benevolently construed.

29–483 Winner Investments v. Hammersmith L.B.C. (1966) 64 L.G.R. 447. Construction of conditional outline consent.

29–484 Trinder v. Sevenoaks R.D.C. (1967) 204 E.G. 803. Although there was no express condition in a planning permission restricting the use of a building, it was clear from the planning permission and related documents that the purpose of the building was for an agricultural worker and therefore designed for such a person alone—the permitted use of the building was as a dwelling for an agricultural worker only.

29–485 Slough Estates v. Slough B.C. (No.2) [1969] 2 W.L.R. 1157, C.A. The word uncoloured in the words 'shown uncoloured on the plan" in the planning permission was an obvious mistake which must be rejected as being absurd; on its true construction permission was in effect an outline planning permission to develop by the erection of factories that portion of the estate which was then shown as undeveloped on the plan.

Per Stamp L.J.: An obvious mistake in a document can be corrected by construing the document according to its clearly intended meaning without resort to rectification if the meaning of the document is clear.

Per Salmon L.J.: Quaere—whether the rule in *Miller-Mead* v. *Minister of Housing and Local Government* about construction applies when a dispute about true construction of grant arises between a planning authority and the original grantee.

29–486 Edmunds v. Cardiganshire C.C. (1969) 113 S.J. 406. Declaration granted as to the correct interpretation of a planning permission.

29–487 W.G. Relton v. Min. of Housing & Local Govt. (1969) 67 L.G.R. 469. Permission to develop by way of building operations does not impliedly carry with it permission to develop by way of a change of use.

29–488 Trustees of Walton-on-Thames Charities v. Walton & Weybridge U.D.C. (1970) 68 L.G.R. 488. As planning permission enures for the benefit of the land and is not a simple matter of contract, there is no place for implied conditions in planning permission. A condition should be express, clear and set out in the document containing the permission.

29–489 R. v. Sec. of State for Environment, ex p. Reinisch (1971) 22 P. & C.R. 1022. Planning permission was not to be construed like a contract and the intentions of the parties has little relevance. A planning permission is effective if it so accurately describes the development to be carried out that anyone taking it and its accompanying plans and applications to the land will be able to see, without doubt, precisely what it is which has been authorised.

29–490 Sutton L.B.C. v. Sec. of State for Environment (1975) 29 P. & C.R. 350, D.C. A condition of planning permission stipulating the type of materials to be used on a building does not include any implied requirement that the work should be done to any particular standard.

29–491 Steggles v. Basildon U.D.C. [1975] J.P.L. 96, C.A. Planning permission for four houses granted in 1937 was modified in 1946 under the Town and Country Planning (Interim Development) Act 1943, s.4 to "permit" only one house—the modification did not amount to a new grant of permission and the 1937 permission had lapsed.

29–492 Manning v. Sec. of State for Environment [1976] J.P.L. 634, C.A. Condition restricting the use of a riding school to disabled riders. Renewal of earlier unlimited permission. Declaration that use was not limited to disabled riders. Permission to be interpreted by reference to previous history, previous application and the previous planning permission.

29–493 Chalgray Ltd. v. Sec. of State for Environment [1977] J.P.L. 175. If permission incorporated documents other than an application they may be considered in construing permission even if it is not ambiguous on its face.

Application was incorporated into permission even though there was considerable difference between the wording of the two.

29–494 Williamson & Stevens (Execs) v. Cambridgeshire C.C. (1977) 34 P. & C.R. 117. Words "occupied by gypsies" in the deemed planning permission have a functional significance and ought to be construed as limiting the proposed use—the difficulty in enforcement did not affect the validity.

Grants of planning permission can be subject to limitations.

Use of land as a site for general caravans where a permission specifies caravans occupied by gypsies would amount to a material change of use.

Use of words in deemed planning permission "for the Huntingdon and Peterborough County Council" did not make it a personal permission.

29–495 Hooper v. Slater (1977) 245 E.G. 573, D.C. Permission to use land for warehousing and as a storage depot did not cover the "storing" of caravans on the land.

29–496 United Refineries Ltd. v. Essex C.C. [1978] J.P.L. 110. Stripping of topsoil was a building operation and amounted to work being commenced to comply with a condition that building operations commence by a certain date. Work costing £30,000 was only a small part of a project costing £15,000,000 but not *de minimis*.

29–497 R. v. Derbyshire C.C., ex p. North East Derbyshire D.C. (1979) 77 L.G.R. 389. A condition attached to a planning permission requiring refilling could be regarded as authorising tipping even though there had occurred a breach of other conditions.

29–498 L.A.H. Ames Ltd. v. North Bedfordshire B.C. [1980] J.P.L. 183. Planning permission requiring the commencement of development within three years was unambiguous and not to be construed in the light of a section 52 agreement requiring commencement within 21 years.

29–499 Edmunds v. Sec. of State for Environment [1981] J.P.L. 52. Plan for a planning application modified by an accompanying letter stating that it was impossible to provide a perfectly accurate plan. Permission to be interpreted by reference to the letter.

29–500 Kwik Save Discount Group Ltd. v. Sec. of State for Environment [1981] J.P.L. 198, C.A. Anglesey case—planning permission impliedly limited to use as a car showroom and not general retail use.

Quaere—whether permission for use as a retail showroom could mean permission for supermarket use.

29–501 Carpet Decor (Guildford) v. Sec. of State for Environment [1981] J.P.L. 806. To exclude a General Development Order or Use Classes Order by condition it must be unequivocal. Here parts of the planning permission were in a common form and printed on the documents. Their purpose was to ensure that the operations were carried out in accordance with the deposited plan and that the premises were used for the purpose described. This did not exclude a Use Classes Order.

29–502 Waverley D.C. v. Sec. of State for Environment [1982] J.P.L. 105. The word "cattle" had just as functional a meaning as, for example, "agricultural" and restriction of a use to use as a depot for cattle lorries, particularly in the context of the application, limited use of the land to one compatible with its other agricultural uses. It did not matter that the use as a depot was not a direct adjunct to its agricultural use. Use as a general haulage depot was not within the permission.

29–503 Centre Hotels (Cranston) Ltd. v. Sec. of State for Environment [1982] J.P.L. 108. What happens after the grant of permission cannot be used to construe the permission itself.

29–504 Watford B.C. v. Sec. of State for Environment [1982] J.P.L. 518. Planning permission was not to be construed too narrowly or nicely. In particular, in the context of the case the phrase "no wholesale, storage or retail business of any kind to be conducted from the premises" meant "no wholesale, storage or retail business of any kind is to be carried on from the premises."

29–505 Curtis v. David O'Morgan [1982] J.P.L. 581. Enforcement notice—construction of the word "vehicle" in planning permission. Whether it was a breach of the planning condition not to exceed a certain number of vehicles.

29–506 Clwyd C.C. v. Sec. of State for Environment & Welsh Aggregates [1982] J.P.L. 696.

(1) Where planning permission is given for the use of part of a site for a particular purpose which necessarily involves the use of motor vehicles and there are no conditions imposed relating to their route the landowner is entitled to use his own rights as a landowner to get from the access to the operative part and special planning permission for such a use is not required.

(2) The words "subject to the following condition" are not sufficient of themselves to make conditions attached to the planning permission conditions precedent.

(3) One could use the planning application as an aid to the construction of the planning permission.

29–507 Irlam Brick Co. v. Warrington B.C. [1982] J.P.L. 709. Permission to extract clay and brick, earth and materials containing a condition that once extraction had ceased the *site* should be made available as a tip and should be filled in within reasonable time. Condition also gave the planning authority a right to reconsider its approval should workings not have been reinstated within 10 years of the workings having ceased. Reason given for the condition was to provide for the reinstatement of the land at as early a date as practicable. Held:

(1) There was an implied planning permission granted for tipping in accordance with the condition.

(2) Entitled to have regard to the reason for the condition as an aid to construction but that merely indicates the purposes of the condition, the reason itself is not a condition.

(3) Notice after 10 years prohibiting any further tipping was within the terms of the condition even though it would prevent reinstatement. Such a possibility was not in conflict with the purposes of the condition as the planning authority could

take the view that if the right was only given for a limited period it would encourage the company to exercise it during that period.

Condition reserving the power to stop tipping if after 10 years works had not been reinstated was valid. Permission to tip was always subject to a planning authority's right to determine it after 10 years of the working having ceased and therefore termination was not a derogation from what had been granted.

29–508 North Norfolk D.C. v. Long (1983) 267 E.G. 251 C.A. Permission to convert two old buildings into a dwelling-house "so as to retain those buildings in good order." Structural problems necessitated the demolition of walls so that the original buildings virtually ceased to exist. Once the buildings had been demolished the new works amounted to operations in breach of planning permission.

Decision of Webster J. reversed: see [1981] J.P.L. 886.

29–509 Meadows v. Sec. of State for Environment [1983] J.P.L. 538. Inspector was wrong to go behind planning permissions and make assumptions about the knowledge of the planning authority at the time the permissions were granted. Permission granted for use as a store. Question whether this permission was implemented by use for storage and wholesale transactions.

29–510 Trio Thames v. Sec. of State for Environment [1984] J.P.L. 183. There can be situations where the Secretary of State can take the view that a mixed use could be carried on under a planning permission for a single, primary use.

29–511 Lobb v. Sec. of State for Environment [1984] J.P.L. 336. Approval of reserved matters in respect of a plot subject to two outline planning permissions. The Secretary of State had failed to consider whether approval of reserved matters could be taken to relate to more than one of the extant outline permissions. Implementation of later outline permission materially affected implementation of the original outline permission.

29–512 Pioneer Aggregates (U.K.) Ltd. v. Sec. of State for Environment [1984] 2 All E.R. 358, H.L. The duration of a valid planning permission is governed by the provisions of the planning legislation which is a comprehensive legislative code. The courts may only resort to the principles of private law to resolve difficulties by the application of common law or equitable principles where the code is silent or ambiguous.

As the legislation makes no provision for the abandonment of planning permission and as by s.33(1) it provides that any grant of planning permission to develop is, except in so far as the permission otherwise provides, to enure for the benefit of the land and of all the persons for the time being interested therein it follows that planning permission cannot be extinguished by mere conduct alone.

A commercial decision to terminate operations on land where there is valid planning permission for such operations cannot by itself extinguish that permission unless the terms of the permission provide that that is to be the consequence.

However, where there are two mutually inconsistent planning permissions in respect of the same land, implementation of one renders the other incapable of implementation.

Pilkington v. *Sec. of State for Environment* approved.

29–513 Wivenhoe Port Ltd. v. Colchester B.C. [1985] J.P.L. 396. Permission authorising a change of use subject to a condition relating to the design of buildings. This did not authorise the construction of the buildings. Whether you can have the equivalent of an outline permission for a change of use. Application form can be used to construe the grant where questions are raised as to its validity.

29–514 Cynon Valley D.C. v. Secretary of State for Wales [1986] J.P.L. 283. A grant of planning permission only covers the initial material change of use, it does not authorise later reversion to the use authorised.

S.29. DETERMINATION OF APPLICATIONS

29–515 Enforcement of a time-limit condition on permission for the erection of a new building. Although some use was made of the outer walls of the former building there was effectively the erection of a new building and could therefore properly require demolition of all of the building. [1966] J.P.L. 116.

29–516 Condition limiting permission for a caravan site to a three-year period to prevent a permanent site. Although there was no specific condition requiring discontinuance of use or the removal of caravans, it should imply that that must be done by the end of the three-year period. [1966] J.P.L. 487.

29–517 Plan with a planning application marking a shop as "Ironmonger-shop" does not restrict the shop to an ironmonger's shop. [1969] J.P.L. 156.

29–518 Planning permission for a petrol service station allows the parking of vehicles whilst waiting for petrol or servicing, but longer-term parking is not within it, nor is it ancillary to it. [1969] J.P.L. 290.

29–519 Outline permission for the erection of buildings to form an industrial estate did not give permission for the industrial use of open land. [1970] J.P.L. 341.

29–520 A planning permission must be taken as a whole, it is not divisible. [1970] J.P.L. 411.

29–521 Condition requiring the turfing and planting of an area did not exclude General Development Order permissions nor did it prevent the erection of a wall as a form of enclosure. [1971] J.P.L. 582.

29–522 Failure to colour distinctively additional stories to a proposed extension misled the planning authority as to the extent of the application—permission was only granted to the limited extent appreciated by the local authority. Knowledge of an official of the local planning authority as to the extent of the application was not to be imputed to the local planning authority. [1972] J.P.L. 725.

29–523 A permission to use a building as a discount warehouse, in the absence of conditions to the contrary, permits retail trading on the premises. [1972] J.P.L. 461.

29–524 Permission granted on an application for a "proposed farmworker's house" is not restricted to its occupation by a farmworker. [1972] J.P.L. 466.

29–525 Implementation of one of two inconsistent planning permissions rendered the other incapable of implementation. [1972] J.P.L. 580.

29–526 In the absence of any condition to the contrary, a permission for residential development, showroom and basement store does not limit storage use to storage in connection with the remainder of the building. [1972] J.P.L. 652.

29–527 Concrete batching plant was not covered by a condition requiring the removal of machinery used in the winning and working of sand and gravel. [1973] J.P.L. 722.

29–528 Planning permission for alterations and additions does not permit rebuilding. [1974] J.P.L. 162.

29–529 Storage of builder's materials properly required for alterations to a dwelling-house for which planning permission had been granted does not involve unauthorised development. [1974] J.P.L. 617.

29–530 Further application following outline planning permission—because of differences in plans the permission given thereon was a fresh permission not an approval of the details of the outline permission. [1976] J.P.L. 384.

29–531/532 Planning permission for the renovation and improvement of an existing dwelling does not permit rebuilding. [1974] J.P.L. 555.

29–533 Planning permission for a builder's merchants covered such wholesale and retail sales as would normally be associated with such premises—5 per cent. retail sales was about the maximum normally expected at a builder's merchant's premises. [1976] J.P.L. 594.

29–534 A "club" is normally taken to imply restricted access and use substantially for and by bona fide club members. A "general entertainment centre" implies a much wider scope of use. [1978] J.P.L. 401.

29–535 Application for permission for part-business and part-domestic use. Permission was given for use as an electrical contractor's business. Permission was to be construed as granted and the planning authority resolution and correspondence was irrelevant. [1980] J.P.L. 61.

29–536 Planning permission is governed by the wording of the written permission. [1980] J.P.L. 352.

29–537 Grant of planning permission for part only of a development for which an application for permission was made. [1981] J.P.L. 698.

29–538 Permission granted for a residential caravan. Structure assembled on site from several separately constructed parts did not meet the legal definition of caravan contained in s. 13 of the Caravan Sites Act 1968. [1982] J.P.L. 265.

29–539 Chalet built for the use of shooting parties and hitherto used for such purposes. Although the original planning permission allowed the erection of a chalet which could have been used as a dwelling-house, it had never been fully implemented and use as a normal residence would be a material change of use. [1982] J.P.L. 393.

E. Judicial Review of the Determination of Planning Applications

29–540 R. v. Harrow U.D.C., ex p. Joiner (1956) 6 P.&C.R. 15. Although the issue of the order of *certiorari* is always a matter of discretion there are many cases in which the court can only exercise its discretion in one way.

29–541 Gregory v. Camden L.B.C. [1966] 1 W.L.R. 899. Town and Country Planning legislation gave rights to the public, not to individuals—a neighbour *per se* has insufficient *locus standi* to challenge the validity of a planning permission. But see later cases.

29–542 R. v. Hillingdon L.B.C., ex p. Royco Homes Ltd. [1973] 2 W.L.R. 805. In planning cases the statutory appeal procedure would normally be more appropriate, but in an appropriate case where, for example, there was an error on the face of the record, an order of *certiorari* could be made to quash a local planning authority's acts.

29–543 R. v. Sheffield C.C., ex p. Mansfield (1978) 37 P.&C.R. 1, D.C. Where it is alleged that a local planning authority has failed to have regard to material considerations under s.29(1), *certiorari* is an appropriate remedy.

Quaere Whether a ratepayer has *locus standi* to apply for *certiorari* to quash a planning decision.

29–544 Bellway v. Strathclyde R.C. [1980] J.P.L. 683.

(1) Applicants for planning permission did not have sufficient title to sue for a declaration that the calling-in of a planning application by the regional planning authority was *ultra vires*.

(2) The remedy of reduction was premature until other statutory means of review were exhausted.

29–545 Steeples v. Derbyshire C.C. [1984] 3 All E.R. 468.

(1) The plaintiff had a private right to seek a declaration on ancillary development as it would involve taking a small piece of his land for a visibility splay. As

S.29. DETERMINATION OF APPLICATIONS

other development was interconnected he would be allowed a declaration on both developments.

(2) If the plaintiff could show that a proprietary interest of his would reasonably and probably be affected by the act in question, that he would probably be prejudiced by it, he suffered in respect of that act damage under a head recognised by the law—here the Plaintiff reasonably anticipated that if development proceeded his view would be impaired, the ambiant noise level would be increased, his use of Pit Lane, at present unhindered, would to some extent be interfered with, and his land would be invaded to a greater or lesser extent, depending on the safeguards, by litter and possibly by vandals or trespassers. The plaintiff therefore would suffer damage.

(3) A person with sufficient interest under R.S.C. Ord. 53, r.3(5) would have *locus standi* in *inter partes* proceedings for a declaration under Ord. 15, r.16.

29–546 I.R.C. v. National Federation of Self-employed and Small Businesses Ltd. [1982] A.C. 617. In deciding on a question of *locus standi* under RSC Ord. 53 in difficult cases, you must take the question of sufficient interest together with the legal and factual context of the application.

29–547 Barrs v. Bethell [1981] 3 W.L.R. 874. Interference with proprietary rights or special damage is a pre-condition to bringing an action by writ.

29–548 R. v. Hammersmith & Fulham B.C., ex p. People Before Profit Ltd. [1981] J.P.L. 869. To object in a planning matter a person need not be a resident or ratepayer, but he must have a legitimate bona fide reason. It is proper to look behind an incorporated body to see if people behind it have a genuine objection. Whether there are any merits in an application relevant to the consideration of *locus standi*.

29–549 Covent Garden Community Association Ltd. v. G.L.C. [1981] J.P.L. 183. Judicial review Order 53—the fact that leave is granted *ex parte* does not preclude the respondent from taking issue as to the *locus standi* of the applicant, although the granting of leave is a relevant consideration.

A group of local residents may have the *locus standi* to apply to quash a planning authority's resolution to grant itself planning permission.

29–550 O'Reilly v. Mackman [1982] 3 All E.R. 1124. Where a plaintiff complains of an infringement of his public law rights he must as a general rule proceed by way of application for judicial review and not by way of declaratory action.

29–551 R. v. L.B. of Haringey, ex p. Barrs [1983] J.P.L. 54. Permission given by a local authority to itself was quashed as wrong and unreasonable because it was in conflict with main planning principles and would not have been given to a private individual (but note that Comyn J's decision was reversed by the Court of Appeal on the merits of the application).

29–552 R. v. Castle Point D.C., ex p. Brooks [1985] J.P.L. 473. Neighbour successfully applied for the approval of details to be held invalid.

F. Liability in Tort Arising from the Determination of a Planning Application

29–553 Evans v. London C.C. (1960) 12 P. & C.R. 172. No jurisdiction to hear a claim for damages against a planning authority for not considering a planning application properly.

29–554 Strabble v. Dartford B.C. [1984] J.P.L. 329, C.A. Where an individual suffers as a result of a local authority decision on a planning application he has no cause of action for damages, his remedy is by way of the statutory appeal system.

29–555 Lyons v. F.W.Booth (Contractors) and Maidstone B.C. (1982) 262 E.G. 981. Although the point was not in issue, it was agreed that the duty set out in *Anns*

v. *Merton L.B.C.* [1978] A.C. 228 applies to the consideration and approval of plans for development under the Town and Country Planning legislation.

SECTION 30. CONDITIONAL GRANT OF PLANNING PERMISSION SPECIAL CASES

A. Conditions Relating to Land under the Control of the Applicant: section 30(1)(a)

30–01 Hayns v. Sec. of State for Environment [1977] J.P.L. 663. Land needed for visibility splays owned by local authority—permission refused because land not under control of applicant. Fact applicant had a right of way gave him no right to have visibility splays. Local authority would be wrong to refuse to co-operate unless they had good reason for not preserving sight lines but court would not interfere.

30–02 George Wimpey & Co. Ltd. v. New Forest D.C. [1979] J.P.L. 314, "Control" for s.30 does not require an estate or interest in land but only such right as was required to implement condition. Whether satisfied that test, a matter of fact and degree for local planning authority or the Secretary of State. Decision quashed as Secretary of State had failed to consider whether negative condition under s.29 would have been sufficient.

30–03 Kember v. Sec. of State for Environment [1982] J.P.L. 383. Example of condition not sufficiently related to the development being granted.

30–04 Atkinson v. Sec. of State for Environment [1983] J.P.L. 599. Condition of planning permission for seven houses that farmhouse be demolished upheld even though sold to somebody else. No need to rely on section 30, when the application included the land which was the subject of the condition. Such a condition not invalid even though it might cause hardship in special circumstances. For section 30(1)(a) to apply land had to be under the control of the applicant at the time of the grant of the permission.

30–05 Benefit of restrictive covenant attaching to application land can provide applicant with sufficient control over other land to enable conditions to be imposed on a planning permission. [1967] J.P.L. 617.

30–06 Use of petrol filling station, planning permission for which subject to condition requiring prior completion of car showroom and office development on adjacent site falsely represented as being in same ownership.—Condition upheld. [1977] J.P.L. 680.

30–07 Condition requiring laying out and maintenance of access land on grant of planning permission for supermarket development. For the purpose of section 30(1)(a) the applicant had sufficient control over the land through an agreement—the fact that agreement later abandoned irrelevant. [1980] J.P.L. 425.

30–08 A local planning authority is empowered by virtue of s.30(1)(a) to impose conditions for regulating the development or use of any land under the control of the applicant, whether or not it is land in respect of which the application was made, provided that such conditions appear to the authority to be expedient for the purpose of, or in connection with, the development authorised by the permission. [1985] J.P.L. 811.

B. Limited Period Conditions: section 30(1)(b)

30–09 Newbury District Council v. Sec. of State for Environment [1981] A.C. 578. In exceptional circumstances conditions can be imposed requiring demolition of building at the end of specified period, even though the building was not being authorised by the permission to which the condition is attached. Need for connection between the condition and the development being granted.

S.30. CONDITIONAL GRANT OF PLANNING PERMISSION SPECIAL CASES

30–10 Imposition of a time limit on a permission for a residential caravan site is not justified unless the land is expected to be required for some other purpose in the future or unless there are valid planning objection to its use as a permanent caravan site. [1967] J.P.L. 621.

30–11 Discharge of condition limiting planning permission for caravan site to 22 years. [1967] J.P.L. 240.

30–12 Limited permission for use of dwelling-house as home for persons with mental disorder to test effect upon neighbourhood. [1969] J.P.L. 665.

30–13 Five-year limit on display of advertisements reasonable. [1969] J.P.L. 668.

30–14 Planning authority may grant a time limited permission for a use notwithstanding fact that that use has become immune from enforcement. [1971] J.P.L. 350.
   See also [1971] J.P.L. 353.

30–15 Time limited permission for continued use of premises as nursery school to allow time for re-location. [1970] J.P.L. 114.

30–16 Temporary permission for use of part of dwelling-house for tuition in typing and shorthand. [1973] J.P.L. 114.

30–17 Planning permission granted for a limited period only, in view of pending compulsory purchase order. [1975] J.P.L. 41.

30–18 Discharge of time limit condition imposed to ensure proper maintenance. [1975] J.P.L. 234.

30–19 Discharge of time limit condition of permission for caravan site, imposed to secure future control. [1975] J.P.L. 362.

30–20 Time-limited permission for the stationing of 4 gypsy caravans on land in open countryside. [1978] J.P.L. 340.

30–21 Reason for temporary permission can never be that a time limit is necessary because of the effect of the development on the amenities of the area. [1981] J.P.L. 695.

30–22 Condition limiting time of permission in view of possibility of development in area unreasonable in absence of firm proposals for redevelopment of the site. [1984] J.P.L. 905.

30–23 Time-limited permission is not appropriate if there are objections to the design and appearance of the building. Durability of materials of construction is properly a matter covered by the Building Regulations and is not a reason for imposing a time-limited permission. [1985] J.P.L. 70.

SECTION 31. DIRECTION AS TO METHOD OF DEALING WITH APPLICATIONS

31–01 Co-operative Retail Services Ltd. v. Taff-Ely B.C. (1979) 39 P. & C.R. 223, C.A. Section 31(1)(*b*), under which the Town and Country Planning (Development Plan) Direction 1975 was made, is procedural only and would not, on its true construction, have deprived the county council of the power to grant planning permission without referring the application to the Secretary of State.

31–02 R. v. St. Edmundsbury B.C., ex p. Investors in Industry Commercial Properties Ltd. [1985] 3 All E.R. 234. Section 31(1)(*b*) does not go to jurisdiction and so the Town and Country Planning (Development Plans) (England) Direction 1981 is not mandatory but merely directory. In any case failure to advertise a technical breach as a proposed departure was widely canvassed in the local press.

SECTION 33. PROVISONS AS TO EFFECT OF PLANNING PERMISSION

A. Permissions Enure for Benefit of the Land: section 33(1)

33–01 Pioneer Aggregates (U.K.) Ltd. v. Sec. of State for Environment [1984] 2 All E.R. 358 H.L. As permissions enure for the benefit of the land they cannot be extinguished by conduct alone.

B. The Purposes for which Buildings may be Used: section 33(2)

33–02 Wilson v. West Sussex [1963] 2 Q.B. 764, C.A. "Design" in s.33(2) is not used in its technical sense and does not mean architectural design suitable for a particular purpose. It was clear that in the general sense of the word the building was designed to be used as an agricultural cottage. The words "agricultural cottage" specified the purpose for which the building might be used under s.33(2).

33–03 Trinder v. Sevenoaks R.D.C. (1969) 209 E.G. 803. Outline planning application stated that the purpose of use was "occupation by an agricultural worker." There was no condition in the planning permission. The building had been designed for occupation by an agricultural worker and permission was granted for that purpose only. This restriction applied to subsequent occupations.

33–04 Wood v. Sec. of State for Environment [1973] 1 W.L.R. 707. Section 33(2) is not applicable to buildings erected under permitted development granted by the General Development Order.

Note

Also see decisions on interpretation of planning permissions.

33–05 Building was not designed for agriculture in the sense of its physical appearance and layout. The shape of the building and the openings suggested a bungalow rather than a building connected with farming. [1986] J.P.L. 384.

SECTION 34. REGISTER OF APPLICATIONS AND DECISIONS

34–01 J.J. Steeples v. Derbyshire C.C. [1981] J.P.L. 582. All documents received by the District Council were kept in one file—this did not constitute a register for the purposes of art. 21 of the General Development Order or regs. 4 and 52 of the Town and Country Planning General Regulations 1976. Therefore notices had not been placed in the required register and so the power to pass a resolution granting planning permission to the county council never arose and the resolution was *ultra vires* and void.

SECTION 35. REFERENCE OF APPLICATIONS TO SECRETARY OF STATE

35–01 Davies v. Sec. of State for Wales (1976) 33 P. & C.R. 330. Application to extend a caravan site called in under s.35 Local planning authority had failed to serve on the applicant the terms and reasons for the direction as required under Art. 15 of the General Development Order 1973; now art. 19 of 1977 Order. It was held that the purpose of art. 15 was to ensure that the applicant was aware of his right to be heard and the requirement that the reasons for calling in an application should be given was merely to assist an applicant in deciding whether or not he wished to be heard. Where an applicant is heard, failure to serve notice had not prejudiced him.

35–02 R. v. Sec. of State for Environment, ex p. Newprop [1983] J.P.L. 386
(1) Section 35 does not require the Secretary of State to entertain any request that he should call in any planning application. His discretion is wholly at large and

is in essence a purely administrative discretion with little hint of any judicial exercise at all. A decision could be challenged if it is wildly perverse.

(2) Secretary of State is not required to give reasons for the exercise of his discretion and so the court was not called on to examine with care the reasons given for refusal to exercise his discretion. If a letter gave the Secretary of State's main reason for not exercising discretion it could not be challenged on the ground that that was the only reason.

(3) If the Secretary of State did give a reason which was clearly a wrong reason the court could interfere and he would have misdirected himself in law.

(4) Except where something was so obviously relevant that no Secretary of State could think otherwise he could not be criticised for failing to take into account something relevant unless it was put to him for his consideration—he is under no duty to find out if there are matters relevant to the exercise of his discretion.

(5) Although Circulars 142/73 and 2/81 laid down a general policy not to call in matters unless they involved planning issues of more than local importance it did allow for exceptions and therefore it did not fetter his discretion.

(6) The court could not say it was wrong for the Secretary of State to exercise a supervisory jurisdiction under s.35 but he was not bound to do so.

35–03 Sir Brandon Meredith Rhys Williams v. Sec. of State for Wales [1985] J.P.L. 29. Section 35 conferred an unqualified discretion on the Minister and its exercise was purely a matter of policy or value judgment for him, though it could be reviewed for error of law or on the *Wednesbury* grounds.

SECTION 36. APPEALS AGAINST PLANNING DECISIONS

A. The Powers and Duties of Secretary of State on Appeal

36–01 Southend Corporation v. Min. of Housing and Local Govt. (1963) 185 E.G. 605. Minister must form his own view. He cannot accept the findings of and legal advice to the Inspector without forming his own view.

36–02 H. Lavender & Sons Ltd. v. Min. of Housing & Local Govt. [1970] 1 W.L.R. 1231. Although the Minister is entitled to have a policy and to decide an appeal in the context of that policy he must give genuine and unfettered consideration to all matters properly put before him.

The Minister had wrongly delegated decision to the Minister of Agriculture in refusing to grant any application opposed by him.

36–03 Stringer v. Min. of Housing & Local Govt. [1971] 1 All E.R. 65. A Minister charged with the duty of making administrative decisions in a fair and impartial manner may nevertheless have a general policy on matters which are relevant to those decisions provided that the existence of the policy does not preclude him from fairly judging all the issues which are relevant to each individual case.

The Minister has power to entertain a planning appeal even though the local planning authority's determination is void because he can deal with the matters *de novo*.

36–04 Miller v. Weymouth and Melcombe Regis Corpn. (1974) 27 P. & C.R. 468. Once the Secretary of State has issued his decision letter, he cannot amend a clerical slip. Discontinuance Order appeal case.

36–05 Glacier Metal Co. Ltd. v. L.B. Hillingdon [1976] J.P.L. 165. The Secretary of State's power to vary the local planning authority's decision does not enable him to give permission for something which is not the subject-matter of the planning application.

An application for a sports centre is very different from a sports ground.

36–06 Price Brothers (Rode Hesth) Ltd. v. Dept. of the Environment (1978) 28 P. & C.R. 579. The hearing by the Secretary of State of an appeal under s.36 is a hearing *de novo*. The inspector is concerned with everything that happens up until the time of the inquiry, and the Secretary of State up until the time of the decision—not confined to the circumstances at the date of the local planning authority's decision. Where a decision letter is quashed the Secretary of State may take into consideration all material matters up to the date of the new decision letter and may still dismiss the appeal on other grounds.

36–07 Robert Hitchins Builders Ltd. v. Sec. of State for Environment [1979] J.P.L. 534, C.A. *sub nom. Britannia (Cheltenham) Ltd. v. Sec. of State for Environment*. Where the Secretary of State regarded proposed conditions as objectionable or potentially *ultra vires* he was not obliged to dismiss appeals—he had power to deal with applications as if they had been made to him in the first instance.

36–08 Niarchos (London) Ltd. v. Sec. of State for Environment [1981] J.P.L. 118. The Secretary of State's decision to reopen an inquiry is perverse where it could only result in further delay and expense—*mandamus* issued to direct the Secretary of State to determine an appeal without re-opening the inquiry.

36–09 McLaren v. Sec. of State for Environment [1981] J.P.L. 423. Although the Secretary of State lacks the power to enter into a section 52 agreement or to require the parties to an appeal to do so, he may intimate to them before issuing a formal decision that if a section 52 agreement were to be entered into in the form of a draft produced at the inquiry he would regard this as a case where he would grant planning permission. He could then adjourn the matter for a reasonable time to consider the further developments.

36–10 M. J. Shanley Ltd. v. Sec. of State for Environment [1982] J.P.L. 380. After rejecting conditions imposed by local planning authority if the Secretary of State did not consider whether could achieve the same end by imposing other conditions he had not performed his duties.

36–11 New Forest D.C. v. Sec. of State for Environment [1983] J.P.L. 178. An appeal on a subsequent application is heard *de novo* by the Secretary of State and he can taken into account any new matters raised.

36–12 Hatfield Construction v. Sec. of State for Environment [1983] J.P.L. 605. Policy statements in Circulars and the like were part of the background to every planning appeal and it could be assumed that they had been considered unless it was clearly demonstrated that they had been ignored.

36–13 Chalgray Ltd. v. Sec. of State for Environment (1976) 33 P. & C.R. 10.
(1) The fact that an application was made for approval of details which did not comply with or which went beyond the outline permission did not make an appeal to Secretary of State against a refusal of approval, which complied with the statutory provisions as to form, automatically invalid. Correct course for Secretary of State is to dismiss the appeal on the ground that the matters for which approval was sought were not within the outline permission.
(2) The Secretary of State declining to consider an appeal, is a decision on an appeal under s.36.

36–14 Co-operative Retail Services v. Sec. of State for Environment (1979) 39 P. & C.R. 428, C.A. A "decision of the Secretary of State on an appeal" in s.36(6) means a decision that disposes of an appeal, not a decision in the course of an appeal. A decision not to adjourn the hearing of an inquiry is not a "decision of the Secretary of State on an appeal."

36–15 Minister's jurisdiction on appeal is limited to development to which the planning application related. [1967] J.P.L. 55.

s.36. APPEALS AGAINST PLANNING DECISIONS

36–16 The Secretary of State has no power to entertain an appeal against a refusal to allow alterations to a detailed planning permission without a further planning application. [1968] J.P.L. 108.

36–17 All matters are before the Secretary of State on an appeal against refusal of planning permission and therefore the appeal need not necessarily succeed just because the local planning authority's reasons were invalid. [1969] J.P.L. 484.

36–18 Outline application for planning permission for a specific number of houses—Secretary of State unable to grant permission for a smaller number of houses. [1973] J.P.L. 185.

36–19 Extension of a garage by the erection of an oil storage tank. Questions as to right of way not a matter for planning appeal. [1973] J.P.L. 327.

36–20 Planning permission refused altogether by the Secretary of State on an appeal against conditional grant of permission. [1974] J.P.L. 739.

36–21 The Secretary of State is not empowered to give permission in respect of part only of the appeal site. [1973] J.P.L. 555.

36–22 Appeal against one condition of planning permission—review of whole decision. [1975] J.P.L. 556.

36–23 Need for office development permit where an application for permission for two office buildings—the Secretary of State has no jurisdiction where a permit is required and lacking. [1975] J.P.L. 619.

36–24 Power of the Secretary of State to decide planning appeal on ground withdrawn at inquiry. [1977] J.P.L. 808.

36–25 Refusal to grant planning permission for a small part of a site to which the application related because it would create a material change in the basis on which the inquiry was held and would result in development substantially different from that for which permission was sought. [1978] J.P.L. 128.

36–26 Refusal of permission for the erection of a building for the production of tallow and bonemeal, and building works to an animal by-product factory, in the metropolitan green belt. Decision on appeal made despite doubts as to whether the proposal required advertisement as an unneighbourly development under art. 8 of the General Development Order. [1985] J.P.L. 578.

36–27 Appeal heard out of time because delay due to planning authority's failure to provide plan relating to condition appealed against. [1985] J.P.L. 665.

B. Appeals Decided by Written Representations

36–28 Lewis Thirkwell Ltd. v. Sec. of State for Environment [1978] J.P.L. 844. Manifestly unfair for an appeal on written representations to fail on a ground that was outside any issue appearing on the documents without the parties being given an opportunity to deal with it.

Where the inspector criticised the alignment of a road junction made by the Highway Authority and accepted by the appellants, they should be given an opportunity to deal with the criticisms.

36–29 Westminster C.C. v. Sec. of State for Environment [1984] J.P.L. 27. Although there was no requirement to provide reasons for a decision made on written representations, if reasons were requested they should comply with the standards set down by the court for decisions on appeals by public inquiry.

36–30 Sir George Grenfell-Baines v. Sec. of State for Environment [1985] J.P.L. 256. Appeal by way of written representations. Duty to give reasons for decision even though this was not expressly required by statute or regulations.

S.36. APPEALS AGAINST PLANNING DECISIONS

36–31 Taylor v. Secretary of State for Wales and Glyndwr D.C. [1985] J.P.L. 792. Appeal against refusal decided by way of written representations. Need for site inspection of the house as this was relevant to the appeal.

Note

See also the decisions on Appeals decided following local public inquiry where relevant.

C. Appeals Decided Following Public Local Inquiry

1. Rules Governing Pre-inquiry Procedure

36–32 Davies v. Sec. of State for Wales (1976) 33 P. & C.R. 330. If an applicant can show that he has been substantially prejudiced by failure to serve a rule 6(1) statement under Town and Country Planning (Inquiries Procedure) Rules 1974, he would be entitled to have the Secretary of State's decision quashed.

36–33 Greater London Council v. Sec. of State for Environment [1983] J.P.L. 793. Guidelines issued by the Minister under Rule 6(1) of the Inquiries Procedures Rules overrode at an inquiry the new policies of the Greater London Council.

Note

See decisions in the next section as to postponement of the start of the inquiry.

2. Rules Governing the Conduct of the Inquiry

36–34 General Poster & Publicity Co. v. Sec. of State for Scotland [1961] S.L.T. 62.
(1) Appointment of a technical assessor for an inquiry is within the ambit of the Secretary of State's administrative powers and reasonably incidental to the proper functioning of the inquiry.
(2) The assessor's report is only one of the elements which the Secretary of State has to consider in reaching his decision.

36–35 T.A. Miller v. Min. of Housing and Local Govt. [1968] 1 W.L.R. 992, C.A. Tribunals are entitled to act on any material which is logically probative, even though it would not be admissible as evidence in a court of law. Hearsay is admissible—the rules of natural justice must be observed, but cross-examination is not essential.

36–36 Ghafoor v. Sec. of State for Environment [1976] J.P.L. 95. Rule 11 of the Appeals (Determination by Appointed Person) (Inquiries Procedure) Rules 1974 provide only for an application for the attendance of representatives and named persons cannot be required to attend an inquiry.

36–37 Snow v. Sec. of State for Environment (1976) 33 P. & C.R. 81. An Inspector is under no duty to formulate questions on behalf of unrepresented parties.

36–38 Performance Cars Ltd. v. Sec. of State for Environment (1977) 34 P. & C.R. 92. Local planning authority failed to allow the appellant to see documents prior to an inquiry in breach of rule 6(4) of the (Inquiries Procedure) Rules 1974. Under rule 10(5) the inspector has to give the appellant adequate opportunity of considering documents and an extended lunch-break was not enough. There was therefore a breach of rule 10(5) and of the rules of natural justice. Even though there was only a risk or feeling on the part of the company that justice had not been done the Secretary of State's decision should be quashed.

36–39 Nicholson v. Sec. of State for Energy (1977) 76 L.G.R. 693. Refusal to allow cross-examination by parties who had no statutory right to cross-examine but who had appeared and given evidence, was a breach of natural justice.

36–40 The Accountancy Tuition Centre v. Sec. of State for Environment [1977] J.P.L. 792. Whether refusal by a planning officer to be cross-examined on certain matters could be challenged.

36–41 Ostreicher v. Sec. of State for Environment (1978) 37 P. & C.R. 9. Whether refusal of an adjournment was fair or unfair and in breach of the rules of natural justice depended on the circumstances of each particular case. It was not unfair when there was no reason to suspect that a date would cause problems when fixed and when the Secretary of State was not aware that no representation would be possible.

Pur curiam: Considerations for adjourning an administrative inquiry are different from those in judicial proceedings. If an objector is unavoidably absent the proper course may be to hear all those present and then hear the absent objector on a later day.

Per Waller J.: An application for adjournment does not have to be made before a date is fixed.

36–42 Gill v. Sec. of State for Environment [1978] J.P.L. 373. Where an application for an adjournment was refused, even though it was not opposed by the only other really interested party and nobody could have been prejudiced by the adjournment, and where it resulted in the applicants being unable to properly answer the local authority's case, the applicants had been denied justice—decision quashed. Proper decision would have been to allow an adjournment but recommend that the applicants pay the costs thrown away.

36–43 Winchester C.C. v. Sec. of State for Environment (1979) 39 P. & C.R. 1. Inspector's conclusion as to the quality of the house and whether it could be extended without spoiling it was not a conclusion on a scientific or technical point, but was on a matter of aesthetic taste or common sense and was one that the inspector could judge for himself so he had rightly held that it was not necessary to call evidence.

Per Waller L.J.: Although the planning authority and the applicant are in the same position before the judge it may be more difficult for a local planning authority than for an applicant to establish that they have a grievance in that they have not had a fair trial.

36–44 Lovelock v. Sec. of State for Transport (1979) 39 P. & C.R. 468, C.A. (Highways Act Case). Where a disrupter is ejected from an inquiry it may continue in her absence and it is not a breach of natural justice because she is not told of the inspector's intimation that she would be allowed back if she behaved herself.

Per Roskill L.J.: Inspectors have power to cause people who disrupt inquiries to be removed. The question of readmission or otherwise was a matter for the inspector and there was no duty on him, after the applicant's earlier behaviour to search her out and have her brought back when she had been properly and lawfully removed on two previous occasions.

36–45 Co-operative Retail Services v. Sec. of State for Environment (1979) 39 P. & C.R. 428, C.A. The Secretary of State's decision not to postpone the start of an inquiry does not preclude or predetermine the exercise by the inspector of his own complete discretion under rule 10(8) of the (Inquiries Procedure) Rules 1974 to adjourn the inquiry from time to time if he thinks it necessary in the interests of justice to any objector or party to do so.

36–46 Behrman v. Sec. of State for Environment [1979] J.P.L. 622. The inspector is not obliged of his own initiative to check that every document was covered by the rule 7 statement.

36–47 Greycoat Commercial Estates v. Radmore, *The Times* July 14, 1981, C.A. When asked for an adjournment of inquiry an inspector may take into account the question of whether some of the participants might consider a refusal of the adjournment as being unreasonable. Important to ensure confidence in the inspector's report.

36–48 Bushell v. Sec. of State for the Environment [1981] 3 W.L.R. 22. (Highways case.) In the absence of statutory rules as to the conduct of a local inquiry the procedure to be followed was a matter of discretion for the Secretary of State and the inspector. The only requirement of the Act was that the procedure has to be fair to all concerned, including the general public and supporters of the relevant scheme. What was fair, including whether cross-examination of a particular witness should be allowed, would depend on the subject-matter of the particular inquiry and was to be judged in the light of the practical realities as to the way in which administrative decisions involving judgments based on technical considerations were reached. The use by the department of the concept of traffic needs in the design year of the motorway assessed by particular methods as the yardstick for determining the order in which particular stretches of the national motorway network should be constructed was a matter of government policy in the sense that it was a topic unsuitable for investigation by individual inspectors at individual local inquiries. Therefore not entitled to cross-examine a witness as to its reliability, nor is Secretary of State required to reopen inquiry if method is revised.

36–49 R. v. Sec. of State for Environment, ex p. Mistral Investments [1984] J.P.L. 516. Decision to adjourn quashed where the appellants were not informed of arguments put forward by the other party and not given an opportunity to reply to them.

36–50 Federated Estates Ltd. v. Sec. of State for Environment [1983] J.P.L. 812. There is no obligation on the inspector to undertake an investigatory role though he has powers to call for information if he consider it necessary. The inspector should arrive at his conclusions on the basis of what the parties (including third parties) put before him, together with his inspection of the site and area, and utilising his own experience, expertise and common sense.

36–51 Halifax Building Society v. Sec. of State for Environment [1983] J.P.L. 816. Inspector cannot be criticised for making clear his view on issues which are advanced or for manifesting a lack of enthusiasm for submissions or evidence before him.

Inspector is entitled to form preliminary views about issues, but if he exhibits a degree of hostility and refusal to pay attention to the evidence so as to give the impression to reasonable people attending the inquiry that justice was not being done (even if it was) the Secretary of State's decision will be quashed.

36–52 Knights Motors v. Sec. of State for Environment [1984] J.P.L. 884. Hearsay evidence is admissible at an inquiry if it is of probative value.

36–53 An officer of the local planning authority is not required to give his personal views at a planning inquiry. [1968] J.P.L. 708.

36–54 In considering noise and its effects, regard must be had to subjective analysis as well as scientific measurements. [1974] J.P.L. 731.

3. Rules Governing Post-inquiry Procedures

(a) **Inspectors report or decision letter**

36–55 Stevens v. Min. of Housing & Local Govt. (1966) 110 S.J. 567. Clear from rule 10(1) of the Town and Country Planning Appeals (Inquiries Procedure) Rules 1962 that the inspector is not obliged to make a recommendation and where a quinquennial review of the county development plan was being considered he did not err in law in declining to make a recommendation.

s.36. APPEALS AGAINST PLANNING DECISIONS

36–56 A.B. Motor Co. of Hull v. Min. of Housing & Local Govt. (1968) 211 E.G. 281. An inspector is not required to record every submission made at an inquiry.

36–57 Deasy v. Min of Housing & Local. Govt. (1970) 214 E.G. 415. Inspector has a discretion to decide which facts are relevant.

36–58 Burwood (Caterers) Ltd. v. Sec. of State for Environment (1972) 224 E.G. 2021. Inspector is not obliged to accept uncontested evidence given at the inquiry.

36–59 Hope v. Sec. of State for Environment (1975) 31 P. & C.R. 120. Where the inspector decided an appeal his decision letter must enable an applicant to understand on what grounds the appeal had been decided and be in sufficient detail to enable him to know what conclusions the inspector had reached on the principal important controversial issues.

36–60 Wholesale Mail Order v. Sec. of State for Environment [1976] J.P.L. 163. Matters of professional opinion held by the inspector and Secretary of State do not require factual support in evidence.

The court is not the forum to question the fact that the Secretary of State may have come to two inconsistent decisions, where conflicting decisions had not been put to the Secretary of State. Doubted whether the Secretary of State committed an error of law in reaching inconsistent conclusions in two cases.

36–61 North Surrey Water Co. v. Sec. of State for Environment (1976) 34 P. & C.R. 140. An inspector is not under a duty to record fully all legal submissions made to him, but the principles of natural justice may require him, in the circumstances of a particular case, to set out the legal argument addressed to him and the authorities cited in order to make the case presented intelligible to the Secretary of State, and to provide him with the proper material.

Irrelevant submissions need not be recorded and the exercise of the inspector's discretion on what was irrelevant should not be reviewed minutely by the courts.

The inspector's report should be construed in a general way to see whether it could be fairly described as a report of the proceedings before him.

If the Secretary of State came to the right conclusion of law there would be no substantial prejudice to a party within s.245 and no ground for quashing the order even though the inspector had failed to record the argument.

36–62 Kentucky Fried Chicken (G.B.) v. Sec. of State for Environment [1977] J.P.L. 727. Inspector is entitled to use his own knowledge and common sense and is not bound to accept the evidence of experts.

36–63 East Hampshire D.C. v. Sec. of State for Environment [1978] J.P.L. 182. The inspector did not have to record everything but as the method of calculation of anticipated population increase was capable of affecting the weight to be attached to it and no explanation was given in the inspector's report, the decision would be quashed for non-compliance with the Inquiries Procedure Rules.

Affirmed by the Court of Appeal: see [1979] J.P.L. 533.

36–64 Banks Horticultural Products Ltd. v. Sec. of State for Environment [1980] J.P.L. 33. Decision quashed as either no evidence or no evidence upon which the inspector could have properly reached the conclusion to which he had come.

36–65 Sears Blok v. Sec. of State for Environment [1982] J.P.L. 248. Unnecessary to decide whether or not inspectors could by their decisions alter ministerial policy though inclined to the view that they could not.

36–66 Westminster Renslade Ltd. v. Sec. of State for Environment [1983] J.P.L. 454. The inspector at a planning inquiry is a technical tribunal entitled to make decisions and make value judgments as subjective judgments about planning matters which fell within his qualifications and expertise. This is not a matter with which the court could or should interfere.

The fact that engineering evidence is all one way and that the inspector has no engineering qualifications does not prevent him from coming to a sound planning conclusion as experts might not always be right and the tribunal is fully entitled to think that they might be wrong.

36–67 Halifax Building Society v. Sec. of State for Environment [1983] J.P.L. 816. Inspector does not have to deal with every single issue. A statement that he had taken into account all other matters raised at the inquiry may be adequate.

36–68 Mason v. Sec. of State for Environment [1984] J.P.L. 332.
(1) Inspector's error as to the distance of the witnesses' house from the appeal site was immaterial.
(2) Expert evidence on noise was somewhat subjective and the inspector was not bound to follow it.

36–69 Gabbitas v. Sec. of State for Environment [1985] J.P.L. 630. Inspector had erred in rejecting evidence because of lack of corroboration of that evidence.

(b) Disagreements between the Inspector and Secretary of State on findings of fact, the taking into account of new evidence or issues of fact, and the rule of natural justice generally

36–70 Blankey v. Min. of Housing & Local Govt. (1967) 205 E.G. 109. Decision based on a matter not canvassed at the inquiry.

36–71 Luke v. Min. of Housing & Local Govt. [1967] 3 W.L.R. 801. Where the Minister differs from the inspector on an expression of opinion upon a planning matter that is not a finding of fact, the Minister is entitled to come to a different conclusion without notifying the applicant or giving him an opportunity to make representations.

Per Lord Denning M.R.: Inspector's heading "findings of fact" is not sacrosanct and the court must look to see which findings are truly findings of fact and which are expression of opinion.

Per Lord Denning M.R. & Davies L.J.: The application of planning policy is the function of the Minister.

Per Davies L.J.: If conclusions are either to be put in the category of findings of fact or recommendations, they should more properly be included in the latter, as they are the inspector's reasons on the facts for his final recommendation.

Per Russell L.J.: If the phrase "finding of fact" is to be construed so as to embrace substantially everything to be found, except a question of law in the inspector's report, it would really make the reference to a finding of fact meaningless.

36–72 Vale Estates (Acton) v. Sec. of State for Environment (1971) 69 L.G.R. 543.
(1) The Secretary of State has to consider policy as well as the facts.
(2) The increase in the bulk of volume of buildings was evident from the plans and therefore where the Secretary of State relied on that as a ground for dismissing the appeal he was differing from the inspector on a question of planning judgment, not a question of fact.
(3) A planning decision by the Secretary of State cannot be quashed by the court simply because he differs on the point of planning judgment from the inspector who conducted the public inquiry.

36–73 Webb v. Sec. of State for Environment (1972) 224 E.G. 889. The issue of whether the site in question was the only one practical for the proposed development, was a new issue of fact within the meaning of rule 12.

36–74 Hodgkinsons (Ringway) v. Buclow R.D.C. (1972) 225 E.G. 2105. In balancing need against amenity more than one judgment is possible and reasonable. The Secretary of State's refusal of a permission on the ground that it was within a proposed green belt area which had been awaiting inquiry for some 10 years was reasonable and upheld, even though this was a reversal of his inspector's views.

36–75 Hibernian Property Co. Ltd. v. Sec. of State for Environment (1972) 27 P. & C.R. 197. (Housing Act Decision.) Breach of the rules of natural justice in asking the views of neighbours on site inspection when the applicant did not have an opportunity to deal with them, even though there may have been no prejudice.

36–76 Camden L.B.C. v. Sec. of State for Environment [1975] J.P.L. 602. Where the Secretary of State disagreed with his inspector on a matter of conjecture or an inference which could occur to anybody, he did not have to give the parties an opportunity to comment on his conclusions.

36–77 Hambledon & Chiddingford P.C. v. Sec. of State for Environment [1976] J.P.L. 502. Compliance with inquiry procedure rules does not mean *ipso facto* that there must have been compliance with the rules of natural justice, but a complainant faced a heavy burden of proof in such a case.

County council changed its policy on the number of caravan sites needed and the parish council was given no opportunity to deal with this, therefore there was a breach of the rules of natural justice.

36–78 Kent C.C. v. Sec. of State for Environment (1976) 33 P. & C.R. 70. Under rule 12(2)(b) of the Town and Country (Inquiries Procedure) Rules 1974 the Secretary of State is entitled to take into account the policy of other government departments even if it is not raised at the inquiry, and such policy cannot be questioned at the inquiry by virtue of rule 8(5) of the 1974 Rules.

Even apart from the 1974 Rules no rule of natural justice could have required another Government Minister to give evidence at the inquiry and the Secretary of State would be entitled to take the views of another Government Minister into account without giving the parties an opportunity to comment on them.

36–79 Granada Theatres v. Sec. of State for Environment [1976] J.P.L. 96. The taking into account of petitions and letters not disclosed to appellants was contrary to natural justice.

36–80 Lake District Special Planning Board v. Sec. of State for Environment [1975] J.P.L. 220. In dealing with an "administrative" process, the question of breach of natural justice has to be approached on broad lines and the test is whether a reasonable person, viewing the matter objectively and knowing all the facts, would consider that there was a risk of injustice or unfairness.

Where the Minister had received correspondence after the inquiry had closed, failure to circulate this correspondence was not automatically a breach of natural justice.

36–81 Fairmount Ltd. v. Sec. of State for Environment [1976] 1 W.L.R. 1255, H.L. (Housing Act 1957.) Contrary to natural justice for the Secretary of State to confirm an order on the basis of facts which the owners had no opportunity of showing were erroneous and on an opinion which they had no opportunity to deal with.

36–82 H. Sabey & Co. v. Sec. of State for Environment [1977] J.P.L. 661. Secretary of State's decision quashed where it was based on a matter raised by a witness from the Ministry of Agriculture and the applicants had had no opportunity to deal with it.

36–83 Ellinas v. Dept. of the Environment [1977] J.P.L. 249. Dismissal of planning appeal on grounds on which the appellant was given no opportunity to comment, it was agreed that the decision should be quashed.

36–84 Pyrford Properties Ltd. v. Sec. of State for Environment (1977) 36 P. & C.R. 28. A finding on an existing state of affairs, not being a finding dependent on aesthetic taste or other subjective opinion, is a finding of fact. In deciding whether firm was a local firm the Secretary of State relied solely on factual and not subjective or opinion evidence. As he disagreed with the inspector he disagreed on a question of fact within rule 12.

Per Curiam: It would have been competent for the Secretary of State, instead of applying the local planning authority's factual test, to have applied his own planning judgment or policy and dismiss the appeal.

36–85 General Accident v. Sec. of State for Environment (1977) 241 E.G. 842. No failure by the inspector or the Secretary of State to take into account material considerations or to disregard immaterial ones and therefore no breach of natural justice.

36–86 Wontner Smith & Co. v. Sec. of State for Environment [1977] J.P.L. 103. Appeal dismissed on the ground that premises could be used for light industry—the local planning authority had not relied on that reason. There was no evidence that planning permission would be granted for such a user nor that an industrial development certificate would have been granted if one were required, nor that there was any market for the industrial use of the premises. There was therefore insufficient material for the inspector to reach the conclusion he had come to, and the applicant had had no opportunity to deal with it.

36–87 Meravale Builders Ltd. v. Sec. of State for Environment (1978) 36 P. & C.R. 87. Finding as to whether the purpose of a proposed road was independent of a proposed housing development was one of fact and, even though described as a conclusion, if the Secretary of State differed from the inspector, he was differing on a finding of fact.

36–88 Thanet D.C. v. Sec. of State for Environment [1978] J.P.L. 250. Secretary of State's decision quashed because he had not complied with Inquiries Procedure Rules when rejecting his inspector's findings of fact.

36–89 Brown v. Sec. of State for Environment (1978) 40 P. & C.R. 285. Where the Secretary of State differed with the inspector as to whether a caravan site would be unduly obtrusive or damaging with landscaping and supervision he did not need to allow the parties to make further representations.

36–90 J. Sainsbury Ltd. v. Sec. of State for Environment [1978] J.P.L. 378. Secretary of State forming a different view from the inspector on the effect of a proposed supermarket on a town centre. This was a matter of planning judgment made on the same material before inspector and therefore the Secretary of State was not coming to a decision unsupported by the evidence and he did not need to allow the parties a further opportunity to address the inspector.

36–91 Winchester C.C. v. Sec. of State for Environment (1979) 39 P. & C.R. 1. A view of a site is real evidence but did not constitute "new evidence" within the meaning of rule 14(1) of the (Inquiries Procedure) Rules 1974 in the present case.

Per Lord Denning M.R.: Important that the inquiries procedure should not become too technical; so long as everything is done fairly and in accordance with the dictates of natural justice that should suffice.

36–92 Hyndburn B.C. v. Sec. of State for Environment (1979) 251 E.G. 473. Secretary of State can take into account his own circulars without having to notify the parties.

36–93 Pollock v. Sec. of State for Environment [1981] J.P.L. 420, C.A. See under enforcement notice appeals at page 161.

36–94 Finlay v. Sec. of State for Environment [1983] J.P.L. 802.
(1) If a party to an appeal wants the appeal to be considered on the basis that some condition could cure the planning objection put forward it is incumbent on

s.36. APPEALS AGAINST PLANNING DECISIONS

him to deal with that condition at the inquiry and if he does not the Secretary of State is not at fault in not imposing such a condition.

(2) If the Secretary of State considers attaching a condition which has not been canvassed at the inquiry he will have to reopen the inquiry to allow the parties to deal with it.

36–95 Hitchens v. Sec. of State for Environment (1983) 265 E.G. 696. In refusing permission for residential development the Secretary of State said that the supply of land available for residential development was 3.5 years when the inspector found as a fact that only 2.07 years' supply was available.

The decision was quashed as the Secretary of State had either failed, in breach of Rule 12 of the Town and Country Planning (Inquiries Procedure) Rules 1974, to notify the parties and to allow them to make further representations with regard to his disagreement with the inspector's finding of fact, or because he had failed to give clear and intelligible reasons for his decision, in breach of rule 13.

36–96 Furmston v. Sec. of State for Environment [1983] J.P.L. 49. Appeal against the inspector's decision was allowed for failure to observe the rules of natural justice where the inspector had been observed talking to Council representatives after the inquiry without any representative of the appellant present.

36–97 Jillings v. Sec. of State for Environment [1984] J.P.L. 32. Inspector should not have granted limited planning permission without giving the parties an opportunity to comment on the proposal.

36–98 D.E. Hudson v. Sec. of State for Environment [1984] J.P.L. 258. Inspector erred in not giving the parties an opportunity to deal with a matter of substance which had influenced him.

36–99 R. v. Bolton M.B.C., ex p. Whitecroft [1984] J.P.L. 875. (Highways Act decision.) Interested parties in a planning inquiry have the right to address the Secretary of State after the close of the public inquiry even though their representations deal with matters that could have been put before the inquiry.

36–100 Simmons v. Sec. of State for Environment [1985] J.P.L. 253. Inspector seen in discussion with the Chairman of the planning committee after the end of the planning inquiry. The decision was quashed on the grounds of natural justice.

36–101 R. v. Sec. of State for Environment and Others, ex p. Greater London Council [1986] J.P.L. 32. New evidence on noise received after the close of the inquiry by the Secretary of State but there was no breach of rule 12 as there was no disagreement with his inspector because of this new evidence. It was also held that the Secretary of State had acted fairly in giving the parties the opportunity to make representations even though he had refused to reopen the inquiry. Further, he had not acted in a way in which no sensible Secretary of State would have acted in refusing to reopen the inquiry.

36–102 Residential development—evidence of the effect on existing sewerage works. Evaluation by the Department, expert opinion under the Inquiries Procedure Rules. [1974] J.P.L. 681.

(c) Duty to give reasons

36–103 Re Poyser and Mills' Arbitration [1963] 2 W.L.R. 1309. (Agricultural Holdings Act Case). Proper and adequate reasons for decisions must not only be intelligible, but must also deal with the substantial points raised.

36–104 Givaudan v. Min. of Housing & Local Govt. [1967] 1 W.L.R. 250. The document containing the Minister's reasons is an important document and is required to set forth with reasonable precision and clarity the matters which are relevant to indicate and explain positively or negatively the reasons for the decision.

The Minister's decision letter in this case was so obscure and would leave such substantial doubts in the mind of an informed reader as to the reason for the decision and the matters which the Minister did and did not take into account it not being a question of trivial error or obscurity or mere failure to give reasons relating to every particular point, that it did not comply with rule 11(1) of the Town and Country Planning Appeals (Inquiries Procedure) Rules 1962 and therefore the decision would be quashed.

Per curiam: When a local inquiry has been held and the inspector has submitted his report to the Minister, there can be no objection to the Minister's letter of statement of reasons and decisions including by reference the inspector's conclusions, provided that they are, in themselves, sufficiently clearly and unambiguously expressed; but the court is not prepared to hold, in favour of the Minister, that the making and inclusion in the letter of a summary of passages in the report is, or is intended to be, irrelevant since the whole of the contents of the letter must be assumed prima facie at least, to be inserted for the relevant purpose of setting forth the reasons for the Minister's decision.

36–105 Ellis v. Sec. of State for Environment (1974) 31 P. & C.R. 130. In giving a decision the practice of inspectors did not have to follow that of the Secretary of State. All that was required was that they gave reasons adequate to the circumstances of any particular case. Unless the reasons were unintelligible or bad on their face it was not for the court to go into their factual accuracy, the weight to be afforded to them or their length or particularity.

36–106 French Kier Developments v. Sec. of State for Environment [1977] 1 All E.R. 296.

(1) The parties to an appeal are entitled to a clear and intelligible statement of the reasons for a decision of the Secretary of State under r. 13(1) of the Town and Country Planning (Inquiries Procedure) Rules 1974.

(2) Where the Secretary of State disagreed with the inspector as to the importance to be attached to the Green Belt but it was impossible to discern why, the decision was quashed.

36–107 The Accountancy Tuition Centre v. Sec. of State for Environment [1977] J.P.L. 792. On appeal the Minister granted permission subject to the condition that permission should be personal to the applicant and lapse after five years. Reasons for imposing such a condition were inadequate.

36–108 Meravale Builders Ltd. v. Sec. of State for Environment (1978) 36 P. & C.R. 87. Always desirable that decision letters should be framed as clearly as possible, particularly when the Secretary of State is differing from recommendations which are favourable to an objector.

36–109 Thanet D.C. v. Sec. of State for Environment [1978] J.P.L. 250 The Secretary of State's conclusion that the restored building would be unlikely to be disposed of was unintelligible as there was no evidence on that point.

36–110 D.F.P. (Midlands) Ltd. v. Sec. of State for Environment [1978] J.P.L. 319. Where the inspector made the decision his letter must be clear and full enough to tell the parties what he had decided and why, but he did not have to deal in it with all the material before him as he did when he reported to the Minister. If his letter was challenged it might therefore be necessary to admit evidence of what material was before him in order to decide whether he had acted according to law or not.

36–111 Price Brothers (Rode Heath) Ltd. v. Dept. of the Environment (1978) 28 P. & C.R. 579. Where a decision letter is quashed because it is unintelligible, the Secretary of State is entitled to issue a fresh letter making his decision intelligible.

36–112 Preston D.C. v. Sec. of State for Environment [1978] J.P.L. 548. If an important part of the Secretary of State's reasoning was omitted in his decision letter there was prejudice in the ordinary way to an applicant for planning permission and to the local authority.

The whole tenor of the letter was that a limited permission was going to be granted and therefore an important part of the reasoning had been omitted when unconditional planning permission was granted and the decision was quashed.

36–113 Grainger v. Sec. of State for Environment [1978] J.P.L. 631. Decision letter has to be reasonably clear to the recipient, but it does not have to deal with every point which has been raised.

36–114 Seddon Properties v. Sec. of State for Environment [1978] J.P.L. 835.

(1) If there has been conflicting evidence at the inquiry the Secretary of State may prefer one piece of evidence to another if the material is there to enable him to do so but he must give valid reasons for so doing.

(2) The Secretary of State is entitled to attach what weight he pleases to the various arguments and contentions of the parties.

(3) "Strategic Plan for the North West" and the Government response were ambiguous and the Secretary of State could resolve it as he chose.

36–115 Millard v. Sec. of State for Environment (1979) 254 E.G. 733. Refusal of permission for the change of the use of a big house to an educational establishment for mature businessmen on the grounds of the generation of traffic was illogical when the alternative would be the construction of seven town houses involving similar traffic generation.

36–116 Shepperton Builders v. Sec. of State for Environment [1979] J.P.L. 102. Permission refused on green belt grounds—the decision was reasonably intelligible and the points raised clearly dealt with.

36–117 L.B. of Camden v. Sec. of State for Environment [1980] J.P.L. 31. Decision quashed because no reasons given, or it was not apparent that the Secretary of State had taken into account the factors he should have done.

It was also found that no reasonable man could have come to the conclusions the inspector came to.

36–118 Sears Blok v. Sec. of State for Environment (1980) 254 E.G. 1195. Inspector's decision letter not to be scrutinised like a statute. The letter was sufficiently clear—construction of paragraph 3.37 of the Greater London Plan.

36–119 Bell & Colvill v. Sec. of State for Environment [1980] J.P.L. 823. Failure to give adequate reasons will not invalidate a decision if there is no prejudice.

In certain circumstances you can assume that arguments have been considered by the inspector even if he does not specifically deal with them.

36–120 Greenwich L.B. v. Sec. of State for Environment [1981] J.P.L. 809. Although the inspector's letter was defective, the local planning authority were not prejudiced—decision affirmed.

36–121 Rogelan Building Group Ltd. v. Sec. of State for Environment [1981] J.P.L. 506. Where the Secretary of State disagrees with his inspector it is particularly important that he makes his reasons for such disagreement clear.

If one is left in real doubt as to what the Secretary of State's reasons were, he has failed to comply with rule 13 of the Inquiries Procedure Rules. Where it is unclear whether the Secretary of State has failed to take into account a material consideration, the applicants are substantially prejudiced.

If the decision letter is quashed for unintelligibility, the Secretary of State need only re-phrase the letter to make his reasons clear.

36–122 Chichester D.C. v. Sec. of State for Environment [1981] J.P.L. 591. References in a decision letter to the inspector's report were inaccurate. It was assumed that the Secretary of State's decision was based on the references in the decision letter, which meant that he had taken into account matters which he should not have taken into account. The errors had not affected the basic reasoning of the decision letter, and they were in any event more favourable to the applicant, therefore the Secretary of State had reached the same conclusion that he would have reached had he relied upon correct information, and had not gone outside his powers.

36–123 J.A. Pye (Oxford) Estates Ltd. v. Sec. of State for Environment [1982] J.P.L. 180. Local planning policy was wrongly reported to the Secretary of State and therefore his decision would have to be quashed.

36–124 Ryan v. Sec. of State for Environment [1982] C.L.Y. 3178.
(1) Decision letter failed to refer to policy documents in the appellant's favour, but it was clear that the inspector took the view that the highway objection outweighed everything else so could assume the inspector found in favour of the appellant on planning merits.
(2) Even where the inspector decides the appeal himself he should state succinctly what the issues are and why he finds some outweigh others.

36–125 Bosies v. Sec. of State for Environment, *The Times*, May 10, 1983. It ought to be possible to ascertain from the letter of refusal of planning permission whether a material point made at the hearing had been taken into account.

36–125 Knights Motors v. Sec. of State for Environment [1984] J.P.L. 884. Decision quashed because the inspector contradicted his own reasoning.

36–127 Southwark L.B. v. Sec. of State for Environment [1984] J.P.L. 263, C.A. Where a decision letter was sent with the inspector's report setting out all the findings of fact, the decision letter set forth "with reasonable precision and clarity" matters which were relevant as explaining the Minister's reasons.

36–128 Hewlett v. Sec. of State for Environment and Brentwood D.C. [1985] J.P.L. 404, C.A. It could be generally assumed that on appeal the Secretary of State took into account the policies in his own circulars.

36–129 Stephenson v. Sec. of State for Environment (1985) 274 E.G. 1385, C.A. Reasoning of the decision was inadequate as it was not clear whether the inspector was disregarding the policy in the structure plan or saying it applied or making an exception to it.
Woolf J.'s decision in *St. Edmundsbury B.C. v. Sec. of State for Environment* [1985] J.P.L. 785, upheld.

36–130/131 Mancini v. Coventry City Council (1985) 25 R.V.R. 132. Counter-notice under section 194 on the grounds that the council did not propose to acquire any part of the land and that the claimant had failed to make reasonable endeavours to sell. Held that:
(1) the relevant date for considering such matters was the date of the counter-notice;
(2) no error in law in the Lands Tribunal following previous decisions made prior to the 1971 Act;
(3) that even if a council can show that land did not fall within section 192(1)(*a*), under section 194(2)(*a*) they were still not compelled to acquire the land;
(4) Hardship and the alleviation of hardship were irrelevant.

36–133/134 Dimsdale Developments (South East) Ltd. v. Sec. of State for Environment [1986] J.P.L. 276. Although it was important to be consistent, a line of ministerial decisions, suggesting that market forces should determine where office development takes place, did not require the inspector to decide the appeal in a particular way.

36–135 Reading B.C. v. Sec. of State for Environment [1986] J.P.L. 115. Correspondence after a public inquiry between the applicant and the Minister—breach of the rules of natural justice as the letters were not disclosed to the local planning authority. Relationship of the Inquiry Procedure Rules and natural justice considered. The rules do not exhaust the requirements of natural justice and although there is no such thing as a technical breach of natural justice, there was no burden of proof where the rules were observed.

Note

As to the award of the cost of appearing at the inquiry, see cases under Section 282.

SECTION 41. TIME LIMITS ON THE LIFE OF FULL PLANNING PERMISSION

41–01 L.A.M. Ames Ltd. v. North Bedfordshire B.C. [1980] J.P.L. 183. A condition requiring development to commence within three years of a contingent future event, the date of which could not be foreseen at the date of the grant of the planning permission, would not comply with the provisions of s.41(1)(*b*).

SECTION 42. TIME LIMITS ON OUTLINE PLANNING PERMISSION

42–01 R. v. Sec. of State for Environment, ex p. Percy Bilton (1975) 31 P. & C.R. 154, D.C. Twenty-two acre site—outline permission subject to the approval of siting details. Impossible to argue that outline permission had been a collection of separate agreements, and there was nothing in the course of dealings to suggest any variation of permission. Therefore, as parts of the site been developed, outline permission was not time-expired.

42–02 Sievers v. London Borough of Bromley [1980] J.P.L. 520. Application lodged within the three year time-limit when lodged on the third anniversary and the two previous days the offices had been closed.

Alternatively, any lateness was *de minimis*.

Note

Also see decisions on the procedures for applying for approval of details at page 366.

SECTION 43. PROVISIONS SUPPLEMENTARY TO SECTIONS 41 AND 42

43–01 Spackman v. Sec. of State for Environment [1977] 1 All E.R. 257.

(1) Construction of a soakaway and trenches, even though not in accord with planning permission plans, were not a colourable operation and related to the implementation of permission and therefore came within s.43(2).

(2) A private drive serving only one house and to which the public would have no access is a "road" within s.43(2)(*d*).

43–02 High Peak B.C. v. Sec. of State for Environment [1981] J.P.L. 366. Digging a trench may keep a planning permission alive even though it is not intended to proceed with the whole development immediately and even though the trench was subsequently backfilled.

43–03 South Oxfordshire D.C. v. Sec. of State for Environment [1981] 1 W.L.R. 1092. A trench dug for a development differently designed from that for which permission had been granted would not keep a planning permission alive.

43–04 Malvern Hills D.C. v. Sec. of State for Environment [1982] J.P.L. 439, C.A. Marking out of the line and width of a road with pegs amounts to an "operation" in the course of laying out part of a road under s.43(2)(*d*).

S.45. POWER TO REVOKE OR MODIFY PLANNING PERMISSION

Per Lord Denning M.R.: An "operation" requires something more permanent than putting in pegs.

Per Eveleigh L.J.: Very little needs to be done to satisfy s.43 so long as it is genuinely done for the purpose of carrying out the development. "Laying out a road" requires placing something in a permanent position on the land to mark the plan of the road on the land.

43–05 Clwyd C.C. v. Sec. of State for Environment [1982] J.P.L. 696. Works undertaken in breach of a condition of a planning permission are not unlawful unless it is a condition precedent and they can therefore constitute the beginning of the carrying-out of the development.

43–06 Salisbury D.C. v. Sec. of State for Environment [1982] J.P.L. 702. The beginning of part of a development is sufficient to lift the time-limit for all of it unless the planning permission is severable. Planning permission for seven bungalows—the building of one lifted the time-limit.

43–07 Engineering works in preparation for the stationing of caravans was not commencement of caravan use. [1966] J.P.L. 418.

43–08 Development begun by digging and filling trenches for the foundations. [1980] J.P.L. 537.

SECTION 44. COMPLETION NOTICES

44–01 Completion notice—prospects of development being completed within a reasonable time. [1979] J.P.L. 184.

44–02 Circumstances governing the confirmation of a Completion Notice. Application for renewal of planning permission under art. 5(3) of the General Development Order. [1979] J.P.L. 480.

44–03 Completion notice allowing three years from confirmation of notice for the erection of an office block and car park. [1981] J.P.L. 605.

44–04 Completion notice on a dwelling-house—the developer's medical and financial condition. Development "little by little" preferable to abandoning the development. [1983] J.P.L. 483.

44–05 Completion notice—completion of construction on a self-build basis of a dwelling for which planning permission was granted over nine years previously. Correction by the Secretary of State of errors in the completion notice. [1984] J.P.L. 820.

44–06 Completion notice confirmed, although time for compliance extended to four years where it was desirable that the second of two proposed dwelling-houses should be built and problems of different weathering might arise. [1985] J.P.L. 125.

44–07 Uncompleted building erected pursuant to planning permission which ceased to have effect by virtue of a Completion Notice. Uncompleted building not constructed in accordance with permission because it differs materially from the completed building authorised by the permission. Permission needed to retain uncompleted building on site. [1985] J.P.L. 496.

SECTION 45. POWER TO REVOKE OR MODIFY PLANNING PERMISSION

45–01 Slough Estates v. Slough B.C. (No. 2) [1969] 2 W.L.R. 1157, C.A. In demanding and obtaining compensation for a refusal of planning permission the applicant abandons rights under earlier permissions. But see *Pioneer Aggregates (U.K.) Ltd. v. Sec. of State for Environment.*

45–02 Caledonian Terminal Investments Ltd. v. Edinburgh Corporation [1970] S.C. 271. The relevant time under s.45 for gauging whether works have been carried out before the revocation or modification of planning permission is the time the order is made by the authority, not the date of its confirmation by the Secretary of State.

45–03 R. v. Sec. of State for Environment, ex p. Reinisch (1971) 22 P. & C.R. 1022, D.C. A planning authority having dealt with a planning application cannot revoke or alter it unilaterally—they must comply with s.45.

45–04 Thomas Langley Group v. Warwick D.C. (1974) 73 L.G.R. 171. Where outline planning permission is granted but subsequent detailed permission is inconsistent with it and is acted on, rights to compensation under the outline agreement will either have been abandoned or consensually varied. But see *Pioneer Aggregates (U.K.) Ltd. v. Sec. of State for the Environment.*

45–05 Pioneer Aggregates (U.K.) Ltd. v. Sec. of State for Environment [1984] 2 All E.R. 358, H.L. Permission cannot be lost by subsequent conduct.

45–06 Confirmation of revocation of planning permission for the re-construction of shop premises although temporary permission for completion of existing premises was appropriate. [1968] J.P.L. 421.

45–07 Revocation order not confirmed as the original conditional planning permission adequately covered the main reasons put forward by the Council for the necessity of a revocation order. [1982] J.P.L. 261.

SECTION 51. DISCONTINUANCE ORDERS

51–01 Re Lamplugh [1967] 19 P. & C.R. 125. Section 51(1)(*a*) and 51(1)(*b*) are alternatives and there is nothing to require a local planning authority to use s.51(1)(*b*) only in a case where s.51(1)(a) would not suffice.

"Amenity" in s.51 includes all amenity past, present and future.

51–02 Miller v. Weymouth and Melcombe Regis Corporation (1974) 27 P. & C.R. 468, D.C. Objection against proposed discontinuance order. Powers of the Secretary of State considered.

51–03 Parkes v. Sec. of State for Environment [1978] 1 W.L.R. 1308, C.A. Sorting, storing and processing scrap with no physical alteration to the land amounts to a "use of land" and therefore a discontinuance order can be made under s.51(1)(*a*).

51–04 Discontinuance order requiring the removal of part of a group of buildings was not confirmed. The fear that the buildings might be made fit for permanent habitation was insufficient to justify the order. [1971] J.P.L. 65.

51–05 In considering a discontinuance order, the Secretary of State is restricted to use as at present, without anticipation of possible future intensification. [1973] J.P.L. 57.

51–06 Confirmation of a discontinuance order requiring partial discontinuance of the storage of bricks and the removal of fences. [1973] J.P.L. 181.

51–07 Discontinuance order requiring the removal of an extension to a dwelling-house not confirmed. [1973] J.P.L. 182.

51–08 Confirmation of a discontinuance order—scrap metal dealer's business in a residential area. [1973] J.P.L. 319.

51–09 Miscellaneous uses and buildings on land within Areas of Outstanding Natural Beauty—discontinuance order not confirmed. [1973] J.P.L. 554.

51–10 Discontinuance order where existing cottage intended to be replaced by a new dwelling for which planning permission had been granted. [1974] J.P.L. 295.

51–11 Power of the Secretary of State to impose conditions on the continuance of use in making discontinuance order. [1974] J.P.L. 607.

SECTION 52. AGREEMENTS REGULATING DEVELOPMENT OR USE OF LAND

52–01 Ransom & Luck Ltd. v. Surbiton B.C. [1949] Ch. 180. Section 34 of the Town and Country Planning Act 1932 enabled a landowner to enter into a restrictive covenant with a local authority whereby his use of the land was restricted but did not allow the local authority to restrict its statutory powers in any way.

52–02 Smith and Snipes Hall Farm Ltd. v. River Doglas Catchment Board [1949] 2 K.B. 500. Covenants running with the land may be enforced by the covenantee and his successors in title by virtue of s.78 of the Law of Property Act 1925.

52–03 National Trust v. Midlands Electricity Board [1952] 1 All E.R. 298. Injunction refused as covenant void for uncertainty because it was impossible to ascertain the limits of prohibition.

52–04 Thackray v. C.L.B. [1952] 1 All E.R. 1374. Consent under agreement made under the 1932 Act does not obviate the need for permission for development under the 1971 Act.

52–05 Bridger v. Shoreham-on-Sea U.D.C. (1956) 6 P. & C.R. 291, D.C. Restriction in force under an agreement under s.34 of the 1932 Act referred to an arbitrator. Whether the agreement's provisions came within s.34.

52–06 Gee v. The National Trust (1965) 17 P. & C.R. 6. *Per* Lord Denning: A covenant made for the benefit of the National Trust under s.8 of the National Trust Act 1937 can be enforced by the National Trust irrespective of whether there is adjoining land to be benefited.

52–07 Crittenden (Warren Park) v. Surrey C.C. (1966) 1 W.L.R. 25. An agreement with a planning authority under s.25 of the Town and Country Planning Act 1947, restricting the use of land but expressly preserving "any rights of whatever nature which the owner has or may have in the future as owner . . . under the 1947 Act or any Act or Acts for the time being amending or replacing the same or otherwise, howsoever" does not affect the rights under a caravan site licence granted on the basis of an "existing site" within s.13 of the Caravan Sites and Control of Development Act 1960 inconsistent with the agreement.

52–08 Jones v. Sec. of State for Wales (1974) 28 P. & C.R. 280. Section 52 does not apply to an agreement with a prospective developer who has no legal interest in land as an owner or tenant.

52–09 Hope v. Sec. of State for Environment (1975) 31 P. & C.R. 120, D.C. Inspector had erred in law in saying that a section 52 agreement might not be binding on successors in title and in saying that the land would be sterilised if such agreement were entered into, for the planning authority could always release the other party to the agreement if its policy changed.

52–10 Augier v. Sec. of State for Environment (1978) 38 P. & C.R. 219 D.C. *Sub. nom.* Hildenborough Village Preservation Association v. Sec. of State for Environment [1978] J.P.L. 708. If the Secretary of State for the Environment was satisfied of the applicant's good faith it was not unreasonable for him to accept an undertaking and not unreasonable to take the risk of sale to somebody else so that the undertaking could not be honoured.

Where an applicant for planning permission gives an undertaking and, in reliance upon that, planning permission is granted subject to a condition in terms broad

S.52. AGREEMENTS REGULATING DEVELOPMENT OR USE OF LAND

enough to embrace the undertaking, the applicant cannot later be heard to say that there is no power to require compliance with the undertaking.

52–11 Pennine Raceway Ltd. v. Kirklees M.B.C. [1982] 3 W.L.R. 987. *Per* Eveleigh L.J.: Section 52 is not limited to apply only to persons who have an interest in land in the strict conveyancing sense.

52–12 Windsor and Maidenhead R.B.C. v. Brandrose Investments Ltd. [1983] 1 All E.R. 818, C.A. A local planning authority is not empowered by s.52(3) to bind itself by an agreement not to exercise the powers conferred on it by s.277 which it had a public duty to exercise.

Section 52 does not empower a local planning authority to grant planning permission otherwise than as provided by ss.26 to 29, and a section 52 agreement made before planning permission has been granted may become irrelevant if permission is not granted and ineffective if conditions are imposed inconsistent with the agreement.

52–13 Re Beecham Group Ltd's Application (1980) 41 P. & C.R. 369.

(1) Lands Tribunal has jurisdiction to modify or discharge restrictions imposed by planning agreements under s.52.

(2) Although the section 52 agreement was not obsolete, the Tribunal was satisfied that the local council would not suffer injury if the agreement was modified as they did not own any land in the area, they had not put forward any objection on aesthetic grounds, there had been surrounding development, the Secretary of State had granted planning permission for the proposed development, and the modification would not weaken the council's power to enforce the restrictions contained in the agreements in future.

(3) The fact that the section 52 agreement was only 10 years old and that the applicants were the original covenantors was insufficient by itself to lead to the refusal of the application.

52–14 Bradford City Metropolitan Council v. Sec. of State for Environment (1986) 278 E.G. 1473, C.A. Doubted whether s.52 could be used to include a covenant that public highway should be widened, but suggested that contribution to costs of widening might have been valid.

52–15 Abbey Homesteads (Developments) Ltd. v. Northamptonshire C.C. (1986) 278 E.G. 1249. Agreement made under s.52 included a covenant that land should be reserved for school purposes. The Court held that this created a permanent restrictive covenant running with the land.

52–16 Secretary of State has no jurisdiction over the enforcement of section 52 agreements. [1975] J.P.L. 692.

52–17 Unreasonable to expect a developer to donate and prepare 33 or 40 acres of public open space in return for permission for housing development of 10 to 17 acres. [1985] J.P.L. 346.

SECTION 53. APPLICATIONS TO DETERMINE WHETHER PLANNING PERMISSION REQUIRED

53–01 Edgwarebury Park Investments Ltd. v. Min. of Housing & Local Govt. [1963] 2 W.L.R. 257, D.C. Section 53 does not give jurisdiction to enquire as to whether a grant of planning permission was valid.

Per curiam: Method of ascertaining whether there was a valid grant of planning permission before the development was commenced is by an action for a declaration.

53–02 East Suffolk C.C. v. Sec. of State for Environment (1972) 70 L.G.R. 595, D.C. Section 53 could not be used to ask for an opinion on the construction of a planning permission or on its validity.

S.53. APPLICATIONS TO DETERMINE WHETHER PLANNING PERMISSION REQUIRED

53–03 Wells v. Min. of Housing & Local Govt. [1967] 1 W.L.R. 1000, C.A. A local planning authority are entitled to make a determination under s.53 without the necessity of a formal written application and an application for planning permission contains an implicit invitation to do so.

53–04 English-Speaking Union v. Westminster L.B.C. (1975) 26 P. & C.R. 575, Ch. A section 53 determination establishes an applicant's rights once and for all and is not invalidated if a subsequent Use Classes Order would have necessitated planning permission for the change of use contemplated.

It was accepted that informal correspondence could constitute a section 53 determination.

53–05 Western Fish Products v. Penwith D.C. [1981] 2 All E.R. 204, C.A. *Wells* v. *Min of Housing & Local Govt.* was followed but the court emphasised the need for the formal procedures to be observed and stated that anything less than a planning application will not suffice for there to be a valid section 53 determination.

53–06 Property Investment Holdings v. Sec. of State for Environment [1984] J.P.L. 587, D.C. No evidence to support the suggestion that the inspector should have treated planning application as an implied section 53 determination.

53–07 Refusal to determine whether planning permission required as the proposed works and use were too indefinite. [1966] J.P.L. 608.

53–08 Determination under section 53 must be related to a particular proposed use. [1970] J.P.L. 722.

53–09 Effect of an agreement between the landowner and the local planning authority as to the use of premises does not fall to be considered on a section 53 application. [1971] J.P.L. 244.

53–10 Onus of proof is upon the appellant to establish that works are deemed not to be development. [1974] J.P.L. 373.

53–11 Reply to a valid section 53 application that the Council did not disagree that it was permitted development is a section 53 determination. [1974] J.P.L. 100.

53–12 Letter from local planning authority was not a valid section 53 determination, but the authority was estopped from serving an enforcement notice. [1975] J.P.L. 105.

53–13 Reply relating to a permitted use was treated as a section 53 determination. [1975] J.P.L. 614.

53–14 On a section 53 application concerned only with the question of whether the proposed operations or use require planning permission, not concerned with construing earlier planning permissions. [1975] J.P.L. 162.

53–15 Expression of a personal view by an officer of the council is not a section 53 determination. [1976] J.P.L. 190.

53–16 A Section 53 determination in respect of building operations cannot be made in the absence of plans and drawings. [1978] J.P.L. 653.

53–17 Estoppel based on a statement made by an officer of a local planning authority. [1980] J.P.L. 418.

53–18 A section 53 application must relate to a proposal and cannot relate to a use begun before an application but where the use was carried out in the past but not at the time of application, the local planning authority can deal with it. [1980] J.P.L. 342.

53–19 Section 53 determination can only relate to a specific proposed use and it cannot determine any purpose for which land may lawfully be used. [1982] J.P.L. 115.

53–20 In a section 53 application the possibility that the use at the date of the application is in contravention of planning control and susceptible to enforcement is irrelevant. [1982] J.P.L. 459.

53–21 Section 53 appeal continued even though the original applicant ceased to have any interest in appeal site as the owners of site were acting as agents for the original applicant. [1982] J.P.L. 657.

53–22 Section 53 application was invalid because it related to a use which had already begun, but formal determination was made and the planning authority accepted that they were estopped from denying that it was a valid determination. Cannot isolate part of a unit referred to in a section 53 determination when looking at the question of intensification—must look at the whole unit. [1983] J.P.L. 493.

53–23 In deciding whether planning permission is necessary you must consider whether the proposed use existed at the date of the application for a determination—the question of whether the use of land at the date of application was unlawful is irrelevant. [1984] J.P.L. 889.

53–24 Following informal inquiry, officer wrote letter stating that proposed works constituted permitted development. It was held, applying *Western Fish Products* v. *Penwith D.C.*, that this did not estop the council, as it was an informal inquiry, the answer to which was not binding on the elected members of the planning authority. [1986] J.P.L. 386.

PART IV. ADDITIONAL CONTROL IN SPECIAL CASES

SECTION 54. LIST OF BUILDINGS OF SPECIAL ARCHITECTURAL OR HISTORIC INTEREST

54–01 Cass v. Platford (1968) 20 P. & C.R. 58, D.C. A building preservation order provisionally confirmed under s.31(2) of the Town and Country Planning Act 1962 ceases to have effect unless it is confirmed again within two months of the provisional confirmation. If it is not, it may be brought back into effect by subsequent confirmation but it will remain inoperative for the period between its lapsing and its subsequent confirmation.

Per curiam: There is no time-limit on the period within which the Minister has to confirm an order under s.30(3) of the 1962 Act.

54–02 Iveagh v. Min. of Housing & Local Govt. [1963] 3 W.L.R. 974, C.A.
(1) A building preservation order could be made under s.29 of the Town and Country Planning Act 1947 by reason of the qualities the building derived from its setting, though it would not, standing alone, be of special architectural or historical interest.
(2) A building preservation order was "made" for purposes of s.31 of the Town and Country Planning Act 1959 when it was confirmed by the Minister.

54–03 Corthorn Land and Timber Co. v. Min. of Housing & Local Govt. (1965) 63 L.G.R. 490. A building preservation order can be made concerning chattels which have been affixed to the freehold so as to become part of it.

54–04 Amalgamated Investment & Property Co. Ltd. v. John Walker & Sons Ltd. [1977] 1 W.L.R. 164, C.A. A building does not become a listed building until the list is signed on behalf of the Secretary of State.

Risk that a building could become listed is an inherent risk all owners of buildings incur.

54–05 Att.-Gen. ex rel. Sutcliffe v. Calderdale B.C. [1983] J.P.L. 310. In deciding whether a structure or object is within the curtilage of a listed building the factors to be taken into account are (i) the physical layout of the building and the structure, (ii) their ownership past and present, (iii) their use or function, past and present.

Terraced houses remained so closely related physically or geographically to a mill that they were still within its curtilage even though ownership had been severed.

54–06 Cotswold D.C. v. Sec. of State for Environment [1985] J.P.L. 407. Erection of a fence in the curtilage of a listed building does not require listed building consent but you do require consent to remove a fence once it has been erected as it was an object or structure forming part of the land: s.54(9).

Debenhams p.l.c. v. Westminster City Council (1986) 278 E.G. 974 C.A. Building connected to listed building by a tunnel at basement level and a foot-bridge at second floor level, was a structure fixed to the listed building or comprised within the curtilage: see section 54(9).

54–07 Fact that buildings were excluded from an earlier building preservation notice does not preclude the making of a subsequent order in respect of them. Buildings not of special interest individually but forming part of a harmonious group. [1966] J.P.L. 548.

SECTION 55. CONTROL OF WORKS FOR DEMOLITION, ALTERATION OR EXTENSION OF LISTED BUILDING

A. The Extent of Control

55–01 R. v. Stroud D.C., ex p. Goodenough [1982] J.P.L. 246, D.C. Although s.55(6) does not say that it would be lawful to demolish a building in a case where the situation was one to which subs. (6) applies, the intent of the legislation was that in an appropriate case a building owner should be able to demolish a building not withstanding the fact that he had not yet got the necessary consent under s.55.

55–02 R. v. North Hertfordshire D.C., ex p. Sullivan [1981] J.P.L. 752. Although not every piece of work by way of alteration or extension necessarily amounted to demolition, demolition referred to the demolition of part of, as well as the whole of a building. Listed building consent was quashed by way of judicial review on the application of a neighbour.

55–02a R. v. Wells Street Metropolitan Stipendiary Magistrates, ex p. Westminster City Council [1986] 1 W.L.R. 1046. The offence created by s.55(1) was one of strict liability and there was no need to prove that person executing the works knew that the building was listed.

55–03 Listed building-installation of window blinds involved either minimal or no alteration to structure of house and were to be regarded as in the nature of internal furnishings. No contravention of s.55. Whether the colour of paint affects the character of a building of special architectural or historic interest depends on the particular facts of each case. Yellow paint did alter the character of a building, but had faded to an innocuous shade. [1972] J.P.L. 650.

55–04 Character of a listed building was adversely affected by a swimming-pool cover. [1974] J.P.L. 376.

55–05 Placing of additional objects or structures on land within the curtilage of a listed building does not require listed building consent. [1975] J.P.L. 690.

55–06 Removal of features of a listed building after accidental damage not preventable by owners could not reasonably be regarded as an alteration affecting the character of building and was unlikely to have contravened s.55. [1981] J.P.L. 443.

S.55. DEMOLITION, ALTERATION OR EXTENSION OF LISTED BUILDING

55–07 Listed-building consent is not required for the erection of an entirely free-standing structure within the curtilage of a listed building. [1984] J.P.L. 55.

B. Applications for Listed Building Consent

55–08 Shop Properties v. Min. of Housing & Local Govt. (1969) 211 E.G. 161. Minister entitled to place a different emphasis on the opinions of the inspector and arrive at a different conclusion whether to confirm a Building Preservation Order.

55–09 Kent Messenger Ltd. v. Sec. of State for Environment [1976] J.P.L. 372. Argument that a building when restored would not be an economic proposition was material to the decision and in failing to deal with it the Secretary of State failed to give adequate reasons for his decision. Left open the question of whether the quality of a proposed replacement building was a material consideration.

55–10 Richmond-Upon-Thames L.B.C. v. Sec. of State for Environment (1979) 37 P. & C.R. 151. When considering whether or not to give consent for the demolition of buildings, the Secretary of State is entitled to consider the merits of a proposed development.

55–11 L.B. Tower Hamlets v. Sec. of State for Environment [1983] J.P.L. 315 Listed-building application for a change from residential to office use. The inspector was entitled to regard as exceptional circumstances justifying grant of permission the facts that (1) the applicant had restored the property, (2) at the time of the inspector's decision the applicant had the right to change the use and would have done so had his fresh application been refused.

55–12 Westminster C.C. v. Sec. of State for Environment, *The Times*, March 24, 1984, D.C.

(1) Reasons for listed building appeal must be given, but they need not be spelt out in detail, so long as their basic outline is clear.

(2) It is proper to grant consent for the demolition of a listed building subject to a condition that no development should take place before a contract for the carrying out of work for redevelopment has been made, and planning permission for the rebuilding works has been granted.

55–13 Consent to demolition of a listed building with structural defects which made rehabilitation to modern standards impossible without virtually reconstructing the building. [1970] J.P.L. 231.

55–14 Listed-building consent to demolish a building of some architectural or historic interest to re-allow redevelopment of the site. The probable high cost of restoration of the building was taken into account. [1972] J.P.L. 729.

55–15 Listed building in a Conservation Area incapable of beneficial use in its existing state. Permission to be granted for office use if applied for. [1973] J.P.L. 719.

55–16 Listed building affected by settlement and decay—conditions of consent to demolition. [1974] J.P.L. 493.

55–17 Refusal of a listed-building consent for demolition of a building not of historic interest or great architectural merit, but with a facade making an important contribution to the street scene. [1974] J.P.L. 552.

55–18 Listed-building consent application—building of little intrinsic merit, but forming part of a group of buildings of interest. [1975] J.P.L. 309 & 423.

55–19 Listed-building consent for the partial demolition of a building where planning permission for redevelopment was granted before the building had been listed by the Secretary of State. [1976] J.P.L. 445.

55–20 Refusal of a listed-building consent for demolition of a building in the course

S.55. DEMOLITION, ALTERATION OR EXTENSION OF LISTED BUILDING

of a large development scheme already partly implemented, with planning permission. [1976] J.P.L. 450.

55–21 Listed building consent for the demolition for redevelopment of a house with architectural interest. Cost of preservation in its existing state. Lack of financial assistance for preservation. Degree of architectural interest. Value of proposed use after redevelopment. [1976] J.P.L. 706.

55–22 Listed-building consent appeal—demolition of a farmhouse. Possibility of economic restoration. [1979] J.P.L. 255.

55–23 Demolition of a listed Wesleyan Church in a remote area next to a graveyard. Need to investigate possible alternative uses before consent given. [1980] J.P.L. 487.

55–24 Demolition of a listed building. Possibility of conversion to an alternative use was not adequately explored. [1979] J.P.L. 496.

55–25 Listed-building consent for demolition of a large country mansion. House was in a poor state of repair and damaged by fire. [1980] J.P.L. 485.

55–26 Listed-building consent to demolish a Victorian ballroom, part of house. [1980] J.P.L. 539.

55–27 Refusal of listed-building consent for demolition of a dovecote in an advanced state of repair even though the full restoration cost could not be justified and it would be difficult to find any use for the building. Possible future vandalism ignored. [1981] J.P.L. 304.

55–28 Listed-building consent—warehouses. If consent was granted it could result in the whole island site being cleared and left vacant, perhaps for years; if refused there was little likelihood of even essential repairs being carried out and the building would be likely to deteriorate to the point of collapse. Redevelopment was the only hope of a viable future. Consent granted. [1981] J.P.L. 72; [1981] J.P.L. 306.

55–29/30 Internal alterations to a listed public house. Appeal against the refusal of listed building consent was upheld. [1983] J.P.L. 751.

55–31 Demolition of listed kiln and chimney was conditional upon the redevelopment of site. [1984] J.P.L. 121.

55–32 Roof with mixed natural and asbestos slates partially reroofed to all asbestos slates. Works for which listed building consent required. Appropriate requirements of a listed building enforcement notice. [1984] J.P.L. 285.

55–33 Listed-building consent for the demolition of a Methodist Church where there were insufficient funds for necessary structural repairs. [1984] J.P.L. 363.

55–34 Alteration to windows and the replacement of the roof with a mansard roof to form an additional room in a Conservation Area. Listed building consent for part only of the proposed works ("split decision"). [1984] J.P.L. 525.

55–35 Listed-building consent to demolish a small listed dwelling-house refused where there was the prospect of purchase by the local Civic Society. [1984] J.P.L. 679.

55–36 Consent for demolition of a listed building will not ordinarily be granted until all reasonable avenues for restoration or conversion to an appropriate alternative use have been explored. [1985] J.P.L. 55.

55–37 Listed-building consent for works of renovation and alteration (including demolition) to Grade I listed building—conditions. [1985] J.P.L. 332.

55–38 Refusal of permission for the installation of doors to the storm-porch of a Grade II listed building. [1985] J.P.L. 416.

SECTION 56. PROVISIONS SUPPLEMENTAL TO SECTION 55

56–01 Phillips v. Min. of Housing & Local Govt. [1965] 1 Q.B. 156, C.A. An "ecclesiastical building" must be owned, in freehold or leasehold, by the ecclesiastical authorities.

Per Lord Denning M.R.: Church open for public worship, vestry, chapter house and theological college are all ecclesiastical buildings.

56–02 Att.-Gen. v. Howard Church Trustees [1976] A.C. 363, H.L.

(1) An "ecclesiastical building" in s.56 is not confined to a building belonging to the established Church.

Quaere

Whether confined to Christian religious buildings or extended to synagogues and mosques.

(2) Section 56 does not apply to total demolition as a building can then no longer be used for ecclesiastical purposes.

SECTION 60. TREE PRESERVATION ORDERS

60–01 Att.-Gen v. Melville Construction Co. Ltd. (1968) 20 P. & C.R. 131. In a case where irremediable injury was threatened by breach of a Tree Preservation Order, the court would and should intervene by injunction without waiting to see whether the statutory remedies proved to be adequate.

While the court retained its discretion it should pay great attention to the fact that the proceedings had been brought by the Attorney-General, and, save in at least exceptional circumstances, an application by him for an injunction to restrain a breach of the law should not be refused.

60–02 R. v. Bournemouth Justices, ex p. Bournemouth Corp. (1970) 21 P. & C.R. 163, D.C. An enabling provision allowing the prohibition of certain matters permits an order covering all aspects of that prohibition and therefore a tree preservation order can prohibit causing or permitting the cutting of trees.

60–03 Bates v. Sec. of State for Environment [1975] J.P.L. 156.

(1) Tree preservation order—whether the Minister had considered the effect on amenity.

(2) Even if trees were wrongly classified the order was valid as trees were sufficiently identified.

(3) Sub-committee of the Forestry Commission—sub-committee Chairman was authorised to make a decision on behalf of the sub-committee.

60–04 Kent C.C. v. Batchelor (No. 2) [1979] 1 W.L.R. 213. Local authority had duties under the Act to protect areas of natural beauty. The duty did not end on making tree preservation orders, they must see that areas of beauty were preserved. It was not just a question of preventing a criminal offence, it was a case of preventing interference with an area of natural beauty, therefore the injunction was appropriate. Power under s.222 of the Local Government Act 1972 was not limited to cases where an emergency or penalties for an offence have proved to be wholly inadequate.

60–05 Kent C.C. v. Batchelor (1976) 33 P. & C.R. 185. *Per* Lord Denning M.R.: Many bushes and saplings are not trees. In woodland a "tree" ought to be something over seven or eight inches in diameter.

60–06 Bullock v. Sec. of State for Environment (1980) 40 P. & C.R. 246. A coppice could be the subject of a tree preservation order as anything that could be called a tree, whatever its diameter, could be the subject of such an order.

The order when applied to smaller trees does not prevent getting out bushes, scrub or saplings with consent.

There is no reason why a practical scheme of management could not be produced in respect of a coppice.

60–07 Vale of Glamorgan B.C. v. Palmer [1983] Crim. L.R. 334. Tree preservation order invalid because the council had failed to deposit it, and keep it deposited for inspection, for so long as it was in force as required by reg. 3(2) of the Town and Country Planning (Tree Preservation Order) Regulations 1950.

60–08 A tree preservation order must be considered on its own merits. One cannot compare the amenity value of the "order trees" with other unprotected trees in the area. Value of a voluntary arrangement for the protection of trees. [1971] J.P.L. 589.

60–09 Form of tree preservation order—the number of trees in relation to the area. [1976] J.P.L. 62.

60–10 Definition of "tree." [1979] J.P.L. 483.

60–11 Permission to fell a tree protected by a tree preservation order where its amenity value was not great and it cast a dense shadow, but subject to a condition that a new tree be planted. [1985] J.P.L. 414.

SECTION 63. CONTROL OF ADVERTISEMENTS

63–01 More O'Ferrall v. Harrow U.D.C. [1947] K.B. 66. Town and Country Planning Act 1932—when deciding whether an advertisement hoarding does seriously injure the amenity of the land to be protected one must ignore the fact that there are already other hoardings near the same place.

63–02 Dominant Sites Ltd. v. Hendon Corp. (1952) 3 P. & C.R. 245. Regulations made under the Town and Country Planning Act 1947 for the control of advertisements were valid and effective even though advertisements were permitted by an existing town-planning scheme made under the Town and Country Planning Act 1932.

63–03 John v. Reveille Newspapers (1955) 5 P. & C.R. 95. Where an advertiser employs a bill-poster to post advertisements he is an independent contractor and if he posts the advertisements in contravention of the 1971 Act the advertiser is not liable.

63–04 Solosigns v. Essex C.C. [1956] J.P.L. 904. An advertisement need not expressly state that the goods advertised were sold on the premises to be "an advertisement displayed on business premises wholly with reference to goods sold." Garage forecourt was part of business premises.

63–05 Cooper v. Bailey (1956) 6 P. & C.R. 261. Advertisements in front of some earth on a kerb which was joined to a wall on each side of a garage building were displayed on part of a structure and erection which was used for building purposes within reg. 2(1) of the Town and Country Planning (Control of Advertisements) Regulations 1948.

63–06 Jones v. Merioneth C.C. (1969) 20 P. & C.R. 106. Merely because a place is within the curtilage of business premises does not mean that it is a "building" for the purposes of regs. 2(1) and 12(3) of the Town and Country Planning (Control of Advertisements) Regulations 1960.

63–07 Blakemore v. Heron Service Stations (1971) 22 P. & C.R. 601. The forecourt of a petrol station is a "forecourt of business premises" within Class V of reg. 14(1) of the Town and Country Planning (Control of Advertisements) Regulations 1969.

63–08 Heron Services Stations v. Coupe [1973] 1 All E.R. 502, H.L. Advertisements on the concrete forecourt of a filling station were not "displayed on business prem-

S.63. CONTROL OF ADVERTISEMENTS

ises" within Class IV of reg. 14(1) of the Town and Country Planning (Control of Advertisements) Regulations 1969.

63–09 McDonald v. Howard Cook Advertising [1972] 1 W.L.R. 90, D.C. The figure of a man, a packet of cigarettes, and a glass of beer are not "figures," "symbols," "emblems," or "devices" within the meaning of reg. 14(2)(*a*) of the Town and Country Planning (Control of Advertisements) Regulations 1969.

63–10 Mills & Allen Ltd. v. City of Glasgow D.C. [1980] J.P.L. 409. Change from an advertisement painted directly on to the wall to an advertisement painted on plywood sheets attached to the wall with a nominal timber frame was not necessarily a substantial alteration, and was not so in this case.

Regulations barred an increase in the size of an advertisement but not a reduction in size.

Alterations refer to changes in the way a site is used to display an advertisement not the matter advertised.

The manner in which one site is used cannot be said to change because use of a nearby site had changed and therefore made the other site more visible.

63–11 Display of illuminated signs—relevant criteria. Renewal of fascia. Whether development was involved.

63–12 On an application for permission for an advertisement the effects of excessive advertising are a material consideration. The interests of business, replacing of the former advertisement, contents of the sign, policy grounds and creation of a precedent are not material considerations. [1971] J.P.L. 470.

63–13 Application for consent for the display of an advertisement must be considered on its individual merits, not on general policy grounds. Illuminated projecting signs are not necessarily out of place in a shopping street in a Conservation Area. [1971] J.P.L. 471.

63–14 Whether the flying of flags amounts to a display of advertisements depends upon the individual circumstances of each case. Visible display drawing attention to itself as part of the setting of a commercial enterprise centred on mill as advertisement. [1979] J.P.L. 628.

63–15 Display of advertisement by a captive balloon. [1983] J.P.L. 574.

SECTION 65. PROPER MAINTENANCE OF WASTE LAND

65–01 Stephens v. Cuckfield R.D.C. [1960] 2 Q.B. 373, C.A. Whether a piece of land was properly described as a "garden," "vacant site" or "open land" is a question to be determined in all the circumstances of each case. A rule of construction should not be laid down defining "open land" as necessarily excluding an open space merely because, by being enclosed by a ring fence, it might be described as part of the curtilage.

Car breakers yard open to the air and unbuilt upon, but fenced, was not open land in this case.

See also *Stephens* v. *Cuckfield R.D.C.* [1959] 1 Q.B. 516.

65–02 Britt v. Buckinghamshire C.C. [1964] 1 Q.B. 77, C.A.

(1) As regulations under the Town and Country Planning Act 1947 could modify the Act, the Court is bound to read the Act together with the regulations made under it.

(2) So read with the Town and Country Planning Act (General) Regulations 1948, s.33(1) of the Town and Country Planning Act 1947 allowed a notice to be given to abate an injury to the amenity of the neighbourhood even if it arose from the use to which the land in question was put, not from mere disuse, the word "condition" in s.33(1) not being limited in any way.

PART V. ENFORCEMENT OF CONTROL UNDER PARTS III AND IV

SECTION 87. POWER TO SERVE ENFORCEMENT NOTICE

A. The Discretionary Power to Issue a Notice: section 87(1)

87–01 Swallow & Pearson v. Middlesex C.C. [1953] 1 W.L.R. 422. No waiver or approbation can turn an invalid enforcement notice into a valid one.

87–02 Davis v. Miller [1956] 1 W.L.R. 1013. Planning authority may serve an enforcement notice before an appeal against the refusal of planning permission is heard.

87–03 Edwick v. Sunbury-on-Thames U.D.C. (1964) 63 L.G.R. 204. A second enforcement notice in the same terms as an earlier notice can validly be served, at any rate if the first is by then of no practical effect.
Per Lord Denning M.R.: It can be served even if it is effective.

87–04 Jeary v. Chailey R.D.C. (1973) 26 P. & C.R. 280, C.A. A local planning authority are entitled to serve an enforcement notice where it appears to them that a breach of planning control has taken place. The fact that such a breach has not in fact taken place does not render the enforcement notice *ultra vires*. There being no allegation of bad faith the planning authority were entitled to issue the enforcement notice.

87–05 De Mulder v. Sec. of State for Environment [1974] Q.B. 792. Although several enforcement notices may be directed to different parts of a planning unit where various uses are carried on, this cannot be done if the effect is more restrictive than just serving one notice applicable to the whole planning unit. An area does not become a separate planning unit as soon as an enforcement notice is served.

87–06 Tidswell v. Sec. of State for Environment (1976) 34 P. & C.R. 152. Local planning authority is under no duty to investigate and satisfy themselves that an appellant could not bring himself within some exception in the General Development Order before serving an enforcement notice. A local planning authority can serve an enforcement notice on the basis that they have not granted planning permission for the use complained of and leave it to the occupier to establish, if he can, some exemption or permission.

87–07 Perry v. Stanborough (Development) Ltd. (1977) 244 E.G. 551. No duty on a planning authority to issue an enforcement notice and therefore its refusal to do so is unchallengeable.

87–08 R. v. Sec. of State for the Environment, ex p. Hillingdon B.C. [1986] J.P.L. 363. No power to delegate the function of issuing an enforcement notice to chairman of planning committee and any such notice will be a nullity.

87–09 Local planning authority estopped from issuing an enforcement notice where the plan showing amendments to permitted development was approved by officer of the authority. [1984] J.P.L. 680.

87–10 Provided a local planning authority has approached the decision to enforce in a responsible manner, taking reasonable care in seeking to ensure that they have had regard to any relevant considerations, then an enforcement notice issued pursuant to such a decision will not be a nullity simply because some particular material consideration was not taken into account.

S.87. POWER TO SERVE ENFORCEMENT NOTICE

B. What Amounts to a Breach of Planning Control: section 87(3)

87–11 Alan Markovits v. Hove B.C. (1958) 9 P. & C.R. 292. Although the manner of the operation of machines did not constitute development it could be a breach of condition of permission.

87–12 Mounsdon v. Weymouth and Melcombe Rehs Corpn. [1960] 1 All E.R. 538. Where enforcement notice served requiring breach of condition it is still open to appellant to argue that no permission for the development was needed anyway: but see now *Kerrier D.C. v. Sec. of State for the Environment*.

87–13 Postill v. East Riding C.C. [1956] 2 Q.B. 386. Discontinuance of user followed by a resumption of user 10 months' later was not the continuance of the original user and there was therefore no breach of a condition in the planning permission that the use cease on a specified date.

87–14 Francis v. Yiewsley and West Drayton U.D.C. [1958] 1.Q.B. 478, C.A. Where development was carried out and then limited permission was subsequently given for it, the development was not carried out without permission for the purposes of enforcement proceedings.

87–15 Wilson v. West Sussex C.C. [1963] 2 Q.B. 764. Limitation on the occupants of a building meant that if the building were to be occupied by different occupants, this use would not be authorised by the permission. It would not be akin to a breach of a condition.

87–16 East Suffolk C.C. v. Sec. of State for Environment (1972) 70 L.G.R. 595. A grant of planning permission for a building limited to "occupation by an agricultural worker" restricts the scope of the permission but does not impose conditions on the use of the land.

87–17 Cater v. Essex C.C. [1960] 1 Q.B. 424. Use of land for more than 28 days could not be classified as unauthorised development because of Class IV of the General Development Order. But now see s.24(6).

87–18 Copeland B.C. v. Sec. of State for Environment (1976) P. & C.R. 403, D.C. New development on previously undeveloped land is a single operation, therefore where a house is built with the wrong type of roof the breach of planning control is the construction of the whole house.

87–19 Rochdale M.B.C. v. Simmonds [1981] J.P.L. 191, D.C. Erection of a fence in excess of the terms of the permission which was granted by way of permitted development was development without planning permission.

87–20 Kerrier D.C. v. Sec. of State for Environment [1981] J.P.L. 193, D.C.
(1) The fact that development is carried out without planning permission because it does not comply with the planning permission which was granted does not mean that planning permission has to be treated as a nullity and therefore there is no reason why conditions to that planning permission should not bite.
(2) Having relied on a permission to build a house the occupiers should not escape the conditions to it by failing to comply with the plans.

87–21 J. Toomey Motors Ltd. v. Sec. of State for Environment [1981] J.P.L. 418, D.C. Not possible to repudiate a planning permission where one was doing that which one had been given planning permission to do and there was no other basis upon which one could do it. Therefore even though the appellants claimed to have carried out development without planning permission they had in fact carried out development in breach of condition of planning permission.

87–22 Deviation from approved plans on the erection of building was insufficient to support an allegation that the building had been built without planning permission. Allegation of breach of limitation of planning permission is inappropriate where the contravention involved is a material change of use without planning permission. [1970] J.P.L. 657.

87–23 Where use continues after expiration of time-limit the breach is a breach of condition not development without planning permission. [1980] J.P.L. 414.

87–24 Condition requiring that estate roads extend to the boundary of estate to obviate a "ranson strip"—road stopping $4\frac{1}{2}$ feet short was a failure to comply with the condition which was not *de minimis* substitution of the condition. [1980] J.P.L. 614.

87–25 Continued stationing of a gypsy caravan after the expiration of limited permission was a failure to comply with conditions rather than development without planning permission. Whether enforcement notices were alternatives. [1983] J.P.L. 566.

87–26 Where planning permission is given on an application which has not been properly advertised it is a nullity and an enforcement notice would properly complain of a change of use without planning permission, rather than a breach of condition in the planning permission. [1985] J.P.L. 201.

C. The Operation of the Four Year Rule: section 87(4)

87–27 Thomas David (Porthcawl) Ltd. v. Penybont R.D.C. [1972] 1 W.L.R. 1526. With mining operations each individual cut is a separate operation and time runs from the date of the cut so that enforcement cannot be taken against mining which took place more than four years ago but can be taken to stop future mining and to take action against mining which had taken place within the last four years.

Per Lord Denning: mining is *sui generis*.

87–28 Bilboe v. Sec. of State for Environment (1980) 39 P. & C.R. 495 at 505, C.A. Tipping constitutes a material change of use, not operations, therefore the four year rule is inapplicable. If tipping commenced before 1964 an enforcement notice could not be served.

87–29 Ewen Developments Ltd. v. Sec. of State for Environment [1980] J.P.L. 404. In dealing with a single operation of construction if enforcement proceedings could properly be brought against the construction as a whole, you cannot retain the part which was constructed four years before proceedings commenced.

87–30 L.B. of Camden v. Balker & Aird [1982] J.P.L. 516. Breach of a condition by the use of a floor for residential accommodation—enforcement notice was bad because it was served more than four years after the date of the breach.

Now see s.87(4)(*d*).

87–31 Worthy Fuels Injection Ltd. v. Sec. of State for Environment [1983] J.P.L. 173. Accepted that if a building which was erected in the course of one operation were to be completed within the four year period, enforcement action could be taken against the whole building even though the work had commenced more than four years ago.

Inspector's decision must be quashed as he had failed to explain adequately whether he had considered that building operations amounted to two or one separate operation in applying the four year rule.

87–32 Howes v. Sec. of State for Environment [1984] J.P.L. 439. Fact that the owner wanted to improve access in the future could not affect the situation at the time an enforcement notice was served. The question is, when did development occur? Where "a single operation of construction" the four year period ran from the time of its substantial completion.

87–33 Peacock Homes v. Sec. of State for Environment (1984) 42 P. & C.R. 20. Continued use of land after the expiration of a time-limited planning permission for

s.87. POWER TO SERVE ENFORCEMENT NOTICE

a building is a failure to comply with "any conditions or limitations" as provided by s.87(4)(b) and therefore an enforcement notice can only be validly served within four years of the breach.

Also see [1983] J.P.L. 543.

87–34 Breach of a condition prohibiting the sale of certain goods. Four year rule did not run from the date of first breach, as the breach continued. (1961) 12 P. & C.R. 406.

87–35 Storage of timber in the open. Continuous breach of a condition. Breach occurs on the first failure to observe the condition. Some parts of the land were not continuously used in breach of the condition but it was impossible to identify them, and generally the land was used in breach since before the relevant date. Immune from enforcement. [1966] J.P.L. 348.

87–36 Enforcement notice in respect of a use carried on on part only of the land for more than four years. [1967] J.P.L. 235.

87–37 Where a breach of condition is continuous the date of failure to comply with the condition runs from first failure to observe the condition. Where the condition applies to only part of the year the breach cannot be continuous over the year. Service of an enforcement notice on the occupants of caravans. [1967] J.P.L. 229.

87–38 Where one of two unauthorised concurrent uses is immune from enforcement one can still enforce against the other. [1968] J.P.L. 299.

87–39 Where a breach of a condition has become immune from an enforcement proceeding that does not render immune a further breach by a materially different use. [1968] J.P.L. 294.

87–40 Use of part of a site in breach of a planning condition for more than four years. [1968] J.P.L. 351.

87–41 Use of premises for car repairs then dual use of car repairs and car sales. Subsequently used only for car repairs. Commencement of the car-repair use dated back to the original sole use for car repairs. [1969] J.P.L. 529.

87–42 Building used as a warehouse and for the sale of cars before 1964 and subsequently for the sale of cars in breach of 1962 planning permission. Use for the sale of cars was immune from enforcement proceedings as carried out prior to 1963. [1971] J.P.L. 57.

87–43 Where external rebuilding of a dwelling was substantially completed more than four years before the date of the enforcement notice it was immune from enforcement even though minor external work was carried out later and it was not immediately fit for human occupation. [1972] J.P.L. 385.

87–44 Use enforced against established on part of land before 1964—that part of the land removed from the enforcement notice. [1972] J.P.L. 515.

87–45 Although building was substantially completed in 1975, a roofing operation in 1979 was part of a single operation to provide a viable building, therefore the operation was only completed in 1979. [1982] J.P.L. 55.

87–46 Date of the completion of building works done over a considerable period of time was no earlier than the erection of the roof. [1984] J.P.L. 601.

D. The Requirements for Service of a Notice: section 87(5)

87–47 Caravans & Automobiles v. Southall B.C. [1963] 1 W.L.R. 690. An enforcement notice under s.23 of the Town and Country Planning Act 1947 must be served on all of the occupiers of the site.

87–48 Courtney-Southan v. Crawley U.D.C. [1967] 2 Q.B. 930, D.C. A husband acting as his wife's agent where the wife was the landowner was not the owner and so an enforcement notice served on him was invalid as incorrectly served.

87–49 Stevens v. Bromley L.B.C. [1972] 2 W.L.R. 605, C.A. Whether or not a man is an occupier entitled to be served with an enforcement notice depends upon the facts and circumstances of the particular case and does not depend upon his status *vis-à-vis* the landlord.

In this particular case, given that the caravan was a permanent home and that it had been on the plot of land for a considerable period of time, and that the appellant's occupation of it was exclusive, he was an occupier even though he was only a licensee.

Per Edmund Davies L.J.: A person living on a caravan site has no legal right to have an enforcement notice served on him unless he can establish a degree of control over and substantial duration of enjoyment of the premises concerned.

87–50 Scarborough D.C. v. Adams [1983] J.P.L. 673. (1) Section 87(5) merely sets out classes of people who must be served with an enforcement notice, it does not preclude the service of other classes of people.

(2) An enforcement notice is not a nullity even if the persons named on it are incorrectly named as occupier.

(3) Occupiers of a caravan parked in a lay-by are occupiers of the land in this case because of length of time the caravans were stationed there, the use to which the lay-by was being put and the exclusive nature of occupation through the whole of the relevant period.

87–51 Effect of failure to serve an enforcement notice on an occupier. [1967] J.P.L. 411.

87–52 Enforcement notice quashed as served on an associated company rather than the owners of the land, but decision still given on deemed planning application. [1968] J.P.L. 39.

87–53 Enforcement notice quashed as not served on the occupier of the premises, even though served on her husband, the tenant. [1968] J.P.L. 41.

87–54 Enforcement notice not served on the owner of land due to incorrect information supplied by him. Notice was not properly served and therefore must be quashed. [1969] J.P.L. 476.

87–55 Failure to serve enforcement notice on all the owners and occupiers of land—failure to make all reasonable inquiries. [1970] J.P.L. 409.

87–56 Enforcement notice covering the whole site served on the owner and notice covering the area of each tenant's holding served on six tenants—failure to serve one enforcement notice on all the interested parties. [1970] J.P.L. 411.

87–57 Enforcement notice quashed because served on the owner and occupiers on different days. [1975] J.P.L. 368.

87–58 Service of enforcement notice not satisfactory. [1975] J.P.L. 230.

87–59 Service of enforcement notice—stall-holders. [1976] J.P.L. 113.

87–60 An enforcement notice sent by recorded delivery but returned marked "refused" is not properly served. A further enforcement notice may be served prior to the withdrawal of an earlier one. [1976] J.P.L. 324.

87–61 Service of an enforcement notice invalid where not authorised by the local planning authority at the time of service, even though subsequently ratified. Effect of service of the notice on (a) persons not having an interest in the land, and (b) the prospective licensee, in addition to persons entitled to be served. [1977] J.P.L. 604.

87–62 Failure to serve an enforcement notice on all the joint owners of the land. [1977] J.P.L. 674.

87–63 Service of an enforcement notice on the owners and occupiers of a priory. [1978] J.P.L. 126.

87–64 Failure to serve the occupier of part of the land with an enforcement notice—exclusion of his part of the land. [1979] J.P.L. 701.

87–65 Owners of caravans stationed on a small caravan site are occupiers for the purposes of s.87(5) and should have been served with enforcement notices. [1983] J.P.L. 271.

E. The Contents of the Notice

1. Matters Alleged to Constitute Breach of Planning Control: section 87(6)

87–66 East Riding C.C. v. Park Estate (Bridlington) Ltd. [1957] A.C. 223, H.L. Enforcement notice must identify which kind of breach of control is alleged unauthorised development or breach of a planning condition. Failure makes the notice a nullity.

87–67 Alan Markovits v. Hove B.C. (1958) 9 P. & C.R. 292. Allegation that detriment by noise and vibration caused by specified machines was sufficiently particularised.

87–68 Findlow v. Lewis [1963] 1 Q.B. 151. Although a fundamental false statement in an enforcement notice may nullify it, a statement that development has been carried out without the grant of planning permission is not false merely because the development occurred before the appointed day when no permission was required.

87–69 Miller-Mead v. Min. of Housing & Local Govt. [1963] 2 W.L.R. 225, C.A. For an enforcement notice to be valid it must "appear" to the planning authority that there had been a breach of the law in that either (a) there had been development without permission, or (b) that there has been failure to comply with a condition or limitation subject to which permission was given. The enforcement notice must specify which of those breaches is "alleged" to have taken place.

87–70 Borg v. Khan (1965) 63 L.G.R. 309, D.C. Use as "a house-let-in-lodgings" is a possible description of a land use for planning purposes—adequate description for enforcement notice.

87–71 Holtby v. Stretford B.C. (1964) 108 S.J. 158. Two enforcement notices served in the alternative. One alleged unauthorised material change of use, while the other alleged breach of a condition attaching to permitted development under Class IV. It was held irregular to serve an enforcement notice based on a Development Order when it was clear that the use was permanent. The first notice was upheld while the second was quashed.

87–72 Ormston v. Horsham R.D.C. (1965) 63 L.G.R. 452. Allegations of development without permission can be combined in an enforcement notice with allegations of overstepping the 28 days' permission under the General Development Order.

87–73 Garland v. Min. of Housing & Local Govt. (1968) 20 P. & C.R. 93. It may be necessary to reconsider whether an enforcement notice, which complains of development without permission where it should have stated that there had been a failure to comply with a condition, was irretrievably bad.

87–74 Burns v. Sec. of State for Environment (1971) 219 E.G. 586, D.C. Open to a local planning authority when issuing an enforcement notice to proceed either for a change of use or operational development.

S.87. POWER TO SERVE ENFORCEMENT NOTICE

87–75 Hawkey v. Sec. of State for Environment (1971) 22 P. & C.R. 610, D.C. An enforcement notice did not have to identify the planning unit, it would normally be directed to the area where it was to take effect. But the occupier still had a right to rely on the planning unit to show that no material change of use had taken place. An enforcement notice could refer to area larger than that in which the activities complained of were carried out.

87–76 Eldon Garages Ltd. v. Kingston-upon-Hull C.B.C. [1974] 1 All E.R. 358. Although necessary to specify in an enforcement notice whether it is alleged that development occurred without the grant of planning permission or in breach of a condition, it was not necessary to use the actual words of the Act. Also, the wording of the notice could be interpreted by reference to its context and background.

87–77 Pilkington v. Sec. of State for Environment [1973] 1 W.L.R. 1527, D.C. *Quaere*—Lord Widgery C.J.: Whether requirement that an enforcement notice should specify which breach of control is alleged has survived the changes in the 1971 Act, especially the power of the Secretary of State to amend the notice.

87–78 Morris v. Sec. of State for Environment (1975) 31 P. & C.R. 216, D.C. Up to the planning authority whether they brought proceedings in respect of the whole planning unit or in respect of some smaller portion of it on which the offending change of use had occurred.

87–79 Lipson v. Sec. of State for Environment (1976) 33 P. & C.R. 95, D.C. Meaning of "multiple paying occupation" depends on the exact context. On appeal against an enforcement notice, it was held that:
(1) houses separately let in bed-sitting rooms with shared bathrooms and W.C.s were aptly described in the notice as multiple-paying occupation;
(2) although the letting of a house in self-contained flats did not necessarily exclude multiple-paying occupation, in this case multiple-paying occupation had not commenced before the end of 1964.

87–80 Duffy v. Pilling (1976) 33 P. & C.R. 85, D.C. Enforcement notice requiring the discontinuance of "multiple-paying occupation." Held that the phrase refers to two or more people occupying parts of the house in the sense of "exercising control" and that physical division is important. See also *Lipson* v. *Sec. of State for Environment*.

87–81 Bristol Stadium Ltd. v. Brown [1980] J.P.L. 107, D.C. An enforcement notice must describe the general activity complained of, but it need not go into greater detail than that and it need not specify the individual steps.
If it specified the general activity it did not matter that it set out some specific activities which were included in the general activity.

87–82 Kerrier D.C. v. Sec. of State for Environment [1981] J.P.L. 193.
(1) If an enforcement notice refers only to the particular respect in which the building departed from the approved plan, without alleging that the building as a whole was built without planning permission, it would be set aside.
(2) If there are breaches by reason both of development without planning permission and breach of a condition the planning authority does not have to enforce both, it can choose to enforce one provided it makes clear the breach it is alleging and that the facts supported that breach.

87–83 Rochdale M.B.C. v. Simmonds [1981] J.P.L. 191, D.C. Planning authority is only required to specify the matter alleged to constitute the breach, it does not need to specify the nature of the breach.

87–84 Scott v. Sec. of State for Environment [1983] J.P.L. 108. An enforcement notice does not have to state the category of development (*i.e.* operational development or change of use) alleged to have occurred.

s.87. POWER TO SERVE ENFORCEMENT NOTICE

87–85 Krueger v. Sec. of State for Environment [1983] J.P.L. 233. Word "land" includes buildings and an enforcement notice alleging a breach of planning control in respect of land extends to activities going on in buildings on the land, even though reference to buildings in printed model enforcement notice may have been deleted.

87–86 Westminster C.C. v. Sec. of State for Environment [1983] J.P.L. 602. Enforcement notice need not spell out the previous use of the premises as in this case the Council had set out the previous use in their statement.

87–87 Backer v. Sec. of State for Environment [1983] 2 All E.R. 1021. Allegation in an enforcement notice that land was used for the stationing of caravans. Held that a vehicle can only be regarded as having been adapted for human habitation where some physical alteration has been carried out with that end in view. Installation of a bed and cooker into a van does not convert it into a caravan, even though someone lives in it.

87–88 Enforcement notice alleging a material change of use and breach of a limitation of 28 days imposed on permission granted by the General Development Order for temporary use of the land. Not a temporary use and therefore the breach of limitation allegation was inappropriate. Not a material error and therefore the notice amended to exclude allegation. [1967] J.P.L. 292.

87–89 Appellant was not prejudiced by a misdescription of the appeal premises. [1968] J.P.L. 700.

87–90 Unnecessary for an enforcement notice to define the former use of the land—erroneous description deleted. [1969] J.P.L. 40.

87–91 Planning permission for a caravan site "for weekend and holiday purposes"—enforcement notice alleging a material change of use to use for permanent residential caravans quashed. [1969] J.P.L. 479.

87–92 Enforcement notice alleging a material change of use where there was only a breach of the condition of the General Development Order permission—notice quashed. [1970] J.P.L. 464.

87–93 Enforcement notice in respect of permanent use must allege a material change of use, not a breach of condition. [1971] J.P.L. 125.

87–94 Enforcement notice void where the extent of land to which it relates is insufficiently defined. [1973] J.P.L. 551.

87–95 Enforcement notice invalid where it alleged a material change of use without permission where the breach consisted of continued use after the time-limit imposed by the condition of a planning permission. [1973] J.P.L. 51.

87–96 Allegation of a change from the storage of builder's materials to the parking of vehicles does not amount to development as both are storage uses. [1974] J.P.L. 159.

87–97 Tipping of soil on land used for the business of a road haulage contractor in order to raise the level to form a parking area was an engineering or other operation, not a material change of use as alleged, therefore notice invalid. [1979] J.P.L. 489.

87–98 Area of land to which an enforcement notice should relate. [1974] J.P.L. 676.

87–99 Dual use of land as a road haulage depot and for the bulk storage of tractors—inadequate description of uses in the enforcement notice. [1976] J.P.L. 117.

87–100 Minor discrepancy in the copy of an enforcement notice served on the wife of the occupier disregarded. [1976] J.P.L. 710.

87–101 Misdescription of land in an enforcement notice was a material irremediable error. [1977] C.L.Y. 2934.

87–102 Permissible to serve an enforcement notice in respect of the use of part of a planning unit. [1977] J.P.L. 264.

87–103 Enforcement notice in respect of part of a planning unit. [1977] J.P.L. 611.

87–104 Use of the first floor of building as a drawing-office amounted to a material change of use and therefore the enforcement notice correctly alleged development without planning permission, even though it was also a breach of a condition of the planning permission attaching to the site. [1978] J.P.L. 203.

87–105 Enforcement notice invalid where an unauthorised use as described was considered by the Secretary of State to be ancillary to a business use, which was part of a mixed one. [1978] J.P.L. 54.

87–106 Enforcement against one use on a site with a dual use—necessary to take care that the notice was drafted to include one use only. [1978] J.P.L. 56.

87–107 Although all of the planning unit must be taken into account in determining whether there has been a material change of use, an enforcement notice can be directed at the actual part of the planning unit where the material change of use has occurred. [1978] J.P.L. 338.

87–108 An enforcement notice must relate to the whole of a composite use and not just to particular elements comprised in it. [1978] J.P.L. 568.

87–109 Enforcement notice defective if the allegation is of a material change of use without planning permission when the use was permitted for a limited period but continued thereafter in breach of the condition requiring cessation. [1978] J.P.L. 724.

87–110 Enforcement notice—error in describing a fence as 6 feet high was an error in labelling and in any event it was unnecessary to specify the height of the fence. The appellant was not misled and the notice was valid. Previous correspondence did not relate to the fence as built and therefore could not found an estoppel. [1979] J.P.L. 47.

87–111 Enforcement notice quashed—defective plan did not include relevant buildings. Use of a stable as a riding school. [1979] J.P.L. 188.

87–112 Stationing of caravans on the site of a holiday camp was one element of use of the land as a whole and not identifiable or severable as an independent use—not possible to enforce against it separately. [1980] J.P.L. 126.

87–113 Where an enforcement notice alleges a material change of use it is sufficient to allege the present use without reference to the former use. [1980] J.P.L. 476.

87–114 Enforcement notice quashed because of an inaccurate description in it of the use enforced against. Storage ancillary to a business use distinguished from storage *per se*. Unable to enforce against ancillary use. [1980] J.P.L. 469.

87–115 Correct allegation for the unauthorised stationing of a caravan should refer to a material change of use. Enforcement notice referring to a material change of use and operational development both within last four years quashed. Notice had so mixed up the two types of development that it was fundamentally bad. [1982] J.P.L. 267.

87–116 Omission to state the actual use of a caravan in an enforcement notice although the use for which it was designed was specified was not material. [1982] J.P.L. 724.

s.87. POWER TO SERVE ENFORCEMENT NOTICE

87–117 Enforcement notice alleging a change of use from a residential use to a mixed residential and storage use when a railway van body was placed within the curtilage of a dwelling-house which already contained another railway van body was quashed as it should have referred to intensification. [1983] J.P.L. 135.

87–118 Where a material change of use occurred pursuant to a conditional planning permission which was granted without the required advertisements of the applications, an enforcement notice correctly described the breach of planning control as a material change of use. [1985] J.P.L. 201.

87–119 Where staircase removed from terraced house with the result that the upper part could only be reached from the adjoining house, the upper part and the adjoining house formed one separate planning unit. Therefore where two enforcement notices served which got the correct planning units wrong, the notices had to be quashed as this could have created difficulties. [1986] J.P.L. 382.

2. Specifying the Steps Required to be Taken: section 87(7) and (10)

(a) The notice must only require those steps necessary to remedy the breach of planning control and should safeguard existing user rights

87–120 Mansi v. Elstree R.D.C. (1964) 16 P. & C.R. 153. No power to prohibit an established use by an enforcement notice—case remitted to the Minister to amend the notice.

87–121 Fordham v. Elstree R.D.C. (1968) 207 E.G. 893. Where use was so small as to be insignificant and then enlarged into a material change of use it was reasonable to require a total cessation of use.

87–122 Decorative & Caravan Paints Ltd. v. Min. of Housing & Local Govt. (1970) 214 E.G. 1355. Enforcement notice allowing such retail sales as would be ancillary to warehouse use upheld.

87–123 Clare & Ridgway Ltd. v. Min. of Health & Local Govt. (1970) 217 E.G. 873, D.C. Case remitted to Minister to amend an enforcement notice to protect legitimate ancillary use.

87–124 Burns v. Sec. of State for Environment (1971) 219 E.G. 586. Power to require restoration of land to its condition prior to the material change of use means that incidental operational development immune from enforcement may also have to be removed.

87–125 Ipswich County Borough v. Sec. of State for Environment (1972) 225 E.G. 1355. Enforcement notice amended to protect established user rights to repair and maintain taxis.

87–126 Trevors Warehouses Ltd. v. Sec. of State for Environment (1972) 23 P. & C.R. 215, D.C. In cases of change of use by "creeping intensification" it may be right to restrict use to pre-1964 use, but where a material change of use created by a dramatic change on a particular date the enforcement notice should not restrict continuance of use that accrued up to that date.

87–127 Lipson v. Sec. of State for Environment (1976) 33 P. & C.R. 95. Enforcement notice cannot require a use to be resumed.

87–128 Day and Mid-Warwickshire Motors Ltd. v. Sec. of State for Environment [1979] J.P.L. 538, D.C. Case remitted to the Secretary of State to amend an enforcement notice so as to preserve any use available under s.23(9) and the Use Classes Order.

87–129 Murfitt v. Sec. of State for Environment (1980) 40 P. & C.R. 254, D.C. An enforcement notice requiring the discontinuance of the use of a site for the purpose of parking heavy goods vehicles may also require the restoration of the land, as a physical matter, to its condition before the development had occurred including removal of hardcore, even if that was operational development.

87–130 Newport v. Sec. of State for Environment (1980) 40 P. & C.R. 261, D.C. Although an enforcement notice may not specifically prohibit a pre-1964 use because this is ancillary to the established use it is important that the limits of what can and cannot be done should be clear and in an appropriate case they should be set out. Enforcement notice requiring discontinuance of use of a forecourt for the purpose of the display of vehicles for sale was sent back to the Secretary of State so that he could make it plain that the sale of three or four vehicles which had been ancillary to the main use of the premises for the repair, servicing and garaging or parking of vehicles was not prohibited.

87–131 Cleaver v. Sec. of State for Environment [1981] J.P.L. 38, D.C. Where breach of planning control was *inter alia* the sale or exchange of items related to general-scrap dealer use, an enforcement notice requiring cessation of any sale or exchange not limited to sale or exchange related to general scrap-dealer use went so far beyond the terms of the breach that it would have to be amended even though the appellant was not misled by it.

No need for further representations before it was amended and no need to give the appellant further time for compliance with the notice.

87–132 Cord v. Sec. of State for Environment [1981] J.P.L. 40. Not necessary to include in an enforcement notice that which must be obvious to everybody. A notice prohibiting the parking and storage of commercial vehicles need not include a specific protection of rights incidental to the use of a dwelling house.

Per Donaldson L.J.: If things which the occupier is entitled to do without planning permission derogate from prohibitions in an enforcement notice there is a strong case for writing them into the notice for the avoidance of doubt.

87–133 Sanders v. Sec. of State for Environment [1981] J.P.L. 593, D.C. Amendment of an enforcement notice by the Secretary of State to include prohibition on use of the land for the "repairing of boilers" is valid on land with rights for use for agricultural purposes and hiring, renovating and dealing in boilers as it did not prevent a use which could otherwise have been independently carried out.

87–134 Perkins v. Sec. of State for Environment [1981] J.P.L. 755. *Murfitt* v. *Sec. of State for Environment* was binding authority for the proposition that an enforcement notice alleging material change of use may be served where operational development is an integral part of a change of use.

Obiter: Operational development may be caught by the requirements of a change of use enforcement notice even though not an integral part of the change of use.

87–135 North Sea Land Equipment v. Sec. of State for Environment [1982] J.P.L. 384. A matter of discretion for the Secretary of State whether an enforcement notice requires amendment to protect an incidental use.

87–136 Haigh v. Sec. of State for Environment [1983] J.P.L. 40. Where an enforcement notice does not prohibit an established use it is not necessary to say in terms that an ancillary use is preserved although it is often desirable to do so. The Secretary of State may wish to consider whether an amendment should be included to make it clear that an ancillary use is not prohibited and he is under a duty to consider this if submissions to that effect are made to him.

87–137 Choudhury v. Sec. of State for Environment [1983] J.P.L. 231. Requirement in an enforcement notice that use must cease "except in so far as the use may be authorised by a letter from the Council dated January 30, 1978" did not sufficiently safeguard existing use rights because it did not clearly define the physical limits of the permitted use.

s.87. POWER TO SERVE ENFORCEMENT NOTICE

87–138 Denham Developments v. Sec. of State for Environment (1984) 47 P. & C.R. 598. Where premises are used for intermingled uses and are then only used for one use an enforcement notice in respect of that use may be in respect of the whole land if it is impossible to clarify which parts of the land had been used for which use.

87–139 Bath City Council v. Sec. of State for Environment [1983] J.P.L. 737. Listed building enforcement case. Consideration of the new powers introduced by the Local Government and Planning (Amendment) Act 1981.

87–140 Green v. Sec. of State for Environment [1985] J.P.L. 323. Where development was completely unauthorised, it was right to require the whole works to be removed even though with alterations the works could have amounted to permitted development under the General Development Order. Section 87(9)(*a*) considered.

(b) Question of "under-enforcement"

87–141 Iddenden v. Sec. of State for Environment [1972] 1 W.L.R. 1433, C.A. *Per* Lord Denning: Local Planning authority have a discretion on enforcement to require the taking only of such steps as they consider necessary, short of complete restoration of land.

87–142 Copeland B.C. v. Sec. of State for Environment (1976) P. & C.R. 403, D.C. Although under-enforcement should be allowed, before an authority can under-enforce they must first correctly describe the breach of planning control.

87–143 Enforcement notice requiring provision of a ramp instead of a stepped entrance to a shop for the benefit of disabled persons quashed, but not to be taken as implying that the needs of the disabled need not be taken into account in dealing with future applications. [1983] J.P.L. 136.

87–144 An enforcement notice may require removal of an uncompleted building erected pursuant to planning permission for the building which has ceased to have effect because of the service of a completion notice. [1985] J.P.L. 496.

(c) Steps must be set out reasonably clearly

87–145 Ormston v. Horsham R.D.C. (1965) 63 L.G.R. 452, C.A. Enough for an enforcement notice to require land to be restored to its previous use if the owner knows what that was, and specific directions need not in that case be given.

87–146 Trevors Warehouses Ltd. v. Sec. of State for Environment (1972) 23 P. & C.R. 215, D.C. Although there might be practical difficulties in complying with an enforcement notice restricting use to pre-1964 use (or some other date) it is not ambiguous and in some cases there may be no better alternative.

87–147 Lipson v. Sec. of State for Environment (1976) 33 P. & C.R. 95. Requirement in an enforcement notice that the premises should be restored to the condition they were in before the development complained had commenced was not invalid because the landowner did not know what this condition was.

87–148 Metallic Protectives Ltd. v. Sec. of State for Environment [1976] J.P.L. 166, D.C. Enforcement notice requiring the installation of satisfactory sound-proofing of a compressor and to take all possible action to minimise the effect created by the use of acryllic paint was so vague as to be a nullity.

87–149 Sykes v. Sec. of State for Environment [1981] J.P.L. 285, D.C. A "paddock" is not a concept of use at all, but perhaps one of enclosure, therefore an enforcement notice requiring cessation of use as a paddock unsatisfactory and ambiguous and therefore invalid.

87–150 L.B. of Hounslow v. Sec. of State for Environment [1981] J.P.L. 510. The wording of an enforcement notice need not strictly adhere to formality, but it must tell the recipient clearly what he has done wrong and what he must do to remedy it. If on the true construction of the notice it is hopelessly ambiguous and uncertain it is a nullity, but if the error can be corrected without injustice it is not a material error. The Secretary of State has a duty to try to put an enforcement notice in order and this is not limited to corrections in favour of the developer.

Words "to comply or seek compliance" with a condition requiring demolition of a building were hopelessly ambiguous and uncertain and the notice was a nullity.

87–151 Lee v. L.B. of Bromley [1982] J.P.L. 778. Enforcement notice requiring a person to discontinue a particular use of land except to the extent to which such use was carried on prior to January 1, 1964 is in its terms perfectly clear and in no way vague or meaningless so as to be void. But a finding by the Secretary of State based upon the inspector's report must be sufficiently precise to enable the user of the land to know clearly what he is permitted to do. It must set out clearly the pre-1964 use.

87–152 Rhymney Valley D.C. v. Sec. of State for Wales [1985] J.P.L. 27. Enforcement notice terminology was reasonably clear and it was not a nullity.

87–153 Ivory v. Sec. of State for Environment & North Hertfordshire D.C. [1985] J.P.L. 796. Enforcement notice requiring the use of land for the holding of show-jumping events and other equestrian competitions to be discontinued was upheld. The notice informed the owner or occupier with reasonable certainty what steps he had to take.

87–154 Dudley Bowers Amusements v. Sec. of State for Environment (1986) 278 E.G. 313. An enforcement notice requiring the use of land as an amusement arcade to cease during the period of summer-time so ambiguous as to be a nullity.

87–155 Requirement in an enforcement notice to reduce the intensity of use of a site to the level existing at December 31, 1963 was too vague and the notice was a nullity. [1972] J.P.L. 337.

87–156 Requirement of an enforcement notice that land be restored in accordance with a scheme to be agreed with local planning authority. [1973] J.P.L. 177.

87–156a Enforcement notice which did not specify the steps to be taken was a nullity. [1979] J.P.L. 633.

87–157 Enforcement notice quashed because the allegations were so widely drawn it was virtually impossible to relate them to the alleged unauthorised uses. [1985] J.P.L. 274.

3. The Date Notice is to Take Effect and the Period for Compliance: section 87(8) and (13)

87–158 Burgess v. Jarvis and Sevenoaks R.D.C. [1952] Q.B. 41, C.A. Enforcement notice not specifying the date on which it came into effect is invalid. Followed in *Mead* v. *Chelmsford* R.D.C. [1953] 1 Q.B. 32 where the Divisional Court held that it must also specify the date on which the works it orders to be done are to be carried out.

N.B. Both points are now expressly dealt with in the statute, *i.e.* s.87(8) and (13).

87–159 Swallow & Pearson v. Middlesex C.C. [1953] 1 W.L.R. 422. Failure to specify the period after which an enforcement notice is to take effect makes the notice invalid.

87–160 Bambury v. Hounslow L.B.C. [1966] 2 Q.B. 204. Enforcement notice which took effect on different dates, because it had been served on the owner and occupier at different dates, was invalid.

But note new procedures for issuing notices.

s.87. POWER TO SERVE ENFORCEMENT NOTICE

87–161 L.B. Redbridge v. Perry (1976) P. & C.R. 176. The period for compliance with an enforcement notice is to be related to the time which it would take those in active occupation of the premises in question, and thus in a position to comply with the notice, to do so; 56 days is sufficient to enable the occupiers of bed-sitting rooms to leave and the fact that it might be insufficient time to enable the landlord to initiate possession proceedings is irrelevant.

Per curiam: An enforcement notice must specify a single period for compliance to different owners and occupiers to match the difficulty or lack of difficulty in complying with it.

87–162 King & King v. Sec. of State for Environment [1981] J.P.L. 813, D.C. Enforcement notice does not have to draw the recipients' attention to s.88(3) and the period for carrying out steps required can be deduced from the information in the notice.

87–163/164 Absence of date on enforcement notice immaterial. [1970] J.P.L. 461.

87–165 An enforcement notice stated to come into effect at the end of 28 days beginning with May 29, comes into effect after 28 days beginning on May 29, not 28 days after May 29.

F. Enforcement of Planning Control by Injunction

87–166 Att.-Gen. v. Bastow [1957] 3 W.L.R. 340. Planning control involved public rights which could be enforced by way of injunction. Once a clear breach had been shown, if the Attorney-General sought an injunction as the most effective method of enforcement it should only be refused in exceptional circumstances.

87–167 Att.-Gen. v. Smith [1958] 3 W.L.R. 81. Town and Country Planning legislation confers a benefit on the public, therefore if somebody shows by his conduct that he intends to avoid the Act and act in breach of it the Attorney-General is entitled to an injunction.

Any development without permission was unlawful, even before an enforcement notice was served.

(Moving caravans from one field to another each time the enforcement notice action taken.)

87–168 Att.-Gen. v. Morris [1973] J.P.L. 429. Injunction granted perpetually restraining the defendant from using a particular site or any other land within the county as a caravan site without authorisation.

87–169 Beaconsfield D.C. v. Gams (1976) 237 E.G. 657. Permission for a bungalow on green belt land conditional upon a farm-house being demolished. Condition was a contractual obligation enforceable by injunction. Injunction granted restraining occupation of the bungalow until the farm-house was demolished or the condition discharged or modified.

87–170 Hammersmith L.B.C. v. Magnum [1978] 1 W.L.R. 50, C.A. (Control of Pollution Act case). Even though statutory procedure had not been exhausted, as the defendants showed no signs of complying with it, entitled to an injunction.

87–171 Solihull M.B.C. v. Maxfern [1977] 1 W.L.R. 127. Section 222 of the Local Government Act 1972 enables a local authority to sue in its own name in cases where formerly the concurrence of the Attorney-General was required.

87–172 Stafford B.C. v. Elkenford Ltd. [1977] 1 W.L.R. 325, C.A. [Shops Act Decision]. As the local council had invoked the statutory remedies available to it and it had been shown that the defendants would continue profitable operations in defiance of the Shops Act 1950 unless effectively restrained, the court could in the exercise of its discretionary jurisdiction ensure obedience by granting an injunction even though the appeal procedure set in train against the conviction under Shops Act had not been exhausted.

Per Lord Denning M.R.: Where there is a plain breach of statute, local councils need not wait for finality anywhere. They can take proceedings in the High Court for an injunction before other proceedings are even started.

Per Bridge L.J.: Only in an exceptional case would the court exercise its discretion to grant an injunction before there has been any resort to the statutory remedies at all.

87–173 Westminster C.C. v. Jones [1981] J.P.L. 750. Change of use to an amusement arcade without permission. Stop notice ignored. The local authority had the power to apply for an injunction under s.222 of the Local Government Act 1972, even though other actions were being heard.

An injunction could be granted to preserve the character of a particular part of the council's territory in accordance with their plans.

See also [1981] J.P.L. 546.

87–174 Stoke-on-Trent City Council v. B. & Q. (Retail) Ltd. [1984] 2 All E.R. 332, H.L.

(1) Section 222(1) of the Local Government Act 1972 empowers a local authority to institute proceedings in its own name in a proper case to restrain anticipated criminal offences without resort to the Attorney-General, but it was limited to the promotion or protection of the interests of the inhabitants of its area and was subject to the well-established principles relating to judicial review of the exercise of an executive power.

(2) To use its powers under s.222(1) to seek injunction restraining breach of criminal law the authority has to show a deliberate and flagrant flouting of the law.

(3) The court would exercise its jurisdiction to grant an injunction with care, but it would grant an injunction where maximum fines which could be imposed would be less than the profits made from breaking the law.

Per curiam: Although a local authority is entitled to have regard to the financial consequences of a prosecution to the ratepayers it cannot say that it will never carry out its statutory duty because of the expense involved.

87–175 Bedfordshire C.C. v. Central Electricity Generating Board [1985] J.P.L. 43. Interim injunction to prevent investigatory drilling refused as no real damage would be caused even if it was unlawful.

87–176 Avon C.C. v. Millard (1985) 274 E.G. 1025. Planning permission granted to mine stone. Covenant entered into by the grantee to construct an access road within two years and to discontinue mining after two years if no further consent granted. Injunction granted to stop mining because of failure to comply with the covenants. Irrelevant that all the powers under the 1977 Act had not been exhausted as this was a question of ordinary civil remedies under the contract.

87–177 Runnymede B.C. v. D.M. Ball [1986] J.P.L. 289. Interlocutory injunction sought to restrain the use of a site for the siting of caravans for residential purposes in breach of enforcement and stop notices. Injunction rejected by the judge in the Chancery Division on the grounds that relief should only be granted where statutory remedies were "inadequate" or there was "deliberate flouting of law." It was held that this was an error of law and that relief could be granted in other circumstances where it is necessary to protect the interests of inhabitants such as when irreversible damage might be caused.

87–178 Runnymede B.C. v. Smith [1986] J.P.L. 592. *Runnymede B.C. v. Ball* distinguished.

SECTION 88. APPEALS AGAINST ENFORCEMENT NOTICE

A. The Grounds of Appeal: section 88(2)

88–01 Mercer v. Uckfield R.D.C. (1962) 60 L.G.R. 226. On an enforcement notice appeal the history of the site is relevant in considering whether a reasonable time was allowed for compliance with the enforcement notice.

88–02 Chelmsford R.D.C. v. Powell [1963] 1 W.L.R. 123, D.C. Appellant is not confined to his grounds of appeal stated in his notice of appeal and the Minister can allow an appeal on other grounds.

88–03 Parker Bros. (Farms) v. Min. of Housing & Local Govt. (1969) 210 E.G. 825. Appeal against an enforcement notice on the ground that a change had occurred before the four-year period was rejected by the Minister. Held that the onus of proof was on the appellants.

88–04 Smith v. King (1969) 21 P. & C.R. 560. The reasonableness of the period of time allowed to comply with an enforcement notice is to be tested as at the date of service of the enforcement notice, regard being had to the background of the matter.

88–05 Stanton v. Sec. of State for Environment (1978) 248 E.G. 227. Scrapyard. Immunity from enforcement proceedings. Burden of proof. Use since 1964.

88–06 Snowdon v. Sec. of State for Environment [1980] J.P.L. 749. In considering whether planning permission ought to be granted there was a duty to compare alternative lawful uses on an enforcement notice appeal, but only where there is a real likelihood that an alternative lawful use will be taken up.

88–07 L.W.T. Contractors v. Sec. of State for Environment [1981] J.P.L. 815. Wrong to require proof "beyond reasonable doubt" in an enforcement notice appeal.

88–08 Thrasyvoulou v. Sec. of State for Environment [1984] J.P.L. 732. On appeal against an enforcement notice the burden of proof is the balance of probabilities.

88–09 Onus of proof on an appeal against an enforcement notice is on the appellant. [1967] J.P.L. 609.

88–10 Grounds of appeal, argued on appeal but subsequently withdrawn, taken into consideration. [1968] J.P.L. 168.

88–11 Enforcement notice appeal not considered because of failure to state facts upon which the appeal based. [1970] J.P.L. 340.

88–12 Enforcement notice—grounds of the appeal which were introduced after service of the notice of appeal were considered by the Secretary of State. [1970] J.P.L. 465.

88–13 Period for compliance with enforcement notice extended, although not a ground of appeal. [1970] J.P.L. 591.

88–14 In the absence of an appeal an enforcement notice becomes effective even though it would have been open to challenge on the grounds that the development was carried out more than four years earlier. [1971] J.P.L. 407.

88–15 In considering the retention of unauthorised buildings it is a relevant consideration that there had been a similar building on the site previously which had been destroyed by fire. [1977] J.P.L. 608.

88–16 Appeal under s.88(2)(*c*) of the 1971 Act provides an opportunity to submit that the breach alleged in the notice has not taken place as a matter of evidential fact, rather than an opportunity to submit that there is no breach of planning control as a matter of law. [1985] J.P.L. 63.

88–17 Challenge to validity of enforcement notice can be heard on re-hearing of appeal because it goes to power of Secretary of State to hear the appeal. [1985] J.P.L. 734.

B. The Procedures for Making an Appeal

88–18 Garland v. Westminster C.C. (1970) 2 P. & C.R. 535. An appeal is finally determined so as to allow an enforcement notice to come into effect when it has been dismissed and the time for any further appeal has expired without the further appeal being made. The theoretical possibility of leave being given to appeal out of time may be disregarded. But see now *Dover D.C.* v. *Sec. of State for Environment* [1985] J.P.L. 627.

88–19 Cookham R.D.C. v. Bull (1972) 222 E.G. 2104. Accepted that notice of appeal was posted in time but received out of time did not constitute a valid appeal, though the point was not argued.

88–20 Howard v. Sec. of State for Environment [1975] Q.B. 235. Requirements that an appeal be made in writing and within a specified time are imperative, and cannot be waived by the Secretary of State. However, it is sufficient to simply appeal without stating the grounds of appeal as the requirement to state grounds is directory. Grounds and details can be supplied later.

88–21 Button v. Jenkins [1975] 3 All E.R. 585. An invalid refusal to accept an appeal has the effect of determining the appeal if it is not challenged by way of s.246. So the enforcement notice takes effect if there is no challenge by way of s.246.

88–22 R. v. Melton & Belvoir Justices, ex p. Tynan (1977) 33 P. & C.R. 214, D.C. Mistaken acceptance by the Secretary of State of an appeal which is invalid because it is out of time does not prevent a magistrate as a competent tribunal on a prosecution from reaching the conclusion that the notice of appeal is invalid.

Per curiam: The Secretary of State is behaving perfectly properly within his jurisdiction if in an appropriate case he says an appeal is hopeless, for example because it is three months out of time. If in those circumstances he overrides an appeal all other authorities dealing with the matter must accept his decision. But he cannot give interlocutory decisions before he is in a position to deal with the matter finally.

88–23 Wain v. Sec. of State for Environment and Waltham Forest L.B.C. [1979] J.P.L. 231. An invalid refusal of an appeal can only be challenged via s.246. Declaration that an appeal was valid was refused by the court. *Howard* v. *Sec. of State for Environment* was not followed as this point had not been argued in that case.

88–24 Scarborough D.C. v. Adams [1983] J.P.L. 673. Although a person with no interest in the land cannot appeal against an enforcement notice and is precluded from raising the matters set out in s.88(2), by s.243(1), when prosecuted he can still argue before a magistrates' court that an enforcement notice is a nullity or invalid, for example because the issuing authority had no jurisdiction to issue a notice.

88–25 Hewlett v. Sec. of State for Environment [1981] J.P.L. 187. Decision of the inspector quashed because he gave inadequate reasons to explain why he considered development had occurred.

88–26 P.A.D. Entertainment v. Sec. of State for Environment [1982] J.P.L. 706. Secretary of State was not obliged to hear an enforcement notice appeal until the appellant had submitted the statement of facts requested by the Secretary of State. Where an appellant refused to submit such a statement the Secretary of State could dismiss the appeal.

s.88. APPEALS AGAINST ENFORCEMENT NOTICE

88–27 Lenlyn Ltd. v. Sec. of State for Environment [1985] J.P.L. 482. Notice of appeal posted but received by Secretary of State after the date when the enforcement notice took effect is invalid and the Secretary of State has no jurisdiction to consider the appeal.

The proper way to challenge the validity of a decision of the Secretary of State not to accept an appeal is by way of judicial review.

88–28 Dover D.C. v. Sec. of State for Environment [1985] J.P.L. 627. The period for compliance with an enforcement notice, where there had been an appeal, ran from the date of the appeal decision even if it was possible to delay the notice by making a further appeal to the courts under s.246.

88–29 R. v. Sec. of State for Environment, ex p. M.T. Crossley [1985] J.P.L. 632. Secretary of State has no power under s.88 to reinstate an appeal once it had been withdrawn. This means that any rights to challenge the notice on the grounds of appeal set out in s.88(1), are lost.

88–30 London Parachuting Ltd. Rectory Farm (Pampisford) Ltd. v. Sec. of State for Environment and South Cambridgeshire D.C. [1986] J.P.L. 279. Court of Appeal, without having to decide the point, expressed approval of the decision in *Dover D.C.* v. *McKeen*, which held that section 88(10) only applied to appeals to the Secretary of State and not to applications to the court under section 246 and so an enforcement notice took effect on the date of the Secretary of State's rejection of an appeal.

88–31 Effect of a High Court judgment as to the validity of planning permission *res judicata* it was not open to the parties on appeal against an enforcement notice to re-open the question of the validity of planning permission and the conditions attached. [1974] J.P.L. 377.

88–32 Person supplied but not formally served with an enforcement notice is allowed to appeal against it irrespective of whether he is an owner or a person with an interest in the land. [1977] J.P.L. 465.

88–33 Appeal lodged on the day that the notice came into effect was out of time and invalid. [1981] J.P.L. 222.

88–34 An appeal posted before an enforcement notice takes effect is lawful. [1973] J.P.L. 666.

But see now *Lenlyn* v. *Sec. of State for Environment*.

88–35 Carrying out tipping of waste-materials on site by way of license is not an interest in land so as to allow a person to appeal against an enforcement notice, but the appeal was considered on basis that it was also made on behalf of a person who had a right to appeal. [1983] J.P.L. 826.

88–36 Appeal charge refunded where the appellant withdrew an appeal under s.88(2)(*a*) and no formal determination given. [1983] J.P.L. 499.

C. Inquiries and the Decision-making Procedure

88–37 Nelsolvil Ltd. v. Min. of Housing & Local Govt. [1962] 1 W.L.R. 404, D.C.

(1) Minister was not bound by the views of the inspector and must exercise his discretion independently, attaching such weight as he thought proper to the findings and recommendations of the inspector.

(2) The burden of proof in an enforcement appeal is upon the appellant to establish that there has been no breach of planning control.

88–38 Knight v. Sec. of State for Environment (1971) 219 E.G. 586. On an enforcement notice appeal as to whether the use is more than four years old, the Secretary of State has the right and duty to re-examine the evidence and come to a different conclusion to his inspector.

88–39 Wild and A.G.M. Car Hire v. Sec. of State for Environment [1976] J.P.L. 432. Appeal against an enforcement notice on the ground that a material change took place before the end of 1963. This was a question of fact and degree and the onus was on the appellant to prove according to the ordinary balance of probability test. Reference to "uncorroborated evidence" did not invalidate the decision as it only showed that the inspector and the Secretary of State had concluded that there was no disinterested evidence and did not show that they had applied a criminal standard of proof.

88–40 Hyndburn B.C. v. Sec. of State for Environment (1979) 251 E.G. 473. Appeal by a local authority against the Secretary of State's revocation of enforcement notice and grant of planning permission:
(1) The Secretary of State is entitled to have a policy and to apply it without giving parties to an appeal the opportunity of commenting on it and could therefore refer to his own Circulars.
(2) Reference to a circular as the basis of a decision made the grounds for the decision tolerably clear.
(3) The Secretary of State is concerned with his own policy not the Council's.

88–41 Warnock v. Sec. of State for Environment [1980] J.P.L. 590. Difference of opinion as to what was the correct planning unit on an enforcement appeal was not a new issue of fact within the meaning of Rule 14 of the Inquiry Procedure Rules 1974.

88–42 T.L.G. Building Materials v. Sec. of State for Environment [1981] J.P.L. 513. In changing a planning unit the Secretary of State had altered the perspective from which the matter should be viewed. It also meant that evidence at the inquiry had been directed to a different unit from that which the Secretary of State was dealing with and natural justice required that the appellant be given an opportunity to make representation in respect of it.

88–43 Pollock v. Sec. of State for Environment [1981] J.P.L. 420. Although the Town and Country Planning (Inquiries Procedure) Rules 1974 did not apply to proceedings brought under s.88 the Secretary of State would allow representations to be made in the same manner and circumstances. The inspector found that repair use had existed unbroken since 1963. The Secretary of State's conclusion that repair use had not been unbroken since 1963 had constituted a different finding of fact.
See also (1979) 252 E.G. 914.

88–44 S.J.D. Properties Ltd. v. Sec. of State for Environment [1981] J.P.L. 673. Although the Inquiry Procedure Rules did not apply to enforcement notice appeals, those appeals had to be carried on in accordance with the rules of natural justice or else there was an error of law. Considerable assistance could be had in looking at the Inquiry Procedure Rules.

In this case, as adequate reasons had been given and as there could be no further submissions, there was no breach of the rules of natural justice and so even if there were a technical breach of the Inquiry Procedure Rules this was not a case where that gave rise to an error of law.

Decisions in *Pollock's* case queried.

See also rule 14 of the Town and Country Planning (Enforcement) (Inquiries Procedure) Rules 1981.

88–45 W. & J. Wass Ltd. v. Sec. of State for Environment and City of Stoke-on-Trent Council [1986] J.P.L. 120. Public inquiry held into enforcement notice appeal. The inspector, in coming to his decision, can rely on personal observations gained on site visit but if allegation of bad faith made at the inquiry against the local planning authority he should make a finding, though failure will not necessarily invalidate his decision.

SECTION 88A. APPEALS AGAINST ENFORCEMENT NOTICES—THE POWERS OF THE SECRETARY OF STATE WITH REGARD TO THE ENFORCEMENT NOTICE

A. The Powers of Correction and Variation: section 88A(1) and (2)

88A–01 Miller-Mead v. Min. of Housing & Local Govt. [1963] 2 W.L.R. 225. If the terms of the notice require more to be done than is necessary to remedy the breach the notice can be cut down by amendment. The Minister has power to correct any informality, defect or error in an enforcement notice if it is not a material one which goes to the substance of the matter.

Per Diplock L.J.: If allegations are wider than are justified by the facts the Minister can cut down the requirements of the notice to fit the facts proved, provided that some facts are proved which support a charge of the kind specified.

Per Upjohn L.J.: The overriding test is, does the notice fairly tell the appellant what he has done wrong and what he must do to remedy it?

88A–02 Nicholls (A.H.) & Sons v. Hertford R.D.C. (1964) 15 P. & C.R. 330. Failure to serve an enforcement notice on the owner is not a defect which can be cured by Minister. But note changes in the legislation since this decision.

88A–03 Lloyd-Jones v. Min. of Housing & Local Govt. (1967) 204 E.G. 1200, D.C. Secretary of State entitled to amend enforcement notice to describe activity as "shop or market" rather than "shop."

88A–04 Bevan v. Sec. of State for Wales (1969) 211 E.G. 1245, D.C. Enforcement notice alleged a change of use from domestic purposes and a pig farm to use partly for a plant-hire and haulage business. The actual change was to composite pig farm and plant-hire and haulage use and then to plant-hire and haulage use. Error immaterial—enforcement notice amended.

88A–05 Hawkey v. Sec. of State for Environment (1971) 22 P. & C.R. 610, D.C. An enforcement notice can only be attacked on the ground that it contains error if those errors cannot be amended without injustice.

Inelegant language and failure to delete parts of a pro forma notice by which no one was misled could if necessary be amended.

88A–06 Burlde v. Sec. of State for Environment [1972] 1 W.L.R. 1207, D.C. Secretary of State is acting within his jurisdiction if he amends an enforcement notice so as to apply to a part only of area included in the original enforcement notice if that is the correct planning unit.

88A–07 Ipswich C.B.C. v. Sec. of State for Environment (1972) 225 E.G. 797, D.C. Amendment of an enforcement notice to preserve established use—deletion of certain activities enforced against.

88A–08 Felton & Sons (Motors) v. Sec. of State for Environment (1973) 227 E.G. 1475. Amendment of an enforcement notice by the Secretary of State. So that the repair of all cars was prohibited. Held that the Secretary of State is entitled to disagree with his inspector and hold that a change of use was more extensive.

88A–09 Morris v. Sec. of State for Environment (1974) 31 P. & C.R. 216, D.C. Where part of a material change of use was the sale of motor vehicles and the local authority stated that this was part of the material change of use but omitted to prohibit the sale of motor vehicles that was an error which could be corrected by the Secretary of State. It is an error for "correction" and the fact that the inspector refers to the correction as a "variation" does not stop it from being a correction.

88A–10 Hammersmith B.C. v. Sec. of State for Environment (1975) 30 P. & C.R. 19, D.C. As the Secretary of State is under a duty to get an enforcement notice in order he is entitled, and in appropriate cases bound, to choose his own label to describe the activity complained of if he thinks that the language used by the draftsman of the notice is unsuitable.

"Guest-house" was not a suitable description of the use of four bedrooms with four beds in each, as it implied something rather more delicate in the way of accommodation and conditions. A "lodging house" or "hostel" would be more appropriate and an enforcement notice could be amended to substitute one of the above labels without injustice.

88A–11 Scurlock v. Sec. of State for Wales (1977) 33 P. & C.R. 202, D.C. Secretary of State is entitled to amend the requirement in an enforcement notice so as to clarify the situation and avoid dispute.

88A–12 Brooks & Burton v. Sec. of State for Environment [1977] 1 W.L.R. 1294, C.A. Allegation in an enforcement notice that land used for Class III of the Use Classes Order when in fact it should have been Class IV did not make the notice a nullity and it could be varied.

88A–13 Patel v. Betts [1978] J.P.L. 109. Enforcement notice dated March 1974 alleged a breach in April 1974. It complained of development by use of the ground floor room instead of alleging a material change of use and did not specify which one of two front rooms it referred to. The appellant was aware of what was complained of and none of the errors were material. Their accumulative effect was no different than their individual effect and therefore could not be material.

88A–14 Murfitt v. Sec. of State for Environment (1980) 40 P. & C.R. 254. Secretary of State has the power to vary an enforcement notice to provide for the land to be restored in accordance with a scheme to be agreed with the local planning authority or determined by the Secretary of State in default of agreement.

88A–15 Royal London Borough of Kensington and Chelsea v. Sec. of State for Environment [1981] J.P.L. 50, D.C. Secretary of States' powers of amendment did not allow him to amend to include an allegation that there had been a change of use by intensification when this had not been previously alleged in the enforcement notice.

88A–16 Dunton Park Caravan Site Ltd. v. Sec. of State for Environment [1981] J.P.L. 511, D.C. Cannot amend an enforcement notice from covering a 67-acre site to covering only one field on the site without causing possible injustice because it distorted the relevance of the inspector's findings of fact and prevented the appellants from arguing their case on the general issue as to the scope of existing storage rights.

88A–17 T.L.G. Building Materials v. Sec. of State for Environment [1981] J.P.L. 513. Beyond a mere formality to call upon somebody to stop using some land for the storage of building materials and to amend it to a much wider concept of prohibiting use as a builder's merchants yard.

An alteration of the planning unit in an enforcement notice would be material in all but exceptional cases.

88A–18 Sanders v. Sec. of State for Environment [1981] J.P.L. 593. Amendment of an enforcement notice by the Secretary of State to include prohibition of the use of land for the "repairing of boilers" was valid on land with rights for use for agricultural purposes and hiring, renovating and dealing in boilers as it did not prevent a use which could otherwise have been independently carried out.

88A–19 Scott v. Sec. of State for Environment [1983] J.P.L. 108.

(1) Even if an enforcement notice does have to state the category of development omission to do so is a defect curable by amendment by the Secretary of State using his power under s.88A(2).

(2) Even though s.88A(2) was not in force at the time of the inquiry it was not a

breach of natural justice to use its provisions without giving the applicant a further opportunity to make representations as it simply applied the same test the courts had previously adopted.

88A–20 Wealden B.C. v. Sec. of State for Environment [1983] J.P.L. 234.

(1) "Variation" is a wider term than "correction." For there to be a "variation" there must be sufficient continuity of identity between the notice before and after the change. In this case continuity of identity was provided by the land and caravan on it.

(2) Amendment of enforcement notice to specify operational development rather than material change of use, would go beyond a "correction" but could be a "variation."

(3) In most cases a variation from material change of use to operational development would cause injustice but not in this case.

(4) As the Secretary of State only considered his powers of correction and did not consider his powers of variation the decision must be quashed and the matter remitted to him.

88A–21 Burner v. Sec. of State for Environment [1983] J.P.L. 459. Where an enforcement notice referred to a change of use as the stationing of caravans the Secretary of State could amend it to the storage of caravans without causing injustice to the appellants.

88A–22 Westminster C.C. v. Sec. of State for Environment [1983] J.P.L. 602. Omission to state previous use can be rectified by the Secretary of State on appeal.

88A–23 H.T. Hughes & Sons Ltd. v. Sec. of State for Environment [1985] J.P.L. 486. Enforcement notice which alleged a breach of contract "after the end of 1963" rather than "within the last four years" could not be corrected on appeal as the mistake went to the substance of the notice and could not be corrected without injustice.

88A–24 Amendment of an enforcement notice to correct an error as to the local planning authority's name. [1966] J.P.L. 118.

88A–25 Change of use from a garage with occasional car sales to the display of cars for sale. Allegation of operational development amended to change of use. [1966] J.P.L. 483.

88A–26 Amendment of an allegation in an enforcement notice to read change of use instead of operational development. [1966] J.P.L. 485.

88A–27 Amendment of an enforcement notice to allege erection of a new building rather than material change of use was a material amendment—notice quashed. [1966] J.P.L. 727.

88A–28 Variation of enforcement notice to prohibit the sale of imported farm-produce but to permit sale ancillary to agricultural use. [1967] J.P.L. 42.

88A–29 In alleging erection of a new building rather than works of conversion an enforcement notice made a material error beyond correction. [1967] J.P.L. 42.

88A–30 Enforcement notice alleging a material change of use and breach of limitation of 28 days imposed on permission granted by the General Development Order for temporary use of the land—not a temporary use and therefore the breach of limitation allegation was inappropriate. Not a material error and therefore the notice was amended to exclude the allegation. [1967] J.P.L. 292.

S.88A. APPEALS AGAINST ENFORCEMENT NOTICES

88A–31 Enforcement notice varied to allow the sale of home-grown agricultural produce ancillary to agricultural use. [1967] J.P.L. 413.

88A–32 Change of use of garages from storage to car repairs. Incorrect inclusion of a dwelling-house in the enforcement notice when the house was not used for repairs was immaterial, and the notice was amended to exclude it. It was unnecessary to add a description of "car maintenance depot" after "change of use to use for repair of motor vehicles." [1967] J.P.L. 607.

88A–33 Minister can amend error in the numbering of the condition which was breached. [1967] J.P.L. 609.

88A–34 Permission for the erection of a flag-staff on a car park. Incorrect height corrected on the enforcement notice. [1970] J.P.L. 226.

88A–35 Correction of plan on enforcement notice appeal to take account of the inspector's findings even though no suggestion that the appellants were misled. [1971] J.P.L. 348.

88A–36 Allegation in an enforcement notice of non-compliance with a condition of planning permission related to a condition other than that intended. Enforcement notice was incorrect and beyond the Secretary of State's powers of amendment. [1973] J.P.L. 380.

88A–37 Power of the Secretary of State to amend an enforcement notice in the appellant's favour. [1974] J.P.L. 373.

88A–38 Power of the Secretary of State to amend an enforcement notice.—Need to specify the allegation correctly. [1975] J.P.L. 166.

88A–39 Requirement to restore land to its condition before development took place deleted. [1975] J.P.L. 484.

88A–40 Power of the Secretary of State to correct a defective enforcement notice. [1976] J.P.L. 255.

88A–41 Requirement of an enforcement notice that land be restored to its condition before the breach of planning control deleted by the Secretary of State contrary to the recommendation of the inspector. [1977] J.P.L. 261.

88A–42 Power of the Secretary of State to correct a plan with enforcement notice. [1977] J.P.L. 675.

88A–43 Amendment of an enforcement notice to allege operations instead of a material change of use (prior to the quashing of the notice). [1980] J.P.L. 348.

88A–44 Extent of an alleged breach could not be clearly identified by reference to the enforcement notice and plan—incapable of correction by the Secretary of State even though the person in breach was probably aware of the extent of the breach. [1981] J.P.L. 831.

88A–45 An enforcement notice which incorrectly alleges a material change of use instead of a failure to comply with a time condition, is a material defect and one not capable of correction under section 88A(2). [1986] J.P.L. 313.

88A–46 An enforcement notice, which alleged unauthorised development rather than breach of a condition, contained a fundamental error and could not be corrected under section 88A(2). [1986] J.P.L. 455.

B. Power to Disregard Failure to Serve Notice on Required Persons: section 88A(3)

88A–47 Skinner & King v. Sec. of State for Environment [1978] J.P.L. 842, D.C. The Secretary of States' conclusion that an appellant is not substantially prejudiced by a failure to serve an enforcement notice on him is to stand, even though he dis-

s.88A. APPEALS AGAINST ENFORCEMENT NOTICES

agrees with the inspector, unless it can be shown that there was no evidence upon which that conclusion could be based or it was shown that the Secretary of State had adopted some erroneous principle by leaving out a relevant factor or including an irrelevant one.

Landowner not prejudiced when one notice served on him and four similar but different notices served on the four occupiers of the land.

88A–48 Failure to serve an enforcement notice on the co-owner of a site disregarded. [1974] J.P.L. 41.

88A–49 Failure to serve an enforcement notice on stall-holders disregarded. [1974] J.P.L. 248.

88A–50 Enforcement notice not served on legal owner—no prejudice. [1973] J.P.L. 381.

88A–51 Mixed agricultural and parachute club use—enforcement notice amended to specify mixed use. [1984] J.P.L. 451.

88A–52 Error in the name of the person to whom the enforcement notice addressed—no prejudice and no need to amend the notice. [1974] J.P.L. 300.

88A–53 Person entitled to be served with an enforcement notice not served. He was aware of the notice and inquiry—chose not to attend and was not prejudiced by non-service. Change of use to the commercial preparation and storage of timber, and to the parking of vehicles not connected with agriculture. [1979] J.P.L. 403.

88A–54 Enforcement notice incorrectly addressed to a limited company due to out-of-date information in Company Search. The Council had no reason to believe it was not the last-known address but the return of a recorded delivery form undated and unsigned meant it was not properly served. However there was no prejudice and therefore the notice was valid. [1979] J.P.L. 693.

88A–55 Plan on an enforcement notice including land not owned or controlled by the appellant and not forming part of the planning unit. Non-service of the owner did not cause any prejudice as this land was not affected. [1981] J.P.L. 382.

88A–56 While caravan owners may have heard of the contents of a notice requiring the re-painting of caravans, the Secretary of State cannot be sure they were all aware of vital contents of the notice and there is a real risk that they may have been substantially prejudiced by lack of precise information as to the nature and purposes of the proceedings such that did not have the necessary facts before them on which to decide whether to appeal. Therefore he was not prepared to exercise his power under s.88A(3) to disregard a failure to serve notice. [1983] J.P.L. 271.

SECTION 88B. OTHER POWERS OF THE SECRETARY OF STATE ON APPEAL

88B–01 Hansford v. Min. of Housing & Local Govt. (1969) 214 E.G. 33, D.C. Deemed application for planning permission on an enforcement notice appeal is for an activity of which the enforcement notice complains and not for some more restricted activity which may be an established use.

88B–02 Richmond-upon-Thames B.C. v. Sec. of State for Environment (1972) 224 E.G. 1555. Power to grant planning permission on appeal against an enforcement notice is limited to the granting permission for actual development enforced against.

88B–03 Moldene v. Sec. of State for Environment [1979] J.P.L. 176, D.C. Matter entirely for the Secretary of State whether it is more appropriate to extend the time for compliance with an enforcement notice or grant temporary planning permission.

88B–04 Planning unit—inclusion of land other than that to which the enforcement notice related. Relevant when considering if there has been a material change of use, but not for deemed planning application. [1973] J.P.L. 261.

88B–05 Extension of time for compliance with an enforcement notice may be preferable to the grant of permission for limited period.[1973] J.P.L. 328.

88B–06 Powers of the Secretary of State on appeal against an enforcement notice to allow retention of part of the development. [1977] J.P.L. 395.

88B–07 Strong planning objections to the grant of planning permission for the stationing of a caravan, but as the stationing of the caravan was now immune from enforcement action a personal, time-limited permission was granted to enable a site licence to be obtained. [1978] J.P.L. 58.

88B–08 Temporary permission for multiple-paying occupation of a dwelling-house on enforcement notice appeal. [1978] J.P.L. 579.

SECTION 89. PENALTIES FOR NON-COMPLIANCE WITH ENFORCEMENT NOTICE

A. General Approach to section 89

89–01 Chiltern D.C. v. Hodgetts [1983] 1 All E.R. 1057, H.L.

(1) An offence may take place continuously or intermittently over a period of time and still remain a single offence.

(2) Section 89 created two types of offences arising out of non-compliance with an enforcement notice requiring either that owner of land does something on the land (a "do-notice") or that the user of the land desists from doing something on it (a "desist-notice"). Both initial and continuing offences for failing to comply with both a do-notice and desist-notice are single offences and an information alleging failure to comply with an enforcement notice "on and since" a certain date is not bad for duplicity.

B. Failure by the Owner to Carry out Steps Required by the Notice: section 89(1) to (4)

89–02 Whitfield v. Gowling (1974) 28 P. & C.R. 386. Where there is evidence that a person is the owner of land at one date it may be presumed that he is the owner at a later date unless there is some ground for thinking otherwise.

89–03 St. Albans D.C. v. Norman Harper Autosales Ltd. (1977) 35 P. & C.R. 70, D.C.

(1) Offence under s.89(1) is a single once-and-for-all offence.

(2) Power to extend the time for compliance under s.89(6) is a power which must be exercised before the previous time for compliance has expired.

89–04 Tandridge D.C. v. Powers [1982] J.P.L. 645. Offence under s.89(4) is a continuing offence as otherwise difficulties would arise. But now see *Chiltern D.C. v. Hodgetts*.

89–05 South Cambridgeshire D.C. v. Stokes [1981] J.P.L. 594. Even if knowledge of the actual time for compliance is an essential element of the *mens rea* required for an offence under s.89(1) a person cannot shelter behind a claim of lack of knowledge if he has taken no steps to inform himself of the time as he has to take all proper care to inform himself of any facts which would make his conduct lawful or unlawful.

Where a tenant appeals against an enforcement notice the landlord should ask the planning authority to notify him of the outcome so that he can know when, if at all, he must comply with the enforcement notice.

s.89. PENALTIES FOR NON-COMPLIANCE WITH ENFORCEMENT NOTICE

89–06 Prosser v. Sharp [1985] J.P.L. 717. Prosecution under s.89(4) after conviction for failure to comply with an enforcement notice. Acquittal by magistrates was quashed as they had wrongly overlooked the continuing validity of the enforcement notice under s.243.

C. The Use or Permitting of Uses Contrary to the Notice: section 89(5)

89–07 Goodbarne v. Buck [1940] 1 K.B. 771, C.A. A person can only permit another to do an act if he has the power to forbid him to do the act.

89–08 Klein v. Whitstable U.D.C. (1958) 10 P. & C.R. 6, D.C. Where an occupier removed caravans to comply with an enforcement notice and shortly afterwards brought them back on to the land he was correctly convicted of the offence of failing to comply with the notice. Whether a discontinuance of a use had occurred was a question of degree for the Justices to determine.

89–09 R. v. Chertsey J.J. ex p. Franks [1961] 2 Q.B. 152. The continued failure to discontinue a use is a continuing offence and the person guilty is liable to a daily fine. But see now *Chiltern D.C. v. Hodgetts*.

89–10 Test Valley Investments v. Tanner [1964] Crim. L.R. 62. Landowner does not "permit" a use of land to continue when he has obtained an injunction restraining its use but has found it impossible to enforce.

89–11 Waddell v. Winter (1967) 65 L.G.R. 370, D.C. "Permit" means to allow someone else to do something—where the Defendant is actually using land himself he is not "permitting" the use of his land for a particular purpose.

89–12 Backer v. Uckfield R.D.C. (1970) 68 L.G.R. 596, D.C. The line between steps causing what was once a vehicle to cease being a vehicle may sensibly be drawn somewhere between removal of the wheels and removal of the chassis. Offence was committed where the owner kept pantechnicons on land in a delapidated condition. *Held* that he had failed to discontinue the use of land for the stationing of "vehicles."

89–13 Johnston v. Sec. of State for Environment (1974) 28 P. & C.R. 424, D.C. A person only commits an offence under s.89(5) if, when in a position to discontinue the unlawful use, he fails to do so or causes or permits somebody else to act in defiance of the enforcement notice.

A landlord who cannot prevent his tenant from acting in defiance of an enforcement notice is not at risk of committing an offence of failing to comply with the enforcement notice if his tenant acts in defiance of it.

89–14 Bromsgrove D.C. v. Carthy (1975) 30 P. & C.R. 34, D.C. If an owner takes reasonable steps to move unlicensed caravans from his land he will not be "permitting" them to remain even if he stopped short of the use of force or of taking legal proceedings.

89–15 Parry v. Forest of Dean D.C. (1976) 34 P. & C.R. 209, D.C. Section 89(5) creates a continuing offence and so a charge that land had been used since a certain date in contravention of the notice was bad for duplicity. However, now overruled by *Chiltern D.C. v. Hodgetts*.

89–16 Redbridge L.B. v. Perry [1977] J.P.L. 247, D.C. Offence of using or permitting use in breach of an enforcement notice cannot be committed until after the date of service of the enforcement notice, therefore it was a defence to show that permission had not been granted for use since the service of the notice.

89–17 Scarborough D.C. v. Adams [1983] J.P.L. 673. An offence under s.89(5) is committed by any person acting in contravention of an enforcement notice be he occupier, squatter or trespasser.

89–18 Ragsdale v. Creswick (1984) 271 E.G. 1268, D.C.
(1) A failure to take steps which on the facts are unreasonable does not amount to "permitting" a use.
(2) Magistrates entitled to conclude that, having regard to a trespasser's itinerant character and lack of means, the launching of possession proceedings would have been unreasonable.

SECTION 90. STOP NOTICES

90–01 Scott Markets Ltd. v. Waltham Forest L.B.C. (1979) 38 P. & C.R. 597, C.A. Section 90(2) prevents service of a stop notice to prohibit the carrying-out of an activity on land where that activity had begun more than 12 months earlier, whether begun in breach of a planning control or not.—Where use commenced under a time-limited permission and continued after permission expired, the 12 months started to run when originally commenced use under permission.

90–02 Bristol Stadium Ltd. v. Brown [1980] J.P.L. 107, D.C. Where a stop notice incorporated the terms of the enforcement notice, a deficiency of particularity in the stop notice may be validated and cured by reference to the original enforcement notice.

90–03 Clywd C.C. v. Sec. of State for Wales [1982] J.P.L. 696. The activity prohibited by a stop notice must come within a matter alleged by the enforcement notice to constitute a breach of planning control.
A stop notice prohibiting the working of minerals on a site based upon an enforcement notice complaining of the failure to fence the site is invalid.

90–04 R. v. Jenner [1983] 2 All E.R. 46, C.A. A person being tried for using his land in contravention of a stop notice contrary to s.90(7) is not precluded from attempting to establish that he is not in fact subject to the prohibition in the notice.

90–05 Runnymede B.C. v. Smith [1986] J.P. 592. A stop notice which requires the discontinuance of use of caravans occupied as sole or main residence is ineffective even as regards such uses which have commenced after the service of the stop notice.

SECTION 91. EXECUTION AND COST OF WORKS REQUIRED BY ENFORCEMENT NOTICE

91–01 Joiner v. Guildford Corp. (1954) 5 P. & C.R. 50, Guildford County Court. The local planning authority cannot extend time further once time for the completion of works required has elapsed even though the authority has complete discretion as to the original time limit and can extend it within the original period.

91–02 Arcam Demolition & Construction Co. Ltd. v. Worcestershire C.C. [1964] 1 W.L.R. 661. Power to carry out works extends to any one or more of the steps required to be taken.

91–03 R. v. L.B. Greenwich, ex p. Patel [1985] J.P.L. 851. Action under s.91 could be challenged by way of application for judicial review where failure to serve enforcement notice on true owner.

SECTION 92. EFFECT OF GRANT OF PLANNING PERMISSION ON ENFORCEMENT NOTICE

92–01 Dudley B.C. v. Sec. of State for Environment [1980] J.P.L. 181, D.C. It may be better to use powers under s.92 to grant permission for part of a development enforced against rather than to try to vary the original planning permission by substitution of a new condition for an old one.

92–02 L.B. of Havering v. Sec. of State for Environment [1983] J.P.L. 240. A planning permission, even if it contains conditions and does not precisely cover the enforcement notice, will deprive an enforcement notice of effect under s.92 if it covers the same area and use as the enforcement notice. The enforcement notice ceases to have effect when the planning permission is granted, not when the conditions are complied with.

92–03 R. v. Sec. of State for Environment ex p. Three Rivers D.C. [1983] J.P.L. 730. Where planning permission is granted after service of an enforcement notice, the fact that under s.92 the notice ceases to have any effect, does not mean notice is no longer in being and so an appeal against it can still be issued.

The words the "enforcement notice shall cease to have effect" mean "actual or potential effect" and so apply equally to a notice which has not yet come into effect because it has been suspended pending an appeal.

SECTION 93. ENFORCEMENT NOTICE TO HAVE EFFECT AGAINST SUBSEQUENT DEVELOPMENT

93–01 Broxbourne B.C. v. Sec. of State for Environment [1980] C.L.Y. 2638. Dutch barn demolished pursuant to an enforcement notice. Nissen hut of the same size erected on site and put to same use.—Nissen hut held to be the reinstatement or restoration of the Dutch barn. Construction of s.93(3).

SECTION 94. CERTIFICATION OF ESTABLISHED USE

94–01 Bolivian and General Tin Trust Ltd. v. Sec. of State for Environment [1972] 1 W.L.R. 1481. Established use certificate could not apply to a situation where use of the land in contravention of planning control arose after 1963 and therefore did not apply to a case where temporary planning permission expired after 1963 and use continued thereafter unauthorised.

94–02 Broxbourne B.C. v. Sec. of State for Environment [1979] 2 W.L.R. 846. The purpose of an established use certificate is to render the use specified in the certificate immune from an enforcement notice and the object of issuing it is to preclude the necessity of an investigation into the nature and extent of an existing use.

Section 94(7) does not permit an inquiry into matters not specifically stated in an established use certificate and therefore since the level of intensity of activity had not been stated in the certificate, the Secretary of State had correctly considered that the certified existing use was without limit.

Per curiam. A planning authority should exercise great care so that the terms of an established use certificate sufficiently particularises the existing use. Such care would not only avoid the conclusive effect of a loosely and widely phrased certificate but would be of assistance to prospective purchasers in determining the value of the land.

94–03 Western Fish Products v. Penwith D.C. [1981] 2 All E.R. 204. The formal procedures for applying for an established use certificate must be followed.

94–04 Bedfordia Plant Ltd. v. Sec. of State for Environment [1981] J.P.L. 122, D.C. Factual basis of any estoppel has to be established by the person relying upon it to the satisfaction of the Secretary of State.

Authority of a rural district council was limited to deciding whether or not to issue enforcement notices and as they had no authority to grant an established use certificate or in any way to determine in a binding manner whether there was an established use, any representation to such an effect by them could not found an estoppel.

94–05 Hipsey v. Sec. of State for Environment [1984] J.P.L. 806. Intensification of use—intensification occurred by the time the established use certificate application was made and the Secretary of State was not entitled to certify that a lesser use was proper.

94–06 An application for an established use certificate can be made notwithstanding that it relates to a single dwelling-house if the condition it is claimed has not been complied with does not itself concern the use of the building as a single dwelling-house. [1971] J.P.L. 417.

94–07 Where a proposed use is same as a previous Crown use no development is involved. In considering whether a use has become established a period of use by the Crown cannot be ignored. [1971] J.P.L. 653.

94–08 An established use certificate should specify the particular use, not the type of use. The Secretary of State has no power to amend the description of the use in the certificate. Power of Secretary of State to grant planning permission on appeal in respect of an established use certificate. [1971] J.P.L. 463.

94–09 Secretary of State has no power to specify uses not specified in an application for an established use certificate. [1971] J.P.L. 467.

94–10 Use of land for a particular purpose by the Crown can create existing use rights from which persons interested in the land other than the Crown can benefit. [1971] J.P.L. 651.

94–11 The establishment of a right to use a building for a particular purpose does not confer any right to use the land on which the building stood for the same purpose after the original building has been demolished. [1971] J.P.L. 714.

94–12 Established use certificate granted in respect of use of which enforcement notice taken effect, but after use established. [1972] J.P.L. 225.

94–13 Refusal of an established use certificate for use commenced before 1964 which had not been a contravening use because it had been carried on under conditional planning permissions. [1972] J.P.L. 226.

94–14 A use cannot become established if a grant of planning permission has been made on or after January 1, 1964 which rendered that use lawful or made the condition which had been breached inoperative. [1972] J.P.L. 230.

94–15 Established use certificate not granted where it was related to one of several uses subsidiary to the permitted use. [1973] J.P.L. 184.

94–16 No established use where enforcement notices served in respect of use before it could become established. [1973] J.P.L. 503.

94–17 Established use certificate refused where use of temporary buildings and plant installed under Class IV in Sched. 1 to the General Development Order 1963 after period for which permitted. [1974] J.P.L. 239.

94–18 Application for an established use certificate must describe a particular use. [1974] J.P.L. 293.

94–19 Application for an established use certificate for a use in respect of which an enforcement notice had taken effect was invalid. [1976] J.P.L. 247.

94–20 An established use certificate will not be granted for a use which at the time of the application is the subject of an enforcement notice as it cannot be a subsisting lawful use at that time.

An established use certificate granted after an enforcement notice would not provide a defence to a prosecution for an offence of failing to comply with the enforcement notice. [1976] J.P.L. 247.

94–21 Established use certificate:
(1) extent of the land within the planning unit, onus of proof;

S.94. CERTIFICATION OF ESTABLISHED USE

(2) estoppel—whether the local planning authority was bound by a statement as to the established use in a letter from the planning officer. [1979] J.P.L. 247.

94–22 If activities are being carried on, notwithstanding that they are prohibited by an effective enforcement notice, in law the use of the land for those purposes does not subsist and no rights can be acquired in respect of it. [1978] J.P.L. 568.

94–23 For established use certificate, the issue is whether use continued "on the ground" throughout the relevant period. The issue of whether use was abandoned does not arise. [1979] J.P.L. 780.

94–24 Statement of fact in an established use certificate is only conclusive for the purposes of an appeal against an enforcement notice in respect of any land to which the certificate relates. [1980] J.P.L. 771.

94–25 Onus of proof on an application for an established use certificate is on the applicant. [1981] J.P.L. 382.

94–26 (1) Normally an application for an established use certificate described only by reference to use class cannot be accepted, but where it is claimed that a building has been used for storing all sorts of things and it is not possible to particularise the use for which the certificate is claimed, will accept an application on the basis that it is a general storage use.

(2) A use can subsist at the time of an application for an established use certificate even if it is not active at that date provided there has been no intervening use and the use has not been abandoned. A use subsisting at the time of an application can be accepted as having continued until the date of the application for the purposes of s.94(1)(a) even if not active for the whole period. [1981] J.P.L. 449.

94–27 (1) Purpose of an established use certificate is to provide a full description of the established use. Fact that it contains specific restrictions does not mean that a breach of planning control will automatically result if those limits are exceeded, but it provides the base against which any intensification can be assessed.

(2) As a use of land attaches to the planning unit as a whole an established use certificate must also relate to the whole of the planning unit. [1981] J.P.L. 527.

94–28 Where a valid enforcement notice was in force before the date of an application for an established use certificate there could not be a subsisting use and the certificate would not be granted for the use which was the subject of the enforcement notice. [1981] J.P.L. 691.

94–29 Refusal of an established use certificate because the use claimed was the storage of old tyres and waste materials and the storage of used tyres was illegal due to a prior enforcement notice. [1981] J.P.L. 691.

94–30 Definition and evidence of uses for an established use certificate. "General dealing in second-hand goods" too wide a description of use to be the subject of an established use certificate. Car-breakers and scrapyard. [1982] J.P.L. 600.

94–31 On an application for an established use certificate, use is still subsisting even though it has ceased, so long as it has not been abandoned. [1982] J.P.L. 800.

94–32 An established use certificate can only be granted for the main use of a site not for an ancillary use and an enforcement notice should be directed to the main use not the ancillary use. [1983] J.P.L. 129.

94–33 Established use certificate—could not limit residential occupation by an agricultural occupancy condition where there was no evidence that the occupant was ever engaged in agriculture. [1985] J.P.L. 494.

94–34 An established use certificate application may properly be made notwithstanding the use of the land to which the application refers is a lawful use as a use started before July 1, 1948.

An established use certificate may be granted for the whole of the land specified in the application, or for part of it—the area of the planning unit is not decisive for the purpose of deciding the extent of land in which there is an established use. [1985] J.P.L. 801.

94–35 Established use certificates granted in respect of siting of touring caravans notwithstanding prohibition of use by touring caravans by condition of 1968 planning permission. [1985] J.P.L. 876.

SECTION 95. GRANT OF CERTIFICATE OF ESTABLISHED USE BY SECRETARY OF STATE

95–01 Cottrell v. Sec. of State for Environment [1982] J.P.L. 443. On appeal under s.95 the Secretary of State can refuse a certificate on grounds not taken by the local authority, even though he rejects the local authority's reasoning, but the Secretary of State cannot allow a certificate granted for part of the land to be overturned on an appeal not relating to that part.

SECTIONS 96, 97 AND 97A. POWER TO ISSUE LISTED BUILDING ENFORCEMENT NOTICES AND APPEALS

96/97/97A–01 Paultons Square Properties v. L.C.C. (1965) 63 L.G.R. 158, D.C. Building preservation order.—Appeal against an enforcement notice refused on grounds of precedent. Question of the relevance of the need to comply with by-laws did not need to be considered.

96/97/97A–02 Bath City Council v. Sec. of State for Environment [1983] J.P.L. 737.
(1) Power under s.96(1)(*b*) cannot be used to punish a contravenor or to require him to carry out works over and above those necessary to remedy his breach which would result in an improvement in building compared to its state prior to carrying out unauthorised works.
(2) Where a listed building enforcement notice requires works which are not reasonably practicable the Secretary of State has power under s.97A(2) to amend or correct the notice and he should consider using that power where the matter comes to him on appeal. If he decides not to use that power he should give his reasons to the local planning authority.

96/97/97A–03 Listed building enforcement notice upheld requiring the partial removal of tiles which had been coated with a black sealing substance. [1973] J.P.L. 56.

96/97/97A–04 Beyond powers under enforcement procedure to require the reinstatement of property damaged or destroyed by accident. [1981] J.P.L. 443.

96/97/97A–05 Painting of the front elevation of a listed building in a Conservation Area. Listed building enforcement notice upheld on its merits. [1979] J.P.L. 782.

96/97/97A–06 Listed building enforcement notice—painting of brickwork and front elevation and the erection of shutters and of a vertical fillet. Notice upheld on its merits. [1981] J.P.L. 607.

96/97/97A–07 Installation of wrought iron railings in place of brickwork on a listed building. Enforcement notice appeal upheld on the ground in s.97(1)(*d*). [1981] J.P.L. 835.

96/97/97A–08 Listed building enforcement notice requiring restoration of a windmill partially dismantled after gale damage. Appeal on grounds in s.97(1)(*c*) and (*d*) upheld. [1982] J.P.L. 731.

SECTION 101. URGENT WORKS FOR PRESERVATION OF UNOCCUPIED BUILDINGS

101–01 R. v. Sec. of State for Environment, ex p. Hampshire County Council [1981] J.P.L. 47.

(1) The purpose of the seven-days notice in s.101 is to enable discussion between the owner and the local authority so that the owner might do the works voluntarily and therefore a notice under s.101(4) should specify in detail the works believed to be urgently necessary.

(2) Section 101 does not cover a case of continuing liability.

101–02 R. v. Stroud D.C., ex p. Goodenough [1982] J.P.L. 246, D.C. Where there was a question of a listed building being demolished without the normal statutory procedure being gone through the planning authority would be failing to perform its functions properly under the legislation if it did not take into account all of its relevant powers, particularly under ss.101 and 115.

101–03 R. v. Camden L.B.C., ex p. Comyn Ching (1984) 47 P. & C.R. 417. A notice under s.101 requiring the owner of premises to take "all such steps as may be necessary" does not state with sufficient particularity the steps required and is bad.

101–04 A notice under s.101 of the 1971 Act should describe in as much detail as possible the work which the authority consider is urgently necessary so that the owner knows what he has to do to comply with its terms, or is forewarned of the work which will be done by the council if he fails to do it himself.

It is important that the works specified should be capable of being completed so that one account for their total cost can be sent to the owner and he is not involved in a continuing liability.

For the powers of s.101 to be properly exercised, the work must be urgently necessary at the time the notice is served and the service of one notice does not enable an authority to recover the cost of additional works not included in the notice. [1978] J.P.L. 637.

SECTION 102. PENALTIES FOR NON-COMPLIANCE WITH TREE PRESERVATION ORDER

102–01 Maidstone B.C. v. Mortimer (1982) 43 P. & C.R. 67. Proof of knowledge by the accused of the existence of a tree preservation order is not a constituent of the offence under s.102(1).

102–02 Barnet L.B.C. v. Eastern Electricity Board. [1973] 1 W.L.R. 430. The purpose of the legislation protecting trees is to protect the amenities of giving pleasure, protection and shade. A tree the subject of a tree preservation order is destroyed when an injury inflicted is such that it is no longer worth preserving as an amenity.

Per curiam: If a person inflicts on a tree so radical an injury that in all the circumstances a reasonably competent forester would in consequence decide that it ought to be felled, that person wilfully destroyed the trees. One of the circumstances a forester could and should take into account in deciding whether an injured tree should be felled is its situation; a tree adjoining a highway needs greater stability and more vigorous life than a similar tree in a field.

SECTION 105. PENALTIES FOR NON-COMPLIANCE WITH NOTICE AS TO WASTE LAND

105–01 Red House Farms (Thorndon) Ltd. v. Mid-Suffolk D.C. (1980) 40 P. & C.R. 119. Positive act required to commit an offence. But note the wording of s.105 has been changed to include a person who does nothing and so fails to comply.

SECTION 109. ENFORCEMENT OF CONTROL OF ADVERTISEMENTS

109–01 R.B. Kensington & Chelsea v. Elmton (1978) 246 E.G. 1011. Replacement of an advertisement which has been taken down because it was committing an offence could not be regarded as a continuation of the original offence.

PART VI. ACQUISITION AND APPROPRIATION OF LAND AND RELATED PROVISIONS

SECTION 112. COMPULSORY ACQUISITION OF LAND IN CONNECTION WITH DEVELOPMENT AND FOR OTHER PLANNING PURPOSES

112–01 Company Developments (Property) Ltd. v. Sec. of State for Environment [1978] J.P.L. 107. For land to be "required" under s.112 it is sufficient if the local planning authority and the Secretary of State think it desirable to acquire the land for the purposes specified in s.112. The land does not have to be essential.

112–02 Thames Water Authority v. Elmbridge B.C. [1983] J.P.L. 470, C.A. Consideration of the meaning of the word "immediately" formerly used in s.112.

112–03 Acquisition of land in a town centre with the intention of being assembled for office development. Compulsory order confirmed despite being a substantial departure from the Initial Development Plan as in conformance with the draft town centre plan. [1974] J.P.L. 39.

112–04 Modification of compulsory purchase orders to exclude premises not necessary for the proposed redevelopment, and intended for acquisition to secure maintenance to a standard compatible therewith. [1980] J.P.L. 697.

SECTION 121. APPROPRIATION OF LAND FORMING PART OF A COMMON

121–01 Third Greytown Properties v. Peterborough Corp. [1973] 3 All E.R. 731. A local authority holding land on trust as an open space may still make an order in respect of it under s.121(1), even though it has been built on.

121–02 Wilcock v. Sec. of State for Environment [1975] J.P.L. 150. Appropriation of public open space land. Whether land, which it was proposed to put to public open space in exchange, was already laid out for public space purposes. Held that the certificate should be quashed.

121–03 Wilson v. Sec. of State for Environment [1973] 1 W.L.R. 1083. The application of the Acquisition of Land (Authorisation Procedure) Act 1946 means that advertisements in local newspapers must correctly describe the land.

SECTION 123. DISPOSAL OF LAND HELD FOR PLANNING PURPOSES

123–01 Crabtree (A.) & Co. Ltd. v. Min. of Housing & Local. Govt. (1965) 17 P. & C.R. 232. Under s.123(7) it is for the local planning authority and Minister to decide whether or not it is practicable to give an opportunity to persons carrying on business within the area to obtain accommodation in the redeveloped area.

Per curiam: The words "on terms settled with due regard to the price at which any such land has been acquired from them" in s.123(7) are a relic from the time when land was often acquired by a planning authority on terms other than its market value, and have no application except in exceptional circumstances where the person dispossessed is entitled to obtain the full market value of his land.

SECTION 127. POWER TO OVERRIDE EASEMENTS AND OTHER RIGHTS

127–01 Dowty Bolton Paul Ltd. v. Wolverhampton Corpn. (No. 2) (1972) 24 P. & C.R. 58. Land validly appropriated for planning purposes could be so used under s.127 (subject to planning permission and payment of compensation) even though the corporation was covenanted in the lease to allow the land to be used for another purpose.
Affirmed (1973) 25 P. & C.R. 282.

PART VII. COMPENSATION FOR PLANNING DECISIONS RESTRICTING NEW DEVELOPMENT

SECTION 136. ORIGINAL UNEXPENDED BALANCE OF ESTABLISHED DEVELOPMENT VALUE

136–01 Re Hasluck (decd.) Sully v. Duffin (1957) 9 P. & C.R. 70. The one-seventh increase is capital because there is no mention of interest in the section.

136–02 Bunce & Bunce v. Min. of Housing & Local Govt. (1957) 9 P. & C.R. 105. Land wrongly regarded as near ripe where a claim pledged to the Board as security for development change by form D.26 was signed by the first appellant only. Signature purported to be on behalf of the partnership—partner was not bound. Not possible, on account of joint interest, to differentiate between the appellants.

SECTION 137. CLAIM HOLDINGS, THEIR AREAS AND VALUES

137–01 Gardiner v. C.L.B. (1957) 8 P. & C.R. 215. Apportionment of development value between 11 areas. Appeal against one apportionment puts the whole apportionment at issue. Aggregate of the parts might exceed the whole and involve scaling down. Effect of road charges.

137–02 Smith v. Central—Land Board (1957) 8 P. & C.R. 357. There is no development value in land separated from a road by land outside the claim area which cannot be added to it and which has no access to the road.

SECTION 146. GENERAL PROVISIONS AS TO RIGHT TO COMPENSATION

146–01 Perris v. Min. of Housing & Local Govt. (1959) 11 P. & C.R. 112. Claim for compensation refused where unable to trace any established claim under Part VI of the Town and Country Planning Act 1947.

146–02 Bridger v. Min. of Housing & Local Govt. (1960) 11 P. & C.R. 335. Maximum compensation recoverable is the unexpended balance of the development value as to which the Central Land Board's decision is conclusive.

146–03 Vallance & Jowitt v. Min. of Housing & Local Govt. (1968) 207 E.G. 893. Claim form improperly filled and so determination of development value had been made. So no right to any compensation.

SECTION 147. PLANNING DECISIONS NOT RANKING FOR COMPENSATION

147–01 Michell v. Min. of Housing & Local Govt. (1957) 8 P. & C.R. 248. No compensation payable where planning permission is granted subject to the siting design and external appearance of the buildings being as determined by the local planning authority.

147–02 Overland v. Min. of Housing & Local Govt. (1957) 8 P. & C.R. 389. On an application for compensation for the refusal of planning permission it is not incumbent upon the applicant to prove affirmatively that if permission had been granted development would necessarily have followed.

147–03 Country Dwellings v. Min. of Housing & Local Govt. [1959] C.L.Y. 3251. No compensation for a requirement to construct a lay-by on the edge of land for which planning permission obtained.

147–04 Grinham v. Min. of Housing & Local Govt. (1958) 9 P. & C.R. 359. Compensation limited to the unexpended balance of the development value.

SECTION 148. NO COMPENSATION IF CERTAIN OTHER DEVELOPMENT PERMITTED

148–01 Hammond v. Min. of Housing & Local Govt. (1957) 8 P. & C.R. 398. No compensation for the refusal of permission for a change of use where there was a permitted use as shop premises.

148–02 Francis v. Min. of Housing & Local Govt. (1959) 10 P. & C.R. 151. No compensation payable for the refusal of planning permission for part of land because planning permission already available even though it was subject to a condition that the permitted house be occupied by members of the agricultural population.

148–03 Hawking v. Min. of Housing & Local Govt. (1962) 14 P. & C.R. 44. Compensation is not payable in respect of a condition relating to the location or design or the materials of construction of a means of access to the highway.

SECTION 152. GENERAL PROVISIONS AS TO AMOUNT OF COMPENSATION

152–01 Briggs v. C.L.B. (1956) 6 P. & C.R. 451. Development charge in respect of part of land is equal to the development value of the whole of land. Apportioned claim holding less than the development value of the whole area.

SECTION 158. APPORTIONMENT AND REGISTRATION OF COMPENSATION

158–01 Styler v. C.L.B. (1958) 9 P. & C.R. 329. District valuer's apportionment approved—costs payable by the appellant.

158–02 Eales-Johnson v. Min. of Housing & Local Govt. (1958) 9 P. & C.R. 350. Effect of possible difficulties as to road access and deferment on a compensation figure.
See also *Fullman* v. *Min. of Housing & Local Govt.* 1958 9 P. & C.R. 358.

158–03 Stock v. Wanstead & Woodford B.C. [1961] 2 W.L.R. 868. Registration of a compensation notice places the Secretary of State within the class of "persons interested under or in respect of matters or documents whereof entries are required or allowed to be registered" in s.17(3) of the Land Charges Act 1925, and the result of a search for a prospective purchaser is conclusive against the Secretary of State.

158–04 Min. of Housing & Local Govt. v. Sharp [1970] 2 W.L.R. 802, C.A. Compensation notice registered on a register of local land charges. The certificate produced for a prospective purchaser is conclusive.
Per Salmon L.J.: A compensation notice is treated as if it were a local land charge from the time it is registered.

PART VIII. COMPENSATION FOR OTHER PLANNING RESTRICTIONS

SECTION 164. COMPENSATION WHERE PLANNING PERMISSION REVOKED OR MODIFIED

164–01 Holmes v. Bradford R.D.C. [1949] 1 All E.R. 381. Question of the entitlement to the recovery of the cost of plans based on wording in section 7 of the Town and Country Planning (Interim Development) Act 1943.

164–02 Halford v. Oxfordshire C.C. (1952) 2 P. & C.R. 358. Estimated loss of profits and goodwill from a business which had not been established was too remote to be loss or damage directly attributable to the revocation of a planning permission.

164–03 Evans v. Cheshire C.C. (1952) 3 P. & C.R. 50. Claim for loss of profits not allowed as the business was not established.

Recovery of expenditure on works of option to defer completion of purchase of land after notification of the revocation order and pending its appeal all allowed.

Costs incurred in an appeal against a revocation order are not admissible as loss or damage directly attributable to revocation.

164–04 Southern Olympia (Syndicate) Ltd. v. West Sussex C.C. (1952) 3 P. & C.R. 60. Architect's fees allowed in compensation on revocation but the words "other similar matters preparatory thereto" in s.164(2) were limited to matters *ejusdem generis* with plans, and could not include costs of raising capital or formation of a company.

Hardcore placed on land was expenditure incurred in the development of the site.

164–05 Biggs v. Buckinghamshire C.C. (1953) 3 P. & C.R. 404. Claimant suffered no loss by personally doing the work of laying-out land and planting trees and shrubs.

Loss incurred in restoring the land based on the depreciation in value of the land is not the subject of compensation.

164–06 Laing (John) & Son Ltd. v. Buckinghamshire C.C. (1960) 11 P. & C.R. 114. Although permission was only for the construction of roads and open spaces a prospective purchaser would have assumed that planning permission for individual factories would have been forthcoming and this was a factor to take into account in valuation.

164–07 Ellis v. Worcestershire C.C. (1961) 12 P. & C.R. 178. The implementation of one permission had prevented the implementaton of another permission.

164–08 Wilson v. West Sussex C.C. (1963) 2 Q.B. 764, C.A. Question of compensation turned on whether permission for an agricultural cottage limited occupants to agricultural workers.

164–09 Upperton v. Hampshire C.C. (1965) 16 P. & C.R. 333. Award reduced by 10 per cent. to take account of contingencies and also by the cost of providing an access road and a sewer.

164–10 Joyce v. West Sussex C.C. (1965) 17 P. & C.R. 34. Permission for the erection of a bungalow "to be used in conjunction with orchard, poultry farm and small holding" modified to add a condition limiting occupation of the bungalow to persons employed, or last-employed, in agriculture or forestry and their dependants—modification decreased the value of the land.

164–11 Hobbs (Quarries) Ltd. v. Somerset C.C. (1975) 30 P. & C.R. 286. Although the Lands Tribunal can award interest from the date of an award, it cannot award interest from the date of revocation as interest is to compensate for the fact that money is not paid immediately and is not compensation for a loss arising from the making of the revocation notice and order, nor is it part of damage to interest in the land.

Loss of anticipated profits is compensatable.

164–12 Loromah Estates Ltd. v. L.B. of Haringey (1978) 38 P. & C.R. 234. Compensation is not payable in respect of development land tax liability.

No power to award interest from the date of confirmation of a revocation order to the date of actual payment.

Mistake to deduct the agreed value of the land remaining after the confirmation of the revocation order from the final figure, which was subject to deferments, since it could not be right to defer a value which had no element in it of either speculation or delayed payment.

164–13 Pennine Raceway Ltd. v. Kirklees M.B.C. [1982] 3 W.L.R. 987. An enforceable contractual right as against the owner of land to use the land in a way prohibited by order under s.45 is an interest in land under s.164.

164–14 Cawoods Aggregates (South Eastern) v. Southwark L.B. (1982) 264 E.G. 1087. Compensation for loss of profit on draft contracts cancelled after revocation of planning permission.

SECTION 165. APPLICATION OF SECTION 164 TO SPECIAL CASES

165–01 Jones v. Stockport M.B.C. (1984) 269 E.G. 408, C.A. Claim for compensation for depreciation in the value of land for revocation of permission in the General Development Order 1973.

SECTION 169. COMPENSATION FOR PLANNING DECISIONS RESTRICTING DEVELOPMENT OTHER THAN NEW DEVELOPMENT

169–01 Green v. Birmingham Corp. (1951) 2 P. & C.R. 220. Although the rebuilding of shops and houses with a limited life would be contrary to by-laws, and therefore the refusal of planning permission could be presumed, for valuation purposes the possible refusal of planning permission should be ignored.

169–02 National Provincial Bank v. Portsmouth Corp. (1959) 11 P. & C.R. 6. Application to redevelop bank premises of which two top floors had been destroyed by enemy action within Class 1 not Class 3 of the relevant schedule.

169–03 Fry v. Essex C.C. (1959) 11 P. & C.R. 21. Compensation for a diminution in value of a dwelling-house due to the refusal of permission for a garage within the curtilage of the house.

169–04 Salisbury (A.C.) Ltd. v. York Corp. (1960) 11 P. & C.R. 421. Compensation refused for the loss of display space caused by the setting-back of a shop to create an "arcaded front" because there was no reduction in the rental value of the shop and the greatly improved flow of pedestrians caused by the arcade led to more custom.

169–05 Burman v. St. Albans Corp. (1961) 12 P. & C.R. 360. Planning permission for the rebuilding of a shop demolished some time previously with a condition requiring detailed drawings of the shop front to be submitted before the front installed. Subsequent permission for the shop front granted subject to conditions. Whole transaction was the rebuilding of a shop and the second permission did not involve the alteration of an existing building, therefore there could be no compensation for conditions imposed on it.

169–06 Sorrell v. Maidstone R.D.C. (1961) 13 P. & C.R. 57. Value of camp buildings where a right to rebuild. There was no requirement to create a slavish copy of the dimensions, appearance and materials of the original on rebuilding, but restricted to sites of former huts.

169–07 Moxey v. Hertford R.D.C. (1973) 27 P. & C.R. 274. Buildings for use as broiler houses "buildings used for other purposes not connected with general farming operations."

169–08 Ivens & Sons (Timber Merchants) Ltd. v. Daventry D.C. (1976) 31 P. & C.R. 480. Where land formerly occupied by a dwelling-house was raised in level by 20 feet the notional right to rebuild was not exercisable.

169–09 Peaktop Properties (Hampstead) v. Camden L.B.C. (1983) 46 P. & C.R. 177, C.A. Under s.169(3) and para. 1 of Sched. 18 where, as a result of the proposed development, the floor space of an existing building would be increased by more than 10 per cent. no compensation is payable, even though it would be put to the same use as the existing building. However, there was a right to compensation, if the enlargement was no more than 10 per cent., if the extension was to be used for the same kind of use as the rest of the building. It made no difference that the extension was going to be used for separate dwelling-houses.

But see now amendments made to s.169 by the Town and Country Planning Compensation Act 1985.

SECTION 170. COMPENSATION IN RESPECT OF DISCONTINUANCE ORDERS

170–01 Harrison v. Gloucester C.C. (1953) 4 P. & C.R. 99. Compensation for loss of trade following discontinuance of use affected by breaches of conditions to which temporary planning permission was subject.

170–02 Blow v. Norfolk C.C. [1966] 3 All E.R. 579, C.A. Open offer made by the District Valuer and doubts that the applicant must have about the existence of existing user rights to be compensated should be taken into account in assessing compensation for discontinuance. See Lands Tribunal Decision (1965) 16 P. & C.R. 342.

170–03 Cartwright v. Dudley C.B.C. [1968] R.V.R. 396, C.A. Where a local authority enters into possession of land as a freeholder and discontinues former use, it cannot claim compensation for loss even though a discontinuance order had previously been served.

170–04 K. & B. Metals Ltd. v. Birmingham C.C. (1976) 33 P. & C.R. 135. Compensation payable for an item of plant purchased after a discontinuance order was made but before it was confirmed by the Minister as the order does not take effect until confirmed by the Minister.

SECTION 174. COMPENSATION IN RESPECT OF TREE PRESERVATION ORDER

174–01 Bollans v. Surrey C.C. (1968) 20 P. & C.R. 745. Compensation in respect of a tree preservation order. Claim for £16,972 rejected and Council's valuation of £26 upheld. Criteria of compensation considered.

SECTION 177. COMPENSATION FOR LOSS DUE TO STOP NOTICE

177–01 Clwyd County Council v. Sec. of State for Wales [1982] J.P.L. 696. Local planning authority ordered to withdraw a stop notice, even though declared invalid, to facilitate a compensation application under s.177.

177–02 Sample (J. Warkworth) v. Alnwick D.C. (1984) 271 E.G. 204. Compensation for wasted labour time restoring deterioration on property, and loss of interest

SECTION 178. GENERAL PROVISIONS AS TO COMPENSATION FOR DEPRECIATION UNDER PART VIII

178–01 Hobbs (Quarries) Ltd. v. Somerset C.C. (1975) 30 P. & C.R. 286. Loss of future business profits may be included in the figure for compensation in a suitable case, subject to an allowance for deferment over the period of the contract.

No justification for drawing a distinction between a company which has started operations and one which has not, nor was there necessarily any difference between a revocation order case and a compulsory purchase order case provided that the rules against double compensation and remoteness of damage were observed.

178–02 Burlin v. Manchester C.C. (1976) 32 P. & C.R. 115. In the case of revocation or modification of planning permission, the assumption as to Eighth Schedule development contained in s.164(4) is the only applicable assumption and cannot import provisions of s.14 to 16 of the Land Compensation Act 1961 so as to make additional assumptions as to planning potential of the site.

Whether you can imply a condition into a planning permission.

Hobbs (*Quarries*) case followed on interest.

178–03 Loromah Estates Ltd. v. Haringey L.B.C. (1978) 38 P. & C.R. 234. Analogy drawn by s.178 between compensation for revocation of permission and compensation for compulsory purchase probably sufficient to import a principle analogous to the Point Gourde principle and any depreciation due to the revocation order itself or its confirmation ought to be left out of account in assessing the market value of the land.

PART IX. PROVISIONS ENABLING OWNER TO REQUIRE PURCHASE OF HIS INTEREST

SECTION 180. PURCHASE NOTICE ON REFUSAL OR CONDITIONAL GRANT OF PLANNING PERMISSION

180–01 London Corp. v. Cusack-Smith [1955] A.C. 337. As to the meaning of "owner" see cases on s.290(1).

180–02 R. v. Min. of Housing & Local Govt., ex p. Rank Organisation [1958] 1 W.L.R. 1093. The meaning of the direction in s.180(2) that no account to be taken of "new development" considered.

180–03 R. v. Min. of Housing & Local Govt., ex p. Chichester R.D.C. [1960] 1 W.L.R. 587. The test is not that land is less useful in its present state than if developed, but whether in its existing state it was incapable of reasonably beneficial use.

180–04 Adams & Wade Ltd. v. Min. of Housing & Local Govt. (1965) 18 P. & C.R. 60. As a landowner may apply for planning permission in respect of any part of his land, however arbitrarily selected, a refusal in respect of any such part may found a purchase notice relating to that part, and there is no principle of "no severance" of land in one ownership.

"Beneficial use" is use which could benefit the owner or prospective owner of the land and benefit or value to the public at large is no bar to the service of a purchase notice.

Cannot have regard to purely theoretical possibilities when considering "beneficial use."

But now see s.184.

180–05 General Estates Co. Ltd. v. Min. of Housing & Local Govt. (1967) 194 E.G. 201. Land used as a sports field is not incapable of reasonably beneficial use.

180–06 West Bromwich C.B.C. v. Min. of Housing & Local Govt. (1968) 206 E.G. 1085. Purchase notice upheld despite present inability to put it to reasonably beneficial use due to the owner's failure to plan the estate properly.

180–07 Brookdene Investments Ltd. v. Min. of Housing & Local Govt. (1969) 21 P. & C.R. 545. At most the fact that land is capable of more beneficial use by the Eighth Schedule of the 1971 Act may be taken into account, along with all other relevant facts, and weight to be given to it is for the Secretary of State to decide. It need not be conclusive in every case.

180–08 Leominster B.C. v. Min. of Housing & Local Govt. (1971) 218 E.G. 1419. History of a building considered—Minister's confirmation of a listed building purchase notice upheld even though present inability to put it to reasonably beneficial use may have been due to past neglect by the owners.

180–09 Hoddesdon U.D.C. v. Sec. of State for Environment (1971) 115 S.J. 187. Land designated as an amenity space is of itself incapable of any beneficial use.

180–10 Smart & Courtenay Dale Ltd. v. Dover R.D.C. (1972) 23 P. & C.R. 408. Expression "the land" whenever it occurs in s.180, relates to the totality of the land the subject of a planning refusal. All the owners of interests in the land the subject of a planning refusal must join in serving any purchase notice, or it will be invalid.

180–11 Rakusen Properties v. Leeds C.C. (1978) 37 P. & C.R. 315. Ownership by a subsidiary or associated company is not sufficient for an application.

180–12 Wain v. Sec. of State for Environment [1982] J.P.L. 244, C.A. A purchase notice may only be served when all of the land to which it relates has become incapable of reasonably beneficial use.

180–13 Purbeck D.C. v. Sec. of State for Environment [1982] J.P.L. 640. In section 180 "has become" incapable of reasonably beneficial use means you look at the position of the land at the time of the application to see if it then could have been capable of reasonably beneficial use.

Where the land is incapable of reasonably beneficial use because of occupiers' actions in breach of planning control s.180 does not apply.

But see now *Balco* v. *Sec. of State for Environment and Maidstone B.C.*

180–14 Balco Transport Services v. Sec. of State for Environment and Maidstone B.C. [1986] J.P.L. 123, C.A. Maxim that a man cannot take advantage of his own wrong has no application to the question whether land has become incapable of beneficial use in its existing state. However, if at the time of the purchase notice, an enforcement notice could be served requiring steps which would restore land to a condition in which it would be capable of reasonably beneficial use, then conditions for a purchase notice not fulfilled. In this case unauthorised development was immune from enforcement and so the land was incapable of beneficial use because of that development. Approach of Woolf J. in *Purbeck D.C.* v. *Sec. of State for Environment* disapproved.

Also see Woolf J.'s initial decision in *Balco* [1985] J.P.L. 722.

180–15 If land "incapable of reasonably beneficial use" it is immaterial that it is due to failure properly to plan the development. [1967] J.P.L. 299.

180–16 Land comprised in a purchase notice must be treated as a whole. The meaning of "in its existing state": look at land as it is, not required to compare with its former state. [1967] J.P.L. 491.

180–17 Incapable of reasonably beneficial user. [1967] J.P.L. 730.

S.180. PURCHASE NOTICE ON REFUSAL OR CONDITIONAL GRANT OF PERMISSION

180–18 Site incapable of reasonably beneficial use despite deemed permission for redevelopment under Class XI of the General Development Order. [1968] J.P.J. 180.

180–19 Lease of 1 acre of land to the Territorial Army and the right to erect one dwelling-house not a reasonably beneficial use of a $9\frac{1}{2}$ acre site. [1968] J.P.L. 420.

180–20 Purchase notice confirmed on a house in a state of disrepair, which was not habitable or capable of reasonably beneficial use, even though it could be repaired. [1969] J.P.L. 48.

180–21 Use of land for "ball knock-about" or by church cricket club at a nominal rent does not amount to a reasonably beneficial use. [1969] J.P.L. 49.

180–22 Words "existing state" refer to the state of the site as at the date the purchase notice served. No need to compare state of the site then with its earlier state. [1970] J.P.L. 276.

180–23 Purchase notice—land in an area requiring comprehensive redevelopment if the site were to be capable of reasonable beneficial use. Notice confirmed. [1971] J.P.L. 535.

180–24 Premises in need of repair before they could be used and which could only be occupied for approximately five years incapable of reasonably beneficial use. [1971] J.P.L. 239.

180–25 "Not capable of reasonably beneficial use"—not an economic proposition to bring land into use as agricultural land. [1972] J.P.L. 520.

180–26 Land with agricultural potential not incapable of reasonably beneficial use. [1972] J.P.L. 523.

180–27 Land capable of reasonably beneficial use even though little demand to purchase it. [1972] J.P.L. 43.

180–28 Land with no practical access incapable of reasonably beneficial use. [1973] J.P.L. 604.

180–29 Land suitable for grazing horses in a residential area still capable of reasonably beneficial use. [1976] J.P.L. 189.

180–30 Whether lack of title to parts of the land of the server of a purchase notice relevant. [1976] J.P.L. 647.

180–31 Relevant consideration for a purchase notice is whether all of the land is capable of reasonably beneficial use, not part of the land. [1976] J.P.L. 649.

180–32 Small site closely surrounded by houses—whether capable of reasonably beneficial use. [1976] J.P.L. 651.

180–33 Although it could be correct to determine whether a small site could be used in conjunction with a larger area, here the viability of the site had to be judged on its own. House was so derelict it was not capable of reasonably beneficial use without being completely rebuilt. [1977] J.P.L. 749.

180–34 Purchase notice. Originally bought as garden land. Owner of adjoining land offered to buy it. Still capable of reasonably beneficial use. [1977] J.P.L. 750.

180–35 Except where planning permission is granted for part of the land to which a planning application relates and refused for the remainder, and the purchase notice relates to the part of the land for which planning permission is refused, a purchase notice must normally relate to the identical land which was the subject of the relevant planning decision.

In considering what other use can be made of land in its existing state account cannot be taken of works which require planning permission—if to make a dwell-

ing-house habitable work requiring planning permission is necessary it cannot be said that that land is capable of reasonably beneficial use. [1978] J.P.L. 195.
See also [1978] J.P.L. 197.

180–36 Cottage subject to an agricultural occupancy condition—it could still be used in conjunction with agriculture and therefore was still capable of reasonably beneficial use. [1978] J.P.L. 198.

180–37 "Incapable of reasonably beneficial use"—prospect of use of the land as garden ground. [1979] J.P.L. 44.

180–38 Purchase notice—the meaning of "owner." Planning permission in lieu of confirmation of notice. [1980] J.P.L. 53.

180–39 Purchase notice invalid as it did not relate to an identical piece of land the subject of the relevant planning decision. [1980] J.P.L. 193.

180–40 Land suitable as garden land not incapable of reasonably beneficial use. [1980] J.P.L. 194.

180–41 In deciding whether land capable of reasonably beneficial use for the purpose of a purchase notice, you must take into account any planning permission granted up to the time of the decision even though granted after service of the purchase notice. [1981] J.P.L. 762.

180–42 Where part of the land is capable of reasonably beneficial use as garden land an owner does not come within s.180 and is not entitled to a purchase notice. [1982] J.P.L. 257.

180–43 Whilst a comparison with the Eighth Schedule (1971 Act) annual values can be a relevant factor in considering whether a purchase notice site has become incapable of reasonably beneficial use it is only one factor to be taken into account. Area of usable land was so small as not to make uses reasonably beneficial to the owners of the land. [1982] J.P.L. 259.

180–44 Reasonably beneficial use—purchase notice. Site of former cottages. [1982] J.P.L. 792.

180–45 Power of the Secretary of State to refuse to confirm a purchase notice where the land has a restricted use by virtue of previous planning permission. [1983] J.P.L. 753.

180–46 Land capable of reasonable beneficial use, where a limited amount of reclamation works would mean that it would be suitable for grazing horses. The responsibility for managing such land should lie with the owners. [1986] J.P.L. 374.

SECTION 181. ACTION BY COUNCIL ON WHOM PURCHASE NOTICE IS SERVED

The Consequences of Confirmation of Purchase Notice

181–01 Devotwill Investments v. Margate Corp. [1969] 2 All E.R. 97, C.A. Where land subject to a purchase notice (because of planning permission) is in fact designated for acquisition for a by-pass to relieve traffic congestion s.16(7) of the Land Compensation Act 1961 requires that in assessing compensation payable such designation shall be ignored, but it is not necessary to presume that traffic congestion will not be relieved by other means.

181–02 Jelson v. Min. of Housing & Local Govt. [1969] 3 W.L.R. 282, C.A. Purchase notice—circumstances at the date of the deemed notice to treat should determine what planning permission might reasonably have been expected to be granted.

181–03 Provincial Properties (London) v. Caterham and Warlingham U.D.C. [1972] 2 W.L.R. 44. Compensation on a purchase notice is not to be assessed on the basis of an assumed grant of planning permission if planning permission cannot reasonably be expected to be granted at all.

181–04 Toogood v. Bristol Corp. (1973) 26 P. & C.R. 132. For compensation purposes the nature of the interest is that which existed on the date of the deemed service of the notice to treat, but generally the valuation will be on the basis of values current at the date of entry disregarding any increase or decrease in value attributable solely to proposals of the acquiring authority.

181–05 Rakusen Properties Ltd. v. Leeds City Council (1978) 37 P. & C.R. 315. Where between the date of service of a purchase notice and its confirmation premises were destroyed by fire and claimants received insurance moneys but did not use them to reinstate the premises because of the purchase notice, they could not recover compensation for disturbance other than the value of the land as it was not attributable to matters relied upon for the purchase notice.

Quaere—Whether ownership by a subsidiary or associated company sufficient and whether can lift the corporate veil.

181–06 I.R.C. v. Metrolands (Property Finance) Ltd. [1981] 1 W.L.R. 637. The deemed service of a notice to treat under s.181 does not constitute a binding contract for the acquisition of the claimants' land.

SECTION 182. PROCEDURE ON REFERENCE OF PURCHASE NOTICE TO SECRETARY OF STATE

182–01 Ealing B.C. v. Min. Housing & Local Govt. [1952] Ch. 856. Minister cannot substitute an acquiring authority without first offering a hearing to the other authority.

SECTION 184. POWER TO REFUSE TO CONFIRM PURCHASE NOTICE WHERE LAND HAS RESTRICTED USE BY VIRTUE OF PREVIOUS PLANNING PERMISSION

184–01 Plymouth Corpn. v. Sec. of State for Environment [1972] 1 W.L.R. 1347. The power of the Secretary of State to refuse to confirm a purchase notice does not apply where part only of the land in respect of which the notice is served has a "restricted use" as defined in s.184.

184–02 Sheppard v. Sec. of State for Environment [1975] J.P.L. 352. Condition that land be maintained for amenity. Not enforceable as the development to which it related had not been carried out. As the condition was not enforceable s.184 did not apply.

184–03 Power of the Secretary of State to refuse to confirm a purchase notice where the use of land was restricted by a previous planning decision. [1974] J.P.L. 38.

184–04 Confirmation of a purchase notice on land with restricted use by virtue of previous planning permission. [1974] J.P.L. 158.

184–05 Where only part of the land covered by a purchase notice has a restricted use by virtue of a previous planning consent, s.184 of the 1971 Act is inoperable. [1978] J.P.L. 394.

SECTION 186. EFFECT OF SECRETARY OF STATE'S ACTION IN RELATION TO PURCHASE NOTICE

186–01 Sheppard v. Sec. of State for Environment [1975] J.P.L. 352. Purchase notice not deemed confirmed under s.186 by reason of the Secretary of State's failure to reach a decision to refuse within the time-limit. As the Secretary of State had notified the applicant within the time-limit that he did not propose to confirm the notice he had unlimited time to reach a conclusion.

SECTION 190. PURCHASE NOTICE ON REFUSAL OR CONDITIONAL GRANT OF LISTED BUILDING CONSENT

190–01 Leominster B.C. v. Min. of Housing & Local Govt. (1971) 218 E.G. 1419. Confirmation of notice upheld.

190–03 Seaside pier—listed building purchase notice. [1971] J.P.L. 587.

SECTION 192. BLIGHT NOTICES: THE QUALIFYING LAND AND INTERESTS

192–01 Oxley v. Keighley Corporation (1960) 11 P. & C.R. 465. Joint town planning committee under the Town and Country Planning Act 1932 was not a local highway authority within s.192 and therefore the local authority could not be required to purchase the land shown or needed for the highway in a plan prepared by such a committee in 1933.

192–02 Bolton Corporation v. Owen (1961) 12 P. & C.R. 231, C.A. Land is not required for the purposes of any function of the authority for the purpose of any of provisions of s.192 simply because it is allocated for a purpose in respect of which the local authority has powers or duties, but which might be effected by anyone.

The onus is on the claimant to show that the authority intend to carry out its function in respect of the land.

See also (1960) 12 P. & C.R. 97.

192–03 Mercer v. Manchester Corporation (1964) 15 P. & C.R. 321. Property was land indicated in the development plan as land on which a highway was proposed to be constructed even though the width of the proposed road was not definite and work was projected after the plan "period."

192–04 Bone v. Staines U.D.C. (1964) 15 P. & C.R. 450. Although planning permission was refused because of a conflict with the line of the proposed highway, there had been no resolution by the local highway authority and it was contingent upon the necessary approval for other proposals, therefore not within s.192.

Confirmed by Court of Appeal: see [1965] J.P.L. 266.

192–05 Link v. Worcestershire C.C. (1965) 16 P. & C.R. 255. Property said to be affected by road proposals in the development plan. Development plan was not approved and not operative, not within the section.

192–06 Williams v. Cheadle & Gatley U.D.C. (1965) 17 P. & C.R. 153. Land affected by a diagrammatic road proposal in the development plan was within s.192(1)(*c*).

See also *Smith v. Somerset C.C.* (1965) 17 P. & C.R. 162.

192–07 Preece & Preece v. Worcestershire C.C. (1966) 18 P. & C.R. 103. Shop affected by improvement line.

192–08 Bryant & Bryant v. City of Bristol (1969) 20 P. & C.R. 742.

(1) Road proposal on review plan—review plan not in force and therefore not a "development plan."

(2) Application to amend claimant's notice refused.

192–09 Sabey & Sabey v. Hartlepool C.B.C. (1969) 21 P. & C.R. 448. Where a blight notice was served in respect of land in an area designated for civic, cultural and other special uses the onus lies on the local authority if it contends that the Council (unless compelled to do so by virtue of the development plan) does not propose to acquire any part of the property.

192–10 Nowell (Executor) v. Kirkburton U.D.C. (1970) 21 P. & C.R. 832. Where there is no structure plan it is irrelevant that it has been indicated that land may be included in action area, and that will not found a blight notice.

192–11 Page v. Gillingham B.C. (1970) 21 P. & C.R. 973.

(1) Draft development plan insufficiently definite to be relied upon for the service of a blight notice.

(2) Plan drawn up by the borough engineer but not officially approved by the local highway authority cannot be relied upon for the service of a blight notice.

192–12 Fogg v. Birkenhead C.B.C. (1970) 22 P. & C.R. 208. Land affected by a dual carriageway approved in principle by the planning committee, but no formal resolution made by the local highway authority, could not be the subject of a blight notice.

192–13 Allen & Allen v. Marple U.D.C. (1972) 23 P. & C.R. 368. An outline plan of local authority proposals affecting property settled and approved by the county council was only an advisory plan and was not a local plan in force for a blight notice.

192–14 Lake v. Cheshire C.C. (1976) 32 P. & C.R. 143. Part of the claimant's land could be acquired without material detriment to the remainder. Meaning of "hereditament."

192–15 McKinnon Campbell v. Greater Manchester Council (1976) 33 P. & C.R. 110. Lands blighted by improvement line—whether improvement line abandoned in subsequent plans.

192–16 Comley and Comley v. Kent C.C. (1977) 34 P. & C.R. 218. A town map which was not part of the development plan and which could not be submitted to the Secretary of State until a local plan was prepared was merely an advisory guide to prospective developers and could not found a blight notice.

192–17 Bowling v. Leeds C.B.C. (1978) 27 P. & C.R. 531.

(1) Shops within an area designated for an approved road-widening scheme on a development plan—came within s.192(1)(*c*). Resolution on the programming or allocation of money by the Council unnecessary.

(2) Diminution in value not wholly due to clearance of the surrounding area.

Note

As to the meaning of "owner occupier" and "resident occupier" see cases on s.203.

SECTION 193. POWER TO SERVE BLIGHT NOTICE

193–01 Stubbs v. West Hartlepool Corporation (1961) 12 P. & C.R. 365. Reasonable endeavours to sell interest—not incumbent on claimant to endeavour to sell at a figure substantially lower than that at which property was reasonably expected to sell.

S.193. POWER TO SERVE BLIGHT NOTICE

193–02 Lade & Lade v. Brighton Corporation (1970) 22 P. & C.R. 737. In most cases the normal procedure for sale of a shop would be by circularising particulars and advertising in the press, but in this case of an antique and second-hand articles shop in a very second-rate street, as the potential buyers were more likely to be drawn from visiting dealers, the owner had made reasonable endeavours to sell by putting a notice to sell his property in the shop window and notifying trade visitors that it was for sale.

193–03 Perkins v. West Wiltshire D.C. (1975) 31 P. & C.R. 427. Claimant under a blight notice must have made a genuine effort to sell the property and that involves placing it on the market.

193–04 Glodwick Mutual Institute & Social Club v. Oldham M.B.C. [1979] R.V.R. 197. It is not a genuine attempt to sell blighted property if prospective purchasers are warned of the authority's compulsory order, but not of the authority's formal disclaimer of any intention to proceed.

SECTION 194. OBJECTION TO BLIGHT NOTICE

194–01 Rawson v. Min. of Health (1965) 17 P. & C.R. 239. Land allocated for hospital land. Ministry disclaimed any intention of buying the land for hospital purposes and Regional Hospital Board resolution that it would not be required for at least 20 years:
(1) Development plan allocation ineffective due to Ministry's disclaimer.
(2) No hardshop to the claimant as he purchased the land knowing of the allocation.

194–02/03 Lockers Estates (Holdings) v. Oadby U.D.C. (1970) 21 P. & C.R. 836. Where a local authority's objection to a blight notice is unfounded the notice must be declared valid even though a valid objection could have been taken.

194–04 Parker & Parker v. West Midlands C.C. (1978) 38 P. & C.R. 720. Both the grounds in s.194(2)(*c*) and s.194(2)(*d*) could be relied on in the same counter-notice but if the ground in s.194(2)(*d*) was established, it deprives the claimant of any right to compensation to which he would have been entitled if the ground in s.194(2)(*c*) had been relied on alone.

194–05 McDermott v. Dept. of Transport (1984) 48 P. & C.R. 351. Blight notice resisted on the ground in s.194(2)(*b*). Objection upheld and it was doubted whether hardship was a factor in deciding whether the counter-notice was well-founded.

SECTION 195. REFERENCE OF OBJECTION TO LANDS TRIBUNAL

195–01 Essex C.C. v. Essex Incorporated Congregational Church Union [1963] A.C. 808. Where an objection, which should have been raised in the counter-notice, is not so referred to the Lands Tribunal, the jurisdiction of the Tribunal being statutory, cannot be enlarged by the consent of the parties.
Per curiam: A hereditament which is exempt from rating is not a hereditament whose "annual value does not exceed" £250 within s.39(4)(*a*) of the Town and Country Planning Act 1959.

195–02 Duke of Wellington Social Club and Institute Ltd. v. Blyth B.B. (1964) 15 P. & C.R. 212. Council failed to establish that it did not propose to acquire premises unless forced to do so within next 15 years. Land Tribunal applied criterion of reasonableness. But see *Mancini* v. *Coventry City Council*.

195–03 Lockers Estates (Holdings) Ltd. v. Oadby U.D.C. (1970) 21 P. & C.R. 836. Where objection taken by a local authority is rejected and they fail to take an objection in the counter-notice which would have been upheld the blight notice is valid and must be upheld.

195–04 Louisville Investments Ltd. v. Basingstoke D.C. (1976) 32 P. & C.R. 419. Material date under s.195 at which the Tribunal has to determine whether an objection to a blight notice is well-founded thought to be the date when the objection is made, *i.e.* the date of service of the counter-notice, but in any case an event which occurred after the service of the counter-notice (revocation of the compulsory purchase order) could not deprive the Tribunal of jurisdiction—all that is necessary for jurisdiction being a valid counter-notice served under s.194.

Counter-notice not invalidated even though authorisation for its service was given by only two of the three persons empowered to do so by district council, as the three persons were a sub-committee, and therefore a majority decision was valid under Sched. 12 paras. 39 and 44 of the Local Government Act 1972.

Revocation of the compulsory purchase order is a matter of expediency and the council had not shown that they did not wish to acquire the land.

Existence of an unconfirmed compulsory purchase order prevented the sale of land—notice valid.

195–05 Parker & Parker v. West Midlands C.C. (1978) 38 P. & C.R. 720. Lands Tribunal's jurisdiction under s.195 depends upon the existence of a valid counter-notice but even if the local authority were not entitled to rely upon s.194(2)(*d*), a counter-notice would not be invalid, as the Tribunal would be justified in declaring under s.195 that objection under s.194(2)(*d*) was, as a matter of law, not to be upheld. This did not take away their jurisdiction.

195–06 Cedar Holdings v. Walsall M.B.C. (1979) 38 P. & C.R. 715. As service of a counter-notice gives the Lands Tribunal jurisdiction that is the date at which its validity falls to be determined.

195–07 Sabey and Sabey v. Hartlepool C.B.C. 21 P. & C.R. 448. In placing the onus upon the local authority Parliament must have intended the Lands Tribunal to look at all of the facts of the case and to dismiss the objection unless satisfied that an effective protection against "blight" is provided.

SECTION 203. MEANING OF "OWNER OCCUPIER" AND "RESIDENT OCCUPIER"

203–01 Ministry of Transport v. Holland (1962) 61 L.G.R. 134. "Occupation" means beneficial occupation. Storage of articles insufficient evidence to constitute a person an owner-occupier.

203–02 Segal v. Manchester Corporation (1966) 18 P. & C.R. 112. Claimant not an owner-occupier where premises empty.

203–03 Webb v. Warwickshire C.C. (1971) 23 P. & C.R. 63. As a personal representative cannot claim to be the same individual as the deceased in qualifying for protection the interest must be a strictly personal one abating on death.

203–04 Sparkles v. Sec. of State for Wales (1973) 27 P. & C.R. 545. Blight notice—the fact that the applicant's husband was an undischarged bankrupt and organised and managed her business was irrelevant. As she was the owner-occupier she could validly serve a blight notice.

203–05 Holmes v. Knowsley B.C. (1977) 35 P. & C.R. 119. As there is no requirement in s.203(1) that to qualify as an owner-occupier the occupation should be or have been as a private dwelling, preparation for residential occupation would qualify, but when a house is put on the market with vacant possession it falls to be considered as being unoccupied.

PART X. HIGHWAYS

SECTION 209. HIGHWAYS AFFECTED BY DEVELOPMENT: ORDERS BY SECRETARY OF STATE

209–01 Ashby v. Sec. of State for Environment [1980] 1 All E.R. 508, C.A. Stopping-up of a highway under s.209 cannot be authorised retrospectively and therefore cannot be authorised where the development has been fully carried out but it is sufficient if part of the development remains to be carried out and the stopping-up is required to carry it out.

209–02 Harlow v. Minister of Transport (1950) 1 P. & C.R. 271, C.A. A valid order can be made under s.209(1) stopping-up highways even though the public had the right of walking over them by virtue of an Inclosure Act.

209–03 Development authorised by the General Development Order is "development authorised to be carried out in accordance with planning permission granted under Part III of the Act." [1977] J.P.L. 388.

209–04 Diversion of a footpath "to enable development to be carried out" where development already completed—order not confirmed. Pointed out that development should not be started if it will have the effect of interfering with the public right of way. [1977] J.P.L. 542.

209–05 Diversion of a public path—form of the order. Diversion to allow development permitted under the General Development Order. [1978] J.P.L. 125.

209–06 Jurisdiction of the Secretary of State to confirm public path stopping-up and diversion orders where development completed over the line of the path. Once an order is made its legal existence may only be brought to an end by an order to revoke it, or a decision not to confirm it, or a decision of the court to quash it. [1984] J.P.L. 362.

SECTION 210. FOOTPATHS AND BRIDLEWAY AFFECTED BY DEVELOPMENT ORDER BY LOCAL PLANNING AUTHORITIES

210–01 Not clear from outline permission that a diversion was needed to carry out development. Also a variation of present permission might be obtained so that the diversion would not be necessary. [1976] J.P.L. 389.

210–02 Failure to cite relevant planning permission in diversion of a footpath order, resulted in the Secretary of State refusing to confirm the order. [1976] J.P.L. 705.

SECTION 212. ORDER EXTINGUISHING RIGHT TO USE VEHICLES ON HIGHWAY

212–01 Saleem v. Bradford M.C.C. (1984) 271 E.G. 119. Claimant failed to obtain compensation when business was bad and could not show that authorised works were the direct cause of his losses.

PART XI. STATUTORY UNDERTAKERS

SECTION 222. MEANING OF "OPERATIONAL LAND"

222–01 R. v. Min. of Fuel & Power, ex p. Warwickshire C.C. [1957] 1 W.L.R. 861, D.C.

(1) It is not necessary for a statutory undertaking to begin operations on land for that land to become "operational land." It can apply to land which the undertaking intend to use in future.

(2) Whether the land is comparable with land in general rather than with land used for the purposes of the statutory undertaking is a question of fact.

(3) It is not necessary that the land to be operational land should be contiguous to other land which is being used for the statutory undertaking.

222–02 East Barnet U.D.C. v. British Transport Commission [1962] 2 Q.B. 484. Discussion of the meaning of operational land.

222–03 Breaking-up of disused railway wagons on operational railway land. Wagons taken to land by rail and scrap removed by rail. Use was an independent business as scrap-metal merchants and not required in connection with the movements of traffic by rail. [1967] J.P.L. 51.

SECTION 238. MEASURE OF COMPENSATION TO STATUTORY UNDERTAKERS

238–01 National Carriers Ltd. v. Sec. of State for Transport (1978) 35 P. & C.R. 245. Section 238(1)(c) only applies where representations are made to the appropriate Minister under s.16 of the Acquisition of Land Act 1981 but no certificate has been given.

PART XII. VALIDITY OF PLANNING INSTRUMENTS AND DECISIONS AND PROCEEDINGS RELATING THERETO

SECTION 242. VALIDITY OF DEVELOPMENT PLANS AND CERTAIN ORDERS, DECISIONS AND DIRECTIONS

242–01 Smith v. East Elloe [1956] A.C. 736. (Compulsory Purchase case.) A compulsory purchase order which was not challenged within the prescribed period was thereafter immune from challenge, even though fraud is alleged.
Also see *R. v. Sec. of State for Environment, ex p. Ostler* [1977] 1 Q.B. 122.

242–02 Cartwright v. Min. of Housing & Local Govt. (1967) 65 L.G.R. 384. Planning permission and compulsory purchase order. Challenge on the grounds of natural justice by application for a declaration excluded under s.176 (now s.242).

242–03 Routh v. Reading Corporation (1970) 217 E.G. 1337, C.A. Section 242 operates to prohibit a challenge to a compulsory purchase order save in conformity with the section, even where the order is a nullity.

242–04 Turner v. Sec. of State for Environment (1973) 28 P. & C.R. 123. A decision on a called-in application for approval of reserved matters on a planning permission does not come within ss.242 and 245.

242–05 Davies v. Sec. of State for Wales (1976) 33 P. & C.R. 330. Only action taken by the Secretary of State falls within s.242(3). Action taken by a local planning authority.

242–06 Co-operative Retail Services v. Sec. of State for Environment (1979) 39 P. & C.R. 428. A "decision of the Secretary of State on an appeal" in both ss.36(6) and 242(3)(b) means a decision that disposes of an appeal, not a decision in the course of an appeal. A decision not to adjourn the hearing of an inquiry is not a "decision of the Secretary of State on an appeal" under s.242(3)(b).

A refusal by the Secretary of State to adjourn an inquiry might, in an appropriate case, amount to "a decision in proceedings on an appeal" under s.246.

Arguable that the expression in s.242(3)(b), "any decision of the Secretary of State on an appeal under section 36," is, contrary to the view of Slynn J. in *Chalgray Ltd. v. Sec. of State for Environment* (1977) 33 P. & C.R. 10, limited to decisions or orders or final results arrived at under s.36(3). A refusal to consider an appeal might well come within s.242(4).

242–07 Westminster C.C. v. Sec. of State for Environment [1984] J.P.L. 27. The provisions concerning planning gain in the City of Westminster district plan could not be challenged as being *ultra vires* in court proceedings by reason of s.242(1) as out of time. Any challenge should be made to the Secretary of State.

SECTION 243. VALIDITY OF ENFORCEMENT NOTICES AND SIMILAR NOTICES

243–01 Somerset C.C. v. Wall (1967) 203 E.G. 939. On prosecution for breach of an enforcement notice, magistrates cannot consider whether a material change of use has taken place.

243–02 Jeary v. Chailey R.D.C. (1973) 26 P. & C.R. 280, C.A. Section 177(1) of the 1962 Act (now s.243 of the 1971 Act) was not directed only at groundless challenges of enforcement notices but also prevented the assertion of vested rights.

243–03 Square Meals Frozen Foods Ltd. v. Dunstable Corporation [1974] 1 W.L.R. 59, C.A. Proceedings started in anticipation of the service of an enforcement notice in which the validity of the notice would inevitably be questioned are barred by s.243(1)(*a*) even though commenced before the notice was served.

Per Lord Denning M.R. and Scarman L.J.: Even if the proceedings were not barred by s.243(1)(*a*) the court would stay these proceedings, as matters involved were better dealt with by the Secretary of State on appeal under s.88.

243–04 Flashman v. L.B. of Camden (1979) 130 New L.J. 885. Section 243(1)(*a*) does not require that an action should be struck out immediately where the grounds of action go beyond those protected by the privative clause or where there is at least an arguable question as to how far s.243 affords a defence to the plaintiff's claims.

243–05 Davy v. Spelthorn D.C. [1983] 3 All E.R. 278. Claim relating to advice by a local planning authority and agreement not to appeal on enforcement notice if not enforced for three years.

(1) Enforcement notice was not being challenged, but even if it were it was not being challenged on any of the grounds specified in s.88(2) and therefore s.243(1)(*a*) had no application.

(2) Action not an abuse of the process of the court because it was for damages in tort and did not raise any issue of public law. It would be an awkward and uncertain process to force the applicant to seek judicial review with a claim for damages attached.

243–06 McDaid v. Clydebank D.C. [1984] J.P.L. 578. Enforcement notice not served on the owner of premises.

(1) The courts' appellate jurisdiction was not excluded where, for reasons beyond the control of the petitioner, procedure provided by statute could not be used.

(2) As the notice was not properly served it was a nullity.

(3) It was relevant that the local planning authority was aware of the interest of the owner and could not explain why the owner had not been served.

243–07 R. v. Smith (Thomas George) [1985] J.P.L. 182. "Proceedings" in s.243 include criminal proceedings. Where there is no appeal against an enforcement notice, precluded from claiming a pre-1963 use on subsequent prosecution for non-compliance with the enforcement notice.

243–08 Prosser v. Sharp [1985] J.P.L. 717. Prosecution under s.89(4), after conviction for failure to comply with an enforcement notice. Acquittal by magistrates quashed as they had wrongly overlooked the continuing validity of the enforcement notice under s.243.

243–08a R. v. L.B. of Greenwich, ex p. Patel [1985] J.P.L. 851. Section 243 operated to oust the jurisdiction of the courts to challenges to enforcement notices on any grounds in s.88(1)(*b*)(*c*); *McDaid* v. *Clydebank* not followed.

243–09 Epping Forest D.C. v. Scott [1986] J.P.L. 603. Enforcement notice incorrectly required that any occupation by person "solely or mainly employed in agriculture" to cease when condition simply required occupant to be "employed" in agriculture. Where appeal against notice but not on this ground, it was too late to challenge requirements of the notice on a subsequent prosecution; *R.* v. *Smith* applied.

Note

Formerly s.243 had been held not to exclude challenge in the magistrates' courts on grounds (*f*) and (*g*) of s.88 on prosecution: see *Smith* v. *King* (1969) 21 P. & C.R. 560; *Hutchinson* v. *Firetto* [1973] J.P.L. 314; *London Borough of Redbridge* v. *Perry* (1976) 33 P. & C.R. 176; *Rochdate M.B.C.* v. *Simmonds* [1981] J.P.L. 171. But new wording introduced by the Planning and Local Government (Amendment) Act 1981 makes clear that all the grounds of appeal are excluded.

SECTION 244. PROCEEDINGS FOR QUESTIONING VALIDITY OF DEVELOPMENT PLANS

244–01 Buckinghamshire C.C. v. Hale Aggregates (Thames Valley) Ltd. and S.A.G.A. [1985] J.P.L. 634. *Per* Purchas L.J.: Section 244 only provides for the challenge to the way the plan has been approved or adopted with regard to the procedures during and after the inquiry. It is not possible under s.244 to challenge the validity of the plan on the grounds of failure to comply with the statutory requirements during the preparation of the plan. However this was doubted by Stephenson L.J.

SECTION 245. PROCEEDINGS FOR QUESTIONING VALIDITY OF OTHER ORDERS, DECISIONS AND DIRECTIONS

A. Who Can Bring Proceedings under section 245 and the Period for Challenge

245–01 Ealing B.C. v. Jones [1959] 1 All E.R. 286. Meaning of "person aggrieved" in section 23(5) of the Town and Country Planning Act 1947.

245–02 Buxton v. Min. of Housing & Local Govt. [1960] 3 W.L.R. 866. "Person aggrieved" is one who has suffered a legal grievance, therefore anybody who is given a right under the planning legislation to have his representations considered is a person aggrieved if those rights are infringed.

But the general public are not persons aggrieved as the scheme of the planning legislation is to restrict development for the benefit of the public at large and not to confer new rights on any individual members of the public irrespective of their proximity to a proposed development. But see *Turner* v. *Sec. of State for Environment.*

254–03 Turner v. Sec. of State for Environment (1973) 28 P. & C.R. 123. Members of a local preservation society were in the ordinary sense of the word persons "aggrieved" and could apply to quash a Secretary of State's decision even though they have been given notice of the inquiry only at the request of, and not by the requirement of, the Secretary of State and had attended and made their representations only at the discretion of the inspector.

There is no jurisdiction to quash the action of the Secretary of State in granting approval of details reserved by an outline permission.

245–04 Bizony v. Sec. of State for Environment [1976] J.P.L. 306. Application by an adjoining land owner allowed. Apparent conflict between *Buxton* v. *Min. of*

S.245. QUESTIONING VALIDITY OF OTHER ORDERS, DECISIONS AND DIRECTIONS

Housing & Local Govt. and *Turner* v. *Sec. of State for Environment* discussed but not resolved.

245–05 Hollis v. Sec. of State for Environment [1983] J.P.L. 164. Applicant who lived near to the site was agreed by the parties to be an "aggrieved person" within s.245.

245–06 Griffiths v. Sec. of State for Environment [1983] 1 All E.R. 439, C.A. Time for application under s.245 starts to run from the date the Secretary of State takes an irrevocable step, *e.g.* when the letter is signed, date-stamped, and put in the tray—the time is not related to receipt of letter.

B. Grounds of Challenge and the Procedures and Powers of the Court

245–07 Hanily v. Min. of Housing & Local Govt. [1951] 2 K.B. 917. Applications by way of originating motion can be amended with the leave of the court.

245–08 Ashbridge Investments Ltd. v. Min. of Housing & Local Govt. [1965] 1 W.L.R. 1320. *Per* Lord Denning M.R.: Where statute requires the Minister to decide a matter, the courts can interfere with his decision if he acts on no evidence, or he comes to a decision he could not reasonably come to on the evidence, or misinterprets the statute, or fails to take into account a relevant consideration, or takes into account an irrelevant consideration.

245–09 William Boyer & Sons v. Min. of Housing & Local Govt. (1968) 20 P. & C.R. 176. The decision as to what are material issues of fact or fundamental facts is for the inspector not the court. The inspector's report and decision letter cannot always be expected to be capable of satisfying the critical analysis of a schoolteacher.

245–10 Continental Sprays v. Min. of Housing & Local Govt. (1968) 19 P. & C.R. 774. Where following a public inquiry the Minister refuses permission for development, the court has no jurisdiction to examine the evidence before the inspector who conducted the inquiry and to determine whether his findings of fact were correct.

245–11 Miller v. Weymouth and Melcombe Regis Corporation (1974) 27 P. & C.R. 468. Where the Secretary of State's decision-making process and decision were unobjectionable the mere fact that a clerical error meant that the order did not accord with the decision letter did not take the order outside the powers of the 1971 Act. In any event the court has a discretion under s.245(4) whether or not to quash an order and in the absence of substantial prejudice will not exercise it.

Where there was no chance that the authorities would take advantage of the error or that it would be enforced by the courts, the applicant had not suffered substantial prejudice within the meaning of s.245(1)(*b*).

245–12 Catton v. Sec. of State for Environment [1976] J.P.L. 633. Weighing of evidence and decisions of fact and degree was for the Secretary of State and his inspector not the court.

245–13 Kent v. Sec. of State for Environment (1976) 33 P. & C.R. 70. Where an amendment is made by the Secretary of State to meet one of the applicant's major objections, the applicant is not entitled to have the decision quashed *ex debito justitiae* under s.245(4)(*b*).

245–14 Eckersley v. Sec. of State for Environment (1977) 34 P. & C.R. 124. (Housing Act Decision.)

(1) While it would be wrong on an application to the High Court to quash a compulsory purchase order, or similar proceedings, for the judge to ask the inspector to make fresh or additional findings of fact, and while where such an application depended on the construction of the inspector's report, any evidence from the

inspector about what he had meant by his report would be inadmissible, the investigation of a possibility that there had been a breach of natural justice must nearly always involve receiving evidence outside the inspector's report and the Secretary of State's decision letter.

(2) Once a question of a breach of natural justice is raised which the judge considers not to be merely fanciful it has to be investigated.

(3) In appropriate circumstances the judge is entitled to ask the inspector to explain his report in an affidavit.

245–15 Performance Cars Ltd. v. Sec. of State for Environment (1977) 34 P. & C.R. 92. There is no direct sanction under s.245(4)(*b*) for a failure of a local planning authority prior to an inquiry to comply with the rules because the "action in question" is the decision of the Secretary of State on the appeal.

245–16 Tarmac Properties v. Sec. of State for Wales [1977] J.P.L. 409. On application under s.245, the Secretary of State withdrew his objections. The court quashed his earlier decision of refusal, enabling him to grant permission.

245–17 H. Sabey & Co. Ltd. v. Sec. of State for Environment [1978] 1 All E.R. 586. New affidavit evidence received by the court in order to determine what evidence had been put to the inspector and whether there had been a breach of natural justice.

245–18 East Hampshire D.C. v. Sec. of State for Environment [1978] J.P.L. 182. If the inspector's account of the hearing was challenged the court would not usually intervene unless there was agreement as to what had occurred, but it was possible for evidence to be given to show that the proper procedure had not been complied with or that there was no material upon which an inspector properly directing himself could have reached one of his conclusions.

Permissible for evidence to be filed to show that a particular matter of real importance in one party's case had been wholly left out, or completely misunderstood, or put in an entirely wrong or misleading way so that the Secretary of State had never been properly instructed as to the case.

245–19 Preston D.C. v. Sec. of State for Environment [1978] J.P.L. 548. Witnesses' proofs considered by the court to check if the inspector had properly recorded the evidence.

After a decision letter is issued the Secretary of State is probably *functus officio* and there is probably no slip rule. In this case, however, the Minister's decision was quite clearly an unconditional grant of planning permission and this could be vitiated by the error in the recital referring to conditions.

245–20 Seddon Properties v. Sec. of State for Environment (1978) 248 E.G. 950. The general principles and grounds of judicial review under s.245 summarised by Forbes J.

245–21 Price Brothers (Rode Heath) Ltd. v. Sec. of State for Environment (1979) 38 P. & C.R. 579. The consequence of a decision of the Secretary of State being quashed is that he is entitled to remake his decision.

235–22 Peak Park Planning Board v. Sec. of State for Environment (1979) 39 P. & C.R. 361.

(1) The true construction of the words in s.245(1)(*b*) "on the grounds that the action is not within the powers of this Act," is that, if the Secretary of State, in the erroneous belief that he had no power to derogate from existing planning rights, did something that was not within his area, he was acting outside his jurisdiction.

(2) In general the court's discretion not to quash an *ultra vires* decision of the Secretary of State should be exercised only if the point was purely technical or there was no possible detriment to the applicant.

Per curiam: Sections 242 and 245 were enacted in order to establish one form of proceedings for challenging decisions and to give certainty to them by prescribing a time-limit, but it was difficult to conceive that it was intended to reduce the powers of review by the courts in other respects.

245–23 George v. Sec. of State for Environment (1979) 38 P. & C.R. 609, C.A. (Compulsory Purchase Order decision). Cross-examination on affidavit should not be allowed unless it is really necessary.

245–24 Behrman v. Sec. of State for Environment [1979] J.P.L. 622. The court could only interfere if it thought an inspector had come to a decision that no reasonable inspector could have come to. The court cannot simply substitute its view of what was reasonable for the inspector's view.

245–25 Elmbridge B.C. v. Sec. of State for Environment [1980] J.P.L. 463. If a decision-maker who was not under a statutory obligation to give reasons in fact gave reasons and the reasons he gave were defective it was open to the court to interfere under s.245(4).

An obvious silly mistake, clerical error or glaring inaccuracy would not amount to an error of law. A mistaken statement that the distance between a new development and pre-existing houses would be 400 feet when the inspector knew it was only 170 feet was such an error. However, an error of fact, if material, would be an error of law.

245–26 Glover v. Sec. of State for Environment [1981] J.P.L. 110. Application to admit fresh evidence to show that a planning decision made on a wrong assumption of fact refused.

245–27 Rogelen Building Group Ltd. v. Sec. of State for Environment [1981] J.P.L. 506. Where a decision is quashed because reasons are not adequate, it is open to the Secretary of State to rephrase his decision.

245–28 Chichester D.C. v. Sec. of State for Environment [1981] J.P.L. 591.

(1) Decision to quash under s.245 is discretionary and the court would not quash where errors in the decision letter were immaterial.

(2) Evidence admitted to show that the Secretary of State had used the correct information in arriving at his decision.

245–29 Hewlett v. Sec. of State for Environment [1983] J.P.L. 105. Where the Secretary of State's decision was quashed by the High Court he did not have to re-open issues not in dispute at the time of the order.

245–30 Bernard Hollis v. Sec. of State for Environment [1983] J.P.L. 164. If it is shown that there was material within the possession of the Secretary of State which must be assumed to have been within his knowledge, which clearly showed that what had been put before that inspector on a material issue was wrong, the court was entitled to, and in an appropriate case should, look at the material to see whether that fact was established. If it were established, it was right to say that the Secretary of State might well have come to a different conclusion had he looked at that material, and thus to quash the decision.

245–31 Graysmark v. Sec. of State for Environment [1984] J.P.L. 115. Where on an appeal to the Secretary of State against a refusal of planning permission the decision of the inspector appointed to determine the appeal was quashed there remained an outstanding appeal awaiting determination by the Secretary of State. The Secretary of State was entitled to delegate the determination of the appeal to an inspector and had the power to appoint a fresh inspector.

245–32 Mason v. Sec. of State for Environment [1984] J.P.L. 332. A mistake of fact by an inspector can make his decision invalid but only if it is material. The inspector is not bound to follow evidence of a subjective nature.

245–33 White Acre Estate U.K. Ltd. v. Sec. of State for Environment [1984] J.P.L. 177. Where a purchase notice was invalid, it had to be quashed under s.245(4)(*b*), as s.245(4)(*a*), which gave power to suspend, was only an interim power and was not an alternative.

245–34 Casburn v. Sec. of State for Environment [1984] J.P.L. 501. Where an inspector wrongly described his findings of fact as findings of law the court had been wrong to interfere with them as if they were questions of law.

245–35 Gill v. Sec. of State for Environment & North Warwickshire D.C. [1985] J.P.L. 710. Both ss.245 and 246 could be used to challenge a grant of planning permission under s.88(*b*)(i), though s.245 was the most appropriate.

245–36 R. v. Sec. of State for Environment, ex p. Centre 21 Ltd. [1985] J.P.L. 865. Decision to re-open inquiry (following a successful application under section 245) quashed on application for judicial review as decision based on a misunderstanding.

SECTION 246. APPEALS TO HIGH COURT RELATING TO ENFORCEMENT NOTICES

246–01 Hoser v. Min. of Housing & Local Govt. [1963] Ch. 428. The Secretary of State cannot be required to state a case under s.246(1) or s.246(1A) because no rules of the court have been made to provide for such a requirement.

246–02 Green v. Min. of Housing & Local Govt. [1967] 2 W.L.R. 192. Right of appeal under s.246 is limited to a point of law and this is not altered by the power to receive further evidence under R.S.C. Ord. 55.

246–03 T.A. Miller v. Min. of Housing & Local Govt. [1968] 1 W.L.R. 992, C.A. No basis for an inquiry into the inspector's notes which should only be done in the rarest cases, by the court.

246–04 Button v. Jenkins [1975] 3 All E.R. 585. Where an appeal against an enforcement notice is rejected by the Secretary of State for failing to specify the grounds of appeal that constitutes a determination of the appeal and should be challenged by way of s.246.

246–05 L.T.S.S. Print & Supply Services Ltd. v. Hackney L.B.C. [1976] Q.B. 663, C.A. *Per* Goff L.J.: If the Secretary of State misdirects himself in law, then unless it is a mere scintilla, the decision should be remitted back to him.

246–06 Horsham D.C. v. Fisher [1977] J.P.L. 178. Secretary of State's incorrect decision that a notice of appeal was defective was "proceedings on an appeal" and as there had been a right of appeal to the High Court under s.246 the validity of the enforcement notice could not subsequently be challenged in the Crown Court.

246–07 Wain v. Sec. of State for Enviornment (1978) 39 P. & C.R. 82. A letter from the Department of the Environment in enforcement notice appeal proceedings to the effect that the Secretary of State has no power to take further action in the matter (even if erroneous) is still a "decision" which must be appealed in accordance with the provisions of s.246.

246–08 Ringroad Investments Ltd. v. Sec. of State for Environment (1979) 49 P. & C.R. 99. Time for appealing against the Secretary of State's decision runs from that date that the decision letter is posted: but see *Griffith* v. *Sec. of State for Environment.*

246–09 Broxbourne B.C. v. Sec. of State for Environment [1980] Q.B. 1 at 9, D.C. Section 246 procedure is not appropriate for the challenge of the grant of planning permission on a deemed application in an enforcement notice appeal: but see *Gill* v. *Sec. of State for Environment.*

246–10 J. Toomey Motors Ltd. v. Sec. of State for Environment [1981] J.P.L. 418. Where an enforcement notice is quashed, because a permission is given for that which is being enforced against, an appellant may appeal under s.246 against the Secretary of State's decision.

246–11 Forkhurst v. Sec. of State for Environment (1982) 46 P. & C.R. 89.

(1) Where there is an appeal under s.246 on the ground that no reasonable inspector could have so decided the appeal and there is foundation for that claim in the appellant's affidavit, the court could look at the uncontroverted evidence as to what had actually been before the inspector.

(2) Duty to apply to the inspector for a signed copy of his note of evidence.

246–12 Weitz v. Sec. of State for Environment (1983) 43 P. & C.R. 150. Where there is an appeal under s.246 on a point of law alone, in the ordinary case it is not necessary for an appellant to comply with R.S.C. Ord. 55, r. 7(4) and not necessary for the inspector's note to be made available to the applicant.

246–13 Rhymney Valley D.C. v. Sec. of State for Wales [1985] J.P.L. 27. Allegation that an enforcement notice was a nullity should be made by way of an application for judicial review and not under s.246.

246–14 Lenlyn v. Sec. of State for Environment [1985] J.P.L. 482. Where the Secretary of State refuses to entertain an appeal under s.88, the correct way to challenge his decision is by application for judicial review, not under s.246.

246–15 Greater London Council v. Sec. of State for Environment and Harrow L.B.C. [1985] J.P.L. 868. Where local planning authority were challenging the reasons for the decision but not the decision itself, the authority was not "a person aggrieved" and could not use section 245; but it might be possible to challenge the reasons by way of an application for judicial review.

246–16 London Parachuting Ltd. and Rectory Farm (Pampisford) Ltd. v. Sec. of State for Environment and South Cambridgeshire D.C. [1986] J.P.L. 279. Application under section 246 to challenge decision of Minister rejecting an appeal against an enforcement notice—whether the High Court had the power to make an order staying enforcement—held that the court could make such an order, but could not hold the enforcement notice to have no effect.

246–17 London Parachuting Ltd. v. Sec. of State for Environment and South Cambridgeshire D.C. [1986] J.P.L. 428. Applications under section 246 to challenge enforcement notice on ground of impropriety at inquiry which was not raised before the inspector. Held that this did not come within the jurisdiction of section 246 as not an error of law and the allegation turned on a question of fact which could not be investigated by the court.

246–18 Dudley Bowers Amusements v. Sec. of State for Environment (1986) 278 E.G. 313. Argument that enforcement notice is nullity should be made by application under section 246, rather than by way of application for judicial review.

PART XIV. APPLICATION OF ACT TO SPECIAL CASES

SECTION 266. EXERCISE OF POWERS IN RELATION TO CROWN LAND

266–01 Ministry of Agriculture, Fisheries & Food v. Jenkins [1963] 2 Q.B. 317. Crown does not require planning permission for development.

266–02 Molton Builders Ltd. v. Westminster L.B.C. (1975) 30 P. & C.R. 182. A contract cannot fetter an appropriate authority's discretion to grant consent to an enforcement notice or other notice under s.266(2).

266–03 Newbury D.C. v. Sec. of State for Environment [1977] J.P.L. 373, C.A. *Per* Goff J.: A purchaser of land from the Crown cannot have enforcement action taken against him with regard to development previously carried out by the Crown.

266–04 R. v. Worthing B.C. ex p. Burgh [1984] J.P.L. 261. Circular 49/63 set out the procedure whereby before Crown land was sold, the Secretary of State for the Environment would give his opinion as to whether planning permission would be granted. It was hoped that local planning authorities would then follow this opinion on a subsequent application. Held that the procedure constrained the local authority and precluded local people from having a chance of making representations and was invalid. Now see Town and Country Planning Act 1984 which amended s.266.

266–05 Jurisdiction of a local planning authority and the Secretary of State where an application was in respect of Crown land. Drilling of an exploratory borehole in a special countryside area.

By virtue of section 266(1)(*b*), Part III of the 1971 Act did not apply to land wholely owned by the Crown: but note now amendments introduced by the Town and Country Planning Act 1984. [1984] J.P.L. 366.

SECTION 270. APPLICATION TO LOCAL PLANNING AUTHORITIES OF PLANNING CONTROL AND ENFORCEMENT

270–01 Att.-Gen. ex rel. Turley v. G.L.C. (1976) 239 E.G. 893.

(1) Where the G.L.C. sought planning permission for development of a site they were the relevant local planning authority.

(2) General nature of the proposals and their difference from what was eventually resolved was not a bar to the validity of the planning permission.

(3) Even if it were the G.L.C. could remedy the defect by a simple resolution.

(4) Minister's decision as to whether there was a deemed planning permission was an administrative act and so final.

270–02 Sunbell Properties v. Dorest C.C. (1979) 253 E.G. 1123. Developer applying for permission to build offices was granted an injunction restraining the local authority from awarding itself deemed permission for office development as the development was to be made and partly financed by private developers and therefore it was arguable that the development was not going to be by the authority as required by reg. 4 of the Town and Country Planning General Regulations 1976.

270–03 J.J. Steeples v. Derbyshire C.C. [1984] 3 All E.R. 468.

(1) Sections 26 and 27 of the Act do not apply to developments to which s.270(1) applies.

(2) A county council could not be required under reg. 4 of the Town and Country Planning General Regulations 1976 to ensure that every recipient of every notice must know exactly what part of his land was affected—a description such as "improvements to alter road known as Pit Lane at its junction with Hassock Lane" was adequate.

(3) All documents received by the district council should be kept in one file. This did not constitute a register for the purposes of art. 21 of the General Development Order or regs. 4 and 5. Therefore notices had not been placed in the required register and so power to pass a resolution granting planning permission to the county council never arose and the resolution was *ultra vires* and void.

(4) Requirement to give notice of the proposed resolution under reg. 10(5) referred only to the resolution to grant permission.

(5) Notice under reg. 10(5) was only intended to provide machinery for consultation under reg. 10(2). At highest failure to give notice under reg. 10(5) would render a subsequent decision voidable at the suit of an aggrieved district planning authority.

(6) Grant of planning permission by a county council after it had entered into a legally enforceable contract to use its best endeavours to obtain planning permission was in breach of natural justice and either voidable or void.

(7) In operating procedure under regs. 4 and 5 the planning authority must be particularly scrupulous to ensure that its decision was seen to be fair, particularly when it was at all controversial. The council should not have been under any obligation to grant planning permission or under any liability should it not be obtained—could have ensured the contract was subject to planning permission being obtained.

270–04 R. v. Lambeth L.B.C., ex p. Sharp (1985) 50 P. & C.R. 284. It is a condition precedent of the exercise of the power to grant deemed planning permission under the Town and Country Planning General Regulations 1976 that the prescribed procedures should be followed. Certiorari was granted to quash a deemed grant as the newspaper advertisement required under reg. 4(2)(c) of the Town and Country Planning General Regulations 1976 had not specified either the period in which objections had to be made nor that they were to be in writing.

PART XV. MISCELLANEOUS AND SUPPLEMENTARY PROVISIONS

SECTION 276. DEFAULT ORDERS

276–01 Relevance of an increase in the estimate of compensation as a reason for the revocation of a discontinuance order. At all material times the true liability was the same. [1966] J.P.L. 288.

SECTION 277. CONTROL OF DEMOLITION IN CONSERVATION AREAS

277–01 R. v. Endersby Properties (1975) 32 P. & C.R. 399.
(1) A direction under s.8 of the Town and Country Planning (Amendment) Act 1972 need not use any particular form of words.
(2) The direction should tell the recipient what he was or was not to do and why.

SECTIONS 280 AND 281. RIGHTS OF ENTRY

280/281–01 R. v. Chief Constable of Devon & Cornwall, ex p. C.E.G.B. [1981] 2 All E.R. 826, C.A. Removal of obstructing protesters who were trying to prevent the exercise of powers under s.280. There may be a right to use common law remedy of self-help to remove obstructing protesters.

SECTION 282. LOCAL INQUIRIES

A. Award of Costs under section 250(5) of the Local Government Act 1972

282–01 Re Wood's Application [1952] C.P.C. 724, D.C. Minister may have a general policy that costs will only be awarded in exceptional cases.

282–02 Wootton v. C.L.B. [1957] 1 W.L.R. 424, C.A. Costs in the Lands Tribunal.

282–03 R. v. Sec. of State for Environment, ex p. Reinisch (1971) 22 P. & C.R. 1022, D.C. As long as the Secretary of State does not apply an inflexible rule he is entitled to have a general policy that costs will only be awarded against a party if he has acted unreasonably. The provisions of Circular 73/65 which incorporate guide lines suggested by the Ministry to the Council on Tribunals do not fetter his discretion.

282–04 Costs awarded against a local planning authority where permission already granted on appeal for similar use of adjoining property. [1967] J.P.L. 668.

282–05 Costs awarded against a planning authority where behaviour unreasonable. [1969] J.P.L. 102.

282–06 Award of costs against a local planning authority where they took into account irrelevant considerations. [1969] J.P.L. 599.

282–07 Award of costs against a local authority after unreasonable imposition of a time-limit on planning permission. [1970] J.P.L. 279.

282–08 Costs awarded against a local authority where they acted contrary to ministerial policy clearly set out in a circular. [1970] J.P.L. 472.

282–09 Award of costs against a local planning authority. A tree preservation order was not confirmed because of an agreement between landowners and the local planning authority for preservation of the trees. [1970] J.P.L. 622.

282–10 Planning authority should not refuse permission simply on green belt policies when the Minister proposes excluding the relevant land from the green belt—costs awarded against the local autority. [1971] J.P.L. 190.

282–11 An objector who succeeds in part may recover his costs on the parts of the appeal on which he succeeds. [1973] J.P.L. 57.

282–12 Appellant awarded 50 per cent. of his costs. [1973] J.P.L. 58.

282–13 Award of costs to an objector following withdrawal of a planning application by the local authority. [1974] J.P.L. 432.

282–14 Costs awarded against an appellant who failed to attend the planning inquiry. [1975] J.P.L. 307.

282–15 Costs awarded against an appellant where the appeal was withdrawn shortly after the inquiry was opened as his maps were inaccurate. [1975] J.P.L. 308.

282–16 Costs awarded against a local planning authority where they refused permission on a planning application in accordance with the inspector's views on a previous appeal. [1976] J.P.L. 129.

282–17 Costs awarded against the appellant where the inquiry was adjourned and the appeal dealt with by way of written representation. [1976] J.P.L. 461.

282–18 Costs awarded against the local planning authority where there was insufficient evidence to justify refusal of permission. [1977] J.P.L. 268.

282–19 Partial award of costs against the local planning authority where one of grounds of refusal of permission was not supported. [1977] J.P.L. 337.

282–20 Costs awarded against the local planning authority where advice in a Development Control Policy Note was not followed. [1977] J.P.L. 544.

282–21 Costs awarded against the local planning authority who had refused to negotiate, in a case where the terms were ultimately agreed. [1977] J.P.L. 547.

282–22 Costs not awarded against the local planning authority where it acted against the advice of its officers. [1977] J.P.L. 549.

282–23 Costs awarded against the local planning authority where refusal of planning permission was not supported by substantial planning objections. [1978] J.P.L. 281.

282–24 Costs granted to an appellant as in the absence of a material change in planning circumstances time-lapsed permission should be renewed. [1980] J.P.L. 202.

282–25 Award of costs on an enforcement notice appeal where the enforcement notice was withdrawn before the inquiry held. The council failed to make reasonable investigation into the situation before taking enforcement action. [1980] J.P.L. 765.

S.282. LOCAL INQUIRIES

282–26 Costs awarded to a district council in respect of an adjournment of the inquiry necessary to consider a proposal by the appellant made immediately before the inquiry. [1981] J.P.L. 214.

282–27 Costs awarded against a district council on an enforcement notice appeal where an allegation in the notice was defective because the breach was a failure to comply with a time-limit condition, not a material change of use. [1981] J.P.L. 218.

282–28 No award of costs against a district council where it held a mistaken but reasonable opinion. [1981] J.P.L. 220.

282–29 Costs awarded against a local planning authority in respect of the second ground of a refusal of planning permission, even though the first ground of the refusal was upheld—award limited to the cost of appealing the second ground. [1981] J.P.L. 773.

282–30 Power to award costs even though there was no inquiry and the appeal was dealt with by way of written representations. Costs awarded against the planning authority as the service of a listed building enforcement notice in the above situation unreasonable. [1981] J.P.L. 443.

282–31 Costs awarded against a local planning authority where the outline planning permission was granted but objection by the authority was taken to subsequent application on a matter which was not within "reserved matters." [1982] J.P.L. 400.

282–32 Costs not awarded to a local planning authority notwithstanding control by them of access to the land to which the application related. No penalty can attach to exercising the option to have a local inquiry once an appeal has been lodged.

282–33 Costs awarded against a local authority where:
 (1) it did not present substantial evidence in support of contentions;
 (2) if the council had correctly considered the matter they would have realised that they did not object to the application. [1983] J.P.L. 334.

282–34 Costs may be awarded against a planning authority in respect of unnecessary and unreasonable expense incurred as a result of issuing an enforcement notice on the authority of a single member of the planning authority. [1983] J.P.L. 323.

282–35 Award of costs to a local planning authority where similar proposal for the erection of a dwelling-house in the green belt had been refused less than three years previously. Circular 22/80 does not suggest that a previous appeal decision of the Secretary of State in a green belt case is likely to be overridden because of the circular. [1983] J.P.L. 337.

282–36 Secretary of State's power to award costs is limited to the costs of and in connection with an inquiry into the matter formally before him. The behaviour of the parties concerned prior to the submission of the appeal is not a matter which can be taken into account by Secretary of State. The fact that full details of the application were not put before the planning committee was disregarded. Councils Rule 7 statement was accepted by the Department. If the appellant was dissatisfied with it he should either request the Department to ask the Council for a fuller statement, or if the matters were raised without prior warning, ask for an adjournment. [1983] J.P.L. 333.

282–37 Costs awarded to a district council against a county council where a direction by the county council was not supported by any substantial evidence. [1983] J.P.L. 329.

282–38 On the basis of evidence before the council it should have been clear to them that an application for an established-use certificate was well-founded. Costs awarded against the council. [1983] J.P.L. 326.

282–39 Costs awarded against a local authority where there was failure to support a refusal of planning permission by substantial evidence. Relevance of the decision being contrary to the recommendation of officers. [1984] J.P.L. 745.

282–40 Costs awarded against a local authority where there was failure to support a refusal of planning permission by substantial evidence. Relevance of fact that the local authority were willing to dispense with a local inquiry. [1984] J.P.L. 747.

282–41 Costs awarded against an appellant where the local plan, recently adopted after a local inquiry, contained a specific policy in relation to the appeal site. [1984] J.P.L. 763.

282–42 Costs attributable to the adjournment of an inquiry awarded against the appellant where he was responsible for the adjournment. [1984] J.P.L. 767.

282–43 Costs not awarded against the appellants despite the withdrawal of the ground of appeal and failure to produce evidence, and continuance of the appeal against the enforcement notice. [1984] J.P.L. 768.

SECTION 283. SERVICE OF NOTICES

283–01 R. v. London (County) Quarter Sessions Appeals Committee, ex p. Rossi [1956] 1 Q.B. 682, C.A. Rebuttal evidence admitted to show that service was not effected by the ordinary course of the post: time was of the essence.

283–02 Borough of Morecambe & Heysham v. Warwick (1958) 9 P. & C.R. 307, D.C. Service at a place of business to somebody else who promises to give the document to the person to be served is good service.

283–03 Moody v. Godstone R.D.C. [1966] 1 W.L.R. 1085, D.C. As time of service of an enforcement notice was not vital the presumption of service was irrebutable.

283–04 Hammersmith L.B.C. v. Winner Investments Ltd. (1968) 20 P. & C.R. 971, D.C. Provision of a fictitious or wrong name cannot deprive a local planning authority of the right to use the alternative methods of service under s.283.

283–05 Hewitt v. Leicester Corporation (1969) 20 P. & C.R. 629, C.A. The court is not bound to deem a notice to have been served at a particular time, within the Interpretation Act, when it knew that it had not been served at all.

Where a letter is returned through the post marked "gone away" it is plain that it has not been served.

283–06 Maltglade Ltd. v. St. Albans R.D.C. [1972] 1 W.L.R. 1231, D.C. As a building preservation notice does not come into effect until served on the owner, the presumption of service can be rebutted by evidence of non-service.

283–07 J.J. Steeples v. Derbyshire C.C. [1981] J.P.L. 582. In placing a box at the end of a path the plaintiff was inviting anyone having anything which did not require a signed receipt to leave it in the box and doing so constituted service in accordance with s.283(1)(*b*).

SECTION 287. REGULATIONS AND ORDERS

287–01 G.L.C. v. Sec. of State for Environment [1984] J.P.L. 424.
(1) Secretary of State is under a duty to make regulations under s.287 so that amendment could be made to the Greater London Development Plan.
(2) Even if under no duty to make amendment regulations, in refusing to do so because of the intended abolition of the G.L.C., the Secretary of State had exercised his discretion for the wrong reasons.

SECTION 290. INTERPRETATION

290–01 Borthwick-Norton v. Collier [1950] 2 K.B. 594, C.A. "Rack-rent" for definition of an "owner" in s.290 means rack-rent at time when the lease was granted and one must have regard to any restrictive covenants in the lease.

290–02 London Corporation v. Cusack-Smith [1955] A.C. 337, H.L.
(1) A freeholder who lets at less than a rack-rent is not an owner within s.290, the owner is the tenant who can sub-let at a rack-rent.
(2) The question whether or not rent is a rack-rent is to be determined according to the value of the land at the time of letting.

290–03 Belmont Farm Ltd. v. Min. of Housing & Local Govt. (1962) 13 P. & C.R. 417. "Livestock" in s.290 does not include any animal whatsoever.

290–04 British Airports Authority v. Sec. of State for Scotland [1980] J.P.L. 260. Applicant was not a "statutory undertaker" as he did not own the airport at the time of the application.

290–05 Crowborough P.C. v. Sec. of State for Environment [1981] J.P.L. 281. Allotments an agricultural use as activities on an allotment fall within the definition of "agricultural" in s.290.

290–06 Gill v. Sec. of State for Environment and North Warwickshire D.C. [1985] J.P.L. 710. The slaughtering of animals in any large numbers did not come within the definition of agriculture in s.290.

290–07 Preparation of horticultural compost was not an agricultural use of the land. [1968] J.P.L. 416.

290–08 Growing of fruit and maturing of bulbs, plants and seedlings was a horticultural activity falling within the definition of agriculture in the Act. [1968] J.P.L. 364.

290–09 Keeping and boarding of dogs is not an agricultural use. [1970] J.P.L. 156.

290–10 The meaning of the phrase "other operations" depends upon its context and it does not only have the meaning associated with building which it bears in the definition of building operations in s.290(1) of the Act. Installation of a protective grille over a shop window and door is an operation within s.22(1) of the Act. [1985] J.P.L. 129.

290–11 Land used solely for the grazing of horses for recreational purposes is not agricultural land when severed from other agricultural land. [1985] J.P.L. 63.

290–12 Breeding and keeping of ponies not used in farming the land is not an agricultural use of the land. [1985] J.P.L. 148.

290–13 Breeding of dogs for show is not an agricultural use. [1985] J.P.L. 201.

290–14 Keeping, rearing and breeding of foxes within definition of agriculture. [1985] J.P.L. 342.

SECTION 292. TRANSITIONAL PROVISIONS

292–01 R. v. Min. of Town & Country Planning ex p. Montague Burton [1951] 1 K.B. 1. Direction for the continuation of pre-existing proceedings after the appointed day.

292–02 D'Aiessio v. Enfield U.D.C. (1951) 2 P. & C.R. 166, D.C. A time-limit specified in determination under the Building Restrictions (War-Time Contraventions) Act 1946 operates as a condition.

292–03 A.G. Campbell (Arcam) v. Worcestershire C.C. (1963) 61 L.G.R. 321, C.A. It is not possible to derive from s.76(6) of the Town and Country Planning Act 1947 any implication that a conditional consent given previous to that Act should operate or be deemed to have operated as planning permission under the Act, which preserves the conditions alone, without the consents.

292–04 Essex Construction Co. v. East Ham B.C. (1963) 61 L.G.R. 452.

(1) Section 4(1) of the Building restrictions (War-Time Contraventions) Act 1946 does not operate to sweep aside a specific valid planning permission granted before the five-year period has come to an end.

(2) Under s.23 of the Town and Country Planning Act 1947 there is power to enforce a breach of a condition of planning permission granted under the Act, respecting development before the appointed day.

292–05 Rose v. Leeds Corporation [1964] 1 W.L.R. 1393.

(1) Section 4(1) of the Building Restrictions (War-Time Contraventions) Act 1946, deems war-time contravention to comply with the earlier planning legislation, but not with the Town and Country Planning Act 1947.

(2) Planning permissions granted under the Town and Country Planning (Interim Development) Act 1943 were not registerable under s.15(7)(*b*)(ii) of the Land Charges Act 1925 (now repealed).

292–06 Bedfordshire C.C. v. Sec. of State for Environment (1972) 71 L.G.R. 420, D.C. Where a development had taken place before 1948, and there had been no written application for and grant of planning permission in accordance with arts. 10 to 12 of the Town and Country Planning (General Interim Development) Order 1945, there was no planning permission in force immediately before July 1, 1948 and para. 7 of Sched. 13 to the Town and Country Planning Act 1962 does not apply.

292–07 R. v. Sec. of State for Environment [1985] J.P.L. 35. A notice of a proposal to enforce planning control was a step for enforcing planning control so as to prevent work done or use begun during the war from being deemed to comply with building laws or planning permission.